THE PELICAN HISTORY OF THE UNITED STATES

General Editor: Robert A. Divine

Volume 3

CONFLICT AND TRANSFORMATION

William Brock was born in 1916 and educated at Christ's Hospital and at Cambridge, where, in 1939, he received the Thirwell Prize for Historical Research. After completing his military service he became a Lecturer in History at Cambridge, a post he held until 1967. Since then he has been Professor of Modern History at the University of Glasgow. Among other books, Professor Brock is the author of *An American Crisis: Congress and Reconstruction* and *The Evolution of American Democracy*. Articles by him have appeared in the *English Historical Review*, *History*, the *Journal of American History*, and other periodicals.

William R. Brock

Conflict and Transformation

The United States, 1844–1877

Penguin Books

Penguin Books Ltd, Harmondsworth,
Middlesex, England
Penguin Books, 625 Madison Avenue,
New York, New York 10022, U.S.A.
Penguin Books Australia Ltd, Ringwood,
Victoria, Australia
Penguin Books Canada Limited, 2801 John Street,
Markham, Ontario, Canada L3R 1B4
Penguin Books (N.Z.) Ltd, 182–190 Wairau Road,
Auckland 10, New Zealand

First published 1973
Reprinted 1976, 1978

Library of Congress catalog card number: 73-77616

Printed in the United States of America by
Kingsport Press, Inc., Kingsport, Tennessee
Set in Linotype Baskerville

Preface

IT is a bold venture to write a single volume about a period that has been more intensively studied than any other thirty years in modern history. The volume of literature is enormous and the controversies keen. The problems and events are discussed with urgency and commitment, because they seem in so many instances to hold the key to contemporary anxieties. Faced with profusion and perplexity, there is a temptation to seek for a new analysis that will explain all, but interpretations that claim this universality no longer commend themselves to those who think about the past. On the other hand, events have a meaning if one can discover it; they are linked together in place and time and produce results that can be ascertained. There is therefore no excuse for abandoning the attempt to produce some kind of coherence, to analyze the influences that crowded in upon men, or to identify the arguments and decisions. I have not hesitated to make clear my own judgments, and those who wish may discover an underlying theory of change and conflict in human society; but I have not presented this analysis in a didactic or dogmatic form, because the essence of historical understanding is the realization that men stand at the vortex of many forces; this may narrow the field of choice but still leaves some options open. At each stage I have tried to show what the options were and why one was preferred to the others, and on several occasions I have indicated my own preference for a choice that was rejected.

Anyone writing about the Civil War must decide how to treat military history. The details are fascinating but cannot be adequately covered in a short survey; the strategy is of the first importance, but a bald account does inadequate justice to the complexity of the considerations that influence a strategic decision. I have decided not to risk distortion and to treat the military events very briefly and only so far as they contributed to the political climate of the day.

It is necessary to summarize, in a few lines, controversies that have occupied much time and energy among professional historians. Anyone familiar with the period will recognize the issues, but I have not thought it necessary to provide elaborate references, and, with a few exceptions, I have confined the footnotes to the source of quotations included in the text. In the final historiographical essay I have indicated the areas of controversy and the principal exponents of contrasting views. In a period such as this no one is ever likely to have the final word; what one hopes is that each new statement will provide a stimulus for further argument.

The organization of this book follows conventional lines. It would have been possible to break away from chronology and write an analytical essay ranging over the whole period, but in a prolonged crisis unfolding events have their own logic. The decisions that men made cannot be separated from the situation as they saw it at a point in time, and too drastic a departure from narrative may obscure the reasons why certain needs were felt to be imperative at given moments in time.

This book is largely about a crisis in white society, and mainly in white society east of the Mississippi River. This requires no apology, because this society made decisions about territorial expansion, the extension of slavery, secession, war, and reconstruction. It also felt most dramatically the impact of economic growth, immigration, urbanization, and intellectual upheaval. In the two final chapters I have ventured some reflections upon black history, the agricultural society of the Great Plains, and the precociously modern society of the Pacific Coast. These are offered as items on the agenda for the future, rather than as full statements about events during this period. Indeed, it is a principal theme of this book that the years from 1844 to 1877 were decisive in the formation of modern American society; but when it closed, many new possibilities had been revealed, and the book must therefore end with tentative and unanswered questions.

W. R. B.

University of Glasgow,
Scotland

Contents

[1]
Introduction

DURING the period covered by this volume the conditions of American life were transformed, new communications changed physical dimensions, and giant strides were taken toward an urbanized, industrialized society. The changes are clear and easy to read; less evident is the extent to which the attitudes and conditions of an earlier period survived. In 1845 there was still a real sense of contact with the formative days of the Republic; in many communities a few old men and women could remember the Revolution. Many of the best-known figures in public life had been born before the adoption of the Constitution and could tell from their own recollections how George Washington had looked and what Thomas Jefferson had said. The old men died, but even at the end of the period the men controlling politics, business, and the professions could remember a time when railway locomotives were novelties. It is often instructive to work out when men lived through their formative years and to remember that most men who had to make decisions during the Civil War had been in their twenties when Andrew Jackson was in the White House and that by 1875 men of middle age had received their strongest impressions of life about the time of the Mexican War. Most men can keep abreast of new ideas in the career to which they are committed and in solving problems to which they are accustomed, but confronted with unusual situations or novel difficulties, they assume instinctively that the knowledge they acquired as young men still contains the wisdom of the matter.

This lag between reality and awareness of reality is always present in human affairs, but it is likely to create most tension when the pace of change is fastest. There is always a former condition that provides the frame of reference for the present, and the greater the gap between the two, the more inadequate is traditional wisdom likely to be. A good deal of the history of the period can be understood when one realizes that men of the nineteenth century had no precedents for life in an era of accelerating change.

Though economic change can be quantified, the psychological consequences of change must be estimated by impressions and hypotheses. If emotional history during this period could be charted, it would show a number of strong impulses, creating major disturbances, with only short intervals of comparative calm. Between 1840 and 1850 there was an emotional upheaval that affected great numbers of Americans in different ways. One can discover evidence in religion, philosophic attitudes, and political rhetoric. Religion was still the core of much thought about man and society, but religion was itself undergoing great changes. In Protestantism there had always been two separate but intertwined strands of thought; one concerned with salvation hereafter, the other with the creation of an environment in which the godly could live. One traditional Christian attitude accepted established order as a part of God's plan for the world; another challenged authority's right to decide what the temporal condition of men should be. The older denominations adhered to the first concept in their official attitudes; the second was expressed by many of the younger and more active members. When existing institutions failed to respond to the demands of those who wished to reform society, ardent men created their own organizations, and there was a tremendous proliferation of societies devoted to every conceivable objective in the spectrum of reform. Sometimes the reformers cut themselves off from traditional church organizations; sometimes they withdrew into a world of philosophic speculation. Ralph Waldo Emerson moved from orthodox religion to forge his own transcendentalist philosophy in which individual men would realize their share in the absolute. Yet even when he seemed most aloof, Emerson epitomized the American dilemma of this age; convinced of the essential goodness of the Great Experiment, he was deeply concerned by the thought that it might somehow be failing the people. He was a philosopher but also a popular lecturer with a special mission to elevate the people. A cynic might add that lecturing was a sure means by which a man of letters could earn some money, but with Emerson lecturing was always more than this, and it had a strong didactic purpose. By 1860 Emerson had come more and more to see slavery as the great betrayal, and the transcendentalist philosopher could deliver an eloquent elegy upon the death of John Brown, the antislavery apostle of violence. In old age Emerson could look back and believe that in spite of all, the universal spirit was working for the betterment of the American people, but by then nearly forty years separated him from the confident faith of 1844 that "one thing is plain for all men of commonsense and common conscience, that here, here in America, is the home of man."

Even in 1844 Emerson stressed the contrast between high aspirations and the poverty of contemporary ethics that recommended "conventional virtues, whatever will earn and preserve property." In subsequent years the feeling of tension grew, and there was a growing belief among sensitive Americans in the northern states that the nation was somehow being betrayed by its politicians. By 1860 they deplored the compromising spirit of politicians and had little respect for Congress; the Presidency had become the tool of obscurantism; the Supreme Court was a bastion of slavery; and if few went as far as William Lloyd Garrison to condemn the Constitution, a great many believed that it had been perverted by "the slave power." Against this background one can understand why so many humane and intelligent men supported the rising Republican party and came almost to welcome the outbreak of war as relief from a tension that was becoming intolerable.

Emotional strain was not confined to the Northeast. Slave-owners were always aware of their dependence upon a social institution that the rest of the civilized world had condemned. The brightest ornaments of plantation culture from Washington, Jefferson, and James Madison to Henry Clay deplored slavery as a social, moral, and political evil. By 1850, however, they had increasingly come to accept John C. Calhoun's doctrine that it was a positive and necessary foundation of a great culture. Whether this came about because of economic pressures, the self-interest of a ruling class, or as a solution to the problem of race relations has been a matter of controversy among historians. The truth may be that the three worked together. Great houses required the economic support of commercial agriculture and the service of domestic labor; this meant the presence of the Negro slaves, and this in turn meant that the relationship between the races had to be stabilized. Once the system had been set in motion, it acquired its own momentum, and each white individual acquired his own vested interest in a part of it. The great danger to the slave power was not, however, attack from outside but from within. The immediate danger of slave revolts could be exaggerated, but the threat of racial violence against isolated families was real. More significant in its long-term consequences was the possibility that nonslaveholders might turn against the system. Much of the proslavery propaganda was consciously or unconsciously directed against this danger. This also explains the violence of southern reactions to Hinton Helper's *Impending Crisis in the South,* published in 1857, because Helper, speaking from the South, linked the backwardness of the lower white people directly to the existence of slavery. It is sometimes said that southern proslavery arguments developed in response to abolitionism, but the first wave of dogmatic justification for slavery was prompted by the debates in Virginia in 1830 and 1831, when a sizable Virginian minority had given articulate support to gradual emancipation; this also coincided with nullification, which rejected the right of the national majority to act as a final arbiter.

The southern upper class genuinely believed that they represented a superior type of civilization; controlling the press, dominating the churches, and exercising a powerful hold upon education, their assumptions spread through many channels. Not all slaveholders believed in the benefits of slavery, and privately many may have shared the old Jeffersonian despair that slavery was a wretched thing but could not be displaced; but with increasing frequency assertions of southern excellence were associated with proslavery arguments. Moreover, the ardent defenders of slavery could stand on common ground with the doubters when they declared that whatever the future of slavery, it must be decided by southerners themselves. In this the upper class could count on much popular support. There was a substantial middle class of farmers and small planters for whom a few slaves were their principal assets, while a man without slaves feared the social convulsion that might follow emancipation.

During this period, however, the constitutional barriers protecting slavery were threatened in two ways. First, southerners themselves felt the need to expand into new areas, and this brought them out from behind the bulwarks of states' rights into the open where only federal law prevailed. Second, and for many different reasons, a majority in the North became convinced that the expansion of slavery ought to be checked. They divided upon whether the right to check lay with the federal government or with the legislatures of newly organized territories. This became the focal point of the controversy. Without slavery there would have been tension between the rapidly developing society of the North and the slower-moving society of the South, but the great arguments of the period clustered around the expansion of slavery and nothing else. All the other arguments were so much window dressing.

The main argument was intertwined with two other themes. The first was the rise of national feeling, the second the difficulty of adjustment when societies with different types of economies at different stages of development have to find the means of coexistence. Nationalism took two forms. One was the strengthening of central authority —or requests for it to be strengthened—in response to the numerous pressures for aid or authority beyond that of the states. This was seen in the demand for a national economic policy, national regulation of banking and currency, and federal aid for roads, canals, and long-distance railroads. The personification of the Union as a great and beneficent institution that made progress and liberty possible could easily slip over into the more aggressive kind of nationalism that justified expansion as the working of Providence and the duty of a chosen people. This kind of emotional nationalism—stirred by concurrent events in Europe—was particularly strong in the West, but it was almost as strong in the South and could rouse the volatile population of eastern cities. It found expression everywhere in a conviction that a people gathered together in a political society acquired a special kind of entity and common purpose. American nationalism differed from European nationalism in its lack of emphasis upon ethnic characteristics. It is true that most influential Americans were of English, Scottish, or Scots-Irish descent and were intensely aware of their heritage, but "American" had to mean a good deal more than this. In Europe nationalist movements were usually able to hold together people of different political beliefs in a common cause; in America the goals of European nationalism had been won long ago, and nationalism fostered contrasting views of what the nation should be.

Simultaneously the unequal fortunes of different regions existing in a great free-trade area produced a multitude of problems. Until the outbreak of the Civil War a majority in all parts of the country believed that on balance their interests were better served inside the Union than out of it, and economic bonds were often as strong as the political; but interdependence necessarily meant that some parts of the economy were stronger and wielded more power than others. As most of the strength was concentrated in the Northeast, and the most striking evidence of growth was visible in the West, southerners had reason to feel that their section was falling behind; they argued that they were being robbed of the proceeds of their greatest asset (cotton) and used their political powers to block the very policies that might have helped them to narrow the gap. Underdeveloped nations of the late twentieth century have come to regard economic aid from the rich as a right, but the leaders of the Old South insisted that they could live on their own. A great agricultural region had a good case for subsidized internal improvements; a section that was usually short of ready money had excellent reasons for favoring a strong central banking system; struggling manufactures in the South were more likely to benefit from protection than established industries elsewhere. Southern spokesmen were not united in the opposition to these things (many southern Whigs supported them), but their most articulate and influential leaders did everything to attack them. This created the illusion that the two sections, instead of having complementary economies, were sharply at variance with each other.

The tensions that arose from nationalism and economic growth were not ended but tightened by the Civil War; economic differences became more marked, the ascendancy of the North and Midwest more obvious, and the control of business more concentrated. Emotional nationalism had become the staple of Union rhetoric during the war, and by the end of it a majority of northerners saw stronger implications in the word "nation" than ever before; by the same process the southerners, having failed to make their own nation, were bitterly opposed to nationalist ideas that could be used to justify the continued ascendancy of the victors. Reconstruction would be, in large part, a series of bitter comments upon these circumstances.

It is a truism that the Civil War was a crisis in the history of democracy, but the relationship between democratic ideas, democratic practice, and the breakdown of the political system is not easy to analyze. There may be a suspicion that the egalitarian impulses of democracy eroded away leadership and caused candidates to focus upon the prejudices of their constituents rather than the needs of the nation. It can also be argued that the weakness lay not in democracy itself, but in the isolation of so many rural communities, so that the voters themselves could form only vague and distorted impressions of problems beyond their own range of knowledge. A complementary line of approach may be to study the channels by which political information reached the electorate. In the South, outside the cities, these channels were controlled by the upper class; though a newspaper might be the independent enterprise of an editor-proprietor, his advertising revenue and much of his sales would depend upon the patronage of the planters. Southern newspapers had party allegiances, but on basic issues affecting southern society they were normally agreed. In the North and Midwest most small towns supported one or two newspapers; these were normally intensely partisan, but as the local basis of party often lay in interest and ethnic groups, there was more diversity of view upon fundamental issues.

Against attempts to throw the blame for collapse upon the democratic processes it must be emphasized that men who could stand for long hours listening to political argument were not unsophisticated. The anxiety of congressmen to see that their speeches were recorded indicates that the *Congressional Globe* was more widely read than its twentieth-century successor. There was also a deluge of pamphlet literature. The great crisis of the period certainly placed an enormous strain upon the political system, but there is no reason to believe that the ignorance of the electorate was its weakest link. It might be fairer to suggest that what one needs to investigate is not so much the failure of the system as the reason why it continued to function so long.

The American federal system was exceedingly complex in its operation. The framework of the Constitution, the separation of powers, the division of sovereignty, and the apparatus of checks and balances were difficult enough in themselves, and experience through the years had introduced further conventions or interpretations. In practice the system had proved to be unexpectedly efficient in dealing with all the normal conflicts of political existence; if it left most people without full satisfaction on some points, it also gave them satisfaction on many others. In the *Disquisition on Government* John C. Calhoun argued that it was essential in a federal system to reconcile the "numerical majority" and the "concurrent majority"—that is, the national and the local majorities—and this thesis was fundamentally correct. Calhoun was also correct in arguing that this system could not function if the two majorities came to be divided on a moral issue and along sectional lines; but paradoxically, he did more than any other man to make the system unworkable by insisting that slavery was the only possible basis for southern society. The constitutional crisis developed because powerful intellectual forces were creating two societies that could no longer meet on the common ground of give-and-take within a system designed to give everyone something and no one everything.

From what has been said it can be seen that the prolonged crisis through which Americans passed during this period does not lend itself readily to any simple interpretation. There are too many different strands of growth and development, intellectual disquiet, moral controversies,

grave social problems, political strain, and deep constitutional issues to permit a monolithic explanation. In the
following chapters the principal emphasis is upon politics,
and space will not permit a full investigation of the social
roots of controversies or of the many forces that build up
toward the point at which political decisions must be
taken. It may therefore assist understanding if some of the
basic concepts that underlie this study are stated at the
outset.

1. Conflict between groups is inevitable in any political
society.

2. These groups are of many different kinds: economic,
occupational, regional, class, status, and idealistic.

3. Individuals may belong to two or more groups. They
may therefore have to resolve inner conflicts before making
personal decisions, and there is no guarantee that they are
capable of making fully rational analyses of either the interests of their own group or the respect due the interests of
others.

4. The more developed an economic and social system
becomes, the more numerous these group interests become;
the growth of a society therefore increases conflict, the
complexity of group aims, and the difficulty of resolving
the issues both in individuals and in society at large.

5. The harmonization of interests is the principal task
of politics, but growth imposes upon political men the
need for decisions about its direction, and this may mean
that some interests are favored at the expense of others.
Thus the "static" task of harmonization is often at variance with the "dynamic" task of deciding the direction and
purpose of change.

6. The direct conflicts that develop are, however, constantly modified and obscured by loyalty to nation, class,
religion, and traditional belief.

7. Faced with the necessity for decision, men are likely
to draw upon the stock of ideas accumulated in their society and select those most appropriate to their situation.

8. The arguments used are therefore unlikely to contain much that is novel, and their relevance is further limited by a tendency to treat concepts that contain a great variety of meaning and experience as though they were simple and self-evident (e.g., "the Union," "the Constitution," "the North," "the South," or, more tendentiously, "the slave power," "the moneyed power").

9. There is a further tendency to treat one admired or detested element in society as characteristic of the whole.

10. Nevertheless, the use of obsolete, oversimplified, or incorrect notions does not minimize their importance. Ideas drawn from the common stock and applied to an existing situation create a new situation with consequences that are impossible to anticipate.

This analysis may seem to minimize the role of individuals. This is not so. There are certain things that would have happened in any event (assuming that the forces of change in the Atlantic world would have remained much the same). There were certain trends that could not be reversed and could have been altered only in detail. The population would have grown, industry would have developed, communications would have been improved, cities would have increased, and thousands would still have wished to migrate across the Atlantic. With only slightly less certainty one can say that slavery would have died before the end of the century, that the transition from forced to free labor would have imposed enormous changes upon southern society, and that nothing was likely to produce an equitable solution to the problem of race relations. It also seems probable that the demands of a growing society would have required central government to assume more and more responsibilities, that the cycle of boom and depression would have continued, that men who controlled economic power would come to have more and more influence, and that whatever happened, sensitive men would have had to face the apparent failure of material betterment to generate moral improvement.

One could add other hypotheses to demonstrate that whatever happened in Congress or on battlefields, modern American society was molded by the long-term forces of social, scientific, technological, and demographic change. The imagined profundity of these arguments can induce a dangerous superficiality. *How* things happen is of greater significance than the possibility that they might have reached the same end by different roads. In many of the crises surveyed in the following pages the decisions of individuals were crucial; in others the opinions and responses of large numbers were the deciding factors. One can narrow the number of options, but choice remains; and the choices made had profound consequences for American democracy and thus for the modern world.

The middle years of the nineteenth century were crowded with change in all the developing countries of the world. Americans regarded their experiences as unique, but it would be more accurate to regard them as the transatlantic manifestation of forces that had all civilization in turmoil. Rationalist, scientific, and technological revolutions; the decay of old institutions, new economic enterprise, and the penetration of interior landmasses by commerce and communications; religious reform, humanitarian reform, wide suffrage, and consent as the exclusive source of authority: these were the momentous and disturbing forces in the nineteenth-century crisis. Even without the impact of slavery the middle years would have seen tension in America, and a most difficult task of historical analysis is to relate these social, economic, and intellectual changes to the conflict that actually occurred.

Figures tell the tale of expansion. In 1840 there were just over seventeen million Americans; by 1880 there were over fifty million. In 1840 there were 2,818 miles of railroad in operation and 491 miles under construction; by 1850 there were 9,000 miles in operation and by 1860, 30,626. Lines completed topped 1,000 miles for the first time in 1848 and reached a peak in 1854 with 3,442; in 1872, on the eve of the great international depression, 7,439 miles were completed, and the first link between the Atlantic and Pacific had been finished three years before. The era also saw steam established as the queen of the oceans, and with it fast, frequent, cheap, and regular shipping services. The domestic telegraph network was built up between 1844 and 1860, and in 1865 the first transatlantic cable was laid. In the Mexican War the fighting fronts were weeks away from Washington; in the Civil War orders could be transmitted immediately to most military headquarters. Newspapers came to employ wire services, and the large-scale organization of business became possible.

American industry expanded tremendously. Imported manufactures continued to play an important part in American life, but American products had a much larger share of a greatly enlarged market. At the same time agricultural exports had leaped forward. In all these fields the Civil War had a disturbing and perhaps a dislocating effect, but over the whole forty-year period the trends indicated a transformation of economic life in both quantity and quality.

The rise in population also saw a proportionately larger number of Americans living in towns: in 1840 about 10.6 percent; in 1888 just under 30 percent. In 1840 there was one city with over 250,000 and only five with more than 50,000; in 1880 there was one city with over a million, and nineteen more with over 100,000.

America had two problems that were unique: the reception and assimilation of huge numbers of immigrants and westward expansion. In 1840, 84,066 immigrants (already regarded as a staggering figure) entered the country. The two main sources were Ireland and Germany, with Great Britain a long way behind. In 1850 the total from Great Britain had risen more than twenty times to 51,085, but Germany and Ireland still led the field with 78,896 and 164,000 out of a total of 369,980. The great rise had begun in 1844 and reached a peak of 427,833 in 1854. There was then a falling off, especially in the early war years, but by 1864 it was back to 193,418 (stimulated by some recruiting in Europe by Union agents) . In 1873 the annual figure reached 459,803, and after a slack rose to a peak of 788,992 in 1882. The later peaks of British immigration were 1854 (58,647), 1866 (94,924), and 1870 (103,677); the Germans contributed most in 1854 (215,009) and 1873 (149,671); the Irish sent 224,253 in 1851 and over 100,000 in every year from 1847 to 1854 inclusive.

The territorial expansion of the United States during this period and the continuing process of settlement and development in new areas formed the second group of experiences unique in America. To some degree the acquisition of Texas, New Mexico, and California and the establishment of American soverignty in Oregon south of 49° paralleled the overseas expansion of western European countries and the Russian colonization of Siberia and central Asia. There was a significant political difference in the assumption that American settlers remained part of the American body politic and that non-Americans of European stock brought under American rule would come to enjoy similar rights. During the debates on the Mexican acquisitions, one could still hear repetitions of earlier fears that this process would endanger the government of the Republic, and these arguments should not be ignored because they were falsified by events. Indeed, the problem of governing distant territories was at the heart of much controversy during the period.

One can imagine the panorama of American society in the middle years of the century as a landscape containing a number of high buildings, varying in size and age but sharing some common architectural features. Each of these buildings had its own internal structure, and in each a multitude of people lived out their lives. These were the separate states with their own political, social, and economic systems. A cluster of six was labeled New England, another group was called the South, and another (more

widely scattered) the West. Others, such as New York and
Pennsylvania, stood alone, whereas some, such as Delaware, Maryland, Kentucky, and Missouri, stood on the
boundaries between two areas, with characteristics of both.
Each state had dominant social groups, but in each the
recipe for success was different, and there was no homogeneous national ruling class. From time to time some individuals came out of the buildings to foregather in central
edifices marked "Congress" or "National Nominating Convention," but unlike those of European countries the national political groupings were unstable and lacked heredi-
tary status and common culture. A few men survived in the
national "establishment" for several years, or even for a
generation, but when the House of Representatives assembled for each Congress, the chances were that half of its
members were newcomers and that about one-third would
not serve another term.

Federalism permeated the whole system. All the states
had similar forms of government and shared in the tensions and conflicts of the age, but even common institutions and experiences took on local colors. The basic
institutions of social life—property, education, and the
common law—came under the state. The state governments were responsible for public order, justice, and the
punishment of crime. They could grant or refuse incorpo-
ration, regulate manufactures and conditions of work;
they could improve rivers, repair bridges, authorize canals
and the new railroads. In some instances the states themselves had become entrepreneurs and financed new communications out of taxes and public loans. The financial
business of the country was conducted by state banks, and
the small scale on which most businesses operated made interstate institutions unnecessary. The daily life of a citizen
was therefore affected at many points by the government of
his state and only indirectly by the government of the
United States. Many American citizens could live out their
lives without meeting an officer of the federal government

save a postmaster, though in seaports they might see revenue officers and in the less developed regions officials of the
Public Land Office.

Yet, unseen by most citizens, though understood by the
majority of them, the Constitution and the law of the
United States determined the framework of society. Goods
could move freely over the whole country, and the states
were prohibited from issuing their own coinage, impairing
the obligations of contract, or interfering with each other's
commerce or social institutions. Once ships left harbor
they came under the maritime law of the United States,
and even in harbor the goods they landed passed through
the Customs House of the United States. The revenue of
the United States was derived mainly from duties on imported goods, and the choice of imports to be taxed affected the development of the country's economy. The
United States also provided for the defense of the country
and the safety of the frontier, though since 1815 had
found it necessary to maintain only a small navy and a tiny
professional army. The relationship with foreign powers
depended upon the initiative of the President and upon
treaties ratified by the Senate. The government of the
United States was a landowner on a vast scale, and its public land policy determined the character of settlement; it
was also sovereign over territories and passed laws that
molded states of the future.

Living in their separate states, engaged in competition
for power, status, and livelihood, immersed in the affairs
of their counties and regarding small market towns as
the hubs of their universe, most Americans lived intensely
provincial lives and were little concerned with external
relations or the views of others. They were not conscious,
however, of political, social, or cultural deficiency. Most
Americans were convinced that their lives were freer, happier, and more rewarding than those of any other people
on earth or in history, and the claim is difficult to disprove.
Social mobility was probably not so marked as some sup-

posed, and it was easy to forget that most successes meant somebody's failure. Even so, there was no other country where a white man of humble origin stood so good a chance of betterment or was more likely to share in the responsibilities of government. The need to succeed carried with it a share of anxiety and social neuroses. Alexis de Tocqueville had insisted upon the extent to which individualism left a man unprotected by the institutions and customs of the older nations. Yet if Americans suffered in some deep psychological way, few of them would admit it. Private doubts were voiced only by a small minority of the wealthy and professional classes of the Atlantic states.

Democracy imparted a special flavor to society. Elections came round with embarrassing frequency, and what has often passed unnoticed was the growing number of offices filled at them. Early in the century county government had normally had an elective body of commissioners. By 1850, in most well-developed counties, the people elected commissioners, treasurers, auditors, sheriffs, coroners, judges, officers of the courts, surveyors, school boards, and a large number of petty local officials. As a result, the opportunities for political participation were frequent, almost every official had to keep his finger upon the pulse of opinion, and a very large number of private citizens expected to fill, in their turn, one or another of these elective offices. Democratic processes were penetrating, tough-grained, and pervasive.

The great majority of Americans lived in rural communities, but for many of them the small town was the dominant political, economic, and social institution. It was in the town that lawyers and merchants had their offices, and it was in the town (and most frequently by the lawyers) that local politics were organized. The town was a market, a distributing center, and its bank was an essential link in the country's financial system. The town probably boasted a newspaper—if not two or three—and it would have an academy and might even be the site of a college; it certainly had several churches and was the undisputed center for whatever culture existed in the region. The rise of large cities has attracted the attention of historians, and few have investigated the characteristics of small towns; yet large cities were still a rarity, they sent few representatives to Congress, and their cultural influence was limited by the comparatively poor communications. By contrast small towns were numerous and provided the home bases for most national politicians. The scale must be grasped in order to understand the institution: In a town of five to ten thousand inhabitants, there might be from one to two thousand adult males, and fewer than this active in business or professional life. It was possible for an aspiring public man to know the majority by sight and many by name; he would certainly be personally acquainted with the leading men. A face-to-face elite operated in an environment in which their personalities were known, and their actions were under the daily scrutiny of those whose support they had to win.

The small town was of exceptional importance in New England and along the line of New England migration to the West. Here its social and economic function was reinforced by the strong traditions of a godly community. It was not that New Englanders had any inherent and superior virtue (though many of them believed that they had) but that traditionally their towns were communities with a moral purpose. Education was a public responsibility and a public pride; moral discipline was an integral part of social life, and even where the old beliefs weakened, the traditions continued. They were not reluctant to conclude that prosperity was the reward of virtue, but they succeeded to a marked degree in reconciling individualism with social obligation. The southern town was less cohesive, usually less well provided with educational institutions, and overshadowed as a political organism by the country-house culture of the great plantations. Nor did the economic life of the southern country town run so strongly as in the North and West; if the district was prosperous, its produce went from the plantations down the rivers or railroads to the ports; if poor, there was little on which to base an urban economy. In either case the small town lacked the vitality and traditions of the North. From this contrast many consequences would ensue.

Religion was universal but so fragmented into the separate denominations that the local congregations, reflecting the preoccupations and views of their members, set the tone. The religious press served a wide audience, and at every census the Christian monthlies and quarterlies were far more numerous than their secular contemporaries; but in the great controversies that were commencing, the writers avoided the issues or swam with the regional tide, and the great denominations spoke with weak and divided voices. In the leading Protestant churches four main currents could be discerned: a conservative strain that had refined Calvinism to a rigid but unspiritual moral code; a philosophic strain, theologically progressive but speaking to a rational and generally wealthy minority; an urgent evangelicalism that turned more and more from the salvation of individual souls to reformation of the world; and a fundamentalism that urged a return to the pure word of Scriptures literally interpreted. These were the principal strains of religious thought, though other influences might be detected among the Episcopalians, Methodists, and minor denominations. All church leaders congratulated themselves upon the decline of "infidelity" among educated men but differed profoundly upon the social implications of faith.

In terms of ecclesiastical politics churchmen were divided between those who struggled to maintain unity by bland insistence upon denominational loyalty and the exclusion of disruptive topics, and those who wished to commit the organization of their church to a cause (which usually meant an explicit avowal of antislavery in the North, and in the South an acceptance of slavery as a divinely appointed institution). The involvement of churches in secular affairs was checked by the separation of church and state; yet separation did not mean secularism. Indeed Horace Mann, the strongest northern opponent of denominational control over education, was also a stout defender of compulsory Bible reading and argued that a universal and basic Protestantism could unite all believers. America was still a Protestant Christian country, and Congress opened its daily meetings with a prayer and invited preachers from all the leading denominations.

While one trend was therefore to counter secularism by claiming that all men could join in a basic faith while organizing denominationally, another trend was toward Christianity as a religion of reform. Drawing inspiration partly from the British evangelicals and partly from indigenous revivals, the crusade for moral reform touched many different aspects of society: home missions, foreign missions, temperance and the moral welfare of seamen, religious tracts, Sunday schools, and the distribution of Bibles. The novel characteristics of most such movements were leadership by pious laymen and national organization. Modeled upon the British societies, the American reformers established headquarters in New York, Boston, or Philadelphia, founded national periodicals, sent out speakers, fostered the establishment of local branches, and brought to their chosen cause the same organizing ability that had won substantial business fortunes for many of their lay leaders. Thus the religious societies cut across both state and denominational boundaries and replaced loyalty to a single church by zeal for an all-embracing cause. It need hardly be added that the most active of all these societies crusaded against slavery.

Internal feuds had done as much as public unpopularity to weaken the drive for abolition. The Garrisonians were divided beyond hope of reconciliation from their former allies; they believed that the only way to attack slavery was by an unremitting onslaught on the conscience of the people. Others deplored extremist intolerance of slaveholders and argued for a more temperate approach, whereas still others hoped that the loose-limbed structure of American politics gave scope for political action. In 1839 the Liberty party was founded, and in 1844 their presidential candidate, James G. Birney, won sixty thousand votes and a good deal of notice because the fifteen thousand Liberty votes in New York would have given Henry Clay the state and the Presidency. Yet in the pages of his *Liberator* Garrison devoted to the Liberty men the invective that he usually reserved for slave-owners and often reported their activities in the column headed "Refuge for Oppression," where he exposed the means by which men in all sections were working for the preservation of slavery. The national antislavery societies were in continual difficulties and could not have survived without the financial help of a few wealthy supporters such as Arthur and Lewis Tappan. There seemed to be nothing to show for fifteen years of agitation and organization, and abolitionism seemed a spent force as westward expansion opened the prospect of more areas devoted to slavery. The paralysis of abolitionism does not, however, tell the whole story, for while the men were condemned as radical troublemakers, more and more sober Americans accepted their assumption that the perpetuation of slavery was incompatible with the aspirations of a nation that claimed to be in the vanguard of civilization.

The press was the channel through which men learned about affairs. No newspaper enjoyed a national circulation, and the vast majority drew readers from only a single town and surrounding countryside. The nearest approach to a national press was achieved through the custom, among editors in different parts of the country, of exchanging copies and reprinting select extracts. As a consequence most Americans outside the larger cities depended upon a local newspaper and extracts from others that the editor chose to insert. The intense partisanship of the day often insured that even a small town would have two rival newspapers, but in both the selection of news and reprinted items papers made no pretense at impartiality and aimed to encourage the faithful rather than to win the confidence of the uncommitted. As a result, though the Americans (at least in the North) were more widely literate than any other people (with the possible exception of the Lowland Scots) , and though a single state could support as many newspapers as a large European country, they were not particularly well informed. Their press was resolutely provincial and ostentatiously partisan. Except occasionally through the correspondence columns, there was little attempt at debate; the vision was narrow, one-sided, and often presented by men whose range of knowledge was little wider than that of their readers. In reprinting items from other parts of the country there was a natural tendency to select what was sensational or shocking. Bowie knives in a southern legislature made news, ponderous but sensible speeches did not; extracts from Garrison's *Liberator* were seen in the South as representative of nothern opinion.

There was, however, a metropolitan press of growing influence. For many years the *National Intelligencer* in Washington had presented the news through Whig eyes in a sober, well-informed, and uninspired way. Over the years a number of different Washington newspapers served as the organs of Democratic administrations. The newspapers published in the capital were the source of frequent quotation in the party press throughout the country. It was in New York, however, that the most powerful journalism of the day flourished. There was Horace Greeley's *Tribune*, Whig in politics but a pioneer of popular journalism that demanded quality from its contributors, and William Cullen Bryant's *Evening Post,* the organ of the radical Democrats. The metropolitan dailies did not circulate much beyond the cities, but their weekly editions circulated widely. A new postal act of 1852, which lowered rates

and allowed them to be paid by the publisher, not the sub-
scriber, proved to be a charter for the popular weeklies.
After 1854 the New York *Weekly Tribune* probably did as
much as or more than any other factor in spreading and
sustaining the doctrines of the new Republican party.

In a changing society groups accustomed to influence
and authority naturally became concerned about their future. In New England the custodians of a traditional culture were still strong. As Henry Adams would observe in
later life:

Down to 1850, and even later, New England society was still directed by the professions. Lawyers, physicians, professors, merchants were classes, and acted not as individuals, but as though
they were clergymen and each profession were a church. In politics the system required complete expression; it was the old Ci-
ceronian idea of government by *the best* that produced the long
line of New England statesmen.

Elsewhere in the North the idea of an established elite
was less firmly entrenched, but nevertheless there existed in
most of the older states a group or groups of men who
would like to consider themselves among "the best" but
found themselves replaced by others with less education or
breeding. In the South the planter gentry, still the "natural" leaders of society, had less cause for disquiet, but even
for them the future was not untroubled.

These old or threatened elites were challenged in their
states and in the nation. In their states new wealth, professional politicians, and diminishing esteem among the
people as a whole weakened their leadership. In national
politics they were forced to yield to men from newer areas
who showed scant respect for the literary culture that had
meant so much in the past. After John Quincy Adams, all
the Presidents were in one sense or another self-made men.
So were the majority of Cabinet members. This did not

mean that they had started at the bottom of the social ladder, but their social background was not that of the men who had wielded authority in the first two generations after independence. Inevitably men of the old elites tended to think that public life had declined.

It is necessary to correct this view to some extent. Despite the privately expressed fears that education and refinement were in retreat, there was a natural resilience and initiative that offset the leveling effect of democracy. Across the country most professions and many businesses were led by men of the old stock, and even if their social origins were comparatively humble, conventional gentility was their model. The commerce of the eastern cities was still dominated by men of inherited wealth and long-established family businesses; in the small towns of the West their descendants were influential; and self-made planters of the Southwest copied the style of Virginia gentlemen. Western men who rose in public life prided themselves upon their plain speaking but also upon their observance of genteel conventions. The most learned man in the Senate—and the one who placed most emphasis upon correct behavior—was Thomas Hart Benton, who had started life as a very rough diamond indeed. Most remarkable of all was the way in which the southern planters retained a monopoly of politics in their section and control over education, the press, and the professions; and despite wide divisions between the classes, smaller freeholders normally used their political power to elect men from the traditional ruling class. Conflicts were occasionally sharp, but they were short-lived and limited in their objectives; moreover, when a man of the lower status was elected to office, he quickly became assimilated, in manners and interests, to the upper class.

In spite of these qualifications the anxieties of members of the old elites did play their part in national life, though their objectives were seldom avowed. The men at the top of a state edifice, who felt themselves threatened, looked with sympathy to those in similar situations elsewhere, and where there were also economic ties the links could be powerful. The merchant classes of Boston, New York, and Philadelphia had more than cotton in common with the southern planters, and the professional men in New England shared sympathies with their brethren across the nation. The lawyers formed a professional guild, not organized as such on a national scale, but speaking a common language and sharing assumptions about the character and purpose of life, and as most politicians were lawyers, these implicit understandings formed a powerful cement in national life. In time these affinities of class, profession, and style of life would not prove strong enough to stand against the great tides released by sectional controversy, but for a time they helped to dam the flow and support the machinery of compromise.

In a curious way the fortunes of the elite groups were bound up with the Anglo-American relationship. Popular rhetoric fed upon abuse of the ancient enemy, but culturally and economically the United States was still heavily dependent upon Great Britain. Literature, literary criticism, classical education, economic theory, and science thrived upon soil that was constantly replenished with British seed. Great Britain was the principal market for American produce, the source of capital for investment, and the supplier of much-needed consumer goods. At the same time it was impolitic, in public, to avow affection for England or even to confess that the United States needed "the old country." Yet it was the elite groups who were both conscious of this dependence and anxious to cultivate British ideas and customs on American soil. There was, indeed, a dichotomy in the emerging spirit of American nationalism. Though most educated men of old stock nourished memories of the Revolution, they also believed that the purpose of the Revolution—and therefore of American national existence—was to preserve and propagate the true principles of British civilization. Aware of the medieval heritage, deeply read in the constitutional conflicts of the seventeenth century, they believed that American civilization had taken over and must develop the best in the English tradition. There was, of course, a difference in emphasis: New Englanders liked to think of themselves as heirs of the Puritans and fellow members of the Commonwealth experiment; southern gentlemen thought of themselves as the descendants of Cavaliers and the champions of authority under the law; but these differences could be resolved in face of a threat to both the older traditions. Did American destiny lie in building upon the old English foundations, or was its inspiration the rejection of the old traditions?

Attitudes to England cut across social and political barriers, and by 1850 they were coming to have a retrospective rather than a contemporary significance. Though fear of British intervention played a major part in the controversy over Texas, and though in the following month some Americans were prepared to fight for the barren wastes of northern Oregon, the interests of the two countries ran on parallel lines. Both had an interest in the peace of the Atlantic; neither wished to see European expansion in the New World. The trading ties were strong and grew stronger; if Britain would find it difficult to flourish without American cotton, the finances of the United States would have been in a sorry state without the annual inflow of British payments. Thus, though attitudes to England symbolized important questions about the American destiny, they did not come to divide the country as the attitude to France had done between 1790 and 1800. Moreover, the questions about the character of the American nation were being presented in a far more challenging form. The debates over Texas, the coming of war with Mexico, and the Wilmot Proviso made it imperative to decide whether slavery followed the flag and what kind of society should be planted on the Great Plains and on the distant shores of the Pacific.

The world had never known a society like this one, and men were amazed, encouraged, and exasperated by its survival. European radicals looked hopefully west for proof of man's capacity to govern himself; conservatives fastened upon violence, naïve culture, and egalitarian discourtesy as evidence of demoralization. Americans themselves were not given to speculation or to philosophic analysis, and the great principles of union, federalism, and democracy were expressed in general, emotive, and imprecise terms. Indeed, political institutions were described in terms that owed more to the impulse of romanticism than to rational inquiry; this did not, however, diminish their force. Romanticism was intuitive; it grasped concepts rather than explored them and expressed beliefs in terms of cloudy grandeur. Eighteenth-century reason had attempted to refine knowledge to self-evident propositions; nineteenth-century romanticism saw self-evident truths as a substitute for reason. There was a magnetism in generalizations that expressed what everyone felt in language that everyone could applaud. It was evident in American oratory, with Daniel Webster providing the model, and it was echoed in pulpits and on the stump in political campaigns. With Emerson common sense acquired a mystic quality, joining individuals with the universal. Antislavery men borrowed something from Puritan demonology, but more from romantic imagery of a war between good and evil. Even the gloomy logic of Calhoun resorted to intuitive concepts when he spoke of "the South" or of the rights of states, and even his more subtle arguments on the rights of the "concurrent majority" soon left the hard ground of fact to voyage upon stormy seas of emotion.

It was a secret of strength that "the Union" became the

most powerful of these romantic concepts. Increasingly it became an act of ritual to proclaim one's devotion to the Union, and even those who would have found it hard to define what the Union did for them were convinced that they would be lesser men without it, and this was as true in the South as in the North. Jackson was still the great hero of the southern democracy, and his best-remembered saying was "Our Federal Union—it must be preserved." For a generation the old nullifiers had been forced into the political wilderness—except in South Carolina—and even they had justified themselves by claiming that their remedy was intended to save the Union, not to destroy it. When William Lloyd Garrison adopted "No Union with slaveholders" as his slogan, he dealt an almost fatal blow to the cause of abolitionism, while his rivals in the Liberty party strove long and with little effect to prove that rejection of slavery was necessary to preserve the Union.

The Constitution had become almost as much an object of romantic veneration as the Union. In an earlier generation Union had been the end, the Constitution the means; but in course of time the two had become inseparable. It was impossible to think of the Union without the Constitution, and it became almost impossible to think of the Constitution existing in any other form. Lawyer-politicians imagined that they were drawing hardheaded conclusions from the text of the Constitution, though most of the time they were making romantic assertions about its spirit. Men refused to recognize that the Constitution could not supply all the answers, that some points could be settled only by political decision, and that constitutional logic could be merely a disguise for emotional issues. In the end the great romantic concepts would come into collision, and the extent of their dependence upon words and emotion would be revealed.

It is a matter for conjecture whether the Union would have been more durable if it had been supported by more national interests of a tangible kind. It is an unfortunate truth that as the economic arguments for Union grew stronger, the internal tensions became more acute. Exchanging goods freely over a wide area, with export crops earning large returns abroad, with undeveloped land and resources in sufficient abundance to attract foreign capital at cheap rates, with an accumulation of commercial and financial skill, and with railroads promising even greater benefits in the future, the Union was a triumphant economic success. Inevitably there was some dispute over the extent to which the rewards were fairly distributed, but no developing country has avoided these tensions. Moreover, the political system enabled the less-developed regions to counterbalance concentration of economic power. Indeed, the question was whether politics had not functioned too well in this respect. The Union might have gathered more strength if the pressure from various economic and regional interests had been allowed to develop stronger stakes in the national government. This, at least, was the lifelong opinion of Henry Clay.

The theory of economic conflict as an explanation for the Civil War has confused a number of separate tendencies in societies undergoing rapid change. Tension is likely to occur when societies at different stages of economic development are thrown into association with each other, but technological advance and financial sophistication have provided the means by which the gap can be narrowed and a community of interest established. Thus, in the United States railroads could link the sections together, industry could supply the needs of the plantations, and a flexible credit system could remedy the shortage of investment capital in an agricultural society. Resistance to these changes may, however, arise when the interests of a class are threatened; it is not exploitation of the poor but challenge to a governing class that transforms tension into conflict. It is a mistake, however, to imagine that these threats are likely to be purely or even primarily economic. Controlling production of crops that had a ready sale in the world market, southern planters were fully capable of surviving economic vicissitudes, whether these came in the form of general fluctuations in demand or rising costs; what they rightly regarded as destructive was an attack on the moral basis of their hegemony. Fully aware that slavery was under attack in all civilized nations, they knew that it was on this point that they must concentrate their defense. Constitutional, economic, social, and religious arguments took their place as required in the logic of proslavery thought. It was not enough that slavery should be allowed to exist; the point to be established was that its existence was essential. This logic ultimately pressed the best friends of the South, and those whose economic aid would be of the greatest assistance, to the point at which they were forced to reject the southern case.

Economic specialization had produced social differentiation, but arguments for economic cooperation remained overwhelming. Only in the wildest dreams of southern separatists did anyone suppose that the South could be better off when deprived of help from northern commerce, banking, and industry. Nor did anyone in the North suppose that their condition could be improved by making the South poorer. The truth is that economic relationships take their place in the total environment in which men have accepted ideas about the structure, character, and purpose of society. These are the beliefs that become the durable facts of life, and material aims must be made to conform with them. The southern upper class was in a position within the South to define its own conditions for survival and then to persuade a majority of white southerners to accept them. The planter gentry were able to do this because the facts of class and race were intertwined in a way that was unique. Nowhere else could an upper class expect the same success in persuading a lower class to accept the economic basis of their power as a social blessing.

Prologue: 1844–1846

VOLUMES of ingenuity and research have been exhausted in discovering the origins of sectional conflict, but if one seeks a proximate cause rather than a long-term hypothesis, there is no more acceptable date than April 10, 1844, when President John Tyler sent to the Senate a secret treaty for the annexation of Texas. In the following weeks most of the arguments that would provide the tragic and dominant themes for the next seventeen years were rehearsed.

There were good and sufficient reasons for joining Texas to the United States—not least that the Texans themselves wished it—but annexation would be controversial. The Lone Star Republic had been virtually independent of Mexico since 1835, but in Mexican eyes Texas was still a rebellious province. Though the Mexicans exercised no authority north of the Rio Grande save in the Santa Fe area, many people were troubled by the morality of annexing a large portion of a neighboring country merely because it had been settled and was now controlled by men of American stock. Then there was a troublesome question of boundaries. The Texans effectively controlled an area from the Louisiana border to the Nueces River and for two to three hundred miles inland. This was large enough—larger indeed than any existing American state—but the Texans claimed the whole of the Mexican province, which ran south to the Rio Grande, west to Albuquerque and Santa Fe, and north to undefined boundaries on the Great Plains. In 1843 a Texan expedition to Santa Fe had failed dismally, and the inhabitants were stoutly opposed to Texan rule, so that by annexing Texas, as Texans themselves defined it, the United States would accept responsibility for the defense of a doubtful frontier and the government of unwilling subjects. Most disturbing to northern Americans was the fact that the Texans had established slavery, and the recognition of their boundaries would carry slavery over a huge area where it had been abolished by Mexican law. From this area perhaps four new states might eventually be carved, and these new states would outweigh the free states that might be added in the foreseeable future and carry slavery far north of the Missouri Compromise line.

Most Americans would, however, agree that if Texas passed under British control, the interests of the United States would be adversely affected, and this seemed not wholly improbable. Texas was bankrupt, rendered insecure by the threat of Mexican attack, and desperately in need of both economic and diplomatic aid. All this Great Britain might be willing to provide but not under conditions that would guarantee the continuance of slavery. Under these circumstances the Texans, whose President, Sam Houston, had no strong attachment to slavery, might agree to abolition as the price of British protection. The possibility appeared to acquire more substance when rumors reached Washington that an Anglo-American abolitionist deputation had seen Lord Aberdeen, the British Foreign Secretary, and secured the promise of a loan for Texas in exchange for abolition. This news provided either the spur or the pretext for secret negotiations that began in the late fall of 1843 and resulted early in 1844 in a treaty annexing Texas to the Union with the status of a territory.

In fact the British Government had no intention of risking good relations with the United States, recently much improved by the Webster-Ashburton Treaty of 1842, in pursuit of hazardous and uncertain gains in Texas. There was no doubt that Great Britain would prefer an independent Texas, linked to Great Britain by a commercial treaty, to American annexation; but it was also clear that Aberdeen would take no positive steps to bring this about. If the Texans offered abolition and appealed for British aid, the case might be altered, so the real danger to American interests came from Texas rather than from Britain. It was the object of the negotiations to anticipate this possibility, while secrecy had to be preserved to prevent any Mexican countermove.

John Tyler was the least happy of American Presidents. A respectable Virginia politician of limited abilities, he had been chosen as Vice-President in 1840; in 1841 the death of William Henry Harrison after a few weeks in office made him the first Vice-President to succeed. Tyler had become a Whig in reaction against what he deemed to be the unconstitutional behavior of Andrew Jackson, and he had little sympathy with the wider aims of the party. Within a short while he had ruined the Whig program through a succession of vetoes but had failed either to initiate an alternative policy or to build up an effective personal following. What ensued was a caricature of the good old Jeffersonian principle that the best government was that which governed least; but in international affairs his administration had been more successful. The Webster-Ashburton Treaty stood to its credit, and Tyler now hoped to identify himself with the annexation of Texas as a great national objective. He himself justified annexation on commercial and strategic grounds but found it difficult to restrain the enthusiasm of southern expansionists who viewed annexation as an opportunity for the extension of slavery.

The man who had been principally responsible for the negotiations was Abel Upshur, the Secretary of State, but he was killed by an explosion on board the U.S.S. *Princeton* in March. After some hesitation President Tyler appointed John C. Calhoun as Upshur's successor. The appointment was controversial, for Calhoun, even more than Upshur, was a confirmed believer in the theory that annexation was necessary to protect slavery in the United States. When he assumed office, the treaty was ready for signature, but Calhoun's logical mind may have realized that the case for urgency and secrecy was deplorably weak. It rested upon British designs that had been emphatically denied by Aberdeen and for which no evidence existed but a gossipy letter written by Duff Green, a private speculator and intriguer, from London in September, 1843. The supposed British threat was to absolve the United States from the necessity of negotiation with Mexico; without it American action would appear high-handed and needlessly aggressive. Presented with a fait accompli, Mexico was almost bound to resist, at least to the extent of securing those portions of Texas where no effective Texan government existed. This would mean war, with America on the wrong side of the moral and legal fence.

It was widely believed that Henry Clay, the Whig leader, would oppose immediate annexation, and the southern Whigs were certain to follow him; some northern Democrats would probably oppose, and the prospect of a two-thirds consent in the Senate was therefore remote. At this juncture, after the treaty had been signed, Calhoun wrote, and added to the papers submitted with the treaty to the Senate, a letter to the British minister in Washington, Francis Pakenham. This letter took up an avowal by Aberdeen that Great Britain must officially deplore the spread of slavery as the occasion to argue that it was a benign institution and the only possible system of relations between two unequal races, that its erosion would gravely damage the South, and that its protection was therefore a national interest of the United States. This argument was likely to cause disquiet in the North, for it implied that the national authority of the United States—drawing upon taxes paid by all Americans and risking a war that all would be required to fight—was committed to the preservation of slavery. Northerners who disliked slavery had hitherto been able to excuse themselves from opposing it actively by arguing that responsibility lay with the states, whose rights could not be abrogated by federal action; but now the federal government of the United States would stand before the world with the avowed intention of protecting and extending slavery under the American flag.

John C. Calhoun is one of the most admired and most censured men in American history. In the South he is still seen as the prophet of southern civilization, and twentieth-century conservatives have found an appeal in his defense of minority interests against majority rule. It was the irony of his career that he was the choice of a majority only when Vice-President under two Presidents, John Quincy Adams and Andrew Jackson, whom he considered unfit for the office. Whenever he advanced to a decisive position on his own, he found himself in a minority and yet remained convinced that the purity of his principles deserved wide support. Even in the South he spoke for a minority of personal followers, and only in the declining state of South Carolina was his word supreme. Constantly torn between the desire for a national constituency and for solid southern support, Calhoun evolved a species of political logic that commands respect for coherence rather than common sense. The typical steps were to suggest that the worst possible consequences of an act were inevitable, that the danger must therefore be "met at the threshold," and that all who valued harmony must sacrifice their own interests and rally on his line. The division between the true men and the false would then be clearly marked.

Calhoun's motive in writing the Pakenham letter has never been fully explained. It may have been a simple error dictated by a compulsive urge to defend slavery wherever it was attacked; but Calhoun was an experienced politician who did nothing without calculation. Several arguments may have converged. He was bitterly offended because some northern Democrats, followers of Martin Van Buren, who was expected to be the presidential candidate, had voted against the rule that forbade the discussion of abolitionist petitions in the House; he may therefore have intended to force Van Buren to choose between accepting slavery as a national interest or opposing annexation and sacrificing leadership of the party. In either event Van Buren, whom Calhoun regarded as corrupt and unprincipled, might be defeated for renomination. Calhoun may also have hoped to persuade southern Whigs to drop their opposition to annexation by demonstrating that their interests as slaveholders were at stake and, as his argument sank in, to break down existing party divisions in the South and establish a single proslavery party under his own leadership. Lack of northern support had recently forced him to withdraw from the presidential race, and he was seeking a new base from which to operate. But Calhoun was not yet purely sectional in his thinking; he believed, rightly, that there was strong popular support for annexation, and by linking slavery and expansion, he might have the elements of a new national party. Northerners who rejected the nationalization of slavery would find themselves in a minority, and as full and frank support for slavery would be identified with union, the outcome would be national strength rather than sectional division. The Pakenham letter might therefore accept the possible defeat of annexation in order to create a new national alliance.

Whatever the arguments that inspired it, the Pakenham letter posed the question whether or not slavery was a national institution. For Calhoun tolerance, based on the hope that slavery would dwindle away, was not enough; Americans must be brought to recognize that slavery was permanent, beneficial, and deserving of all the aid and protection that the federal government could supply. This, in essence, was the proposition that would haunt America for the next seventeen years.

If Calhoun wanted to force Van Buren's hand, he need not have bothered, for the former President had already decided to oppose immediate annexation, and, by coincidence, he and Clay published simultaneous letters condemning the treaty. This ensured its failure in the Senate but led to Van Buren's defeat for renomination by his party. Instead, the Democrats, after an ugly fight in their convention, chose James K. Polk, of Tennessee, who was firmly committed to annexation. Polk had been Speaker of the House of Representatives and had had one term as governor of Tennessee, but compared with Clay and Van Buren, he was comparatively unknown, and his nomination came as a shock. Nevertheless, he made a good candidate and narrowly defeated Clay. The Democrats, however, ran well ahead of their nominee in the congressional elections, and their victory almost assumed landslide proportions. It is a fair assumption that Clay's stand against immediate annexation won him votes for the Presidency, while his party suffered a severe defeat in the constituencies where the Whigs completely failed to hold the gains they had made in 1840 or to recover the ground they had lost in the midterm elections of 1842. Be that as it may, the election of Polk was interpreted as a mandate for annexation.

Indeed, annexation did not wait for Polk's inauguration. Tyler proposed that Texas should be acquired not by treaty but by the normal process for the admission of a new state, that is, by concurrent resolutions in the two houses of Congress. This had an important consequence for the future. The treaty had proposed to admit Texas as a territory, leaving Congress with control over boundaries and the creation of new states; the joint resolutions admitted Texas as a state with boundaries at her own valuation and with the constitutional right to refuse partition into new states. A move to commit Tyler to further negotiation for annexation—which would have brought the boundaries of the new state back to Congress for determination—failed, and what was finally agreed left him a choice between negotiation and an offer of unconditional admission. In the course of the final debates on annexation some interesting arguments were produced to limit the extension of slavery. In the final form it was agreed that slavery should be prohibited in any state formed from Texas north of 36° 30′ but that states formed south of that line would be admitted with or without slavery as the inhabitants wished. This early adoption of what subsequently became known as popular sovereignty has usually passed without comment, for no new states were formed from Texas.

For the older leaders of the parties that contended for mastery in 1844 annexation was a distracting and unwelcome question. From 1834 to 1853 there was a national two-party system in operation; both Democrats and Whigs had organizations in every state, and in many states elections were closely fought and uncertain in their outcome. The Whigs won a great national victory in 1840 but failed to sustain the momentum of their triumph, because the breach with President Tyler deprived them of a legislative achievement. In 1844 the Democrats won both houses of Congress, but Henry Clay won a larger popular vote than William Henry Harrison in 1840. The Whigs would win again in 1848; and in 1852, though the Democrats won overwhelmingly in the electoral college, their popular majority was narrow, and the Whig candidate, Winfield Scott, won more votes than any previous Whig candidate. Votes, of course, rose with population, but Whigs almost held their own in an expanding nation. Thereafter this great party, which had promised so much in its first days, broke up. On their side the Democrats preserved the organization built up by the Jacksonians. They suffered from the panic of 1837 and the subsequent depression but were fortunate to win in 1844 on a tide of returning prosperity and expansionist enthusiasm. Internal party dissensions were mainly responsible for their defeat in 1848, but the growing confusion of their opponents secured them victory in 1852 and

1856. The disruption of the party in 1860 is numbered among the immediate causes of the Civil War.

Attempts by historians to define and describe the two parties have often misled. The Whigs have been characterized as the party of slave property and northern business, without explaining how such a top-heavy organization could retain so large a popular following at a time when the majority of voters were small rural landowners. The Democrats have been characterized as the party of the common man; some recent studies have found "the common man" to be a man on the make and the advance agent of laissez-faire capitalism, but others have seen the core of the party as a backward-looking protest against the methods and morals of a commercial society. This last view of the party accords well with its increasing conservatism and southern domination in the years before 1860. Difficulties of analysis have arisen because historians have ignored the complexities of interest and organization that they would immediately recognize in a modern party. The Democrats of this period displayed slightly fewer internal contradictions than their modern descendants, and the Whigs contained somewhat more disparate elements than the modern Republicans; but with necessary qualification one can emphasize the underlying similarities.

The life history of an American political party is familiar. Generated by negative reactions to a positive situation, it draws together a loose alliance of groups that have little else in common. The elements in the alliance may be classes, economic interests, regional interests, and local party organizations. Success in a national election provides the opportunity and occasions the need for a positive policy; if this is successfully achieved, it provides a nucleus around which party traditions can be built. Building upon familiar themes but elaborating and adapting them to explain and signify the new policy, politicians acquire ready-made arguments for the future, which force the dissident elements in the party to adapt their attitudes so that future success will not be jeopardized. The dominant party now becomes a political "establishment"—loosely organized but with strong motives for continuing association.

The original impetus of the Democrats had been a protest movement against the management of national affairs by an inner circle composed mainly of eastern gentlemen, and its traditional base was formed by small farmers of the West and South. The Democratic stream was fed by various tributaries to become a great river. There were old Jeffersonian Republicans who were alarmed by the increase of federal power at the expense of the states. There were a few younger representatives of the old Federalists (they would contribute a Democratic President in James Buchanan and a Democratic Chief Justice in Roger B. Taney). There was the powerful political organization of Martin Van Buren in New York, built on the support of upstate farmers, the rural Dutch, and low-paid city workers (especially the Irish Catholics). There were zealous businessmen, lawyers, and newspaper editors from rising western communities. The popular origins of Democracy tended to be overlaid by later accretions, though Democratic politicians preserved the rhetoric of a party of protest. By 1840 the Democrats had been the established party for many years and had attracted bankers, businessmen, planters, and ambitious lawyer-politicians, so that the leaders of the party were often socially indistinguishable from their opponents. To offset this, however, the Jacksonians attracted movements among the eastern craftsmen and petty bourgeois who organized locally in ephemeral Workingmen's or Equal Rights parties and who were described by 1840 as "the radical democracy" or more graphically and confusingly as "the Locofocos." They also preserved a strong rural base where neither commerce nor radicals were popular. Finally, if the bulk of the highly educated were Whigs, some of the most active intellectuals were Democrats, including such familiar names as James Fenimore Cooper, George Bancroft, and William Cullen Bryant.

The Democrats had less difficulty than might be imagined in holding this heterogeneous collection together, because their principles of government were negative. Inheriting the Jeffersonian suspicion of government in any form, and, if government functions had to be performed, preferring to see them done by the states, the Democrats could appeal to a popular dislike of intervention by the remote federal government in Washington. They felt that the revenue from the tariff should be kept at the minimum level required for "wise and frugal" government and deplored the protective principle that used the tariff to exclude imports or raise prices to a level at which less efficient American production could compete. There were exceptions to this rule, especially in Pennsylvania where protection was popular with the small masters and skilled men concerned with iron mining and manufacture. Most emphatically the Democrats agreed that financial control should should not be concentrated in a national bank, but the apparent unanimity on this point could mean a crude hostility to monopoly, a sophisticated preference for private and state banking, protest against unduly restrictive credit policies, or a moral condemnation of paper currency as the instrument of speculators at the expense of the credulous.

In line with their suspicion of governmental activity the Democrats opposed federal aid for "internal improvements"—roads, waterways, railroads—but here again there were some confusing crosscurrents. The idea of a nationally sponsored system of roads and canals had Jeffersonian origins in proposals by Albert Gallatin and at one time had attracted the support of John C. Calhoun. The first great public work—the national road westward from Baltimore over the Appalachians—had been launched by the Republicans. Presidents James Madison and James Monroe had opposed internal improvements, but less on principle than on the legalistic ground that subsidies could not be given without a constitutional amendment, and Andrew Jackson had not seemed to exclude a truly national scheme though opposed to appropriations for local projects with spurious claims to national importance. There was an opening wedge, even for strict constructionists, in the constitutional power of the federal government to improve harbors and provide for safe navigation; and what was legitimate on the coasts might be extended to lakes and rivers; another loophole was the constitutional power to establish post roads and provide military communications, and a good deal of support for local improvements could thus be reconciled with rejection of a national policy. The argument over internal improvements also became linked with the tariff question: If there were a surplus in the treasury, should it be used to finance internal improvements or to reduce duties; and if there were a deficit (as there was after 1837), should not additional expenditure be avoided?

It may seem perverse that the Democrats should exalt executive influence at the expense of the representatives of the people. This was partly an accidental result of the personal ascendancy of Andrew Jackson but could also be rationalized by the argument that local and special interests were likely to predominate in Congress. This respect for presidential initiative could be an element of both strength and weakness, because it tied the fortunes of the party to personalities and inhibited the evolution of legislative skills. Martin Van Buren was adroit and experienced but lacked popularity in the West and South. James K. Polk was strong inside his administration but little known or appreciated outside it. The two later Presidents, Franklin Pierce and James Buchanan, have become bywords for vacillation. In addition to personal failings it should be remembered that the administrative structure of government was far from adequate for the task of centralized direction. Polk worked himself almost to death keeping pace with administrative tasks that would have been performed by subordinates in a more professional system; under less industrious Presidents the administration would simply come to a halt. With all its deficiencies Congress, with experienced membership and its system of specialist committees, would have been better equipped than the executive branch to study problems in detail and in depth.

The Whigs were regarded by their opponents as old Federalists, but Henry Clay always claimed that he was a Jeffersonian. Indeed, the National Republican party, as he and John Quincy Adams had known it, had grown within Republicanism and not outside it. According to Clay, the Whigs respected the rights of states and rejected loose construction of the Constitution but took the realistic view that a growing nation demanded positive policies from its government. The protection of American industries and federal aid for internal communications were the twin bases of Clay's "American System"; to this was added support for a national bank that could ensure a steady flow of credit to developing enterprise without the risk of financial instability. Constitutional objections to the use of federal money had been met in 1841 by a proposal to distribute the revenue from land sales to the states without laying down conditions for its use, but on the understanding that most of the money would be used to subsidize public works or meet debts already incurred for that purpose. Clay was, however, fully aware that the separation of land from customs revenue would strengthen the case for raising what he regarded as the ruinously low tariff rates.

The Whigs went into 1841 with a coherent policy: restoration of a national bank, a protective tariff, and distribution. Behind this lay an instinctive belief that the future of the nation lay in recognizing and fostering a national community of interest. The United States should not be regarded as a number of competing regions and interests but as a single whole in which local activities complemented each other and mutual interests were served by improvement in any one of them. Northern, southern, and western Whigs showed a remarkable solidarity behind these concepts, and the voting record of the party demonstrated consistency and coherence. Unfortunately for the Whigs there was one dissenter in the party; John Tyler had been chosen as Vice-President in 1840 (ironically enough to conciliate the southern supporters of Henry Clay when their leader was turned down by a combination of northerners and westerners), and in 1841 he became President on the death of Harrison. Tyler was a strict constructionist whose vetoes wrecked the Whig program, and the one survivor from this political disaster—the protective tariff of 1842—was the least popular with southern Whigs. The failure to enact a coherent policy was a fatal blow to the Whigs, and their defeat in 1844 left them with nothing to offer the country. Nevertheless, they continued as an organized, vigorous, and national party for a further eight years.

The Whigs comprised three main elements: the older dominant groups, such as northern merchants and southern planters, who were fighting to retain their ascendancy; representatives of new wealth—especially in finance and industry—whose interests were bound up with national development; and western and southern areas that were dependent on (or had been deprived of) internal improvements. The geographical pattern of Whiggery holds some surprises for those who have accepted conventional accounts. The impression is often given that New England was strongly Whig; in fact, New Hampshire was a Democratic stronghold, and Connecticut and Rhode Island were marginal states. Western New York—an area of farms and small towns that benefited greatly from the Erie Canal —was Whig. In Ohio the northern counties were normally Whig, and the southern were Democratic (though there were some exceptions). In Indiana a large block of rural counties voted for Harrison in 1840 but were afterward normally Democratic. Four states went Whig in every presidential election from 1840 to 1852. Three are predictable —Massachusetts, Vermont, and Kentucky (where Clay's personal influence was paramount). The fourth was, surprisingly, Tennessee, where a combination between commercial towns and the small farmers of the eastern mountains prevailed in the home state of Jackson and Polk. In the South as a whole it is usually said that the Whig map corresponded with the "black counties" of large plantations, but the "white counties" of eastern Tennessee, western Virginia, and western North Carolina were strongly Whig, and these areas would provide several Unionist enclaves within the Confederacy during the Civil War. It may be true that the Whig was the party of wealth, but its deeper significance lay in a commitment to economic development that attracted many who were not wealthy but wished to become so.

Other elements in the Whig syndrome were New England descent, recent immigration from England or Scotland, piety, and affiliation with one of the older Protestant denominations. In the North antislavery men who stopped short of abolitionism were much more likely to be Whig than Democrat. In the South most Whigs were stout defenders of slavery but opposed to giving it prominence in national politics. Finally there was a reform movement within the Whig party for whom the influential Horace Greeley was spokesman and writer in chief. Jacksonian financial policies had driven many over to the Whigs, and these included many southern planters who were shocked and materially damaged by the attack upon the bank. In 1841 all but a small minority of southern Whigs voted for a restored national bank. Those who were less hostile to Jackson's bank policy were alienated by his assumption of authority and defiance of Congress. In 1840 "executive tyranny" was the most popular Whig slogan, and in office the Whigs were expected to provide congressional government.

Both parties were national alliances, and both had local organizations; both offered to advance some interests and defend others. Heredity, group traditions, and local needs were powerful influences in determining party allegiance. In a city a ward of solid middle-class respectability was far more likely to be Whig than Democrat; but in the country a prosperous and stable farming region was more likely to be Democrat. There was a difference in rhetoric and style. Democrats attacked monopoly, governmental expenditure, and English influence; the Whigs attacked "executive tyranny," political corruption, and the Locofocos (by which they implied senseless equalitariansim). Democrats accused the Whigs of manipulating government in the interests of favored individuals or occupations; Whigs accused Democrats of sacrificing the interests of the people as a whole to their unrealistic ideas of strict construction. Neither party willingly brought slavery onto the national stage, but a note of negrophobia could often be heard in Democratic oratory. Both parties proclaimed a stout adherence to the Constitution, and both claimed that their policies would strengthen the Union, whereas those of their opponents would weaken it. In a distant prospect it may be difficult to detect marked differences, but to contemporaries they were real, profound, and important.

For the majority of men actively engaged in politics it was the local scene that mattered. Aspiring politicians hoped to build up a network of friends and followers whose mutual efforts would establish a center of power in the state. Rival groups contended at elections, competed for patronage, and hoped to build up an organization with some chance of survival through slack times as well as profiting from the good. For many who gave themselves to politics this was the reality while national organization was remote; but the two were indissolubly linked. The national administration or its supporters in Congress could help local factions by federal patronage, federal aid for local improvements, and assistance at election time. On the other hand, a national party could not hope to carry a state without strongly based and tightly organized local parties. Unfortunately, the equation was seldom simple. There were rival groups within the national party and rival factions within the state party; there were first preferences, second preferences, and temporary alliances of convenience. The pattern of politics was intricate, and miscalculations through ignorance were more probable than masterly management.

What is seldom noticed by political analysts is the extent to which the politicians needed the traditions of their party. It was the tradition rather than interests or factional loyalties that drew most voters to the polls. It was agreement upon use of the familiar rhetoric that enabled rival factions within a party to close ranks once their struggle for power had been determined. At a predestined point in the political game loyalty to a factional leader gave way to party regularity; and regularity could be explained only by the demands of a common tradition. The decade following 1840 was one of unusually high voter participation, and party allegiance was particularly strong. This was mass democracy in action for the first time, and Americans preceded other peoples in giving to party the kind of allegiance that had formerly been reserved for kings or religious faiths. Loyalty was often unthinking but nevertheless symbolized convictions based upon historical experience.

Both parties had several faces. Old-fashioned Virginia gentlemen who had accepted Jackson with misgivings, and Van Buren and Polk with distaste, had much in common with conservative Bostonians who lamented the onset of democracy and believed that Daniel Webster offered the best hope for the nation. The self-made planters of the Southwest who talked cotton, niggers, and states' rights were socially more like northwestern entrepreneurs than South Carolinians who traced their lineage to the seventeenth century. Both parties cut across many different so-

cial groups and brought together diverse elements.
Broadly speaking, the Whigs were men of old wealth, men
with overseas trading interests, men with national economic connections, and men who believed that they and
their regions would develop if good roads or canals were
subsidized by the federal government. In spite of their bottom weight of men who fought to defend status against
change, the Whigs thought of themselves as the party of
improvement—both material and moral. One axis of the
party linked the merchants of the North with southern
planters; another, which Henry Clay had spent his energies in forging, linked the commerce of the ocean with the
developing West; and yet another linked industrial progress with the interests of skilled labor and the traditions of
the Puritan community.

The Democrats adhered to states' rights and strict construction; they claimed to be the party of the common man
and the persistent foes of monopoly. In practice they were
more complex: States' rights could mean the rights of the
dominant group in the state; strict construction did not inhibit a somewhat enlarged view of presidential authority,
and monopoly could be curbed only by federal authority.
The common man was likely to be a westerner of southern
descent, a farmer in a stable rural society, an Irishman or a
recent immigrant from anywhere except England or Scotland; never, by the wildest flight of fancy, could he be a
Negro. The Democrats prided themselves on the destruction of the Bank of the United States and the low tariff;
they opposed federal aid for internal improvement, and
they tended to be suspicious of all banks that did not subscribe to the party funds. Their one positive commitment
was to territorial expansion. Their record was the most barren and their rhetoric the most persuasive of any party in
the modern world. Their organization, if amateurish by
modern standards, was superior to that of their rivals and
would sustain them with few internal dissensions to the
fatal days of 1860.

The hard core of Democratic support was not uniform throughout the country. In some regions it rested upon the farmer vote in relatively prosperous districts with easy access to river or sea communications. In some western regions it depended upon farmers and small entrepreneurs who believed that private enterprise and state action were sufficient to promote development without federal aid. In eastern cities it relied upon what was often called "the Democracy," which meant an alliance between small entrepreneurs, urban craftsmen, and low-paid laborers; where the Democratic party had controlled a city for years (as in New York) or (as in Chicago) had always been in the ascendant, a considerable number of bankers, large merchants, and prosperous lawyers were prominent in the party. Everywhere, in the rank and file, there were strong ethnic influences; the party had an unchallenged hold upon the Catholic Irish and took most of the German vote. English immigrants were most likely to vote Whig; so were recent Protestant arrivals from Northern Ireland. On the other hand, in the South the Scots-Irish who descended from eighteenth-century immigrants were Democrats. Recent arrivals from Scotland and Wales were divided but inclined to the Democrats.

The prospect of territorial expansion offered a new opportunity that the Democrats were able to seize. Once the embarrassment of Van Buren's opposition to the annexation of Texas had been shaken off, the party was able to commit itself wholeheartedly to "manifest destiny." If the Whigs were the exponents of national consolidation, the Democrats identified themselves with the romantic implications of national growth. In the late 1850's some Democrats, particularly Stephen A. Douglas, were trying to broaden the concept of expansion and identify the party with the interests of progressive western business. Others hoped to continue the momentum of growth into the Caribbean, Central America, and the Pacific. Southern planters, whom the party also wished to attract, were firmly committed to the Atlantic trade and to close economic ties with Great Britain but could be interested in the expansion of slave-based culture in the Gulf of Mexico. The pursuit of a political formula for expansion would become an explosive issue in 1854.

Both major parties tried to steer clear of the anxieties and bitterness of nativism. As Irish and German immigrants, with a preponderance of Catholics, moved into the eastern cities, there were spontaneous reactions uniting genuine fears for the future of Anglo-Saxon civilization, religious bigotry, and resentment at foreign competition in the labor market. The 1840's saw a rising tide of anti-Catholic sentiment with Native American candidates doing well in many local elections. By 1850 they were well represented in most state legislatures, and there was a chance that a more responsible party would emerge from the earlier phases of violence and intimidation. The Democrats had obvious reasons for resisting this attack and for trying to associate their rivals with it, but in many cases they turned the fire of resentment against Negroes. Contempt for free Negroes was not an issue in the South, where their defects were held to be self-evident, but in the free states Negro rights could become a major issue. Racial violence could flare out in the back streets of big cities and in backward rural areas, but even in the calmer atmosphere of state legislatures few men would dispute the fact that law should recognize the inequality decreed by nature. Only in Massachusetts could Negroes vote on equal terms, and in most states they were denied both the vote and the expectation that they could ever rise to full citizenship. Democrats who indignantly rejected the nativist demand that the naturalization period for European immigrants should be extended from five to fourteen years were equally vehement in proclaiming that America was a white man's country in which Negroes must live (if they lived at all) in a state of permanent inferiority.

Few Whigs disputed the basic premise of racial inequality, though some believed that this should not justify the denial of the basic rights of citizenship. There were rare exceptions in the major parties, but only the abolitionists accepted a positive commitment to racial equality; and even they qualified their stand by admitting that immediate equality was impracticable and that it might take generations to overcome the degrading consequences of slavery. Apart from the abolitionists, a conviction of permanent and inherent white supremacy was one of the bonds of the Union. It would be challenged not by a sudden conversion to new concepts of racial justice, but by arguments over what kind of white man should be supreme and whether some of them should be allowed the privilege of employing slave labor.

President James K. Polk was one of the least attractive and most effective of Presidents. The dour, self-righteous little man with few words and a sharp eye knew what he wanted, kept his administration and party up to the mark, and finished his single term having accomplished everything that he intended. He remained little known in the country and sacrificed both social life and public appearances to the unremitting demands of toil at his White House desk. Even men who worked close to him left scanty information about his personality, and one would know little of him (save for official acts) if he had not decided to keep a diary that survived as an intimate picture of the man and a unique record of a President at work.

President Polk was committed to the annexation of Texas and the acquisition of Oregon to 54° 40′ (the Alaskan boundary). The decision on annexation was taken before his inauguration, but in his first hours in office he had to decide whether or not to endorse an important decision by his predecessor. As a compromise between those who wanted immediate annexation and those who wanted a further round of negotiation, the joint resolution had authorized the President to choose either course. It had been expected that Tyler would leave the choice to his successor, and it was believed that Polk would choose negotiation; but Tyler sent the offer of unconditional annexation to Texas, and Polk decided not to recall the messenger. Doubtless he was secretly glad to have the question settled and to await Texan acceptance without the necessity of a further round of congressional controversies over boundaries. He already had his own reasons for preferring the Rio Grande boundary, which he rightly saw as a key to further expansion, and this would have certainly been challenged in Congress. The main difficulty would not lie with the defeated Whigs, but with Van Buren's supporters and with Thomas Hart Benton. Benton was one of the grand figures of Jacksonian politics; as senator from Missouri, he represented the interests of the small farmers rather than the slave-owners of that state, and though a product of the roughest days of the frontier and largely self-educated, had become a prolix but formidable authority on congressional history, diplomacy, and almost every other political question. Himself a slave-owner, Benton was nevertheless opposed to any positive action to extend the institution and had taken the lead in proposals to limit the geographical extent of slavery and to ensure that free settlers would have a fair deal in the western and northern portions of the new state. If negotiation resulted in a further treaty, Benton might well be able to block ratification in the Senate unless it met his requirements.

Oregon was an even more difficult question, for it promised collision not with a weak Mexico, but with enormously strong Great Britain. Since 1826 the Oregon territory had been jointly occupied by the two powers, and the Hudson's Bay Company had become the principal authority on the Columbia and Fraser rivers and on Vancouver Island. Great Britain was unlikely to sacrifice these interests. At the same time American migrants had crossed the continent and established agricultural settlements in the southern coastal area. The sensible solution was to partition the region, leaving the northern part to Great Britain, but agreement would not be easy when it involved the navigation of the Columbia and control of the Puget Sound area and of its outlet, through the straits of San Juan de Fuca to the Pacific. Reviewing the history of the dispute, Polk was in a dilemma; he was politically committed to accept nothing less than the whole of Oregon, but it seemed that the United States was already committed to negotiate on the line of 49° north. He decided to offer negotiation but with the implication that British claims to the Columbia would not be ceded, and he made this offer to Packenham, the British minister at Washington, who unwisely rejected the overture without reference to his government. Nothing could have suited Polk better, for he could now stand by his commitment to all of Oregon while leaving the next move to Great Britain. When Congress met in December, 1845, he proposed formal notice of intention to terminate the agreement of 1826.

The congressional debates on Oregon were interesting. Most Whigs, several southern Democrats (led by Calhoun), and Benton were opposed to any step that would precipitate conflict with Great Britain. Benton argued that American claims north of 49° could not be sustained and that even if they had substance, the mountainous and arctic north was not worth a war. Webster stressed the importance of good understanding with Great Britain, particularly on economic grounds, and Calhoun insisted that the Atlantic Coast would bear the brunt of a war in which only a handful of western expansionists could expect to gain, while even they could hardly expect material benefits. In contrast to the sectional divisions that had emerged over Texas—and would become far more bitter in succeeding years—the Oregon debates illustrated a truly national alliance that crossed party lines. At the same time the tone of debate convinced the pacific Lord Aberdeen that the Senate would ratify a treaty that offered a fair division of the territory.

The Senate toned down the inflammatory wording of the notice as it passed the House of Representatives and deliberately left open the door for negotiation. In the meantime the British had offered a new treaty, which Polk decided to refer to the Senate. This proposed division at 49° with a southward deviation to leave the whole of Vancouver Island and part of the strait in British hands. Free navigation of the Columbia River was proposed for a twenty-year period and only for servants of the Hudson's Bay Company. This the Senate accepted.

The Oregon settlement divided the area of Puget Sound and the straits, which had a natural geographic unity, but given the history of the area and the established interests of the two countries, it was a fair and statesmanlike agreement. Some historians have seen in the chagrin of the western expansionists the seeds of later opposition to the extension of slavery, but it is difficult to attach much importance to this. It is true that there was some bitter criticism of the way in which southern expansionists had got all that they wanted in Texas, while westerners had to forgo "all Oregon," and this may have persuaded a few westerners to look for opportunities to embarrass Polk's administration; but the mainsprings of opposition to the expansion of slavery were already present and would be operated by other and more important causes.

While the Oregon question was still unsettled, Polk had turned his attention southward. He had determined from the outset that the acquisition of California should be a major objective of his policy, and he hoped (following the precedent of Louisiana) that Mexico might be persuaded to sell, but Mexican resentment over Texan annexation made voluntary accommodation unlikely. There were good reasons why pressure should be brought to bear on Mexico to settle substantial debts owing to American citizens, and these might be compounded for California, but the precarious state of Mexican politics made it unlikely that any government could risk concession to the United

States. If the proposal for purchase would not be considered, the road to California must be won by war.

Texan annexation made the United States responsible for extended and vulnerable frontiers, and Polk decided to order General Zachary Taylor with a strong military force south to the Rio Grande. Was this a legitimate and necessary step to defend American soil, or was it needless provocation of a neighbor who had not yet displayed more hostile intentions than a refusal to negotiate for the surrender of half her territory? The Mexicans were bound to view it in the latter light, because they had never recognized Texan independence, and south of the Nueces the Texans had never exercised any authority. On the other hand, by the act of annexation the United States had accepted responsibility for whatever boundaries Texas might claim. Moreover, if war was to come, it was obvious strategy to secure the line of the Rio Grande.

Polk decided upon war when the Mexican Government refused to receive John Slidell, whom he had sent to negotiate for the recognition of Texan annexation and the purchase of California. Before sending his war message to Congress, however, Polk heard that a Mexican force had crossed the Rio Grande and that American soldiers had been killed in a skirmish. The situation was not easy to handle; the news was two weeks old, and for all one knew in Washington the incident might have been followed by a general attack upon Taylor's force; but there is no doubt that President Polk welcomed the news that enabled him to announce to Congress that "American blood had been shed on American soil."

By all counts this was a war of aggression, and it is no mitigation to say that Polk would have preferred to pay than to fight. Mexico had been an unsatisfactory neighbor and had been unwise not to agree at an earlier stage to a de facto recognition of Texan independence; but apart from the foray across the Rio Grande into territory that she still regarded as her own, Mexico had committed no hostile act.

If Polk is to be justified, it can be only on wider and hypothetical considerations. The eventual separation of California from Mexico was probable, and the British had already shown some interest in the Pacific Coast. It is extremely unlikely that Britain, at this stage in her history, would have voluntarily accepted a new commitment, but when Polk made his decision, the fate of the Oregon negotiations was still uncertain, and he may have thought it necessary to forestall any possibility of British action in the Pacific. But the fact remains that Mexico was deliberately forced to choose between humiliation and war and was denied the opportunity of making a rational decision. Moreover, having once entered upon war, Polk was not going to desist until he had all the acquisitions he desired. At one stage he would even consider the possibility of bringing all Mexico under American rule.

The year 1846 was also a turning point in domestic policy. Polk intended to force the country along the road laid down by his own interpretation of Democratic orthodoxy. He would restore the Independent Treasury, repeal the tariff of 1842, and close the back doors and side alleys to internal improvements. The Independent Treasury was the Democratic alternative to a central bank. Its virtue was that it would cut the government off from any connection with commercial banking. The treasury would establish subtreasuries in commercial centers and act as its own depository for government funds. The Whig objection was that in a capital-hungry country substantial funds would be frozen in government custody and play no part in providing the country with its working capital. Nevertheless, this was a measure upon which all Democrats were united and to which the Whigs could offer but feeble resistance.

The tariff was a more difficult party issue. Some downward revision was certain once the Democrats obtained power, but during the campaign Polk had appeared to assure the Pennsylvania Democrats that he would continue protection for their iron products. It was said that without this assurance he could not have carried the state and might have lost New York as well. Nevertheless, Polk encouraged his Secretary of the Treasury to prepare a tariff bill that abandoned the protective principle and to accompany it with a report that laid out the theoretical case for low tariffs. In Congress the measure proved to be bitterly controversial, with some northern Democrats in open opposition. At one stage it was saved in the Senate only by the vote of the Vice-President and finally passed because a Whig from Tennessee decided to obey instructions from his state legislature, though announcing that he did so only because he thought that the low tariff should be tried and shown to fail. A North Carolina senator resigned rather than vote for the bill while unwilling to take responsibility for its defeat. Though many northern and all western Democrats voted for the bill, it had far more the appearance of a sectional measure than the tariff of 1842. Taken alone, it would hardly have been seen in this light, but taken in conjunction with Texas and the Mexican War, many northerners concluded that a southern President was deliberately forcing a southern policy upon the nation. Polk was himself convinced that the tariff bill was a great victory over predatory interests (which had flooded Washington with propaganda and personal solicitations) and a vital step toward the separation of government from the unwholesome influence of private business.

The third domestic issue of 1846 was the President's veto of a rivers and harbors bill. This action was wildly unpopular in the West, where many communities expected to profit by the doctrine (even endorsed in that summer by Calhoun) that the Great Lakes and the river system of the Mississippi had as good a claim for aid as the Atlantic Coast. It was indeed notorious that a number of purely local schemes had been brought into the bill, and little exception could have been taken if Polk had singled out particular schemes for disapproval; what he did was to announce his general opposition to anything that went beyond the strongest case justified by the strictest construction of the Constitution. Privately he feared that the Mexican conflict might stimulate nationalizing tendencies in the same way as the War of 1812. This veto probably did more than any other single measure to put faithful Democrats into a bad humor.

In the immediate future, Polk's domestic policy was a success. In the long run the nation would not have suffered and industry might have gained by protection, but the negative consequences were far outweighed by returning prosperity, which set America upon a course of rapid development that would continue with few checks for over a decade. Similarly, the restrictive consequences of the Independent Treasury were little felt; private business was better able to supply capital, British investment was beginning to flood in after the dull period of the depression, greater banking skill was leading to increased use of paper instruments in place of cash, and before the end of the decade gold would come flooding in from California. The Polk policies were thus a personal triumph for the President and firmly imprinted his doctrines upon the future. The Whig concept of a community of interest fostered by national policy was lost for a generation, and if the economic consequences were barely perceptible, the psychological importance of this void at the center of the Union was important and incalculable.

President Polk, surveying with satisfaction the work of Congress, hoped to extract one further useful measure before its dispersal in August, 1846. The early success of American arms encouraged him to believe that the Mexicans would be forced to negotiate, and he hoped to have the cash in hand to offer the purchase of California as the price of peace. To this end he requested an appropriation of two million dollars for unspecified purposes in the event that peace became possible. It hardly seemed that the passage of the bill would occasion much comment save some warnings from old fogies about the danger of overambitious territorial acquisitions. But at a late stage in the House a Pennsylvania Democrat named David Wilmot rose to propose a proviso that in any lands acquired from Mexico "neither slavery nor involuntary servitude" should be allowed to exist. This famous and portentous Wilmot Proviso used the same words as the Northwest Ordinance and was accepted by most northerners as an extension of traditional policy in changed circumstances. It passed the House by a comfortable margin and reached the Senate in the last hour of the session. John Davis, a senator from Massachusetts, had the floor and proceeded to speak at length. His object was to delay a vote on the bill until it was too late to move any amendment deleting the proviso. Amid a scene of great confusion, with messages arriving from the House in a last-minute rush to complete business for the session, and with several senators appealing to him to allow a vote, Davis continued to speak. Finally a message arrived that it was now noon and the House had adjourned. Davis had mistimed it because the Senate clock was eight minutes slow. The "two-million bill" was lost, and the Wilmot Proviso remained as the focal point of sectional discord. Had Congress the right to prohibit slavery in the territories, had an antislavery majority the right to demand acquiescence from a proslavery minority; and if the right existed, ought it to be exercised?

It is natural that controversy has gathered around the motives for the proviso, which had been prepared by a small group of northern Democrats among whom Jacob Brinkerhoff, of Ohio, was a leading spirit. Wilmot was probably delegated to propose it because, as a regular Democrat in good standing with no reputation as a troublemaker, he was most likely to catch the Speaker's eye. One argument has been that the proviso was intended to repay the President for his betrayal of the western expansionists over Oregon, but it is impossible to establish any

connection between the two groups. A more subtle argument suggests that Wilmot, as a Pennsylvanian who had
supported the 1846 tariff, needed some dramatic cause to
save his seat from angry constituents; this argument is fine-
drawn and hardly persuasive. It is, however, possible that
the proviso was the outcome of a more generalized dissatisfaction with the meager rewards that northern Democrats
derived from their support of the administration. If so, it
was a hint rather than an ultimatum; in the form proposed, as a proviso to an appropriation bill, it would settle
no principle and could mean only that Polk must defer the
question of slavery for determination by Congress. On the
other hand, it gave warning that the mere extension of the
Missouri Compromise line west to the Pacific would be unsatisfactory to many northern Democrats, because it would
mean the establishment of slavery where it had been abolished and might close a large part of southern California
to free white settlement. The most convincing explanation
of the proviso is therefore the simplest one: Wilmot, Brinkerhoff, and their friends disliked slavery. They would not
lift a finger to help the abolitionists, but they served notice
that the national authority of the United States should not
be employed to establish slavery where it had not previously existed.

[3]
Free Soil and Frustration

THE Mexican War occupies an uncertain place in American history. It added half a continent to the United States, secured the Pacific Coast, and established American power irrevocably on the Rio Grande. These enormous gains were won by adding a volunteer force of less than 100,000 to a professional army of under 7,500; 1,721 were killed in battle or died of wounds, and 11,155 died of disease. The battles were remote, all the major engagements were American victories, the terrain and the colorful uniforms provided excellent material for grandiose pictures, and adventures in the largely unknown West had all the trappings of romance; yet outside Texas and California the war itself has almost disappeared from American folk memory. Americans who stayed at home had little idea of how the war was being fought, and the fighting men left few literary records. The contrast with the Civil War is remarkable; the latter would be the most literate of all wars, with thousands of surviving diaries, letters, and reminiscences, and every engagement recorded in exhaustive detail. Even allowing for the far smaller number engaged and the shorter period of conflict, a singular obscurity shrouds the conduct of the war with Mexico. Congress debated the rights and wrongs of war, discussed the acquisitions to be made, but paid little attention to the way in which it was fought. Faulty supply, the disproportionately high incidence of disease, and the quarrels between the generals in the field could have provoked justifiable criticism and investigation, but little was done.

From the outset the Whigs were caught in a trap. When Polk announced the commencement of hostilities, they had no means of knowing whether they were dealing with a border incident or the beginning of an all-out attack on Taylor's army. If the first, the case against war was strong, but if the second, they would incur odium by opposing action. Once they had voted for supplies, they were committed to war and dared not refuse to support the armies in the field. Their criticism of the government was fortified by heavy Whig gains in the congressional elections in 1846 (restoring many of the losses of 1842 and 1844 and winning a small House majority) and by the knowledge that General Zachary Taylor, commanding in the field, was bitterly critical of Polk's administration. They were now able to attack the government by praising the general.

In point of fact Polk had good reason to think that Zachary Taylor's campaign in northern Mexico was losing its momentum by the end of 1846 and that a new military initiative was necessary; but he then hesitated until February, 1847, before ordering General Winfield Scott, with whom he was also on bad terms, to head an expedition to take Vera Cruz and advance inland to Mexico City. Scott's campaign included an amphibious operation against Vera Cruz, six major battles fought with inferior numbers in hostile country with ever-lengthening lines of communication, and ended with a triumphant entry into Mexico City. Yet popular acclaim underrated much of Scott's achievement and fastened upon Taylor's principal victory—won at Buena Vista after advancing against orders and occupying a position in which his force would have been eliminated by a competent enemy—as a glorious triumph of American arms. Buena Vista was to make Zachary Taylor President of the United States, whereas the capture of Mexico City brought Scott cool public praise, private recrimination, and smoldering disputes with his subordinates.

To complete the sequence of misunderstanding the peace commissioner sent by Polk after Vera Cruz was Nicholas P. Trist, who first quarreled with Scott, then won his support, and finally negotiated a treaty ten weeks after receiving orders for his recall. By this time Polk was on the point of yielding to pressure from expansionists who pressed for the annexation of all Mexico and deprecated Trist's treaty of Guadaloupe Hidalgo, which gained a mere 1,193,061 square miles of territory for the United States. However, he sent the treaty to the Senate, where it was quickly ratified. The administration pointedly refused any expression of thanks to Trist, and for many years thereafter he attempted unsuccessfully to get his expenses paid. Unkind rumor said that it was not the opportunity of negotiating a treaty but the attractions of a Mexican lady that had kept him from obeying his instructions to return to the United States.

In the Senate debate on the Mexican Treaty an attempt to add the Wilmot Proviso had been voted down (38–15), but in August, 1848, the House, by a large majority, added a prohibition of slavery to a territorial bill for Oregon. The real issue was not Oregon, where slavery was opposed by the settlers and unlikely to be established, but California. In the Senate there was an attempt to compromise by extending the Missouri line to the Pacific and prohibiting slavery north of it, but this was as unacceptable to Calhoun as the Wilmot Proviso. In extended and increasingly bitter debates he insisted that the United States Government could not prohibit, in any territory, the possession of property that was recognized by the law of a state. In addition, he maintained that American conquest had invalidated Mexican laws; some existing laws might be recognized as a matter of temporary expediency, but none could abridge the privileges and immunities of any American citizen. While the Wilmot Proviso men argued for congressional prohibition of slavery in all territories and Calhoun maintained that only a state had the right to abolish it, Lewis Cass, who was the most likely candidate for the Democratic presidential nomination, put forward the proposition that although Congress had no constitutional power to prohibit slavery, a territorial legislature could do so if it wished.

Here, then, were the positions around which controversy would revolve interminably. Of these solutions to the problem the Wilmot Proviso was logically valid but politically impossible. The power to prohibit slavery had been exercised in the Northwest Ordinance and in the Missouri Compromise, and there seemed to be no constitutional reason why the same principle should not apply elsewhere; but between August, 1846, and the end of 1847 it had become apparent that even moderate southerners would not sacrifice the right to take slaves into the Southwest and especially into southern California. Calhoun had some logic in arguing that no man could be deprived of his property by act of Congress, but in order to sustain his case he had either to say that the Northwest Ordinance and the Missouri Compromise were unconstitutional or, by tortuous argument, to distinguish these precedents from what was now proposed. In any event his solution was also politically impossible, for no amount of argument would persuade the northern majority (or even some slaveholders such as Henry Clay or Thomas Hart Benton) that slavery could be legislated into a territory where it had not existed, and even less into one where it had been previously abolished. The advocates of extending the Missouri Compromise had a good political argument, in that this solution was more likely to win a majority, but there was no logic in the proposition that the limits of slavery should be set by an arbitrary geographical line. The Cass solution had political possibilities but even greater political dangers; it proposed to leave the decision on an issue that affected everyone to small groups of newly arrived settlers in remote territories; nor was it clear when the decision should be made or for how long it would be binding. Thus it would merely postpone the day of reckoning while imposing upon distant settlers the awful burden of immediate decision. The hollow constitutional logic of the Cass argument involved first denying to Congress a power that had twice been exercised and then claiming this power for a legislature that derived its authority exclusively from Congress. The proposition that Congress could delegate a power that it did not possess was obvious nonsense, and Cass had to fall back upon a specious argument that settlers possessed a natural right of self-government that could be neither conferred nor denied by Congress.

Behind these furious arguments—with all their extremes, lack of political realism, and mishandling of precedents—lay a fundamental issue. What kind of nation was the United States to be? And who had the right to decide? The ultimate authority lay with two-thirds of both houses of Congress and three-fourths of the states; but the possibility of deciding a contentious issue by amending the Constitution was so remote that other means had to be found. The southerners would not accept decisions on slavery by a simple majority, but their legal power to resist depended upon the willingness of three or four senators from the North to vote with them. This precarious situation could easily be altered, for it was unlikely that northern pressure against the expansion of slavery would be relaxed, and the addition of one more free state and changes in the senatorial delegation from two old ones would place the South in a minority in both houses. Nullification was dead and would, in any event, be ineffective when the points at issue concerned distant territories under direct rule by Congress. This left only the threat of secession as a defensive weapon, and it was in this direction that an increasing number of southerners began to look.

Legally the status of slavery in the new territories was exceedingly complex. On one side it was argued that Mexican law remained in force until superseded by legislation altering it. This would certainly apply to laws affecting contracts, titles to property, and commercial law, but they could have only local effect and could not abridge general rights of American citizens. In law this argument seemed somewhat stronger and might carry weight with the Supreme Court. There was, therefore, sufficient southern support in the Senate to pass the Clayton Compromise of July, 1848; this proposed that territorial legislatures (when established) in California and New Mexico should have no power to legislate on slavery while allowing cases concerning the status of slaves to be carried on appeal to the Supreme Court. The House of Representatives refused to accept the Senate bill.

Nor would a decision by the Supreme Court have satisfied many southerners, for if the judges settled the conflict between Mexican law and the Constitution, they would leave untouched the power of Congress to prohibit slavery in the territories. Indeed, at the very moment that the House majority was rejecting the Clayton bill, it was passing a bill prohibiting slavery in Oregon. Another line of argument was therefore evolved to demonstrate that limitations upon the power of Congress did exist and that the clause giving Congress the power over the territories of the United States had never been intended to confer unlimited sovereignty over vast areas. As a matter of expediency Congress governed the territories but did so as agent of the states and ought therefore to prejudice none of their interests. The territories had been won not by an abstract entity called the United States, but by the people of all the states acting in union; they should be governed on the same principles.

In the argument on the validity of Mexican law the slave interest seemed to have the better case, but their second argument was historically and logically weak. In 1787 the makers of the Constitution had been aware that very large territories had recently been ceded to the United States and that the old Congress had just passed the Northwest Ordinance; some convention delegates also had experience of land purchase and speculation in the public domain. It was therefore disingenuous to suggest that they either ignored the problem of government or intended the word "territory" to apply only to forts, dockyards, and other small pieces of land acquired by the federal government. The government was an agent of the states, but as long as it acted within the Constitution, it had plenipotentiary powers. Even Calhoun, who unsuccessfully urged Polk to veto the Oregon bill on constitutional grounds, subsequently admitted the weakness of his argument by urging an amendment to the Constitution that would give the power of veto to the "concurrent majority" (that is, to a majority in a minority of the states). With his customary consistency Calhoun would then argue that the power to prohibit slavery had always been unconstitutional but that bad precedents made new safeguards necessary.

The legal maze into which these arguments led, and the impossibility of emerging from it with any agreement, generated increasing support for the solution propounded by Lewis Cass. Though his first step involved the legal absurdity of allowing Congress to delegate a power that it could not exercise, it had the apparent advantage of taking the debate out of Congress and permitting decision by those most affected by it. Later events would prove that the question must return either to Congress or to the Supreme Court or to both, but in 1848 "popular sovereignty" seemed to offer a formula upon which the Democrats could agree; avoiding the politically impossible extremes, it offered a middle road for consensus and common sense. Cass had other qualifications for the Presidency: identification with expansionism and the interests of the Northwest, experience as minister to France, and a reputation for aggressive anglophobia. Nothing in his career suggests that he possessed superior qualities of statesmanship, but he had a grasp of political realities, and if he won little personal devotion, he enjoyed a good deal of respect. In the early months of 1848 he emerged as the strongest contender for the Democratic nomination (Polk having declared that he would not run again).

It is a common fallacy that the Whigs were a party of talents rather than numbers. In fact their voting strength had been demonstrated in the midterm elections of 1846 and could be mobilized behind an effective presidential candidate. Henry Clay had lost in 1832, lost in 1844, and was over seventy by 1848. Daniel Webster was the same age, and his popularity as an orator had always far exceeded his support as a politician. If these two were ruled out, the Whigs were hard pressed to find a presidential candidate. Willie P. Mangum, of North Carolina, the most experienced and respected of Whig senators, was slipping prematurely into despondent and alcoholic senility. Alexander Stephens, of Georgia, was erratic and in poor health. William H. Seward lacked national experience and had a precarious hold upon his home base in New York. John M. Clayton had made a strong impression in Congress, but he was little known in the country at large and came from the state of Delaware, which was electorally insignificant. Associate Justice John McLean, of the Supreme Court, was a perennial but uninteresting and superannuated aspirant for the Presidency. It was therefore logical to look for a popular outsider, and the man of the hour was Zachary Taylor.

The general began by refusing to consider himself as a presidential candidate, but it did not take much to convince him of his error. Indeed, it was not long before he began to swing upon the opposite tack as a nonparty candidate, who might win without a partisan commitment; this had to be corrected, and he was soon brought to realize that the Whigs were odds-on favorites for the election and that it would be better to ride a winning horse than to run against the field. His candidacy was promoted principally by the younger and more progressive Whigs of the North, with W. H. Seward and Thurlow Weed setting the pace.

It might seem inconsistent for northern Whigs to back a southern slave-owner, but Taylor, like Andrew Jackson, could be represented as a national man, and unlike Jackson, he announced in advance his willingness to accept the decisions of Congress and forgo use of the odious veto. This could be taken to mean that he would not block the prohibition of slavery if both houses of Congress wished it. This fitted well with the belief of many antislavery Whigs that, in the long run, the will of the majority must decide the character of the nation and that a national President would accept this principle. At the same time, as a southerner, he might allay sectional fears and assure slaveholders that they need fear no immediate attack upon their institution.

Apart from Taylor's popularity, the Whigs had little to offer. The project for a national bank was dead, rising prosperity killed the case for a protective tariff, and private enterprise was forging ahead without federal aid. It was possible that victory would bring them the opportunity of restating the idea of the harmony of interests—which most of them sincerely believed—but the heat of a campaign precluded fresh thinking, and Taylor himself was hardly the man to formulate a policy. It is possible to exaggerate his simplicity and lack of talent; even when his luck was discounted, it still required ability as well as courage to lead an outnumbered army to victory over difficult terrain, with complicated and unprecedented problems of supply. Even so, compared with all his predecessors, Taylor was a political novice. Andrew Jackson had been a senator, governed territories, and been prominent in the public life of his state. Harrison had been in public life since the first years of the century. Polk had been Speaker of the House and governor of Tennessee. Taylor had held neither executive nor legislative office, and his only symptom of political aptitude was his willingness to act upon the advice of Thurlow Weed, who enjoined silence on every controversial issue. The Whigs turned to Taylor as the inevitable candidate, but the fact that he had no serious rival was proof of political bankruptcy.

Even before a majority of the Democrats had agreed to nominate Cass, there was abundant evidence that the party divisions were too deep to be bridged by easy formulas. The New York followers of Van Buren had not forgiven the defeat of their leader in the 1844 nominating convention, they resented bitterly the favor that Polk had shown toward their more conservative rivals, and they believed that the hostility of these conservatives (or "hunkers") had ruined the political career of their other hero, Silas Wright, and driven him to premature death. They detested Calhoun, whose influence had undermined Van Buren's hold on his party, and did not forget that in 1844 it had lain within the power of Cass to deliver his votes to Van Buren but that he had chosen rather to block the convention until it turned to Polk. In addition to these discontents, the radical Democrats of New York included some of the firmest supporters of the Wilmot Proviso.

Smoldering resentments, bitter local rivalries, and personal hostility to Cass persuaded the radical Democrats (or "barnburners") of New York to stage a revolt. In a hastily contrived convention they nominated Van Buren on a platform condemning the extension of slavery and supporting the Wilmot Proviso. In August they called a national convention at Buffalo and drew together an extraordinary collection of dissident elements in what was perhaps the largest political gathering ever assembled. The estimated forty thousand included, in addition to the New York barnburners, a strong delegation of antislavery Whigs from New England, Ohio, and points west; from Pennsylvania, David Wilmot; a scattering of border-state Democrats; a few old Clay men who could not accept Taylor; and (with considerable misgivings) a majority of the abolitionist Liberty party. If the various elements had few points of contact, they were united by an enthusiasm expressed in a song that, like the movement itself, showed signs of hasty improvisation and defective craftsmanship.

> O, what a mighty gathering
> From the old free states,
> Of the friends of freedom,
> And the tillers of the soil.
>
> We'll not vote for Cass or Taylor
> In the old free states;
> We're the friends of freedom
> And our motto is Free Soil.
>
> Heaven bless the brave barnburners
> In the old Empire State,
> For their fires of freedom
> Are lighting up the land.
>
> And the old Whig party's rotten,
> All that's left is damaged cotton,
> In the old free states.
> But freedom's fires are burning
> And will soon clear out Free Soil.
>
> Then three cheers altogether,
> Let the people shout forever—
> Freemen's hearts none can sever
> In the old free states.

The barbarous rhythm pointed up several truths about the movement. It was a revolt, but it drew upon the banked-up fires of northern sentiment. It appealed to laboring men, repudiated the Whigs, whose advocacy of economic nationalism was pictured as subservience to cotton, and identified freedom with the defeat of slavery. Amid enormous enthusiasm the convention confirmed the nomination of Van Buren and selected for Vice-President Charles Francis Adams, son of the redoubtable and recently deceased John Quincy Adams. As a name the new party chose "Free Soil"; as a slogan, "Free Soil, free labor and free men."

The Free Soil party came too late in the year, left too many questions unanswered about its other objectives, and failed to carry a single state. Its intervention gave New York to Taylor and may have given Ohio to Cass; on balance, however, it probably helped Taylor more than Cass. At least the former won by a decent but not wide margin in the electoral college; but many Democratic Free Soilers must have voted with their old party in congressional elections to win a small majority over the Whigs in the House, though a small band of Free Soilers held the balance. There could hardly have been a more unfortunate outcome to an election in an hour of crisis; no principle had been settled, and no party or person had authority to decide anything.

Nevertheless, the sudden emergence of the Free Soil party was an event of profound significance. In retrospect it is seen as a rehearsal for the later Republican upsurge. Indeed, many of the same groups and leaders would come together in and after 1854, but the syndrome was not complete. Seward campaigned vigorously for Taylor; so did a lone Whig from Illinois named Abraham Lincoln. In Massachusetts a rising star called Charles Sumner campaigned as an antislavery Democrat but was chosen for the Senate by a combination of Free Soilers, Democrats, and dissident Whigs. In Pennsylvania Thaddeus Stevens was an ardent Taylor man. Unkind critics represented the new party as the last fling of Van Buren's frustrated ambition and the dying gasp of political abolitionism; with great realism one can see it as a major alliance against the expansion of slavery, as a revolt against the old leaders, and as the first party claiming that "the old free states" spoke for the nation.

While Americans were absorbed by the political frustrations of 1848, news began to come in that gold had been discovered in California. The distant region was no longer an abstraction but a magnet for thousands of ambitious, shiftless, unscrupulous, and violent men. By the end of 1849 the territory would contain 100,000 people with many of the problems and none of the restraints of civilized society. The principal goldfields were northeast of San Francisco, but no one could tell what more might lie hidden in the great spine of mountains running from north to south, and new immigrants continued to flood in. Yet Congress, in its lame-duck session of December, 1848, to March, 1849, was deadlocked once more upon the insoluble problem of slavery and adjourned without having passed an enabling act to organize the territory. President Polk, as he performed his last official act by riding with the President-elect to the inauguration, was desperately unhappy as Taylor spoke casually of letting California become independent; he may have misunderstood the drift of the general's remarks, because what Taylor intended was to encourage the Californians to seek immediate admission as a state.

If the Californians would organize themselves for admission to the Union as a state, slavery would quickly be removed from congressional jurisdiction. If New Mexico followed the same course, the admission of both territories as states would take the slavery question out of Congress and leave it to be decided by the newly admitted states. During 1849 the Californians went through this process, made a constitution, and applied for admission as a state; by unanimous vote their constitutional convention had prohibited slavery.

The apparent simplicity of Taylor's solution raised more problems than it solved. There was first the question of size and boundaries: California included the present state together with modern Nevada; New Mexico included not only the modern state of that name but also Utah, Arizona, and a part of Colorado. The Californians had assumed authority over the whole Mexican province, and the inhabitants of the small settlement around Santa Fe and Albuquerque would have the right to settle the future of a vast and largely unexplored inland empire. By the normal processes for the admission of states, Congress would first have decided boundaries in enabling acts; moreover, a part of New Mexico, including the only permanently settled area, was claimed by Texas. Once admitted, states had unqualified control over their own domestic institutions and could not be subsequently subdivided without their own consent. Unilateral action by the Californians, and the threat of similar action in New Mexico, was therefore the virtual and probably irreversible implementation of the Wilmot Proviso.

There is little wonder that senators and representatives from the southern states assembled in Washington in December, 1849, in an excitable mood and resolved to do battle for southern rights; it was equally predictable that Free Soilers, holding the game in their hands, were in no mood for compromise. The immediate issue was the Speakership of the new House. The Whigs hoped to continue Robert C. Winthrop, of Massachusetts, in office, but the Free Soilers blocked the election of a "Cotton Whig" who had (so they believed) deprived antislavery men of their rightful representation on committees during the previous Congress. The rules required a majority of the House, not a plurality, for the election. While President and Senate waited impotently for the choice of a Speaker, the House witnessed scenes of repeated disorder, violent speech, and the bitterest statements of sectional animosity yet heard in official Washington. After three weeks, some southern Whigs joined with Democrats to alter the rules and choose the man with the largest number of votes. On the sixty-third ballot Howell Cobb, of Georgia, was elected under the amended rule; his considerable ability would be exerted uniformly on the proslavery side of the great controversy.

At this stage it is worthwhile to consider the forces that were building up behind the dams. Generations of writers have submitted sectional differences to minute analysis, but the mainsprings of controversy must be found in the character of the regions themselves and in their internal tensions. These forces, more than anything else, made men who shared the same traditions, enjoyed similar political institutions, and were largely of similar ethnic origins regard each other as bitter enemies.

The most obvious fact about the South was its biracial character; second was the existence of sharp class divisions among the whites. Wide suffrage among white males gave numerical superiority to the small landowners, but social prestige, economic power, and educational advantage lay overwhelmingly with the planters and tended to concentrate among the wealthiest of them. The economic base of this power was slavery, but political weight lay with the white majority who owned few or no slaves. The upper classes, though sharing a style of life, were far from homogeneous. Breeding and prestige derived from tradition lay with those whose economic position was precarious; new wealth and bright prospects for the future lay with the plantation magnates of the cotton belt of the lower South, and the relative decline of the old Atlantic states was directly attributable to their competition. Even in the more advanced states the majority of free white men lagged far behind other civilized societies in education, material standards, and economic opportunity. All made for what is now recognized as a classic situation in an underdeveloped country. The ruling elite had to exploit emotional issues, because they could not or would not offer tangible benefits to their constituents; poverty, backwardness, and lack of progress had to be blamed upon external enemies; but the authors of their misfortunes had to be found within the same political nation and among men with whom on other issues they would have been pleased to cooperate. Southern leaders were torn constantly between the need to demonstrate their unique qualifications for ruling their own society and the desire to associate with those elements in the other society upon whom they depended for economic and political support.

The differences between the sections were formidable, but they need not have been impossible to resolve. On the major question of race relations there was little dispute, for the great majority of whites, North and South, believed that the blacks were intellectually, morally, and biologically inferior. On the crucial question of the future of slavery in the nation, it required only two conclusions to restore harmony. It was necessary for southerners to accept the fact that slavery was neither permanent nor beneficial and for the North to agree that the adjustment of race relations in a free society was a national responsibility. Both propositions could call upon deeply rooted traditions of the past, and the refusal to accept them is evidence that the internal forces of the two societies were driving on to the point at which their converses seemed to be logical and unavoidable. The South came to assume that slavery was necessary, permanent, and beneficial and that southerners could not remain in a Union that refused to accept this. The North came to insist that because slavery was morally wrong, slaveholders must make all the concessions while the rest of the nation accepted no responsibility for the problems of a biracial society.

By some modern standards society in the South was simple and unsophisticated. It is important to realize that compared with all preceding societies, it was complex and depended upon accumulated knowledge and skill for its effective operation. It belonged to a great international economic system, producing large-scale commercial crops for the world market. It was a very large region with districts at very different levels of development: declining areas of the old tidewater, booming areas of the cotton belt and the new Southwest, piedmont and valley areas with a settled and economically conservative class of middle-class farmers, and everywhere enclaves or remote districts in which occupiers of the soil lived at subsistence level in an environment of ignorance and apathy. The nexus between old and declining areas and new and prosperous areas was an internal slave trade that the best of the old-style paternalist planters regarded with intense distaste, but without which their economy would collapse and that of their newer competitors would not thrive.

The white South could never get far from the facts of race. Most southerners could not imagine what life would be like with a free black population. They had a preview in the southern cities, where the free blacks were most numerous and the discipline of slavery was withering away, and what they saw most of them disliked. The poor white freeholder in the South was caught in a dilemma; he had little love for the great planters who dominated politics, held down the level of expenditure, and did less than any other nineteenth-century ruling class to supply their poorer neighbors with the elements of civilized life; yet the planter enforced discipline upon the blacks, segregated them from the rest of society, provided for their health while working and their maintenance in old age. No one else was likely to perform these functions; certainly no one else would do so without any charge upon the public. Free Negroes would swarm over the country, force themselves onto the poorer lands where too many already struggled for subsistence, foster violence, and breed shiftless poverty. In addition, emancipation would impose financial losses upon the very large numbers of small slave-owners who were least able to bear them. It was clear that the free states of the North and West would do nothing to ease the social and economic burdens that would be placed upon the South.

If the circumstances of a biracial society caused men to converge upon support of slavery—whether as an unavoidable necessity or as an essential support for civilization— they differed upon other issues much as the men of other advancing societies did. The planter gentry controlled politics and the press, they exercised a predominant influence over the churches, and the lawyers were their professional dependents. There were divisive issues, most of them running along class or regional lines, but politics also tended toward equilibrium. The Democrats were broadly identified with the small farmer of the "white counties," but they could not have been effective without a minimum number of leaders drawn from the planter gentry. The Whigs were the party of the larger slave-owners and their commercial and professional allies, but they could never win an election without substantial support from the poorer farmers. Given leadership for the Democrats and a popular following for the Whigs, there was no reason why party politics should not remain stable.

Yet tension existed; it could hardly be otherwise in a society with so unequal a division of wealth, so little economic opportunity for the poor, and so many occasions upon which political dissatisfaction could be voiced. The power of the planter gentry was always under pressure, and their most effective political leaders (drawn from the Atlantic states) operated from an insecure economic base.

In this situation there were three principal responses from the dominant class: insistence upon the racial aspects of slavery and the need to maintain white control over black; recrimination against "the North" for depriving "the South" of a fair share in national wealth; and determination to keep open the doors of westward migration, which had been the traditional safety valve for southern discontents. The first response was comparatively easy in a race-conscious society, but the southern political leaders were able to exploit fully the abolitionist criticism of slavery. The abolitionists said that the Negro was a man and a brother, that his apparent depravity was the consequence of slavery, not its justification, and that blacks should have equal rights with whites. It was this plea for equality that was particularly odious in the South (and in most parts of the North), and it provided the southern leaders with an object lesson that they used with alacrity; the alternative to slavery was not segregation but amalgamation. The second proposition—that southern backwardness was the result of northern "aggressions"—was more difficult to maintain. Southerners had played prominent parts in every government, in every Congress, and in every phase in party evolution. Whatever political decisions had been taken and whatever policies had been pursued, the southerners must share the credit or blame. It was necessary to credit northern politicians with exceptional skill and southerners with remarkable blindness to maintain the contrary, and all the evidence pointed in the other direction. Calhoun could, indeed, accomplish this difficult feat, but many southerners were puzzled rather than enlightened by the argument. The economic problem was equally puzzling. Free trade was the popular economic theory in the South, and free trade fostered specialization. Large-scale commercial agriculture became the specialized activity of the South; banking, shipping, and the handling of international trade became that of the North. The rise of northern industry and its comparative lack of success in the South might be attributed to the protective tariff, but after 1846 it was difficult to sustain this argument. Moreover, many southerners held to the Jeffersonian faith that agriculture bred a superior and purer race of men; they might wish to counteract the economic power of the North, but they were not convinced that they should themselves undertake these questionable activities. A few writers, among whom J. D. B. De Bow was prominent, preached the doctrine of economic development to the South; but rhetoric against the mysterious and faceless men of the North made far more impression than constructive proposals for southern manufactures, railroads, and shipping. Above all, these writers helped to convince southerners that whether or not they diversified their economy, slavery must remain its essential base.

The perplexities of the economic enigma made it likely that attention would focus upon the third proposition of southern political leadership: that the roads to the West must be kept open for migratory southerners. For the larger planters there was little in this of direct or material interest. As would be pointed out all too frequently in the future, the natural limits of plantation slavery had been reached or almost reached; and those who wanted to try their luck on new lands had the vast plains of Texas as their safety valve. A few might have an eye on southern California, but this could be only an abstract speculation about a region of which little was known. In any event the large planters of the upper South and Atlantic Coast, who were under the greatest economic pressure, were the least likely to pull up their roots. The migration by large planters was mainly to establish plantations and good lands in Mississippi, Louisiana, or Arkansas. In this situation the strident complaints of southern leaders about the prohibition of slavery in the territories seem exaggerated and unbalanced; the case is altered when one realizes the extent to which they were the result of internal pressures. The plain people of the South got little enough out of their political leaders and might have been stirred to revolt if their freedom to move had been bargained away.

For generations southerners had, of course, been migrating into free states and free territories, but in the difficult and largely unknown terrain of the West the possession of slaves would be an enormous advantage. Too much attention has been concentrated upon the possibility of using slaves in large-scale agriculture and too little upon the importance of a few slaves—even of one or two—in a new land where hired help was impossible to obtain. Even in the pioneer household a female slave would lighten the wife's burden of incessant toil; in the fields a slave working alongside the owner (as they had always done on the small farms of the South) would be a valuable asset. Whether the optimistic migrant from the South thought of himself in the future as a farmer, rancher, or miner, a single slave would give him a start on new land, and success would be secured if more could be purchased at a later date. This was the rationale behind the assertion that southern rights would be impaired if slavery were excluded from the territories; it was the logical response from a ruling class that could not ignore democratic pressures.

Southern resentment over northern attitudes to fugitive slaves showed a similar logic behind what was apparently a largely emotional issue. Though running away was a normal occurrence in a slave society, comparatively few reached the free states. Most were recaptured soon after escape, and of the successful, more found a refuge in swamps, forests, or remote mountain districts than crossed the Mason-Dixon line or the Ohio; of those who did flee to the free states, comparatively few were pursued. Naturally fugitives were most numerous from the upper South, and sometimes the loss suffered was serious, but in an area with redundant slave labor the owners were not always sorry to lose a mouth to feed. For though it is impossible to be precise before the days of modern accountancy, it is probable that on declining estates too many slaves consumed more than they produced. It is true that a redundant slave might be more profitable if sold to a trader, but this was not a popular remedy, even though many resorted to it. However, special cases made bad practice, and for slavery as a whole it was essential to maintain the maximum deterrence against fugitives, and obstacles to their recovery could not be tolerated. The constitutional obligation to return "fugitives from labor" was inescapable, but several northern states honored this in the letter, not the spirit; in effect the slave-owner was told that he could come and look for fugitives but that no one would help him to do so, and that he ran the risk of prosecution if he picked the wrong man or could not prove the identity of the right one. A few states went even further and forbade their officers from assisting recovery in any way. Even if some stopped short of this, they could rely upon the decision of the Supreme Court in *Prigg v. Pennsylvania* to maintain that they had no power to pass laws on a matter over which Congress had exclusive authority. Whatever the arguments, the underlying assumption was that owners had no *moral* right to recover slaves and that no man's hand need be lifted to help him. Slave-owners were correct in saying that with every other kind of lost property, it was assumed that the obligation to assist recovery went far beyond the letter of the law. Again, the real threat was felt by the small slave-owner. The large plantation owner could afford to lose an occasional fugitive, but the small man might lose his life savings and could certainly not undertake the costly and difficult task of recovery. What southern leaders wanted was a procedure that would be quick, relatively cheap, and willingly administered by the men on the spot, and they could not accept less without betraying the interests of their constituents.

Southerners had become exceedingly sensitive to attacks upon slavery in the District of Columbia. The abolitionists had concentrated their attack at this one point where Congress had undivided sovereignty. It was improbable, in the immediate future, that majorities in both houses would abolish slavery in the nation—or that a President would sign such a bill—but it was conceivable that a majority might regulate the slave trade, pass a slave code to enlarge the rights of slaves, and accept some plan of gradual and compensated emancipation in the District. If this should happen, the resistance of southern states to similar proposals elsewhere would be weakened, and it was not forgotten that in 1831 a substantial minority in Virginia had pressed for action on these lines. It therefore became a major objective of southern men in Congress to prevent discussion of slavery in the District. Calhoun's argument that Congress could not discuss an institution over which it had no jurisdiction was far-fetched, but his contention that debate on slavery in the District constituted a political threat that had to be "met at the threshold" was realistic. Hence the famous "gag law" and Calhoun's accusation of betrayal when, in 1844, some northern Democrats voted to end it.

It was not, as his enemies claimed, an "abstraction," but a well-founded belief that if Congress discussed slavery in the District, it would soon move to regulate it, and that once slavery was brought under the law in this way, its days as a national institution were numbered.

Speculation and statistical inquiry have been exhausted by the profitability of slavery. Was the institution in good economic health, or was it languishing under the weight of diminishing returns? At one end it seems clear that on new land, under efficient management, slavery was profitable; all the evidence points to a good return on investment, and the rising price of slaves indicates competitive buying and an expectation of profit. At the other end of the scale there are examples in which it seems that a large slave force was being employed simply to maintain itself. At every level, of course, efficient men could do well, and inefficient men did badly, so that generalization becomes difficult. Also, most of the available evidence comes from large plantations, and one knows little of the economic fortunes of the large number who owned fewer than ten slaves. It has been argued that only the internal slave trade kept the economy of the upper South viable, yet this may be too broad a generalization. The sale of slaves undoubtedly kept some inefficient planters in business and some poor lands in cultivation, but if these had failed, the men who remained might have succeeded rather better than they did. It may be true that the slave trade kept the marginal producer in business, but this does not mean that the whole region would have been bankrupt without it. The effect of the internal slave trade may therefore be compared to that of government subsidies for an inefficient producer in an otherwise healthy economy.

There are plenty of examples of plantations going downhill, but any expanding economy has its toll of dislocation, lack of adaptation, and failure. In the upper South men who clung to old methods, poor land, and unremunerative crops paid the price, but there were opportunities for diversification, enterprise, and experiment; outside some worn-out tidewater lands, the whole band of upper slave states, from the Atlantic to the Mississippi, experienced an era of bustling prosperity in the middle years of the nineteenth century.

No calculus of slavery can be based exclusively on economic considerations. For many southern gentlemen the valued aspect of slavery was the domestic service that it provided; in the life of the great house the butlers, cooks, coachmen, gardeners, household servants, stable boys, and craftsmen made possible leisure, conviviality, parties, balls, dinners, discussion, politics, and public life. These things persuaded so many southern gentlemen that slavery was the best foundation for civilization. Lower in the social scale, it was still the social assets rather than the economic functions of slavery that were often valued. Under these conditions there was nothing incongruous in a system that barely kept solvent but was valued for the way of life that it made possible.

It is necessary to emphasize these social and psychological advantages of slavery for the owners in order to understand their apparent indifference to other aspects of a developing society: innovation, availability of capital, consumer demand, diversity of opportunity, improved education, and the cultivation of new skills. On good land cotton was profitable, but the profits were used to buy more land and more slaves; this in itself might not have been a disadvantage if there had not been a companion tendency to hold on to redundant labor and keep poor land under cultivation and for unsuccessful employers to cling to their land rather than seek occupation elsewhere. The commercial class remained small when compared with that of other developing societies, and the more ground it yielded to the superior skill of northern men, the less incentive was there to enter it. Nor was there much recruitment from below, for the plain people of the South, relieved from the burden of economic exploitation, produced neither entre-

preneurs nor working-class organizations and were content
to live at a low economic level. By the middle of the nineteenth century the South was caught in an economic and
social trap from which it would be difficult to emerge.

It has sometimes been argued that this situation had little direct connection with slavery and that sectional tension was merely an extreme example of the stuggle
between agriculture and industry that occurred in so many
nineteenth-century societies. According to this analysis, the
tragedy lay in the geographical separation of the two cultures that prevented them from finding a way of living
with each other; slavery became the symbol of conflict, not
its cause. It would be possible to draw different conclusions
from this comparison. The tension existed in every developing country but deteriorated into war only where the
agricultural society depended upon slave labor. Or it can
be argued that the benefits of economic cooperation were
so great, and the political power of the South so effective,
that only the existence of slavery could have obscured the
first and caused a loss of confidence in the second. In any
case, and whatever logic may be adduced, there seems little
point in arguing that slavery had nothing to do with the
rising tide of controversy, when almost all contemporaries
believed that it did. The men of the age tried to deal with
the world as they saw it, and slavery could be neither ignored nor exorcised. It was certainly the central and inescapable fact of southern society that influenced (when it
did not determine) every southern action.

It is possible to speculate upon the extent to which slavery conditioned the behavior of slave-owners. In many respects the southern planters were similar to the country
gentry of England. They were accustomed to local authority and accepted it as a right and a duty. They possessed no
privileges in law, but they expected deference as a matter
of course. They alone enjoyed higher educational opportunities but gave more acclaim to physical than to intellectual prowess; they were contemptuous of men who earned

their living in commerce and had little inclination to leave
their plantations for more profitable occupations. All this
was characteristic of large landowners everywhere and of a
good many smaller ones who imitated their wealthier
neighbors. Was there something more? Southern gentlemen adhered to a code of honor that included such obso-
lescent customs as dueling. They used a style of rhetoric
that was becoming outmoded, and the high culture of the
age of Jefferson (never sustained by more than a small minority) was fading into the past. Much of this could be
explained by provincialism and lack of criticism in the
South itself, but antislavery men maintained that cultural
decline and violence disguised as chivalry were consequences of slavery. On the one hand it was said that the
habit of absolute authority over other human beings corrupted the spirit, and on the other that the inner guilt of
slavery made slave-owners sensitive, aggressive, and intolerant of reasonable dissent. Abolitionists made great play
with the sexual morals of slavery. Southerners might reply
that no part of the South witnessed the hordes of prostitutes and rampant depravity of northern cities, but it remained true that nowhere else was the dual standard of
male morality so apparent or so likely to invade the home.
Less considered at the time but of significance in retrospect
was the slave-owner's experience of living out his life
under the scrutiny of black people; he might command but
never knew what kind of judgment was being made behind
those dark faces. Obedient, respectful, sometimes syco-
phantic, the slaves had their own secret lives, and the masters watched constantly for signs of deceit, unvoiced
criticism, or more daring insolence.

The psychological effect of these experiences can be
conjectured rather than proved, but contemporaries may
have been right in attributing to them the mixture of ar-
rogance and sensitivity that characterized southern public
men. Criticism of a southern man was not an expression of
a point of view, but a challenge to his honor; but he him-

self treated critics of his institutions with abusive contempt. This behavior earned its reward as northerners who
were apathetic about slavery came to conclude that it corrupted white society; instinctively, too, they often realized
that the posture of the upper-class southerner was necès-
sary in order to maintain his prestige among his humbler
white neighbors who were the real sufferers from the slave
system.

The internal structure of southern society can therefore
explain the force behind southern expansionism, but the
drive might have expended itself and dwindled away if it
had not met resistance. On the face of it, there was little
to arouse northern fears; the most that southerners demanded was the right to take slaves into an area where the
risks were high and the prospects dubious; and whatever
might be the status of slavery during the territorial period,
no one questioned the right of a state to determine the
character of its own institutions. The distinction between
a territory and a state was (in some sense) a legal fiction.
At one moment people enjoyed limited rights of self-
government under a constitution that was no more than an
act of Congress; at a stroke of the pen they became citizens
of a state that was sovereign over most matters affecting
life, liberty, and property. The quarrel focused upon the
twilight stage during which the people of a territory enjoyed local self-government under congressional authority,
and it would not seem to be beyond the political wit of
men to discover a formula. The major difficulty was that
once slavery had been established, it might be difficult to
remove; and even if slavery were ended, the problems of
a biracial society would remain.

Yet even if this were so, who would suffer? It seemed unlikely that any economic interest would be jeopardized,
and many would reap immediate benefits from the opening of the Great Plains. The settlers in the unmapped West
would enter a vast region in which there was room for all,

and the vast northern trade with the South and West was likely to grow ever larger. There seemed to be strong arguments for allowing the South to have the shadow while economic power and westward migration would give the substance to the free men of the North and West. This, in essence, was the solution propounded by Cass, and after him by Stephen A. Douglas. Popular sovereignty was a means of shelving the problem of slavery until new states were ready to solve it for themselves. The solution appealed equally to men who believed that the problem of slavery was insoluble, to hardheaded men of business, and to settlers who wanted quick access to new land. For all of them the intrusion of slavery into new territories might be unwelcome but need be neither a disaster nor a great moral crisis.

This was the foundation upon which northern and midwestern Democrats would try to build their system. If most of them would prefer to see slavery excluded (and believed that it could not make headway against popular disapproval), they were content to stand on the proposition that communities should decide for themselves. That this involved a further proposition that white men had an inalienable right to settle the status of black men seemed immaterial, for the inferiority of Negroes seemed to require neither argument nor proof. The abolitionist counterproposition that Negroes were everywhere entitled to the right of life, liberty, and the pursuit of happiness commanded little support. The intermediate ground, taken by antislavery Whigs and Free Soilers—that the laws of states legalizing slavery must be respected but should not be extended beyond the boundaries of the existing states—was logically the weakest of the three positions. If the white people of a state could decide the status of Negroes, why not the people of a territory; alternatively, if slavery was immoral in a territory, was it not immoral everywhere? As so often happens, the least logical position proved to be the one upon which it was easiest to rally, and in course of time resistance to the extension of slavery combined with respect for slavery where it already existed became the central tenet of both the Free Soilers and the later Republicans. The inconsistency would plague Republican leaders, produce deep conflicts of opinion during the Civil War and Reconstruction, and render it impossible in later years to maintain a firm commitment to equal citizenship.

To understand why the Free Soil argument came to occupy this important position, it is necessary to investigate the internal tensions of northern and western society. Rapid expansion, economic growth, the swelling tide of immigrants, and the great rewards offered for enterprise created an atmosphere of excitement focused upon material success. At the same time deep and persistent currents of idealism pressed men to clothe their ambitions in moralistic terms. There was little hypocrisy in this. From the beginning of American civilization mastery of the material environment had been associated with the preservation of rights and the attainment of a better society. The dualism had been explicit in old Puritanism; it was implicit in much recent experience. Settlers went west to recover lost innocence, but hopes remained dreams without economic success. Europeans escaped from the restraints of the Old World to make a new life in a new land, but they were forced to depend upon such hard facts as savings, employment, and adaptation to an unfamiliar environment. Inevitably material welfare became the object of endeavor and the index of individual success. It also meant enhanced prestige for the entrepreneurs who created employment, brought railroads, commerce, and manufactures to entire regions, and upon whose collective enterprise depended the personal success of thousands of individuals. Yet the prestige and rewards given to coarse vigor never destroyed the underlying conviction that it was the destiny of America to build and become a morally superior society.

It is easy at this distance of time to underrate and misinterpret ideals but doubtful whether any vigorous civilization can live without faith. Whether the rhetoric seized upon a phrase such as "manifest destiny," drew upon the well-springs of religious revival, or rested upon revolutionary traditions and the Declaration of Independence, the outcome was a conviction that America was both the land of opportunity and one in which a better life could be lived. There was a tremendous buoyancy in this civilization and few doubts, but this very confidence made it necessary to define the national spirit in idealistic terms. The imperative can be illustrated in many ways: It was a constant theme of Horace Greeley's New York *Tribune,* it was dominant in many of Emerson's writings, it inspired William Cullen Bryant and (in a slightly soured and eccentric version) James Fenimore Cooper. Across the country it was the theme of many humble newspaper editors, essayists and poets of local reputation, and (perhaps most significant of all) hundreds of Protestant clergy.

The contrasts between the ideal of a more perfect society and the realities of actual existence were always apparent, but they became of special significance when every speech and every newspaper proclaimed that the road to earthly paradise lay over American soil. There were many obstacles and lions in the path. The climate, with its extremes of temperature, required the romantic touch of a Currier and Ives print to endow it with magic. The immigrant worker might find harder toil demanded of him in the poor streets of ugly towns than he ever experienced in his own fields. Skilled workers could live considerably better than their European counterparts, but they were at the mercy of violent fluctuations in the economy. Higher up the ranks of business the rate of failure was high, and the unsuccessful could seldom fall back, as in Europe, upon family or community for support. Charitable institutions were few; public welfare hardly existed. Pennsylvania had penitentiaries that attracted worldwide interest from penal reformers but did little for the sick or aged and nothing for the unem-

ployed. Massachusetts had excellent schools but did nothing to regulate the hours and conditions of work even
when health was endangered. The eastern states prided
themselves upon their high standards of behavior but witnessed personal and mob violence (including the destruction of schools, churches, and orphanages) directed against
immigrants (particularly if they were Catholics) and free
Negroes.

Things were quieter in the rural West, but frustration
could be just as bitter. In the dream every settler became a
successful farmer, every village became a city, and every
community was close-knit by bonds of friendship and
shared the experience of improvement. It requires no doc-
umentation to prove that this was not always so. Beneath
every record of successful development there is an untold
story of failure, shiftless men, and dispirited laborers; a
few found their way into remote rural or frontier areas,
some might end as subsistence farmers or as hired help for
their more prosperous neighbors, and others would end up
in low-paid work in the towns. This shifting population in
the lower strata of society contributed nothing to the dyna-
mism of American society but gave a sense of urgency to
the efforts of those who meant to get on in the world. Nor
was this compulsion purely individualistic; success was
unlikely in an unsuccessful community, and personal ambition blended naturally with the advancement of towns
and districts.

Within this spectrum of individual drive, anxious energy, and social aspirations the antislavery movement
played a comparatively small part. It was natural that
idealism should manifest itself in several forms, and the
religious preoccupations of many nineteenth-century men
clothed most causes with a crusading spirit. There was
therefore nothing exceptional about abolitionism, but the
recent success of emancipation in Great Britain and the existence of a well-organized antislavery movement in that
country gave abolitionism an international aspect and

identification with universal principles of betterment. It would be unrealistic to suggest that large numbers of Americans were deeply moved by the injustice done to slaves, but increasingly they came to regard the society that slavery produced as the antithesis of what America should be. Southern society spurned free labor, raised a few slave-owners to the zenith of power and influence, but denied both education and opportunity to poor white men. In addition, the political power of the South, inflated by counting slaves as three-fifths of a person for the purpose of apportionment, had a long record of obstruction to what was regarded as legitimate economic objectives. In Pennsylvania and the Northeast the tariffs of 1833 and 1846 were major grievances; in the West it was opposition to national aid for internal improvements. Less keenly felt by the rank and file, but an embarrassment to business, was the ruin of the Bank of the United States and the establishment of the Independent Treasury.

These material grievances created irritation but were seen as symptoms of a disease rather than as its cause. None of them would have grown to the magnitude of bitter controversy if they had not been associated with what generations had learned from Jefferson and Clay (both slave-owners) to call "a moral, social, and political evil." It is true that the majority of northerners showed little respect and scant consideration for the free Negroes in their own states, and it is equally true that most of them did not want black people, slave or free, in the new territories; but it is an error to rush with some recent writers to conclude that Free Soil and its variants were "racist" and therefore to be condemned. In common with most white men of the nineteenth century, northern Americans believed that Negroes were lower on the scale of creation, and even if some were tolerantly disposed to allow black men an equal chance, they knew the difficulties of a biracial society and can hardly be blamed for wishing to avoid them. These prejudices do not alter the significant fact that they came to regard slavery as a monstrous institution and resolved to do what lay within their power to prevent its nationalization.

These were the forces that converged upon the center when the application of California for statehood gave them point and direction. Basically the issues were very simple: Would the representatives of the South accept an extralegal act that excluded slavery from the Pacific? If they were forced to accept it, what price would they demand? If the same process were to be repeated in New Mexico, would they accept this also? On the other hand would a majority of representatives from the North be ready to open a door for slavery in the territories? And if they won on the major issue of California, what would they give in return? Beneath these superficial issues were deeper questions of American national character. To many on both sides it seemed that a decision against slavery, however qualified, would release the dammed-up waters of abolitionism and eventually drown southern society; equally it seemed to many in the North that concession would recognize a national interest in the retention of slavery. To this were added two further questions of profound emotional significance: Would abolitionism die down; would southern separatism fade away?

The politicians who had to confront these issues were ill equipped for the task. The leaders were old, with ideas rooted in the past. Most men in the second rank depended for survival on majorities that combined provincialism with grandly stated principles. The world was a blend of rhetoric and Main Street. President Taylor was honest, inexperienced, and totally lacking in finesse. He had succeeded in convincing himself that the only way to get slavery out of politics was to accept California and New Mexico as states, when they would be able to control their own destinies. Himself a great slaveholder, enjoying economic and social security, he had little sympathy with southern farmers; thoroughly national by upbringing and profession, he had a simple detestation of all talk of holding the government to ransom with talk of southern rights. With somewhat greater shrewdness he sensed that if the case for compensation whenever slavery had to yield a point were admitted, one had set out on a long road with neither end nor turning.

The Senate contained a number of aging men with a last chance to make a reputation in the world. The generation born in the dawn of the nation were playing out their last act. Henry Clay—twice unsuccessful in bids for the Presidency, once most unjustly passed over by his party, and recently discarded as a superannuated man—came back to the Senate with incredible vigor for all his seventy-three years. Daniel Webster, who had delivered one of the greatest of American orations twenty years before, was determined once more to stand out as a national figure. John C. Calhoun, robbed of his national constituency, still smarting from the defeat of nullification, hoped to grasp a dying reputation as a profound political theorist and resolute spokesman of the South. Thomas Hart Benton, in some ways the wisest but most erratic of the four, was obstinate and opinionated. Of the younger men who would play an active role Henry S. Foote had a violent temper and uncertain judgment; Stephen A. Douglas was deeply distrusted by Free Soilers and antislavery Whigs and regarded as a coarse parvenu by men of the older school; Jefferson Davis was self-righteous and inflexible; while William H. Seward had a reputation (not altogether deserved) for antislavery "ultraism" and was envied for his influence with the administration.

During the course of the controversy three other major issues emerged. In January Senator James M. Mason, of Virginia, had introduced a new fugitive-slave bill; it was little debated but remained in the wings as an essential ingredient for any settlement acceptable to the South. Concurrently Texas claimed western boundaries that would have brought Santa Fe under her authority. The status of slavery in the District of Columbia had long been a target for antislavery agitation; was it not at least possible to end its role as one of the nation's greatest slave markets?

Clay's compromise, presented in a set of resolutions in February, tried to build on realities without treading the dangerous sands of abstract right. There might once have been a case for dividing California, but Congress had failed to agree or to act; it would now be folly to deny the Californians orderly government, pretend that they were too few for statehood, or ignore their wishes because their procedure was technically irregular. The people of New Mexico had repeatedly expressed their wish to remain outside Texas, but as the United States had admitted by implication the justice of Texan claims, there was a moral obligation to assume a substantial portion of the Texan debt in compensation. For Texans the payment would indicate that their boundary claims had been accepted but adjusted on grounds of expediency while assumption was justified because the debt had been raised on the security of customs levied by independent Texas and since brought within the United States revenue system. An important though unmentioned bonus would be the support of Texan bondholders who had much influence in New York and in some southern states. Between the restricted boundaries of Texas and the new boundaries of California, the enormous area acquired from Mexico would be divided into New Mexico and Deseret (Utah), and both would be organized as territories. Northern supporters of the Wilmot Proviso were asked to abandon it (without accepting that it was unconstitutional) because it was made redundant by climate and terrain; proslavery men were asked to drop their claim that slavery followed the flag; in place of both positions the territorial legislatures should be left free to act as they wished. Clay accepted the antislavery case that Congress could abolish slavery in the District of Columbia but insisted that it would be improper as long as slavery remained in Maryland and Virginia; on the other hand both northern and southern men disliked the slave market in Washington, and no one would be seriously inconvenienced by its prohibition. Clay accepted without qualification the southern case for a new fugitive-slave law but did so without entering into the merits of slavery itself and rested his argument upon obligations voluntarily accepted under the Constitution.

For some weeks the Senate was engaged in intensive debate upon the principles enumerated by Clay. At issue were not the measures themselves, but the demand that extremes must be rejected and some middle ground occupied. On March 4 Calhoun, then in the last weeks of his life and in appearance like one from the grave, presented his case against compromise; too weak for sustained speaking, his speech was read for him. His underlying assumption was that the federal system depended upon an "equilibrium" maintained between all the great interests of the Union, but he spoke only of the balance between the South and the North. The numerical power of the North had been manifest in a series of "aggressions" against the South. It was natural that wealth should be drained from the rural South toward the commerce, cities, and industries of the North, but this imbalance had been made worse by a series of calculated acts. On the one hand restrictions on the expansion of southern civilization in 1787 and 1820 had ensured that the North would enjoy increasing political power used to exact tariffs, monopolize banking, and subsidize the internal communications and shipping of the North at the expense of the South. This preponderance might not of itself endanger the Union (for some interests and regions had to accept a minority status), but for two generations or more, northerners had been brought up to believe that slavery was sinful, whereas southerners had come to recognize it as the surest support for a civilized society and the only possible way of adjusting relations between the two races. This division had already disrupted the churches, both political parties were endangered, and the Union itself could not endure unless the slaveholding minority had some safeguard against an antislavery majority.

Calhoun's analysis has commended itself to some modern writers who reject the concept of the great state controlled by a sovereign majority, and his argument embraced a universal truth that a democratic system cannot endure unless its people are agreed upon the fundamentals of their society. Yet it was unrealistic to expect that in a crisis all the concession should come from one side, and that whatever had to be done for the restoration of harmony northerners alone must do it. "The South asks for justice," he asserted, "simple justice, and less she ought not to take. She has no compromise to offer but the Constitution, and no concession or surrender to make." The concessions had to come from the North, for the South had nothing left to offer; there must be "equal right in the acquired territory," "the stipulations relative to fugitive slaves [must] be faithfully fulfilled," agitation of the slave question must cease, and there must be an amendment to the Constitution "which will restore to the South in substance, the power she possessed of protecting herself, before the equilibrium between the sections was destroyed by the action of this Government." Calhoun closed by asking for "an open and manly avowal on all sides, as to what is intended to be done. . . . If you who represent the stronger portion, cannot agree to settle them on the broad principle of justice and duty, say so; and let the States we both represent agree to separate and part in peace. If you are unwilling we should part in peace, tell us so, and we shall know what to do, when you reduce the question to submission or resistance." The bleak alternatives presented by Calhoun probably defeated his own argument and did much to promote the cause of compromise. By presenting disunion as the only alternative to politically impossible remedies, he pushed a significant number of southerners toward a compromise. Prominent among them was Henry S. Foote, of Mississippi, who had been an explosive defender of southern rights.

Calhoun said that the South had "no compromise to offer but the Constitution" but demanded an amendment to the Constitution as an essential condition. What this amendment was to be he did not specify, but in his *Disquisition on Government*, published posthumously, he proposed a dual executive, with one President elected by the free and one by the slave states, each with a veto on legislation and on the executive acts of the other. In the *Disquisition* this was accompanied by a theory of the "concurrent majority" under which a local majority would have the right of withholding consent to the laws of the "numerical majority." What he proposed, in effect, was constitutional recognition of nullification with a southern President able to veto a force bill. Behind this lay the argument that "equilibrium" was the essential characteristic of a federal union; but "equilibrium," however attractive it might sound to the ear, was a confusing and deceptive idea. A few days later Lewis Cass was to comment:

I do not know precisely what is meant by an equilibrium in a Government. I do not know in what way legislation is to be exactly weighed or measured, with reference to the various sections or interests of the country. . . . Is every section of this country— North, South, East, and West—is every interest, manufacturing, agricultural, commercial, and mechanical, to be weighed against the other? Is each to hold the Government in a state of equipoise? What it would become in such a case, while in nominal operation, no man can tell. We can all tell, however, what it would not do; it would leave its great functions unperformed and would, ere long, die in the affections of the people, as it would already be dead to their interests.[1]

[1] *Congressional Globe*, 31st Cong., 1st sess., March 14, 1850, p. 529.

Calhoun's demand for restoration of "equilibrium," Cass continued, was in fact an innovation "which, when translated into English, means a plan by which a sectional minority may, at its pleasure, control or suspend the operations of Government. . . . Such an equilibrium, instead of being a balance-wheel, would be a check-wheel—it would stop the whole operation of the Government—it would, in fact, place it under the control of a minority."

Three days after Calhoun's legacy of despair, Daniel Webster delivered an oration on which he had been working for many weeks.[2] There had been a good deal of speculation on his intentions, for though he was expected to offer a strong plea for the Union, it was not known how he would weigh the balance between Clay and Taylor. He reviewed the whole course of the controversy, with some passing shots at northern Democrats who had voted for the annexation of Texas and acquisitions from Mexico and then supported the Wilmot Proviso. He condemned the methods of the abolitionists while giving them credit for good intentions; their views were not generally endorsed, but in a free society controversy must be allowed. He then moved to an emphatic repudiation of the idea that the Union could be dissolved by agreement:

Peaceable secession! Peaceable secession! The concurrent agreement of all the members of this great Republic to separate! A voluntary separation, with alimony on one side and on the other. . . .

To break up! To break up this great Government! To dismember this great country! To astonish Europe with an act of folly, such as Europe for two centuries has never beheld in any Government! No, sir! No, sir! There will be no secession. Gentlemen are not serious when they talk of secession.

Webster emphasized that slavery was excluded from California and New Mexico by physical causes. There was no

[2] Webster's speech has been reprinted many times. The original will be found *ibid.*, March 7, 1850. It was reprinted as a pamphlet and widely distributed.

need "to reaffirm an ordinance of nature nor to reenact the will of God." He added that he would "put in no Wilmot Proviso, for the purpose of a taunt or reproach." The part of the speech that made a deep impression, and was to tarnish the memory of Webster in the minds of his anti-slavery constituents, was his indictment of northern obstruction to the return of fugitive slaves.

Here is a ground of complaint against the North, well founded, which ought to be removed . . . which calls for the enactment of proper laws, authorizing the judicature of this Government, in the several States, to do all that is necessary for the recapture of fugitive slaves, and for the restoration of them to those who claim them.

The speech of William A. Seward on March 11 lacked Calhoun's intensity and Webster's oratory; to a sparsely filled House, and reading from careful notes, his argument had few adornments, attracted contemporary attention only because of one misunderstood phrase, and has been brusquely dismissed by historians. Yet in many ways it was a significant and prophetic statement. Seward emphasized the realities of California's situation and pointed out that the application for statehood was irregular only because Congress had failed to pass an enabling act. Nor was it reasonable to suggest that every apparent gain for free soil should be accompanied by compensation for the slave interest. Calhoun's idea of "equilibrium" implied that:

The free States having already, or although they may hereafter have, majorities of States, majorities of population, and majorities in both Houses of Congress shall concede to the slave States being in a minority in both, the unequal advantage of an equality—that is, that we shall alter the Constitution so as to convert the Government from a national democracy, operating by a constitutional majority of voices, into a Federal alliance, in which the minority shall have a veto against the majority.[3]

³ *Ibid.*, March 11, 1850, Appendix, p. 263.

Moreover, this equilibrium was not truly general; it could not protect all interests but only that of the slaveholders. He attacked the proposed fugitive-slave law, which ran counter to the settled convictions of the northern people, and asked:

Has any Government ever succeeded in changing the moral convictions of its subjects by force? . . . We are not slaveholders. We cannot in our judgment be either true Christians or real freemen, if we impose on another a chain that we defy all human power to fasten upon ourselves.[4]

On the question of slavery in the territories, he pointed out that there was no firm rule enunciated by the Constitution and that therefore one had to resort to other precepts.

The Constitution regulates our stewardship. . . . But there is a higher law than the Constitution, which regulates our authority over the domain. . . . The territory is a part—no inconsiderable part—of the common heritage of mankind bestowed upon them by the Creator of the universe. We are His stewards, and must so discharge our trust, as to secure, in the highest attainable degree, their happiness.[5]

This "higher law" doctrine would frequently be held up, by southerners, as an example of antislavery contempt for the Constitution and an attempt to substitute the erratic claims of conscience for the known rules of law. What Seward had intended to say was that when the Constitution was silent, the moral law provided the only rule upon which one could act, and though the passage followed a condemnation of the proposed fugitive-slave law, he had not suggested the invocation of conscience against the law of the land.

The main burden of Seward's speech was that southerners must learn to live in a country where the majority dis-

[4] *Ibid.*
[5] *Ibid.*, p. 265.

approved of slavery, and for all to recognize that wisdom
lay in preparing for its eventual demise. In a prophetic
sentence he said that the great issue was

> whether the Union shall stand, and slavery under the steady,
> peaceful action of moral, social, and political causes, be removed
> by gradual, voluntary effort, and with compensation, or whether
> the Union shall be dissolved, and civil wars ensue, bringing on
> violent but complete and immediate emancipation.[6]

The outcome of the great debate in March was agreement to appoint a Senate Committee of Thirteen with
Clay as chairman. Its reference was based upon Clay's resolution of February, but by this time Clay had accepted the
strategy originally proposed by Senator Foote of uniting
the California, New Mexico, Utah, and Texas boundary
measures into a single "omnibus bill" (the phrase was
adopted by Clay before he had accepted the principle of
uniting all the bills in one). A tactical reason for the omnibus was that if a vote on California's admission came up
first, the President would be free to veto the other bills as
they came to him, and none could win two-thirds in both
houses to override. A more respectable argument for the
omnibus was that men who were anxious for California's
admission would vote for the territorial bills, the Texas
boundary, and the assumption of Texan debts, while
southerners who wished to secure freedom to carry slaves
into New Mexico would commit themselves to the admission of California. The compromise would therefore
emerge as the act of a national majority, and no part of it
could be seen as a purely sectional measure.

Stephen A. Douglas was to claim later that the Committee of Thirteen merely joined together two bills,

---

[6] *Ibid.*, p. 268. I have devoted a considerable amount of space to Seward's speech because it has been unjustly neglected by most writers
on the compromise and because it contains the key to future Republican argument on slavery, its extension, and the implications of both
for the Union.

for California and New Mexico (and settling the Texas boundary), already reported by him as chairman of the Committee on Territories. This was true of the measures as they finally passed, but before then there were several attempts to define or limit the power of the territorial legislatures over slavery. One of Clay's original resolutions stated that slavery did not exist in New Mexico and proposed that the legislatures should be given no power to pass any law in respect to African slavery. This tilted the issue against the South but would have left it open to them to test the status of slavery, and Calhoun's doctrine that it was established by the Constitution, in the courts. The committee dropped the declaratory clause but stuck to the restriction on the territorial legislature. This left it open to test slavery in the courts while avoiding argument in Congress on the validity of Mexican law. During the debate in the Senate John M. Berrien, of Georgia, carried an amendment that the legislature could pass no law establishing or prohibiting slavery; this left open the appeal to the courts, did not prevent legislatures from passing laws to protect "property" but prevented them from prohibiting slavery. The various versions became the focus for complicated congressional maneuver. As finally passed, the territorial bills adopted Douglas's original version that made no mention of slavery and left the legislatures free to act as they wished.

Two deaths promised well for the compromise. Calhoun died during the night of March 30–31 and President Taylor on July 9. The removal of Calhoun meant that southern opponents of compromise lacked a leader around whom they could rally, and Vice-President Millard Fillmore, who succeeded Taylor, was a man of accommodating temper, personally hostile to Seward, and indicated his endorsement of the compromise by appointing Webster as Secretary of State. A fortunate omen was the moderation shown at the southern Nashville Convention in June, when moderates were able to outvote the extremists and present a comparatively mild statement without accompanying threats of disunion. Nevertheless, the omnibus still encountered stormy weather in the Senate; so far from drawing support from the extremes, it left both dangerously strong and capable (in unnatural alliance) of defeating the bill if it were abandoned by a few moderates. Finally, on July 31, the bill was amended out of existence, leaving the Utah bill as the sole survivor of the omnibus, and Clay—now a saddened, angry, and defeated old man —withdrew from Congress.

Leadership of the compromise forces was now assumed by Stephen A. Douglas, who took up the various measures separately, and in a form similar to that first proposed by him; obtaining different majorities for each of the measures but leading the main body of northern and southern Democrats—with help from some Webster and southern Whigs—he was able to carry the day. In the Senate the Texas bill passed on August 9, the admission of California on August 13, the New Mexico bill on August 15, the fugitive-slave bill on August 23, and abolition of the slave trade in the District of Columbia on September 16. The House followed suit from two to three weeks later in each instance except the last, which was passed on September 17.

The compromise achieved after so much congressional time, and with such acclaim, therefore consisted of six separate acts: Texas, Utah, New Mexico, California, the Fugitive Slave Law, and suppression of the slave trade in the District of Columbia. The Utah and New Mexico acts provided that they should eventually be admitted as states "with or without slavery as their constitution may prescribe at the time of their admission," and all restrictions on the power of the territorial legislatures over slavery were dropped. Proslavery men could read some meaning into the proviso that the legislative power extended "to all rightful subjects of legislation, consistent with the Constitution of the United States," and that the Constitution was declared to be in force "so far as the same, or any provision thereof may be applicable." On the other side antislavery men had insisted that writs of error and appeals from the territorial supreme court should be taken to the Supreme Court of the United States; this would ensure that the validity of the Mexican law would be fairly considered by the highest court and not be settled in the lower courts as would normally be done in cases concerning property worth less than one thousand dollars. Without leaning heavily one way or the other it could therefore be said that the territorial bills offered a little more to the opponents of slavery than to its friends. Given the presumption that it was politically impossible either to enact the Wilmot Proviso or to follow Zachary Taylor's original plan to take no action while awaiting New Mexico's application for statehood, it was probably the best that antislavery men could expect.

It is only this that can explain the attitude of many northerners to the Fugitive Slave Law. It was widely believed that the loss of the bill might cause the South to reject the settlement as a whole. Nothing could, of course, undo the laws that had been enacted, but the election of persons hostile to sectional adjustment in the South would reopen the issues that were almost closed. In the event the southerners were allowed not only to have their Fugitive Slave Law but to write it as they wished. There is no reliable evidence about anyone's motives, but on the crucial vote on August 23 twenty-one senators were absent, of whom fifteen were northern Democrats or Whigs.[7] In the House of Representatives twenty-eight northerners were

[7] The absentees when the vote was taken in the Senate included Clay, who left Congress after the defeat of the omnibus; Douglas, who subsequently claimed that he had been called away on urgent personal business after making sure that the bill would pass; John P. Hale, the senatorial spokesman for Free Soil; and Seward. There must have been some certainty that the vote would not be close and that these absences of prominent men on both sides would not be crucial. It passed 27–12.

absent. It seems a fair presumption that a number of northerners were persuaded to let the bill pass without recording their votes in its favor.

From the early stages it was assumed that a fugitive-slave bill would be necessary if southern moderates were to beat off the challenge of the disunionists, but the details were not subjected to the same intense scrutiny as the territorial provisions. It was debated at some length in the Senate, but most of the speakers were southern; in the House it was rushed through without discussion. The law gave the circuit courts of the United States authority to appoint federal commissioners, with the power of justices of the peace or other magistrates and having concurrent jurisdiction with the judges on all matters affecting the recovery of fugitive slaves. Federal marshals were to execute all warrants issued by the commissioners, to call bystanders to their assistance in making an arrest, and to invoke the help of the posse comitatus if necessary. A person claiming a fugitive slave, or his agent, could either obtain from a court or from one of the commissioners a warrant "to pursue or reclaim such fugitive person" or do so without legal process if the arrested runaway were taken before one of the commissioners who had power to deal with the case summarily, and "in no trial or hearing . . . shall the testimony of such alleged fugitive be admitted in evidence." Persons obstructing the return of fugitives were liable to a fine of one thousand dollars, imprisonment for six months, and payment of one thousand dollars compensation to the claimant for each slave lost. There had been some hope that claimants would be required to deposit a bond as surety that the fugitive would be tried before a jury in the state from which he was alleged to have escaped, but the bill's sponsors rejected this. The section of the act that laid down the fees payable to officers assisting in the recovery of runaways included the provision that the commissioner should receive ten dollars if he authorized recovery but only five dollars if he found the proof of possession or identity insufficient. If a claimant anticipated attempts at rescue, he could call upon the officer making the arrest to assume responsibility for custody and return of the fugitive, and this officer was "authorized and required to employ so many persons as he may deem necessary to overcome such force, and to retain them in his service so long as circumstances may require."

It is difficult to imagine an act that violated more elementary principles of justice. The proceedings were summary, the accused could not be heard in his own defense, it was entirely within the discretion of the commissioner to admit or reject evidence in his favor, there was no requirement for trial by jury, and the officer of the court making the arrest was given full discretion to employ as many persons and to use as much force as he saw fit. Designed to deal with recent and readily identifiable runaways, the act provided no safeguards for persons who had been long resident in a free state, and it expressly debarred anyone claimed as a slave from giving evidence in his own defense. This was the measure that was acclaimed in the South as compensation for the loss of equality in the Senate and widely accepted in the North as the price of Union.

What had been the product of nine months of political controversy? The California, New Mexico, and Utah acts were identical, save for a few unimportant verbal alterations, with the bills that Douglas had presented in the early spring; so all the involved debate and heated exchanges had ended with a result that might have been achieved in March. The great debate of that month may have moved some southerners toward compromise and enabled some northerners to support it with a clear conscience, but some features of the compromise can best be explained by sheer weariness. It is probable that most southerners would have fought the prohibition of the slave trade in the District of Columbia and that northerners of both parties would have put up a stiff fight against the Fugitive Slave Law if these measures had been tackled early in the session; the more objectionable provisions of the latter measure might not have survived. Public delight at the achievement of the compromise was emphatic only because there had been so much serious talk of disrupting the Union; but common sense and mutual forbearance might have achieved the same result without having to steer past the rocks of secession. In the closing weeks of the session Douglas demonstrated his leadership; alliances and combinations that had fluctuated and broken throughout the spring and summer stood firm in August and September to ensure the passage of all the bills. To him, more than to anyone else, is due whatever credit may attach to the Compromise of 1850.

There were a number of incidental casualties. The Whig party had almost dissolved under the strain, and though it would rally to fight one more presidential election, its days as a national party were numbered. The temperate vision that had kept southern and northern Whigs together was fading, and if the party was to have any future, it must be the outcome of agreement between sectional wings to avoid discussion of the most important issues of the day. Preoccupation with the territorial issue had prevented the Whigs from developing any new momentum, and the party that had blossomed in time of depression was unable to evolve a new character in a period of rising prosperity. More serious for the future of the party was the preoccupation of the old leaders with controversies of the past and the failure of new men to develop common policies. The Democrats had fared much better than the Whigs; with a few exceptions they had been able to rally behind Douglas, and the anti-Negro bias of most northern Democrats made it easy for them to accept the Fugitive Slave Law. The real failure of the Democrats lay in the next decade, but it was the long shadow of the 1850 controversy that stopped up the springs of innovation.

The controversy had done something to thicken still further the cloud of frustration hanging over the House of

Representatives. The great issues had been discussed in the Senate, and it was upon this body that public attention focused. For the best part of nine months the House had occupied itself with little besides speeches on the familiar questions while waiting for decisions to be made in the Senate. The directly elected representatives of the people were paralyzed and presented no new initiative. The one contribution of the House had been to foster discord by the unseemly wrangle over the Speakership. The year 1850 had therefore helped to distort the processes of constitutional government by depressing the reputation of the House.

At the outset there had been some hope that the South would meet the fears of the North by returning once more to the possibility of gradual emancipation. Perhaps the hope was slender, for apart from a few slaveholders such as Clay and Benton (who were regarded as "unsound" on this question), no southerner echoed the old Jeffersonian hope that slavery might wither away; it had become, on the contrary, a settled part of the southern faith that slavery would endure and was beneficial. Even in Kentucky, where there was considerable antislavery feeling, a proposal for very gradual emancipation, supported by Henry Clay, had been decisively rejected. By the time that the argument was over, a majority of northerners had accepted the idea that slaves and fugitives must pay the price of Union. It was symbolic that in the one gain for antislavery—the District of Columbia bill—a slave was identified by the neuter pronoun.

The compromise, which is sometimes seen as a triumph of political art, was therefore the ruin of one political party, committed the other to negative attitudes, and weakened the machinery of the Constitution. Most of all it had persuaded many men that great issues could be solved by legal and verbal juggling. There had been a moment of truth when some had realized that the survival of the Union, and restoration of harmony, depended upon a willingness to examine the moral foundations of society; but the opportunity had been lost and would never recur. As Seward said, in his speech on March 11, "All our difficulties, embarrassments, and dangers, arise not out of unlawful perversions of the question of slavery, as some suppose, but from want of moral courage to meet the question of emancipation as we ought." [8]

[8] *Congressional Globe,* 31st Cong., 1st sess., March 11, 1850, Appendix, p. 268.

4

Growth, Deterioration, and a New Party

IN economic growth the decade that opened in 1850 was the most striking in American history, and the contrast between spectacular advances and political inadequacy has led historians to speak of a "blundering generation." It is beyond question that the political leaders committed some grievous errors. The tone of antislavery invective was not calculated to conciliate, persuade, or suggest realistic ways in which the grip of slavery could be slackened. The handling of the Kansas question would be a classic example of sustained error flowing from unwise initial decisions; the movements of the southern secessionists in the Democratic party and after Lincoln's victory would display every kind of calculated miscalculation; nor would Lincoln's decision for war be beyond question or reproach. Yet there is little to suggest and impossible to prove that the politicians of the age were inferior to their predecessors. Deeper explanations than the failure of individuals must be sought, and judgments on "a generation" should be suspect even before they have been pronounced.

A more subtle explanation suggests that the problems were not insoluble but that the form and process of American government imposed serious obstacles to their solution. It has been argued that American democracy eroded away traditions and leadership, leaving the people exposed to emotional exploitation. To retain power the politicians cultivated provincial, unrealistic, and uncharitable themes. Lacking the moderating influence of established leadership aware of national needs, American democracy had a centrifugal force that could not be resisted. As a generalization this theory is too broad. In the majority of constituencies, both North and South, stability rather than volatility was often the keynote. In the South men often held their seats in Congress for many years; in the North and West there was a more frequent turnover of representatives, but they were the products of a party system that until 1852 was comparatively stable. If men took their turn, the organization went on. A comparison with the experience of other nations might suggest that the entrenched power of institutions is a formidable threat to political sanity, and it may be that Americans were not suffering from democratic excitability but premature paralysis.

Nor is it realistic to assume that there was an alternative leadership that would have been wiser and stronger than that resulting from the process of democratic life. Indeed, the Senate, which was indirectly elected and where even northern men held their seats for long periods, was equally swayed by the passions of the age. Nevertheless, the nature of the national leadership is a relevant consideration. The United States had never had a national "establishment," but there had been enough continuity in Washington to build up traditions of forbearance and accommodation. Behind all the fights of factions and interests there had been recognition of the responsibilities of government. Within the parties there were tacit understandings that somehow the different claims must be placed in an order of priority and that issues on which the largest number were agreed must be preferred to those with only minority support. This understanding made possible the operation of party caucuses. Between the parties there was an equally firm though unacknowledged convention that when a party could mobilize enough support for a measure, and when a fair opportunity had been given to the minority to express their views, legislation should be allowed to go through. The rules of the Senate allowed unlimited obstruction, and no business could ever be done without this recognition of the ultimate right of a majority to pass its measures. The House was more tightly organized, but there was still great scope for obstruction. The fine distinction between what was allowable delay and what would infringe the spirit of the legislative process was most evident in the closing hours of a session when many long-debated measures were rushed through. There was normally a tacit understanding that, at this stage, procedural delays should not deprive a majority of the right to pass the measures to which they were committed.

It was this network of understandings at the center that was placed under great strain after 1845 and suffered severe damage in 1850. It became apparent that on some issues the minority would not accept the decision of the majority. The inspiration behind Clay's omnibus bill had been the re-creation of a central body of political men, capable of disagreeing with each other while recognizing that, when all had been said, those with most votes should be allowed to win. The omnibus was intended to gather a sufficient body of support for proposals that would take slavery out of politics and thus restore a situation in which minorities could recognize the rights of majorities. The compromise, as it was achieved, lacked this healing function. Subsequent attempts to return to the omnibus principle, by pressing upon Congress resolutions that the compromise was "a finality," merely emphasized the unfortunate loss of a national consensus. There were men in the South who would inflate the idea of southern rights in the hope that they would become incompatible with allegiance to the Union; there were men in the North who would insist upon the divorce of the national government from slavery and welcome opportunities to emphasize the evils of a slave-owning society. These extremes had more leverage than ever before, because at the center large groups had come to believe that some measures or policies were politically intolerable. On the southern side a large body of men who regarded themselves as moderates and Unionists nevertheless believed that there must be no further encroachment on southern rights, and it might not be difficult for the secessionists to move the sticking point further in their direction. On the northern side there was an even larger body of men who agreed that the national government must not assume responsibility for the protection and perpetuation of slavery, and it was comparatively easy for the dedicated antislavery men to demonstrate that events were moving in this direction. On both sides it became impossible to have any rational discussion about the real problems and future prospects of a biracial society.

If the great divide of 1850 had occurred over economic differences, harmony could have been restored, for the American political system was admirably designed to resolve conflicts of material interest; but the moral fissure that had been exposed affected the whole character of the nation. On this issue the slave-owning states set themselves against the reforming instincts of the age and turned willfully blind eyes to the weight of moral support that lay behind the censure on slavery. In demanding that their brethren of the North should align themselves with the cause of slavery they demanded the impossible, and no appeal to law, custom, or Constitution could alter the situation. Indeed, the hardening of the southern mind made it difficult if not impossible for men in the North to share responsibility for slavery and the burden of emancipation. Neither compensation nor colonization could be discussed while southerners insisted that slavery was permanent and beneficial. In the Fugitive Slave Law they had claimed and been given the protection of the law and a diminution of the rights of others. The eagerness with which Clay Whigs, Webster Whigs, and northern Democrats proclaimed their willingness to comply with the law merely demonstrated the inroad that slavery had made into the mind of a people who prided themselves upon their righteousness and freedom. The sectional crisis thus became also a struggle for the conscience of the North, and there could be little doubt that in the long run this conflict would end with the defeat of those who defended the rights of slave-owners.

If the spokesmen of the South committed a gross strategic blunder in asking others to surrender that which could not be abandoned without losing self-respect, the antislavery men of the North erred in demanding that the South should come penitent to the bar of judgment. Under happier circumstances many slave-owners would have been glad to abandon slavery, even at some personal loss, but in a biracial society such an answer could not easily be given. Voluntary emancipation had become an antisocial act threatening calamity to those who were poorer and weaker than the slave-owners themselves. How could the plain and quiet white people of the South be protected against free Negroes? How could old, infirm, or infant Negroes be protected against the animosity of white society? And what of the widows and fatherless whose sole asset was the possession of slaves? In the circumstances of the South unqualified attack upon slavery generated defiance, and non-slaveowners joined slave-owners in the chorus. In the North there was much lack of charity in attacks upon slaveowners, but more and more tolerant men were driven to the conclusion that at some point the slave power must give ground and make the first confession of error.

Whoever gained or lost from the Compromise of 1850, the blacks were expected to pay the price of white harmony. The basic assumption on which the compromise rested was not the inferiority of the Negro—on this there was no debate—but the conclusion that because inferior, he could enjoy only those rights conceded by permission of the superior race. In the territories white men had the right to hold African slaves provided that they were supported by local law. In the "free" states a Negro had the scales of justice weighted against him, and if claimed as a fugitive, must rely upon the charity of others to defend his freedom; and though crimes might be buried in oblivion, society could not forget a slave mother or grandmother. For this encroachment upon what many regarded as the rights of man, the slave-owners offered no compensation. They would not recognize slave marriage; they would not regulate the domestic slave trade. Their vulnerability was shown when Harriet Beecher Stowe's *Uncle Tom's Cabin* became a best-seller in the civilized world. The strength of the indictment lay not in the portrayal of a brutal Simon Legree, nor in the money-grubbing slave-trader, but in the revelation that slavery compelled well-intentioned men to behave iniquitously. A law in the South, with the same teeth as the Fugitive Slave Law, could have enlisted authority against the abuse of power and imposed upon individuals a humane code of conduct. Instead, southern law went even further than before in entrenching the rights of slave-owners and condemning the Negro to perpetual servitude. Before the decade was out, there would even be clamor for reopening the African slave trade and the enslavement of free Negroes.

The Compromise of 1850 brought about major changes in the parties. The Democrats realized the advantage of appropriating whatever credit might be won from preserving the Union. Though associated with Clay, supported by Webster, and steered home by Millard Fillmore, the compromise measures had been opposed by Zachary Taylor and by the most active northern Whigs; the bond between "Cotton Whigs" of the North and South still held, but it seemed fragile when the distinction between "Conscience Whigs" and Free Soilers was so finely drawn. On the Democratic side many of the radical northern Democrats had lost status in the party by deserting to Free Soil; some came creeping back to the party after 1850; others stayed in the wilderness and eventually joined the Republicans. As the Whigs shifted toward the North and reform, the Democrats shifted toward conservatism and the South. There would be no more southern Presidents, but so long as the Democrats remained unified, there would be no northern nominee who was unacceptable to the South.

This was not what Stephen A. Douglas had hoped. Strongly identified with economic expansion and the aggressive entrepreneurial interests operating out of Chicago, he hoped to lead the Democrats in his own direction. With slavery taken out of politics, the way would be open for a new departure under the banner of Young America. Douglas did not intend to abandon the traditional Democratic principles of states' rights and strict construction but hoped that government policy could be harnessed to the wide-ranging interests of western entrepreneurs. He looked for a transcontinental railroad, anticipated the growth of American power on the Pacific Coast, and linked expansionist policy with liberal aspirations by advocating American aid for European nationalists, the Irish, and Cuban opponents of Spanish rule. Douglas played little upon the idealistic chords in his Puritan heritage but had the imagination to link material advance with human betterment the world over. Yet in spite of his services to the party Douglas could not win the nomination in 1852; he was too rash for the conservative, too vulgar for the fastidious, and had little support in the South. After a lengthy deadlock in the convention, the Democrats turned to Franklin Pierce, of New Hampshire, who had made no enemies outside his own state and no commitments to anything except the compromise including (emphatically) the Fugitive Slave Law. Like Polk, Pierce was a dark horse, but whereas Polk had emerged as a champion of a positive program, Pierce stood for a negation. What was required was a man who would forget the past and open a new chapter, but Pierce's only positive contribution was respect for the compromise and his one principle the avoidance of innovation. He was elected over the Whig, Winfield Scott, by a landslide majority.

The Whigs had chosen Scott because they had won twice with a popular general and had no other serious candidate for nomination. Fillmore was unacceptable to the northern antislavery Whigs because he had signed the Fugitive Slave Law; Webster was unacceptable and dying. Clay was dead. Seward was too young and had alienated the South. Scott had an excellent military record and was more cultured and politically more experienced than Taylor had been, but his attempt to hold the party together was a failure. When he equivocated over support for the compromise, leading southern Whigs deserted him, and though he received more votes (even in the South) than any previous Whig candidate, the Democrats took a larger share of an increased total. Even if he had been successful, it is difficult to know what Scott would have done; all parties tend to fight elections on generalities rather than policies, but in 1852 the Whig generalities were even less convincing than usual. The economic promises were echoes of the past and irrelevant in a period of rising prosperity; without achievements to defend they could only repeat platitudes. There were two underlying themes, a quest for respectability and a quest for reform; but they could not be voiced without losing support and were largely at odds with each other. When southern leaders deserted in 1852, the Whig party could no longer stand as the party of national union. Before 1853 was out, it seemed unlikely that the once great party could ever again fight a successful national election.

The political scene was littered with the debris of disappointed hopes. The Democrats were triumphant and were apparently secure in their national union, but this facade concealed internal fractures. Radical northern Democrats who rejoined the party could not be entirely happy about its drift. States' rights southerners and former southern Whigs looked to the party as their safeguard but profoundly distrusted Douglas, whom they regarded as an opportunist and demagogue. Douglas disliked the domination of the party by conservatives and old fogies, but he was also alienated from many of the old Jacksonians, of whom Thomas Hart Benton remained the most articulate and opinionated representative. Outside the major party citadels, small disorganized bodies occupied the political plain. Antislavery seemed to be completely fragmented. The Garrisonians would still acknowledge no political associations, the rump of the old Liberty party kept a flickering light alive, the bulk of the Liberty men had lost their separate identity in Free Soil, which was itself an amalgam of men with varying antecedents and could not sustain the momentary enthusiasm of 1848. Its vote in 1852 was almost halved. The largest and best-organized opposition group was still the reform Whigs of the North; some kind of leadership was offered by W. H. Seward, but his writ ran only in constituencies where antislavery was dominant. Conservative Whigs of the Atlantic cities were almost without a political home; by temperament and recent experience they were cut off from the "Conscience Whigs." Some gave reluctant support to the Democrats (as proved exponents of sectional harmony) ; others looked hesitantly toward the American, or "Know-Nothing," party movement, which was being stirred into nativist virulence by the influx of foreign and Catholic immigrants. Border-state Whigs opposed the extravagance of southern rights and pinned their faith to the economic growth of their region, but most of them were wedded to slavery.

Leaderless and lacking any sense of direction, these political fragments nevertheless included some of the most dynamic and ambitious elements in American political life. With varying qualifications they shared the ideals of nineteenth-century middle-class liberalism, which is a cumbersome and colorless description of a great international reservoir from which has flowed most of the forces that move in the modern world. They were the heirs of Puritanism and had been deeply affected by evangelical revivalism; they distrusted privilege and believed that the world could be made anew by men of goodwill; they believed in freedom and equal rights, in opportunity and education; they knew something of classical economics and certainly thought that material improvement was a royal road to the betterment of man. They included some genuine idealists, and though most prided themselves on being practical men, all could be moved by sentiment to attitudes that were romantic rather than rationalist.

This was the diffuse but powerful movement that Emerson turned into a philosophy (or something like one). In 1856 he published *English Traits,* a sustained reflection upon the relationship of the new American to the old English culture. Out of this came the conclusion that it was the destiny of America to fulfill in the future those great principles of justice and freedom that England had fostered. As he told Thomas Carlyle, "I surely know that as soon as I shall return to Massachusetts I shall lapse at once into the feeling, which the geography of America inevitably inspires, that we play the game with immense advantage; that there and not here is the seat and centre of the British race."

This stress on the British heritage was not acceptable to all Americans; for some the destiny of America lay in the rejection of England or in the judicious selection of only those attributes that were useful in an American environment. Emerson's stress upon the Anglo-Saxon character of America was echoed in a debased form by nativism, but from Britain also flowed the currents of antislavery and humanitarian reform. No one who thought about these matters in the northern states doubted that the idea of American nationalism was bound up with the ideals of human betterment. This explains the intensity of emotion that focused upon the word "Union"; it was not a mere political arrangement but the only way in which an American could summarize his romantic concept of national existence. As Abraham Lincoln would later say in his first message to Congress, it was "that form and substance of government whose leading object is to elevate the condition of men—to lift artificial weights from all shoulders; to clear the paths of laudable pursuit for all; to afford all an unfettered start, and a fair chance in the race of life."

In the 1850's the great popular vehicle of these opinions was Horace Greeley's *Weekly Tribune*. The daily *Tribune* achieved great success in and around New York City, but it was the weekly edition that circulated widely to all parts of the northern and midwestern states. When Pierce was inaugurated, Greeley was a powerful voice without a political home; he had given strong backing to Winfield Scott, though aware that defeat was in the air. With the ruin of the party with which he had been identified since 1839, Greeley was temporarily a voice crying in the wilderness, but this did not diminish his enthusiasm for reform. Indeed, he could speak more freely now that it was no longer necessary to look over his shoulder at the southern Whigs. Across the northern states hundreds of lesser editors reacted in the same way. They expressed the anguish of all those who saw 1850 as a betrayal of American ideals or believed that devotion to the Union had been exploited to undermine what the Union ought to be. It would not take much of a spark to ignite the mass and fuse it together into a river of molten metal.

At a lower level of activity the breakup of the Whig party and the failure of Free Soil dismayed many political aspirants. In many towns and districts the fragmented parties still existed but without a national alliance to give them life and hope. The northern Whigs, the radical Democrats, and even the Liberty party were still organized locally. They had their newspapers, would-be officeholders, voters ready to answer the call, and friendly interests ready to back their campaigns; yet there was nowhere to go. A new movement, whatever it might be, would inherit all these carefully cultivated bases of local power.

The expanding society of the decade provided the environment in which middle-class liberalism could flourish. It was a period of unprecedented growth. The population increased by over eight million (by more, that is, than the whole population of the United States in 1810). The national rate of increase was 35.65 percent, or over 3.5 percent per annum. The highest rate came in the Midwest and West, but New England, New York, New Jersey, and Pennsylvania increased by nearly 23.3 percent and the South by over that figure. Southern whites increased by 25 percent, blacks by 20.6 percent, and as the South attracted few immigrants, the natural increase was remarkable. In 1850 there were only six cities of more than 100,000; by 1860 there were nine; and the total number living in these large cities had increased from 1,200,000 to 2,600,000. The next group of cities, with population between 50,000 and 100,000, increased from four to seven, with population rising by 168,000, while those with between 25,000 and 50,000 increased from sixteen to nineteen, with a rise of 59,000. The most spectacular urban growth came, however, in the smaller towns, ranging from 2,500 to 25,000; these increased from 200 to 257 and in population from 1,472,000 to 2,354,000. The lower one went down the scale of the smaller urban places, the greater was the proportionate increase. The total urban population increased from 3,500,000 to just under 6,250,000. In 1852 less than one-eighth of the population lived in towns; by 1860 about one-fifth did so. The northern states had by far the largest share in this increase, and urbanization was a more potent influence than industrialization in accentuating the differences between the sections.

The influence of towns cannot be understood merely by a record of numbers. Towns were markets, distribution points, and banking centers and contained a high proportion of the nation's schools, churches, and newspapers. They were the bases from which most lawyers conducted their business and the focus for local politics. They drew in life from the countryside, and though a large majority in the North and Northwest still lived on farms, they relied more and more upon urban institutions. In business, politics, and culture it was more and more likely for decisions to be made in the towns and for men of influence to be found in urban environments. By contrast decisions in the South were made in rural courthouses or wherever else the larger landowners gathered; the southern towns were fewer in number, more primitive in their economic functions, and dependent upon the plantations for political direction and cultural influences.

Urbanization is a question of scale as well as institutions. Most urban historians have concentrated upon the greater cities, but in the mid-nineteenth century most towns were very small. They formed societies in which all the men of influence could know each other and be familiar with many of their humbler fellow-townsmen. Moreover, most northern and western towns had very distinct traditions of communal activity. The influence of New England upon so many of these towns was shown in adapting the idea of a congregation. The town was a gathering-together of like-minded people before it became an economic unit, and churches and schools preceded material success. The original concept of towns as environments in which the godly could live was diluted, and so was the New England heritage, but the idea of the town as a community with social functions remained strong. Though expansion would eventually destroy the ethos of the small town, this stage had not been reached in most towns by the middle of the nineteenth century; on the contrary, the experience of growing up with a town, of playing a part in its development, and celebrating its success in civic rituals, made the town-dwellers even more self-conscious. The towns in existence also demonstrated the survival of the fittest; many had dreamed of founding cities, many rural settlements had looked forward to urban develpment, but not all had won through to prosperity and sustained growth. If the successful small town was self-satisfied, its citizens also knew that efforts must not be relaxed. The small town was not sleepy but dynamic, not complacent but economically aggressive, and material success was closely associated with moral and educational progress.

Lack of detailed study makes hypothesis necessary, but one cannot escape the conclusion that the driving forces in northern American society were focused in the small town. Reform movements and antislavery societies flourished in small towns; colleges and churches provided forums for debate; town lawyers became county and state politicians; this was also the starting point for most entrepreneurial careers. The small town was active, busy, interested, proud of success, and impatient of obstruction. In the 1850's slavery and the landowners who depended upon it would offer an increasingly sharp contrast to this urban world and to the middle-class liberalism that flourished in it.

Many aspirations and hopes were still concentrated upon the Democratic party. The controversy over the Wilmot Proviso and resentment of the radical northern Democrats had placed the party under a severe strain, but it had greater resilience than its rival. The loss of some northern Democrats to Free Soil was outweighed by gains in conservative support, especially in the South. The party organizations emerged almost unscathed and fully equipped to demolish their opponents. Since Jacksonian times the party had offered more opportunities for the ambitious young politician, and on the lower rungs of the political ladder the Irish and Germans could find a place. If the keynote of Whiggism was respectability, that of the Democrats was opportunity. Old antimonopoly traditions persisted, and the Democrats could present themselves as the foes of established oligarchy. In practice the Democrats included many men of wealth, and in states where the party had long been ascendant it had attracted the support of commercial interests. In New York, New Jersey, and Pennsylvania, where the Democrats normally controlled state politics, they could count leading bankers and merchants among their supporters. In the river cities of the Ohio and its tributaries there was a predominance of Democrats among the leading citizens, and in Michigan and Illinois one had to be a Democrat to get anything done. In a period when laissez-faire was increasing its hold in theory and in practice, many businessmen were well suited by a doctrine of states' rights and nonintervention, and prosperity seemed to prove its validity.

In foreign affairs the Democrats had attitudes rather than policies; they were anti-British, looked hopefully toward Central America, and for expansion in the Caribbean. They were critical of the Clayton-Bulwer treaty with Great Britain, which had been the one major achievement of Zachary Taylor's administration and which was intended to prepare the ground for an isthmian canal as an international waterway. Otherwise "manifest destiny" had not much to offer in these years; and though the Democrats favored the development of the newly acquired West, their practical proposals tended to become enmeshed in sectional controversy and traditional hostility to federal subsidy for economic enterprise. Plans for a Pacific railroad would play a significant part in the great Kansas controversy; northerners, westerners, and southerners quarreled over the projected routes, and by 1860 nothing had been done.

In the South the Democrats had claimed to be champions of the plain people, and in the lower South their principal strength had lain outside the plantation belt. New recruits from the planter class were not altogether welcome, and in the upper South many of the former Whig landowners and merchants held aloof. Politically, however, the South seemed to profit by the turn of events, for during the two Democratic administrations of the 1850's, the southern leaders enjoyed an ascendancy in the national government that even they had not experienced before. The two northern Presidents, Franklin Pierce and James Buchanan, almost abandoned the convention that a federal administration must represent a national alliance.

The key posts went to southern Democrats, and both Presidents seemed to display a deference toward the South that their northern supporters found increasingly irksome.

The economic history of the South has long been a matter of controversy. Contemporary evidence is often contradictory. The most notable southern publicist, editor, and statistician was J. D. B. De Bow, and the pages of his *Review* were filled by articles deploring the failure to develop indigenous economic activities and the dependence upon the North. At the beginning of the decade De Bow recalled with gloom the hopeful prospects announced ten or fifteen years before by southern commercial conventions, emphasized the decline of direct shipping services between Charleston and Europe, and lamented southern weakness in banking, credit, manufactures, and commercial services. Yet other articles celebrated the success of southern agriculture, the increase in cotton production, and the possibilities of economic expansion. Appointed superintendent of the United States census in 1853, De Bow had a unique opportunity of surveying the economic condition of the whole nation, and he concluded that though there were faults (as in every system), the economic foundation of the South was sound. Antislavery men, on the other hand, emphasized southern backwardness and the low standards of the mass of the people, who had been sacrificed to the interest of a minority of slave-owners producing far less efficiently than they would with free labor. Toward the end of the decade this analysis was reinforced by a powerful voice from the South itself: Hinton Rowan Helper, speaking from experience in a middle-class farming family in a poor but not poverty-stricken area of North Carolina, drew upon De Bow's census figures to demonstrate that even in agriculture the South lagged far behind. He attributed this backwardness to inefficient labor and a social structure that denied opportunity to the poorer whites.

Frederick Law Olmstead, publishing at the end of the decade books based on materials collected mainly in 1852 and 1853, emphasized the low living standards, ignorance, and lack of enterprise among the farmers and small planters of the back country. In the lower Mississippi cotton lands he found the cotton planters prosperous but boorish, crude, and ostentatious. They might benefit from the cotton boom, but they were not the stuff of which a civilization could be made. He also believed that this was shallow prosperity, dependent upon soil fertility and brutal slave driving and unlikely to maintain its momentum. Only occasionally did he encounter plantations that seemed to be run on sound principles, made efficient use of labor as a long-term investment, were ready to use new agricultural methods, and produced good yields while also conserving resources.

A later generation of prosouthern historians tended to accept gloomy estimates of the southern economy. It seemed important to them to show that slavery would have collapsed under its own weight and that but for war and northern interference there would have been a slow but steady transition from slave to free labor. The shrinking of slavery in Delaware, Maryland, and even in parts of Virginia seemed to prove the point. More recent study of slavery in the southern cities has shown how urban conditions eroded away the discipline upon which slavery depended, and that the system of slave hiring could produce a situation in which slave craftsmen lived almost as free men. Less sympathetic historians, however, have rejected the thesis that slavery was withering away.

The most recent econometric studies of slavery appear to demonstrate that the system as a whole was profitable. On the large cotton plantations an investment in slaves could yield as good a return as that in other activities not wildly speculative. Where production was less profitable, the internal slave trade provided a safety valve when a plantation ran into difficulties and a regular income for plantations with a recurrent surplus of labor. Indeed, southern agriculture achieved a degree of mobility of labor that a modern industrial economy might well envy. The precise way in which the balance sheet is drawn is bound to remain a matter of dispute, for planters were not cost accountants, and it is difficult for the future investigator to decide how the overheads should be weighted or how expenses are to be distributed over a slave's lifetime. However, there seems to be fairly wide agreement that slavery was profitable, continued to be so (with the normal fluctuations that might be expected in a capitalist economy) until the Civil War, and that expectations of future profits continued to run high. The 5 percent of slaves engaged in industry were disciplined and profitable to their owners. On the eve of the Civil War the price of slaves was higher than ever before.

Another recent calculation, not yet fully tested, suggests that the picture of low standards in the South has been overdrawn or even misinterpreted. The per capita income of the whole population in the South was lower than the national average in 1860 and much lower than in the Northeast, but 15 percent higher than that in the north-central states. And from 1840 to 1860 the per capita income in the South grew at an average of 1.7 percent a year against a national average of 1.3 percent. This reckoning treats slaves as consumers; if the free population alone is considered (taking the slaves as "intermediate goods" used to produce for the consumers), the southern per capita income was above the national average, and the average per capita of white southerners exceeded that of the north-central region by nearly 70 percent. The growth rate of the southern economy on this basis is more than one-third that of the rest of the nation.

If these figures are to be taken seriously (and they cannot be lightly dismissed), it may show that observers without the aid of modern quantification paid too much attention to large plantations on marginal land and too little to the solid achievement of small planters and small farmers. Literary evidence about the "plain people" is hard to come by, but studies based on the manuscript census schedules reveal a farming society that was not adventurous but stable and making a good living. Slaves were men and women of all work, and also investments to be raised and sold in their prime. All this helps to explain the broad-based support for slavery in the South, whereas the comparatively low per capita income in the north-central area may explain something of the resentment felt in this region when proslavery threatened to march across the West.

There are, however, other factors to consider. Within the South the surprisingly high per capita income is explained by the very high rate of the growth in the Southwest. In 1860 the per capita income of all population in this region was $184, compared with a national average of $128, and the free per capita income was $274. For the southern Atlantic states the figures were $84 and $124, compared with $181 for the Northeast. The east-south-central figures were very little better than the southern Atlantic. In these regions the growth rate was about the national average of 1.3 percent from 1840 to 1860, but it was much below that of the Northeast. So the region that produced a majority of the southern political leaders was growing at a slower rate than the Northeast. Although an econometric look at the whole South may destroy the idea of a stagnant economy, figures for the politically important regions give a clue to some of the anxieties of southern leaders as they saw political power slipping away.

Whatever the outcome of these arguments, some facts about southern society are indubitable. The rate of urbanization was far slower in the South than in the North, and the principal function of the southern towns was to provide services for the plantations. Manufactures grew slowly and attracted little investment. The rate of growth of railroads may not have been quite so slow as is sometimes believed, but southerners failed to build the long-distance lines that would have fed the seaports. The Baltimore and Ohio was an exception that proved that opportunity existed if only the will could be generated. Most important of all, the South failed in education. No state had a system of public schools, and many people had no schooling at all. Higher education was poor in quality and monopolized by the upper classes. Analysis shows the weakening of literary culture even among the highly educated, and rhetoric increasingly played upon old images. Thus, though the South was not a stagnant economy, it was not becoming a modern society.

Nor were there signs that slavery would wither away if left undisturbed. There had, it is true, been an upward trend in voluntary emancipation in Delaware and Maryland, but south of the Potomac there was little evidence that slave-owners would themselves end slavery. In 1849 there had been an attempt in Kentucky, strongly backed by Henry Clay, that would have introduced a scheme of gradual emancipation. It would have been slow in operation, and under it many Negroes would have continued in bondage well into the twentieth century. The proposal was decisively defeated in Kentucky, and Clay (a lifelong slave-owner) was branded in South Carolina as no better than an abolitionist. In 1855 Abraham Lincoln, whose opinion was both representative and pregnant with future significance, wrote to a Kentucky friend:

You are not a friend of slavery in the abstract. . . . You spoke [in 1819] of "the peaceful extinction of slavery" and used other expressions indicating your belief that the thing was, at some time, to have an end. Since then we have had thirty six years of experience, and this experience has demonstrated, I think, that there is no peaceful extinction of slavery in prospect for us. The signal failure of Henry Clay, and other good and great men, in 1849, to effect any thing in favor of gradual emancipation in Kentucky, together with a thousand other signs, extinguishes that hope utterly. On the question of liberty, as a principle we are not what we have been. . . . That spirit which desired the peaceful extinction of slavery, has itself become extinct. . . . Our political problem now is "Can we, as a nation, continue together *permanently—forever*—half slave, and half free?" [1]

Early in 1854 Stephen A. Douglas introduced a bill to organize the territory of Nebraska, which then comprised all the land west of the Missouri, east of the Rockies, and north of 36°30'. Subsequently, the proposal was amended to divide the area into the territories of Kansas and Nebraska. The bill used the same wording as the 1850 New Mexico and Utah acts: "that when admitted as a State or States, the said Territory, or any portion of the same, shall be received into the Union with or without slavery, as their Constitution may prescribe at the time of their admission." This would be of little advantage to slave-owners if the Missouri Compromise prohibiting slavery north of 36°30' remained in force, and Douglas agreed to add a clause that this restriction, "being inconsistent with the principle of non-intervention by Congress with slavery in the States and Territories, as recognized by the legislation of eighteen hundred and fifty, commonly called the Compromise Measures, is hereby declared inoperative and void." This ill-fated measure was directly responsible for the formation of the Republican party, indirectly for the disruption of the Democratic party, and led by inexorable steps to secession and civil war. The opposition to the extension of slavery might have taken a different form, wiser presidential leadership might have averted the troubles of the Democratic party, and the acute phase of sectional controversy might have been deferred; the Civil War was not inevita-

[1] Quoted in Roy P. Basler (ed.), *The Collected Works of Abraham Lincoln,* Vol. II (New Brunswick, N.J.: Rutgers University Press, 1953), p. 318. This seems to be the first use of the famous phrase "half slave and half free."

ble, but whatever hypotheses may be proposed, it is undeniable that the actual sequence of events flowed from the repeal of the Missouri Compromise and the proposal "to leave the people ... perfectly free to form and regulate their domestic institutions in their own way."

Douglas's motives have been variously interpreted. He was keenly interested in the project for a railroad to the Pacific, and the route chosen was of crucial concern to those who hoped to profit from it. Crudely, the issue was whether Chicago, St. Louis, or New Orleans would become the gateway to the overland route. Southerners pressed for a southern route, made possible by the Gadsden Purchase of 1853, providing a way around the difficult mountain and canyon country. A northern route would favor Chicago, but a central route through Kansas could serve both Chicago and St. Louis, and southern support might be won by opening Kansas to slavery. Douglas had also to consider the situation in Missouri, where he wished to advance the interests of the powerful Senator David R. Atchison against the declining fortunes of Thomas Hart Benton. Atchison was a spokesman of the business and planting interests in Missouri, and his supporters would reap immediate benefit if they were allowed to carry slavery across the river. Douglas was, however, too ambitious a man to think merely of material and local interests; his broader concern was to unite the Democratic party behind a program of western development and to clamp down sectional controversy by giving southerners the hope of more slave states and northerners the substance of land and profits. On this political base Douglas hoped to make himself President.

The moment seemed propitious for a new initiative. The disorganized condition of the rival political groups made it improbable that they could unite on any coherent program; 1850 seemed to have inflicted a decisive defeat upon Free Soil and driven abolitionism beyond the pale of effective influence. Moreover, Douglas was aware of a new force: apparently powerful, certain to capture some following among the old Whigs, and equally certain to cement the Democratic allegiance of foreign-born and Catholic voters. This was the Know-Nothing, or Native American, movement.

Between 1845 and 1854 the United States experienced a deluge of immigrants. In the latter year nearly half a million were officially recorded, and the figure may well have been swollen by unrecorded immigrants entering from British North America. The large majority came from southern Ireland, the Rhineland, or southern Germany and thus were predominantly Catholic and unfamiliar with Anglo-Saxon political traditions. The same romantic concept of nationalism that Emerson turned into a transcendental spirit (with a strong emphasis upon racial destinies) became among simpler men a violent anti-foreign and anti-Catholic prejudice. It is difficult, in the present age, to imagine the depth of feeling invested in Protestantism; it was not that Americans were particularly pious (though many were) but that they had been taught from childhood that Catholicism meant the rule of priests, the secret influence of the Pope over civil institutions, and the subversion of republican government. More prosaically, the foreign-born added to the growing problems of congested and ill-governed cities and competed with the native-born for employment. It was significant that Baltimore, with a large inflow of unskilled southern whites, was a center of nativism.

There was no questioning the patriotism of the Know-Nothings or their determination to uphold the Union and the Constitution, and if they disassociated themselves from violence and crude manifestations of bigotry, they might emerge as a new national and conservative party. The idea appealed to many old Whigs, particularly in the border states and eastern cities. In 1854 the Know-Nothings won many local successes and a few seats in Congress and began to look confidently toward nominating a presidential candidate in 1856.

From the start, however, the Know-Nothings had intrinsic weaknesses. Though most Americans were anti-Catholic to a greater or lesser degree, they were also keenly aware that religious toleration was a principle of republican government and realized that Native Americanism rejected the confident hope that the oppressed of Europe would be saved by the free institutions of American government. If some politicians dallied with nativism, few who carried great weight did so; locally powerful, it produced no leaders of national stature. Moreover, American parties have habitually developed around opposition to established national power, and the enemies of the Know-Nothings were too localized or too hypothetical to rouse the enthusiasm necessary for sustained activity. Finally, the Know-Nothings could not avoid slavery, however much they wished to do so. As they presented themselves as a party of American nationalism, it was inevitable that some should ask whether slavery must be accepted as a national interest; when no answer was forthcoming, many northern "Americans" held aloof from the new party, however much they might sympathize with its local objectives. The movement that Democrats first welcomed as a divisive element among their disheartened opponents ended by providing new recruits for the far more formidable party that was to capture the national government in 1860.

As soon as the details of the Nebraska bill were made known, spontaneous protest meetings were held in various parts of the country. Though some were held predictably in old antislavery strongholds (this Douglas must have anticipated), some appeared in traditionally Democratic areas such as northern Illinois and many in newly developed regions such as Wisconsin and Iowa, where the Democrats hoped to establish themselves as the party of the common man. There was still a good way to go before this movement of protest could become a new party, but its vitality was evident from the start. Himself insensitive to the moral implications that many northerners saw in slavery, Douglas had also failed to realize the extent to which the slave power was becoming a feared symbol.

The Liberty party had first claimed that abolition was consistent with the Constitution, but their original doctrine—that the Constitution implied a positive grant of power to attack slavery—was too strong a potion even for most antislavery Americans. With the abolitionist pamphleteer Lysander Spooner and with Salmon P. Chase, of Ohio, who was emerging as one of the most effective political figures of the period, the argument took on an apparently less radical but eventually more drastic form. They argued that a majority of the makers of the Constitution had been opposed to slavery; it had been necessary to accept its existence, but the word had been deliberately excluded from the document, and the "founding fathers," knowing that emancipation was accomplished or near to accomplishment in the northern states, expected it to move south within a generation. Unfortunately, their expectations were disappointed because a powerful interest based on slave labor had established itself in the Union, and to counter the normal operation of democratic and constitutional government against slavery, the slave power had taken control of the national government, perverted the Constitution into a proslavery document, and was now determined to nationalize slavery. The repeal of the Missouri Compromise seemed to fit exactly this interpretation of history, and many northerners awaited the next step in fear that it would provide further evidence of the slave-power conspiracy and convinced of their duty to resist.

The strength of the slave-power theory lay in its appeal to conservatives and radicals alike. The former were urged to return to the true principles of the Constitution; the latter were assured that something could be done if they ceased to quarrel over words and united with more cautious men against the common enemy.

There were organizational reserves for a new movement. All over the country there were men who had carefully, through the years, nourished local political power. In recent years too many had seen this power threatened and had been forced to find new appeals to voters and new hope of eventual nourishment from federal sources. The Van Buren Democrats had found themselves squeezed out between 1844 and 1848. Many had gone into Free Soil; some had returned in 1852 but without enthusiasm. The Free Soilers had suffered a setback but still had active organizations in some northern districts. Old Whigs of the Clay and Webster school were left without a political home; they would scatter between Know-Nothingism, reluctant support for the Democratic party, and cautious endorsement of the anti-Nebraska movement. There is no need to doubt the sincerity of all who eventually committed themselves to the new party—some were opportunists, the majority were not—but it is a fact of life that men are more responsive to ideals when they have lost their political anchors.

It would still, however, be difficult to unite behind leaders or agree upon programs. Some New England "Conscience Whigs" were suspicious of the New Yorkers and looked to Charles Francis Adams; in New York itself the most eloquent writer on behalf of reform, Horace Greeley, was hardly on speaking terms with William Henry Seward, the most prominent antislavery Whig; Senator Charles Sumner, of Massachusetts, publicly committed to radical antislavery, was too much an individualist to fit into any combination. The northern "Americans" were an active body, with good local organizations to add to the common cause, but no national leader. Senator Salmon P. Chase was, with Sumner, the most dedicated and able antislavery man in high elective office, but his intense ambition was not matched by personal popularity; as a political maneuver he favored the aging John McLean, an associate justice of the Supreme Court, a perennial seeker after the Presidency, and the author of statements on the slave issue that were remarkable for ambiguity rather than clarity.

With these disparate groups, and with dislike of one bill as their only point of agreement, an astute Democratic President could have postponed if not prevented the rise of a new party. But pressed on one side by Douglas and on the other by southern friends, Franklin Pierce made the repeal of the Missouri Compromise an administration measure, used federal patronage and influence to bring reluctant northern Democrats into line, and thus kept this single contentious issue at the center of the stage. Every lifelong northern Whig whose instinct to oppose was not too strongly diluted with caution, every alienated northern Democrat, all the Free Soilers, and many of the northern Native Americans were given an easily recognizable standard to which they could rally. There was some hesitation over the name, but for reasons that are not altogether clear, "Republican" emerged as the title that was most emotive and least likely to offend.

"Popular sovereignty" left some important questions unanswered. When was the decision for or against slavery to be made? This was vital, for experience showed that once slavery had been admitted into a territory, it was there to stay, and that once excluded, it would not be subsequently introduced. If the earliest settlers had the right to decide, was it equitable that a remote minority might settle forever a question in which all were vitally interested? And the admission of slaves would bequeath to the future a biracial society even if slavery were subsequently rejected. An early decision might precipitate a struggle for control of the first legislature, but if decision were deferred until the territory applied for admission as a state, the status of slavery during the intervening period would be contentious. Could it be prohibited by the territorial legislature, or was it protected by the Constitution? Finally, it was vain to hope that controversy could be kept out of Congress, for a ruling power could not escape responsibility. All these questions were asked during the Kansas-Nebraska controversy, and all plagued the nation as soon as the measure had been passed.

The obvious interest of proslavery Missourians in preventing the establishment of free soil on their western boundary, and the attraction of land across the river suitable for commercial agriculture, inspired an "invasion" to control the polls and return a proslavery majority. This was done, though it was said that many of the voters were "border ruffians" with neither homes nor property in the territory. Meanwhile, a New England Immigrant Aid Society was organized to send out antislavery settlers. More important, though less publicized, were the large number of migrants from Iowa, Illinois, and Indiana who came west to create a society without slavery and without Negroes. Interwoven with proslavery and antislavery passions were hardheaded opportunists who came west to see what profitable speculations might be made in an area with so much land and undeveloped resources. Oddly enough, the railroad promoters, who had formed an important pressure group behind the organization of the territory, were slow off the mark, and no railroad was built or even surveyed.

The story of "bleeding Kansas" was exaggerated, but violence impeded whatever progress toward orderly government had been envisaged by the administration. Before long there were two territorial legislatures—one proslavery, the other Free Soil—with the former recognized by the President but the latter commanding more support in Kansas. Senator Atchison, of Missouri, who was in the best position to exercise restraint over his followers in Kansas, was arrogant, tactless, and used his influence as a prominent Democrat to hold the weak President to a proslavery line. The nascent Republican party was presented with a cause that was easy to propose and appealed clearly to the normal canons of fair play. The sack of Lawrence (the seat of the Free Soil "government") by proslavery men was a gesture rather than a serious threat to life and property; but it was singularly ill timed and added further evidence to the argument that what the slave power could not get by chicanery it would seize by force.

On May 19, 1856, Senator Charles Sumner began a two-day speech on the "crime against Kansas," characteristically laden with literary flourishes, historical references, and personal invective. On May 23 Sumner was attacked while sitting at his desk in the Senate chamber by Representative Preston Brooks, of South Carolina; asserting that Sumner had libeled his uncle (Senator Andrew P. Butler) and his state, Brooks began to beat the senator over the head with his cane. "I gave him about thirty first-rate stripes," Brooks recalled later. "Towards the last he bellowed like a calf. I wore my cane out completely but saved the Head which is gold." The incident created a sensation and was represented in the North as a typical slave-owner's response to criticism, while Brooks received congratulatory addresses and gold-topped canes from admirers in all parts of the South. Sumner was seriously injured and did not recover quickly, but for the next three years his friends ostentatiously kept his seat in the Senate empty, and Massachusetts reelected him for the next twenty years. Sumner had hitherto been regarded as an extremist with a small following, whose support might be more damaging than his opposition. His misfortune made him spokesman for the conscience of the North and a central figure in the new movement, though his injury and absence probably made it easier to go forward with the practical tasks of pulling together a great but so far unwieldy political alliance.

It would be neither fair nor accurate to attribute the rise of the Republican party merely to circumstantial events or political ambitions; it sprang from deep sources and repre-

sented irresistible impulses. Whether one begins with ideological commitments and works one's way around to
material aspirations, whether one believes what the men
themselves said or prefers a modern explanation of what
their motives ought to have been, Republicanism remains
a unique blend of confidence and anxiety. Confident that
they represented the best hope of mankind, fearful that in
some way the promise was being betrayed, Republicans
took their place in the great torrent of middle-class liberalism that flowed on both sides of the Atlantic. Historians
have labored to demonstrate the inconsistencies of men
who declared slavery a moral wrong but promised not to
interfere with it where it already existed; were sworn to
prevent the extension of slavery but in their own states
(and, indeed, in the new territories) denied equal rights to
free Negroes; proclaimed the universal truths of the Declaration of Independence but insisted on the superiority of
the white race; and spoke the language of idealism while
encouraging selfish businessmen and shady politicians to
march under their banner. These contradictions matter little; all successful parties present a similar record, and the
most effective leaders are those who are least disturbed by
inconsistency. The strength of the party lay in its synthesis
of all elements in the syndrome of nineteenth-century reform; it was idealistic and materialistic, rational and
romantic, traditionalist and revolutionary.

There were several possible claimants for the Republican nomination in 1856, but what was wanted at this stage
was a symbolic figure rather than a practiced politician.
John C. Frémont—soldier, explorer, adventurer, and
(thanks to a romantic elopement) son-in-law of Thomas
Hart Benton—filled the bill. He had taken a prominent
(though perhaps unconstructive) part in the conquest of
California, quarreled with his commanding officer, and
earned a court-martial that increased his popularity.
"Free Soil, Free Labor, Free Men, Free Speech, and Frémont" (borrowed with two additions from the Free Soilers

and emphasizing their continuity with the earlier movement) was perhaps the best campaign slogan ever coined.

In the presidential campaigns of the day the candidate
was expected to take little active part, and Frémont, with a
nationally known name, no previous political activity, and
an unequivocal acceptance of the Republican commitment to prevent the extension of slavery, was a good candidate who would probably have made a poor President. It
was easy to associate him with the romantic heroes of the
European liberalism and nationalism. Carl Schurz, newly
arrived from Germany as a liberal exile, would later recall
how the new party caught his imagination and inspired
him to take an immediate plunge into the troubled waters
of American politics.

The Republican platform sounded to me like a bugle-call of liberty, and the name of Frémont, "the Pathfinder," surrounded by
a halo of adventurous heroism, mightily stirred the imagination.
Thus the old cause of human freedom was to be fought for on
the soil of the new world. The great final decision seemed to be
impending.[2]

The men of '56 were to be prophets and movers of men for
twenty years to come, and the historian who ignores the
compulsion of their beliefs does so at his peril.

The surprise of 1856 was not that the Democrats won,
but that the Republicans did so well. The Democrats had
had enough of Pierce, but they would not go for Douglas.
James Buchanan was qualified by experience; in public
life since 1820, he had been Secretary of State and minister
to England, had almost unchallenged control of his party
in the predominantly Democratic state of Pennsylvania,
and, in spite of a wry neck, looked the part of a distinguished elder statesman. He was not inspiring, but he
seemed safe. Personal inclination had led him to associate
more with southern than with northern politicians, and

2 *The Reminiscences of Carl Schurz*, Vol. II (New York: 1917),
p. 67.

nowhere in his record could anyone detect a criticism of southern institutions. In the South the Democrats were at the height of their power and carried every slave state except Maryland and (apart from a few seats carried by Know-Nothings, old Whigs, and states' rights men affiliated to no party) won sweeping victories in the Congressional elections.

The Know-Nothings nominated former President Millard Fillmore, who carried Maryland and provided the main opposition to the Democrats in the upper South. In the North he did badly, though his party picked up some congressional seats in the larger cities. The failure of nativism to maintain the momentum of its local successes in 1854 meant the end of its national hopes, but its memory would plague city politics for years to come.

Frémont carried all but five of the free states; in those five the Democratic margins were not large. With them he would have been President without a southern vote, and anyone looking to the future could do the necessary electoral arithmetic. The extraordinary thing is that during the next four years almost every nationally prominent Democrat seemed to conspire to make certain the loss of these five vital states in 1860. This is not, of course, what they intended, but their actions could hardly have been better planned to achieve a result that was tragic for themselves and the nation. Whatever the merits or demerits of popular sovereignty, whatever criticisms might be made of the negative attitudes toward national responsibility, the Democratic party was national and the only significant organization in which southerners and northerners worked together. Not party interest alone but true statesmanship dictated a charitable attitude to men of tender conscience in both sections. Yet Franklin Pierce's last state of the Union message showed no token of sympathy or understanding for northern attitudes. The blame for the difficulties in Kansas lay, he claimed, exclusively with the Free Soil element; the activities of "border ruffians" went unnoticed, while the entire blame for refusing to accept a legal decision was laid upon the antislavery men. The troubled President may have believed this, but to a majority in the North it sounded like the special pleading of a man with a bad case.

Buchanan had an opportunity to make a fresh start; belief in his judicious temperament had won him the vote of many conservative Whigs, and though dramatic gestures were improbable, his career inspired confidence that he could bend in the storm without breaking. His inaugural address included bland appeals for understanding and an assurance that the whole issue would shortly be settled by a decision of the Supreme Court. He referred to the celebrated case of *Dred Scott v. Sandford,* which everyone knew raised important issues relating to slavery in the territories. Dred Scott, a slave, was claiming his freedom on the ground that he had been taken by his master in 1834 into the territory north of 36°03′ where slavery was prohibited by the Missouri Compromise. Did Buchanan know that aging Chief Justice Roger B. Taney intended to deliver an opinion, with the concurrence of a majority of the Court, which declared unconstitutional the congressional prohibition of slavery in territories of the United States? If he knew that this would be the outcome, it is a singular reflection on the belief (not of Buchanan alone but of many in his generation) that deep emotional conflicts could be settled by a one-sided opinion from a divided Court. Respect for the law, as urged by conservatives, had drifted away from the great corollary that governments derived just power from consent of the governed.

By the time that he commenced suit in 1847 Dred Scott had passed by inheritance to an owner with antislavery sympathies, and his backers probably hoped to obtain an opinion, following Lord Mansfield's judgment in Somersett's case, that slavery being contrary to natural law could be established only by the positive law of a political sovereign. What they got was an opinion that the Constitution protected slavery in the territories against legislative prohibition. Taney chose first to decide whether Dred Scott, a Negro, could sue as a citizen of the United States; he answered that Negroes had not formed part of the political people in making the Constitution and were therefore "not included . . . under the word 'citizen' in the Constitution." A state might treat a Negro as one of its own citizens, but this did "not put it into the power of a single State to make him a citizen of the United States, and endue him with the full rights of citizenship in every other State without their consent." Granted his premise—that Negroes, slave or free, had not formed a part of "We the people"—Taney's argument had some kind of logic; it meant that only a state could decide what rights a Negro possessed, that these rights could be recognized in law only by the courts of that state, and that the Supreme Court had therefore no jurisdiction. In the next part of his judgment he turned from the status of Negroes to the rights of citizens. Slaves were property, and in this instance the law could not distinguish between one kind of property and another. It followed that to deprive a man of his slaves was a breach of the Fifth Amendment (that no person could be deprived of life, liberty, or property without due process of law) , and "upon these considerations . . . The Act of Congress which prohibited a citizen from holding and owning property of this kind in the territory of the United States . . . is not warranted by the Constitution, and is therefore void."

It has sometimes been held that Taney said more than was necessary; that the mere denial of Negro citizenship would have enabled him to refuse jurisdiction and that he went beyond this because Associate Justices John McLean and Benjamin Curtis were preparing dissenting opinions that embraced the whole question of congressional jurisdiction over slavery. It seems more probable that Taney, who was the most experienced judge in the country, intended from the start to tackle congressional prohibition of slavery but thought it necessary to strip Dred Scott of his United States citizenship as a preliminary step in the argument. Without this the slave himself might have been able to claim protection of the Fifth Amendment, and it was essential to establish that although a United States citizen could not be deprived of his property, a noncitizen could be deprived of his freedom. McLean and Curtis delivered dissenting opinions upholding the power of Congress to prohibit slavery and while denying Taney's argument over Negro citizenship, argued that even if true, Congress had jurisdiction over all "persons" in the territories. One justice concurred in Taney's judgment without an opinion; three others delivered opinions that supported Taney's conclusion on different grounds; but it was Taney's attack on the Missouri Compromise that attracted universal attention. For southerners it was a vindication of their rights against northern "aggressions"; for antislavery men it was a great betrayal; for northern conservatives it destroyed the ground of Webster's 1850 argument that the status of slavery was everywhere fixed by law or nature; for many it was further evidence of the slave-power conspiracy; and for Douglas and his supporters it was a two-edged weapon. *Dred Scott* sealed with approval the repeal of the Missouri Compromise and denied the right of Congress to prohibit slavery in the territory; but whereas Cass and Douglas had opposed to congressional authority the inalienable right of self-government, Taney fettered both with the Fifth Amendment. If slave property were protected by the Constitution, how could it be destroyed by a mere territorial legislature deriving authority from an act of Congress? The natural right of self-government would be akin to Seward's "higher law" (or the popular interpretation thereof) if it claimed the right of territorial legislative assemblies to override the Constitution when they chose to do so.

This trap was also prepared for Buchanan. It was probably now his private opinion that if there was interference
with slavery in the territories, it would be the President's
constitutional duty to protect the guarantees of the Fifth
Amendment as interpreted by the Supreme Court. Rather
than risk a confrontation between federal authority and
Free Soil, Buchanan preferred to accept the dubious Lecompton constitution as the true will of the people of Kansas and to pretend that self-government had fortunately
coincided with the mandate of the Constitution by legalizing and protecting slavery.[3] If Kansas were admitted as a
state, there could be nothing to stop the Kansans from subsequently doing exactly as they liked; few slaves had actually been carried into the territory, and they were unlikely
to be carried farther north; southerners would be satisfied
with the legal victory, while Free Soil would soon have the
reality of power. Such may have been Buchanan's rationalization of the situation, and it certainly explains the haste
with which he now tried to get Kansas into the Union as a
slave state under the Lecompton constitution.

As a subtle political maneuver Buchanan's policy had
much to commend it, and if quietly accepted might have
created the atmosphere in which a dialogue at the center
could recommence. Unfortunately, the policy depended
upon too many expectations that could not be publicly expressed. For the Republicans it was simply a barefaced attempt to force another slave state into the Union, with

[3] In 1857 the proslavery legislature of Kansas called a constitutional
convention to meet at Lecompton. The Free Soil settlers refused to
recognize the legality of these proceedings and abstained from voting
in the election for the convention. The convention drew up a constitution that legalized slavery; the Free Soilers again refused to vote on
ratification. Whether the action of the Free Soilers was wise or unwise,
it was undeniable that the move for a convention had been initiated
by a legislature that no longer represented a majority and that the
convention had been chosen by less than a quarter of those entitled to
vote and the constitution proposed had been ratified by an even
smaller proportion.

more to follow, since the Dred Scott doctrine allowed slave-holders to carry their property farther north and west. For Douglas the Buchanan policy was a travesty of popular sovereignty; it placed the vital decision in the hands of the first men across the border, ignored all subsequent indications that they no longer represented the majority, and re-fused to submit the constitution to a fair vote. With vigor and skill Douglas had recovered by 1857 much of the popularity that he had forfeited with the repeal of the Missouri Compromise; but he could hardly survive a second surrender to slavery, and his opposition was inevitable. Personal feelings reinforced his decision; he had little respect for Buchanan, whom he had hoped to overtake in the presidential race, and he was bitterly offended by what he regarded as the bad faith of leading southern Democrats. Once he had decided upon opposition, he acted with characteristic vigor, and his anger was not diminished by Buchanan's threat to destroy him politically if he abandoned the Democratic principle of "regularity." Moreover, his senatorial term expired in 1858, and he intended to seek reelection; the Republicans were becoming ominously strong in Illinois, and Lecompton might drive doubtful Democrats into their ranks. Early in 1858 he combined with the Republicans to beat back the admission of Kansas as a slave state, forced the administration into a position where the Lecompton constitution had to be submitted to the vote in a fair election, and though he opposed the final form of the compromise bill, because the conditions were too heavily weighted in favor of accepting the Lecompton document, the victory was his and recognized as such. In the summer of 1858 he returned to Illinois to campaign for reelection with reasonable confidence of success; he believed correctly that the administration Democrats could be ignored and that his personal following in the southern counties could not be shaken. He hoped also to gather in some former Whigs and reluctant Republicans in the center of the state and to win a majority in the Illinois legislature with their support. Early in August his hand was strengthened still further when the voters of Kansas voted overwhelmingly to reject the proslavery constitution, and though the Dred Scott decision made slavery legal in the territory, the Free Soil victory ensured that it would make no headway.

The Republicans nominated Abraham Lincoln. He was almost unknown in the East, though he had served one undistinguished term in the House of Representatives as "the lone Whig from Illinois." His obscurity has become one of the great American legends, and he was certainly a self-made man of humble origins; but so was almost every other prominent man in Illinois, though the shiftless Kentucky family from which he sprang was a little lower down the social scale than most. By 1858 he was an extremely successful lawyer in a thriving small town, with a reputation that extended beyond his own state. He had been prominent in state politics for over a decade, but loyalty to the Whig party had limited his political horizons until the great upheavals of 1854–1856. He would gain a reputation (from historians rather than contemporaries) for cautious deliberation; in practice, in all the crucial decisions of his life, he seems to have made up his mind quickly and firmly, though timing his announcements with care. The rise of the Republican party presented an opportunity that he grasped immediately. In 1855 he was its leading candidate for the Senate and only after a somewhat unhappy contest threw his support to Lyman Trumbull, a former Democrat, who would bring fresh support to the party. It is a curious reflection that if Lincoln had won in 1855, there would have been no epic battle with Douglas in 1858 and that his role as a freshman senator in the single Congress would hardly have made him a national figure in 1860. The small and factious group in the Illinois legislature in 1855, who refused to give Lincoln the few votes he needed, may therefore have made him President in 1861.

As with other astute politicians it is often difficult to separate Lincoln's real convictions from expedient opinions. The urgent need was to broaden the base of Republicanism in Illinois, and this meant drawing in Free Soilers, Whigs, and discontented Democrats. He had to appeal to men who were long-standing critics of slavery, to men who disliked slavery but would not agitate to end it, to abolitionists, and to men who reacted violently against the idea of racial equality even as a remote possibility. In spite of these difficulties it was easier to build a statewide alliance on opposition to the extension of slavery than on any other issue, while other traditional items in the party policies divided many whom it was necessary to unite. In his public utterances he had remarkably little to say about other issues, but his views on slavery were always consistent, though the emphasis might vary with different audiences. In the first flurry of opposition to the repeal of the Missouri Compromise he said:

The Judge [Douglas] has no very vivid impression that the negro is human; and consequently has no idea that there can be any moral question in legislating about him. In his view, the question of whether a new country shall be slave or free, is a matter of as utter indifference, as it is whether his neighbour shall plant his farm with tobacco, or stock it with horned cattle. Now, whether this view is right or wrong, it is very certain that the great mass of mankind take a totally different view. They consider slavery a great moral wrong; and their feeling against it, is not evanescent, but eternal. It lies at the very foundation of their sense of justice; and it cannot be trifled with. It is a great and durable element of popular action, and, I think, no statesman can safely disregard it.[4]

In 1857, arguing against Douglas and the Dred Scott decision, Lincoln maintained that the Declaration of Independence applied to *all* men, and while confessing that "there is a natural disgust in the minds of nearly all white

---

[4] Speech at Peoria, October 16, 1854. Quoted in Basler, Vol. II, pp. 281–282.

people, to the idea of an indiscriminate amalgamation of the white and black races," added a protest against

that counterfeit logic which concludes that, because I do not count a black woman for a *slave* I must necessarily want her for a *wife*. I need not have her for either, I can just leave her alone. In some respects she certainly is not my equal; but in her natural right to eat the bread she earns with her own hands without asking leave of anyone else, she is my equal, and the equal of all others.[5]

Slavery brought the races together; Free Soil kept them apart. "A separation of the races is the only perfect preventative of amalgamation but as an immediate separation is impossible the next best thing is to *keep* them apart *where* they are not already together." In the same speech he advocated colonization.

The enterprise is a difficult one; but "when there is a will there is a way"; and what colonization needs most is a hearty will. Will springs from the two elements of moral sense and self-interest. Let us be brought to believe that it is morally right, and, at the same time, favorable to, or, at least, not against our interest, to transfer the African to his native clime, and we shall find a way to do it.

Finally, he summed up the differences between the parties by saying:

The Republicans inculcate, with whatever ability they can, that the negro is a man; that his bondage is cruelly wrong, and that the field of his oppression ought not to be enlarged. The Democrats deny his manhood; deny or dwarf to insignificance, the wrong of his bondage; so far as possible, crush all sympathy for him, and cultivate, and excite hatred and disgust against him; compliment themselves as Union-savers for doing so; and call the indefinite outspreading of his bondage "a sacred right of self-government." [6]

---

[5] June 26, 1857. *Ibid.*, p. 405.
[6] *Ibid.*, p. 408.

From these views Lincoln never wavered throughout the rest of his life. He always believed that slavery was morally wrong, never accepted any theory that justified the enslavement of one man by another, always argued that separation of the races was the only long-term solution to the racial problem, continued to advocate colonization, and always refused to admit that it was impracticable. He never claimed to provide an easy solution for racial problems but consistently maintained that of all solutions slavery was the worst.

In these opinions Lincoln was neither original nor, in his generation, unique; he was influential because he was representative. He would apply his keen but reflective mind again and again to this one problem; and, for good or ill, he did much to keep the public mind of the North focused upon it. Rightly or wrongly he saw slavery as a fundamental fact that could not be evaded and was convinced at the outset that the whole future of the American nation depended upon the way it was handled; being fundamental, it was linked with all other commitments, values, and promises of American society.

The great debate between Lincoln and Douglas, argued out in the late summer and fall of 1858 before audiences of farmers, storekeepers, and clerks in unexciting little towns, attracted nationwide attention. Douglas was the man of the hour, struggling for his political life, but by the perversity of fortune his fame made Lincoln the spokesman of antislavery sentiment throughout the free states. Douglas had an opportunity of making popular sovereignty, fairly applied, the rallying standard for a revived Democratic party in the North, while his stand for repeal of the Missouri Compromise and acceptance of the Dred Scott decision were expected to reconcile southern Democrats to his nomination in 1860. At the same time he intended to associate the Republicans with abolitionism, "amalgamation," racial equality, and disunion; against them he would show himself as a moderate and conciliatory statesman and thus win over administration Democrats (who ran a separate campaign in the state) and conservative Whigs. These tactics left Lincoln with very little room for maneuver. The weak points in his case were his attitude to the Dred Scott decision (he could not appear to defy the Court without losing conservative support), his apparent rejection of the right of men to decide local issues for themselves, the association of the case against slavery with racial equality, and the "house divided" theme, which could be represented as either disunionist or a threat to the South. Lincoln planned his tactics with two main aims in view. First, he would insist that slavery was a moral issue, force Douglas to deny this publicly, and so cut him off from the mainstream of antislavery opinion in the North. Second, he would force Douglas to admit that in the light of the Dred Scott decision popular sovereignty could not be a reality without nullifying in some way the constitutional rights of slaveholders; this might help Douglas in Illinois but would drive a wedge between him and the southern Democrats. In neither instance would he extract from Douglas any new admission; the novelty lay in the reporters and newspaper editors who would carry the debates across the nation.

Near the end of the first joint debate Lincoln attacked Douglas's attitude toward self-government and slavery:

When he invites any people, willing to have slavery, to establish it, he is blowing out the moral lights around us. When he says he "cares not whether slavery is voted down or voted up"—that is the sacred right of self-government—he is, in any judgment, penetrating the human soul and eradicating the light of reason and the love of liberty in this American people.

In the second debate, at Freeport, he put a direct question to Douglas:

Can the people of a United States Territory, in any lawful way, against the wish of any citizen of the United States, exclude slavery from its limits prior to the formation of a State Constitution?

The question was not a new one, and Lincoln could anticipate that Douglas would answer:

It matters not what way the Supreme Court may hereafter decide
as to the abstract question whether slavery may or may not go
into a Territory under the Constitution, the people have the lawful means to introduce it or exclude it as they please, for the reason that slavery cannot exist a day or an hour anywhere, unless it
is supported by local police regulations. These police regulations
can only be established by the local legislature, and if the people
are opposed to slavery they will elect representatives to that body
who will by unfriendly legislation effectually prevent the introduction of it into their midst.

To many of the audience it probably seemed that Douglas had made an effective response to Lincoln's challenge,
yet Lincoln had considered carefully whether or not he
should put the question. He probably considered the effect
on southern opinion, but it seems likely that he also
aimed at two further points. Douglas had been attack-
ing the Republicans for their attitude toward the Supreme
Court, and Lincoln wished to draw the contrast between
his own position—that the Dred Scott decision was bad in
law and erroneous in fact but must be respected until a majority was found to reverse it—and Douglas's suggestion
that it could be accepted in the letter and nullified in practice. Of the two, a conservative might well prefer the former. Douglas had also represented Lincoln, on the basis of
the "house divided" speech, as a disunionist; but was not
the nullification of what southerners claimed as a constitutional right as likely to disrupt the Union? As the issue of
the contest was to be decided in the central counties of the
state, with conservative Democrat and Whig traditions
predominant, it was important for Lincoln to establish
that the attempt to run with the proslavery hare and hunt
with the Free Soil hounds would have consequences more
radical than his own straightforward stand.

Lincoln won a popular majority in the state, but the senatorship was decided by the Legislature, and the overrepre-

sentation of the Democratic southern counties and the holdover Democrats in the State Senate gave Douglas a safe majority. Once more Lincoln had failed to achieve that legitimate ambition of every aspiring politician, a seat in the United States Senate. He prepared to return to private life and to develop his law business, but the result indicated that the Republicans had a good chance of carrying Illinois at the next presidential election, and whatever Lincoln's own role in that contest, it was clear that he had become indispensable to the party in the state.

In a well-known passage in his biography of Lincoln, James G. Randall wrote of the 1858 contest:

Swinging up and down and back and forth across Illinois, making the welkin ring and setting the prairies on fire, Lincoln and Douglas debated—what? That is the surprising thing. With all the problems that might have been put before the people as proper matter for their consideration in choosing a senator— choice of government servants, immigration, the tariff, international policy, promotion of education, westward extension of railroads, the opening of new lands for homesteads, protection against greedy exploitation of those lands (a problem to which Congress gave insufficient attention), encouragement to settlers, and the bettering of agriculture, not to mention such social problems as guarding against economic depression, improving the condition of factory workers, and alleviating those agrarian grievances that were to plague the coming decade—with such issues facing the country, these two candidates for the Senate talked as if there were only one issue.[7]

As a statement of fact this is correct, but historians should necessarily be more concerned with what men wished to talk about than with what they ought to have discussed. Lincoln and Douglas stuck to the one issue, but there is no indication that the voters of Illinois expected them to do

[7] James G. Randall, Lincoln the President, Vol. II (New York: Dodd, Mead; London: Eyre and Spottiswoode; 1945), pp. 121–122.

otherwise. Any political campaign must necessarily be selective in the points presented for discussion, and the maturity of a political society may well be judged by the discussion of one or two issues in depth rather than by touching superficially upon a large number. Certainly it appears that in the history of all nations, at some periods, certain questions become paramount and seem to contain the answer to all others. The truth was that each of the other problems mentioned by Randall did not engage the interest of more than segments of the population; some deserved serious discussion but were less important than the character of the nation. The voters of Illinois in 1858 knew that either man would do the best for the state within the guidelines of well-understood political philosophies, that on many of these issues they were likely to differ in detail rather than in principle, and that the political system was well-adapted to work out compromises on such matters. Of the problems mentioned by Randall the choice of government servants was of little public interest. The tariff was of little direct interest in Illinois, and the voters did not have to be told that Lincoln would vote for a higher and Douglas for a lower tariff. Foreign policy was of no significance to the ordinary voter in 1858. On education, immigration, western railroads, and homesteads there was little difference between the two men. The other more speculative questions hardly impinged upon the public conscience.

Some writers have accused Lincoln, and other Republicans, of exploiting antislavery sentiment to win political advantages. Horace Greeley, who was a formative influence upon Republican opinion though a doubtful judge of popular reaction, took a different view of the relationship between antislavery and material interests. In April, 1860, he wrote privately that

I know the country is not Anti-Slavery. It will only swallow a little Anti-Slavery in a great deal of sweetening. An Anti-Slavery man *per se* cannot be elected; but a Tariff, River-and-Harbour,

Pacific Railroad, Free-Homestead man, *may* succeed *although* he is Anti-Slavery.[8]

This was, however, written when Greeley was backing Edward Bates, of Missouri, for the Republican nomination, and Bates was an old-line Whig who tried to be as noncommittal as possible on slavery. The fact, rather than the hypothesis, is that Lincoln was nominated and elected in 1860 as a man opposed to the extension of slavery.

The debate over the primacy of material or ideological issues is not likely to end in this generation or the next, but if men had been so minded, there would have been good reason to discuss economic issues. The long upward movement of the economy had been halted by a sharp financial panic in 1857, and though the shock did not penetrate so deeply as in 1819 or 1837, it was still severe. In 1858 men were still bewildered, and Republicans were eager to blame Democratic policies and particularly the low tariff that had been pushed through Congress in the previous year. There had also been continuous debate over federal aid for rivers and harbors, the Pacific Railroad, and homesteads for western settlers. There was a developing contest within northern society on these questions, but it hardly coincided with traditional party lines. The old Whigs were divided, as were the Democrats; on both sides were groups seeking for new alignments, but nowhere within the political spectrum could anyone see the coherent national alliances that might offer defined policies. A new society was struggling into being, with diverse and confused economic interests, and it was neither perverse nor unexpected that men should seek to discover the moral and intellectual bonds of union in preference to argument over what was local, uncertain, and fluctuating. This does not imply that American politicians were not intensely aware of local issues, but that as they found their

---

[8] Quoted in Jeter A. Isely, *Horace Greeley and the Republican Party* (Princeton, N.J.: Princeton University Press, 1947), p. 266.

way toward wider alliances, material interests dropped into the background, and the broader issues of national character came to the fore.

The "slave power," "popular sovereignty," and "black Republicanism" became the focal points for emerging ideologies. These specific issues symbolized more generalized conflicts between attitudes rooted in the past and molded by changing events. In this conflict the South was, in a sense, irrelevant, for little that happened in that section could change opinion in the North and West; yet southern society, southern aims, and southern slavery became references for the interior conflict of northern society. Relationship to the South, and especially to the slave power, became the test and symbol for a range of attitudes that embraced everything from religious conviction to economic calculation. Just as earlier Americans had defined their national character as "not English," so northern Americans now defined themselves as "not southern." Throughout history emergent nationalism has been forged by the realization and definition of differences with others; themes of conflict, association, and definition of aims become the essence of a new relationship between a society and the world; normal struggles for power in a developing society are thus transformed into revolutionary change.

A parallel conflict developed in the South. Superimposed upon the class structure of southern society was the argument over separatism or association with the North. There has, as yet, been insufficient study of the sociology of secession to permit generalization. The upper class became divided, but it would seem that a majority of the larger planters remained Unionist as long as it was possible to do so. Separatism was the creed of a minority excluded from power and was in some respects the political aspect of men on the make in southern society. Even the great Calhoun had come from a comparatively humble family and had

depended upon his own talents. Nor had separatism
struck roots in the mass of the people. Nullification, the
first separatist experiment, had failed and failed completely, but the resolute response by Andrew Jackson had
been effective because the southern people did not want
a separate or autonomous South. The argument over slavery in the territories, with all its attendant themes of northern "aggressions" and abolitionist invective, had, however,
provided the separatists with themes that promised to
broaden the base of activity, for behind the argument over
the extension of slavery was the problem of race, the universal reaction against the prospect of competition between the races or eventual amalgamation, and implied
criticism of southern society in all its aspects.

Just as the "slave power" had emerged in the North as
the reference point for northern political behavior, so in
the South "abolitionism" and "southern rights" became
the negative and positive ways of explaining and popular-
izing the idea of a separate southern identity. Although
many of the separatists still talked of states' rights, they
meant the rights of the section; the actions of states were
to be the means, but an independent South was the end.
The so-called fire-eaters in the South were enthusiasts for
southern nationalism; as yet they spoke for a minority, and
the very need to capture a majority impelled them to
fasten upon every point at which the interests of the South
were incompatible with those of the North. In their vocabulary free settlers excluding slavery by refusing to protect it by law were little different from a northern majority
excluding it by act of Congress. Thus the great conflict
that was developing in the North was really irrelevant to
southern politics, or relevant only insofar as the arguments
might provide separatists with that power over the minds
of their fellow citizens that would make them true nationalists. All nationalist movements have been led by
minorities who claim to know, better than either the estab-

lishment or the mass of the people, the true mind and character of the nation. The South was no exception.

The paradoxical aspect of southern nationalism was that its exponents were often political outsiders who were nevertheless driven to extol the merits of society as it was. They might look forward to southern independence, but in other respects they wished to keep things as they were. With the exception of a few advocates of commerce and manufactures their politics were anchored to plantations and commercial agriculture. The paradox can readily be understood when the racial dimension of southern nationalism is understood. There was a neat syllogism that southern society could not exist without slavery, the plantation could not be run without slavery, therefore plantation agriculture was essential to southern society. There were more attractive elements in the southern case; they wanted local autonomy and the protection of a face-to-face society against dictation by impersonal political and economic forces, they protested against "wage slavery," and they valued dignity and responsibility in public life; but these admirable features were harnessed to the ascendancy of large landowners and the dependence upon slave labor.

5

The Collapse of the Union

THE year 1859 was not an auspicious one in American history. Save for a few tragic hours at Harpers Ferry, it contained few moments of drama. The country was beginning to recover from the depression of 1857, but business was still slack. The old Congress served out its lame-duck session to expire in March; the new Congress did not meet until the close of the year. Politically, the year formed a twilight period during which the intentions of the Republicans and the future of the Democrats remained uncertain. Everyone anticipated that in 1860 Stephen A. Douglas would make a supreme bid to capture the national organization. Avowed secessionists studied the political cards attentively to show how events could be manipulated to generate a concerted move for southern independence. Republicans staked their claims for 1860 but without knowing who would lead them or on what principles.

This year rather than the secession crisis provides convincing evidence that James Buchanan lacked the qualities of statesmanship. Though his party was divided and weakened by Republican election successes, he was President of the United States and would be so until March, 1861; he alone had power to reunite his party and stimulate the efforts of Unionists in all parts of the country. Yet Buchanan seemed to be preoccupied by his feud with the Douglas Democrats and with putting the blame for all that might ensue upon the Republicans. It is possible that any attempt to avert the coming conflict would have failed; yet it was surely the duty of the President to give public warning of the dangers that lay ahead. The most urgent task was to provide an opportunity for moderate men to confer, and the President was the one man in a position to act or to understand the gravity of the crisis.

It must be admitted that even if Buchanan had been minded to stop treating his own vindication as a major political objective, he would have received little help from the Republicans. They now felt assured of a permanent place as a major party; most of them believed that talk of disunion need not be taken seriously, and they continued to act as though the political situation were normal. As former Whigs, Free Soilers, or dissident Democrats they had long operated in a political environment controlled by their enemies, and they saw no reason why others should not accept the same role when their turn came. Most of them were convinced that when it came to the test, a majority in the South would accept the exclusion of slavery from the territories as a very small price for the preservation of the Union and one that would do no damage to the real interests of the southern people. These views were fortified by a book, *The Impending Crisis in the South,* by Hinton Rowan Helper, first published in 1857, and now in July, 1859, published in an abridged form with endorsement by leading Republicans. The bulk of the book consisted of an argument, buttressed by history and figures from the United States census, that slavery had retarded southern progress, corrupted public life, and done grave injustice to nonslaveholders. *The Impending Crisis* advocated the abolition of slavery, but it was not "abolitionist" as the term was generally understood in the North. Helper intended to consider slavery "with reference to its economic aspects as regards the whites—not with reference, except in a very slight degree, to its humanitarian or religious aspects." Indeed, he reflected the antipathy to Negroes that was common among the class of small farmers of North Carolina where he had been born and bred, and wanted separation, not integration.

Once for all, within a reasonably short period, let us make the slaveholders do something like justice to their negroes by giving each and every one of them his freedom, and sixty dollars in current money; then let us charter all the ocean steamers, packets and clipper ships which can be had on liberal terms, and keep them constantly plying between the ports of America and Africa, until all the slaves shall enjoy freedom in the land of their fathers.

Helper's carefully documented but highly emotional work made it appear that anyone who worked for the end of slavery would be serving the true interests of the southern white people by saving them from their own leaders. He told his fellow southerners:

The slaveholders, the arrogant demagogues whom you have elected to office of honor and profit, have hoodwinked you, trifled with you, and used you as mere tools for the consummation of their wicked designs. . . . By a system of the grossest subterfuge and misrepresentation, and in order to avert, for a season, the vengeance that will most assuredly overtake them ere long, they have taught you to hate the abolitionists, who are your best and only true friends.

It was slavery that made the South dependent upon others for capital and manufactures, while slaveholders had cast the blame upon the North.

It was Horace Greeley's hope to spread Republicanism among the plain people of the South, and Helper's arguments (which had been little noticed when the book first appeared) seemed a means of achieving this objective. In July, 1859, a compendium of *The Impending Crisis* was printed, advertised, and distributed by the New York *Tribune*, endorsed by Republican leaders, and presented as a campaign document. It sold in large numbers and provided a quarry of material for hundreds of Republican speeches. To most Republicans it seemed common sense that antislavery would benefit the South, and they did not anticipate the storm of southern fury that burst when Congress met in December, 1859, and a Missouri Democrat moved that no man who had endorsed *The Impending Crisis* was fit to be Speaker of the House. The Republicans were the largest party but without a majority, and the balance of power was held by a small group of Native Americans and Whigs from the border states; for nearly two months the House was deadlocked because the Republican nominee, John Sherman, had been an endorser. Finally the Republicans had to withdraw his name, but not before the House had sat through weeks of sectional invective during which even hardened politicians were shocked by the intensity with which familiar arguments were uttered. When Congress was finally organized, a prominent southern senator wrote:

There are no relations—not absolutely indispensable for the conduct of joint business—between the North and the South in either House. No two nations on earth are or ever were more distinctly separated and hostile than we are here. . . . How can the thing go on? [1]

To understand this deterioration in sectional relations, one must look back to two significant events, one now forgotten except for a phrase, the other forever remembered. The first was a speech in October, 1858, by William H. Seward; the second was John Brown's raid. Seward was the most probable Republican nominee for the Presidency, so his words carried weight, but his sophisticated rhetoric had the unfortunate knack of crystallizing in a phrase arguments that appeared uncompromising. In 1850 it had been "higher law"; in 1859 it was "irrepressible conflict." Seward's purpose was to reject the southern argument that antislavery was the work of fanatical agitators; rather he wished to emphasize that deep differences existed and must be understood sympathetically. The avowal of an "irre-

[1] James H. Hammond (South Carolina) to M. C. M. Hammond, April 22, 1860. Quoted in Harold S. Schultz, *Nationalism and Sectionalism in South Carolina* (Durham, N.C.: University of North Carolina Press, 1950), p. 205.

pressible conflict" was not a call to battle but an urgent plea for men to face realities. In the North the speech was understood as it was intended, but in the South the "irrepressible conflict" was seen as a declaration of war against southern society by the party, and perhaps by the man, who might soon control the national administration; it required little effort to link the philosophy of the irrepressible conflict with the armed attack upon the South that followed within a year.

On the night of October 16, 1859, John Brown led eighteen men across the Potomac to the little Virginia town of Harpers Ferry. Set in a fine valley amid the mountains, it was an important strategic point commanding a railroad bridge and containing the Federal Armory. Brown intended to raise southern slaves in revolt and establish an antislavery stronghold in the Virginia mountains. He was a man of unstable temperament, fierce imagination, and violent determination. In manner, appearance, and speech he modeled himself upon the conventional image of an Old Testament prophet and believed himself to be the chosen instrument of divine wrath against slaveholders. In 1856 he had been in Kansas and was responsible for the murder of five proslavery settlers under particularly unpleasant circumstances, but despite this he was well received in eastern abolitionist circles. Clearly he possessed a personal magnetism that persuaded intelligent and humane men to accept him as a man of destiny, and though the extent of the aid he received is unknown, some was certainly given.

The raid itself was a fiasco. No slaves rose in revolt, the invading force was quickly surrounded in an engine house by United States marines, and after the inevitable surrender the remnant of Brown's force was handed over to the state of Virginia. Just two weeks later Brown was convicted of treason against Virginia and murder. On December 2, 1859, he was hanged, and six of his followers were also executed. In calmer times the raid might have been recognized as a minor act of violence committed by a paranoid man; in 1859 it was seen throughout the South as proving the falsity of Republican claims that there would be no interference with slavery in the states. In the North most public men rushed to deplore the raid, but with the rank and file of the antislavery movement the episode was seen in a different light. John Brown had struck a blow for freedom; while politicians prevaricated, he had acted and in a noble cause had sacrificed his life. The blood of such martyrs had advanced the cause of Christian freedom throughout the ages, and conscious of his historic role, John Brown had behaved during his trial with tragic dignity; he expressed no regret—except for having failed—and in a final and moving speech claimed that he had done what he did for the poor and oppressed. The abolitionists had a martyr; thousands who had not been convinced of the need to act were won over to a positive antislavery view; Ralph Waldo Emerson spoke for New England intellectuals in a eulogy, and John Brown's memory would be carried over the nation in the most famous of all marching songs.

In the South the coming political struggle was complex and the outcome uncertain. Separatists looked for the breakup of the Union and the winning of southern independence. Their characteristic argument was that the movement for independence could not begin unless the individual states were ready to act and that each southern state should go forward with its own plans for secession. Only when this was accomplished would it be possible to reconstruct a southern Union. The men of this group were strongest in South Carolina and Alabama; weaker in Georgia, Mississippi, and Louisiana; and a minority in the upper South. The next group were the cooperationists who stressed the right to secede but argued that it would be inexpedient for states to do so in isolation. A concerted movement would be required, perhaps initiated by a southern convention. Cooperation offered a haven for large numbers of conditional Unionists, moderates, and others who hoped for firmer guarantees of southern rights within the Union. The requirement for common action among the states was in fact a plea for delay and negotiation rather than the action advocated by the "fire-eaters."

The distinction between the two groups was often one of temperament rather than fundamental beliefs. Secessionists were violent in their denunciation of northern aggressions, uninhibited in their defense of southern rights, and apt to emphasize that because the majority in the North would not recognize slavery as a positive good, the Union could not endure. Cooperationists were milder in their denunciations, ready to work with northerners whom they regarded as friendly to the South, and not prepared to force the issue by requiring the northern majority to give positive support to slavery. The cooperationists controlled the majority political organization in all southern states, though as one moved north, they had to share power with unconditional Unionists. The Dred Scott decision, by providing a theoretical case for the federal protection of slavery in the territories, had, however, built a bridge between radical separatists and the conservative cooperationists, who could now unite in demanding that guarantees for a right recognized by the Supreme Court must be accepted if the Union were to survive.

Unconditional Unionists were drawn from both the old major parties and included Jacksonian nationalists and Clay Unionists. This divided ancestry weakened their impact. Except on the single issue of preserving the Union, a lifelong Democrat such as Senator Andrew Johnson, of Tennessee, found it difficult to combine with former Whigs led by members of the planter gentry. Unconditional Unionism was strong in some of the "white counties" of the Appalachian uplands and valleys and among the planters and businessmen of Maryland and Kentucky. There was a tendency for unconditional Unionism to crumble away as the defense of slavery became a major issue and as subsequent events convinced upper-class Unionists that there would be a real danger if the Republicans captured national power.

In any situation moving toward revolution the men who know what they want and where they are going are likely to have the advantage. It was so in the South. The men who wished to head straight for southern independence were a minority in the South as a whole and a small minority in the upper South; but they knew that events were moving in their direction and could plan ahead to turn the situation to their advantage. It was logical that the Democratic party, as the sole remaining national institution, should first bear the weight of their attack. They could exploit the animosity between Buchanan and Douglas and demand a commitment to a federal slave code that would be unacceptable in principle and politically suicidal in the North. Either way the coming election would be fought on sectional lines, and the outcome would demonstrate the impossibility of continuing in the Union.

There was thus nothing accidental about the crisis forced upon the Democratic party when delegates gathered in April, 1860, at Charleston for their national convention. In 1856, in the mood of harmony following Buchanan's nomination, it may have seemed appropriate to compliment the South by choosing the nerve center of separatism for the next party convention and perhaps to hope that Calhoun's state might be drawn back into the political mainstream. In 1860 there could hardly have been a worse place for a national meeting or an easier one in which to effect the disruption of the party. Northern delegates were made to feel like outsiders, secessionists were encouraged at every turn by popular approval, and rational conversation about slavery was impossible in a city where its positive benefits were articles of faith. Douglas came to the convention with a large majority of northern Democrats pledged to support him, and in spite of opposition from the administration, most politicians looked to the rising sun from Illinois. In the South Douglas had some support and under normal circumstances could have expected a safe nomination accompanied by the usual demonstrations of party harmony. He himself hoped that the territorial issue was dead; Kansas would eventually come in as a free state, New Mexico might come in nominally as a slave state, but for the rest it was folly to argue about abstract rights that would never be exercised. In spite of the storms through which it had passed, popular sovereignty had won the game and would make the West a white man's country without imposing upon the South the affront of a Wilmot Proviso. With this fair prospect ahead it seemed wholly unreasonable for a block of southern delegates (led by Alabama but inspired mainly by South Carolina) to insist upon federal protection for slavery in the territories. Until very recently every southern leader had accepted nonintervention by Congress as essential to their cause; now it was proposed that Congress must intervene to protect slavery not merely against unfriendly action by people of the territories but even against a failure to act.

In the confused episodes that followed it was clear that a majority of the convention wanted Douglas but that he might fall short of a two-thirds majority without more support from the South. A majority in the South would pledge support to no candidate who did not endorse a federal slave code, but neither Douglas nor realistic northern politicians could possibly accept this. Douglas was publicly committed to his Freeport doctrine, and the political managers foresaw a Republican landslide if the point were conceded. Even so, northern Democrats were ready to accept a meaningless reaffirmation of their 1856 platform, and many showed themselves ready to accept any form of words short of a positive commitment to a federal slave code. But nothing less would satisfy the delegates of the lower South who were more intent upon finding the issue on which to divide the party than a formula to enable a requisite number of southern Democrats to join the Douglas camp. On

April 30 the delegations from Alabama, Arkansas, Louisiana, Florida, Mississippi, Texas, and South Carolina withdrew from the convention.

The convention still attempted to make a nomination, but a ruling that nomination required two-thirds of all the delegates, not merely of those present, effectively prevented a choice, and the best that the Douglas men could obtain was an adjournment to Baltimore in June. The Douglas Democrats were angry, bitter, and convinced that the real objective of the lower South leaders had been to draw a line that few northern Democrats could cross without committing political suicide. Many southern Democrats had been carried much further than they would have wished in demanding the nationalization of slavery as an essential condition. The final breakup of the party took place at Baltimore, when a majority of the delegates (including some elected from the South to replace the seceders and recognized by the convention) voted to nominate Douglas, while a majority of the southern delegates, with a sprinkling of northern men, met in separate convention to adopt a slave-code platform and nominate John C. Breckinridge, of Kentucky.

The rupture of the Democratic party is rightly seen as a prelude to disunion, but the division was neither purely sectional nor exclusively concerned with slavery. Ever since the rise of Jackson the Democrats had wrestled with contradictory principles. Their Jeffersonian legacy made them adherents of states' rights and limited government, but their Jacksonian precepts made them nationalists and upholders of majority rule. The Buchanan Democrats believed that when compromise failed, the national majority must recognize the limitations imposed by state sovereignty; the Douglas Democrats believed that though the rights of states ought to be respected, they must ultimately yield to the wishes of the majority. The disciples of Calhoun were therefore right in seeing their action as a protest against the tyranny of the majority, and the heirs of Jackson were right in believing that the old battle against nullification was being fought again in a new guise. Yet because the dispute was also over slavery, the argument had taken a new and unexpected course. The southern extremists now demanded that the national government must act to curb the will of local majorities and not stand aside to allow them to make an unfettered choice.

The Republicans also embraced discordant views and mixed ancestry but knew what they wanted and were not disposed to quarrel over details. The further extension of slavery was to be prevented, but identification with abolitionism was to be avoided. Slavery was the enemy of progress, and though most Republicans believed it to be immoral and unjust, their public condemnation stressed the damage inflicted upon white society. Horace Greeley, the best-known publicist of the Republican cause, was a man of many enthusiasms, and his *Tribune* editorials constantly made the point that the Republican party was not confined to one idea; deeply impressed by the arguments of Hinton Helper, he even believed that support could be won in the upper South, and his chosen candidate for the Presidency was Edward Bates, of Missouri, a Whig of the Clay school, who would hardly go beyond opposition to positive measures for the establishment of slavery.

At the very time, therefore, that the future of slavery was becoming the dominant and divisive issue among the Democrats, their opponents were trying to treat it as an incidental issue, important less for itself than because its containment was the key to so many other desirable improvements. It was the slave power that had to be defeated, and the attack upon slavery became the means only because slave-owners themselves insisted upon treating it as the paramount issue; but most Republicans hoped that once the slave power had been overthrown, the people of the South would find their own way of ending slavery. The

Republican cause in 1860 therefore appeared more aware of political calculations, more emphatic upon material issues, and less idealistic than in 1856. This changed character has misled many commentators, particularly those who have not understood the character of an ideology.

Many years ago John R. Commons, the historian of American industrial society, announced that the Republican was not an antislavery party, but a homestead party, and this impression was a legitimate deduction from the party propaganda appearing in the newspapers circulating among skilled workers and farmers. The Republican was also a Pacific Railroad party and a protection party. Despite some temptations and local alliances, it was not a nativist party; nor was it a party of bankers and merchants. It was strongly nationalist, and commitment to the betterment of man was indissolubly linked with the idea of American superiority. In its philosophy of history the Republican party became the spearhead of a great drive to lead America into fruitful ways in economics, moral elevation, and humanitarian action. This awareness of standing at the head of a great endeavor, which was intensely national yet truly international, provided the deep springs of Republican enthusiasm. It was a new party committed to the enlargement of life in a new country, and in the view that had been built up over the years the slave power stood athwart all the roads to improvement.

Even within the antislavery tradition the Republicans of 1860 were less inconsistent than is sometimes supposed. They were prepared (and this would be said still more emphatically before the outbreak of war) to support a constitutional amendment denying the right of Congress to abolish slavery in states where it existed by law. This was an abandonment of the position taken up by the former Liberty party that the general-welfare clause, interpreted in the light of the Declaration of Independence, gave the national government power to act against slavery in the states; but it was in line with the Garrisonian argument that slavery could not be abolished by political action until slave-owners themselves had become convinced of its iniquity. Indeed, the Republican position of 1860 was more consistent with earlier abolitionist thought than with the postwar determination to reconstruct southern society by national power. Moral pressure remained the best hope for ending slavery, and this could work more freely if slaveholders were guaranteed against arbitrary political action. This point is worth making because the Republicans of 1860 have so often been accused of betraying the antislavery cause.

William Henry Seward seemed to be the obvious candidate. Charles Sumner had been the zealot of the antislavery cause in the Senate, men like Salmon P. Chase and Ben Wade had been the shock troops, but Seward had been the statesman of the movement. He was subtle, humane, intelligent, and had shown a marked talent for maintaining his principles while enjoying good personal relations with his rivals. Yet he had serious handicaps. He had much respect but little popularity; his lifelong friend and mentor, Thurlow Weed, had much skill but little respect; and Seward himself neglected the small arts that might gratify vanity and secure support. He had offended Horace Greeley by failing to consult him, and the influential editor was determined to prevent his nomination. The existence of a still powerful Democratic party in New York and the alienation of some Republicans made it doubtful whether he could carry his own state. The "higher law" and the "irrepressible conflict" made it likely that his candidacy would trouble conservative men and end Republican hopes of making inroads into the upper South.

Eastern Republicans failed to realize how much strength Lincoln had built up in the Midwest. They thought of him as a favorite son who would be backed by his state for a few ballots, but Lincoln appealed to western pride in a way that no other candidate could match. The Republican party had originated west of the Appalachians, and veterans (if there could be veterans in so young a movement) did not welcome the suggestion that the rewards of success should pass to experienced eastern hands. Lincoln had proved his worth in the great contest with Douglas, and he alone had a fair prospect of stealing from Douglas moderate and conservative votes in most trans-Appalachian states. There was also good reason to believe that he would be more likely than Seward to break the Democratic ascendancy in Pennsylvania. Added to these calculations, Lincoln had few enemies while Seward had many, the Republican convention was held in his home state, and his campaign was organized by shrewd men who were equally adept in the stimulation of popular enthusiasm and the arrangement of matters behind the scenes. These factors led to Lincoln's nomination after a short though dramatic convention battle.

Even so, the nomination of Lincoln remains an unusual episode in American political history, and only the great reputation he subsequently acquired makes the choice appear logical and wise. Lincoln had no executive experience; his legislative experience was confined to his own state and to one undistinguished term at Washington. All that most people knew of him outside Illinois was that his speeches read well on paper and that he had risen from humble origins (a not unusual attribute among public men of the day). He had never traveled abroad and had spent little time outside his own state. On the other hand, it is wrong to overemphasize his obscurity; he was not an ignorant "prairie lawyer" but an extremely successful member of the Illinois bar; he was not a political novice but had long been prominent in the Whig and then in Republican organizations; he had been a strong candidate for the Senate in 1856 and had won a popular majority in

1858. There were several men in the Republican party with equal or superior attainments, but Lincoln's unique asset was the experience of standing up to Douglas in sustained argument; and this, more than anything else, commended him to professional politicians. The split in the Democratic party eliminated Douglas's chances of winning the Presidency, but Republicans and Democrats would still be locked in combat in every northern and western community, and men at the head of the local Republican organizations wanted a standard-bearer who had proved himself a match for the most formidable public man of the day. It was the typical but understandable ambition of small-town politicians to win in their own states that turned the scales in Lincoln's favor, with little thought about the part that the candidate might play upon the national stage.

Before the Chicago nomination a meeting had been held in Baltimore, where (in Allan Nevins's words) "Clay's despairing ghost was invoked for almost the last time," and a Constitutional Union party was launched. Most of the delegates were former Whigs from the upper South; a few came from other parts of the Union. The most prominent man in the movement was J. J. Crittenden, of Kentucky, but he was too old to run for the Presidency, and the choice fell upon John Bell, of Tennessee, a strong Union man whose votes in Congress had often been too close to the antislavery line to please his constituents. In a bid for conservative support in the North Edward Everett—a fine representative of the Boston intelligentsia, former minister to Great Britain, and one of the best-known orators of the day —was nominated for the Vice-Presidency. The Constitutional Unionists avoided all divisive issues and adopted the shortest possible platform. A few years earlier a new party that gathered up so much talent and goodwill might have made a decided impression, but when the waters were dividing in furious torrents, its impact was likely to be limited.

The contest of 1860 was not in any true sense a national election.[2] In most northern and midwestern states the votes were virtually confined to a choice between Lincoln and Douglas; in most slave states to Breckinridge or Bell. Only on the Pacific Coast and in Missouri and New Jersey was it truly a four-party struggle. In the nonslave states the Republican victory was overwhelming. Lincoln carried every county in New England despite the fact that one of the most distinguished sons of Massachusetts was the vice-presidential candidate of the Constitutional Union party. Lincoln also carried most counties in New York and Pennsylvania. In the east-north-central region he won 252 counties to 136, with an absolute majority in every state. In the west-north-central region Douglas got a plurality—125,471 to 109,496—but Lincoln carried more counties and won every state except Missouri. The Douglas vote was largely concentrated in Missouri, southern Illinois, southern Indiana, and traditionally Democratic areas of Ohio. In the mid-Atlantic region Lincoln carried 109 out of 147 counties, even though the opposition was most commonly a fusion between rival parties. In Pennsylvania, so long dominated by President Buchanan, the Republican triumph was extraordinary, with "a nearly complete obliteration of those areas which had been counted strongholds of the party of Jackson." [3] Lincoln had therefore won by an electoral landslide in the free states and would still have won even against a united opposition.

Though Douglas was on the ballot in several southern

[2] The information in this and the following two paragraphs is drawn from W. Dean Burnham, *Presidential Ballots, 1836–1892* (Baltimore: Johns Hopkins Press, 1955) , pp. 71–87.

[3] *Ibid.*, p. 79.

states, he made a poor showing; he won 43 counties in Missouri (where he won over Bell by 140 votes) but only 52 in all the other slave states. Bell did well in the upper South but won no county outside the slave states. In the south Atlantic states (from Delaware to Georgia) Breckinridge had 19,552 more than Bell, but the Republicans and Douglas Democrats had 45,714. In the lower South Breckinridge had an absolute majority, though a plurality in Louisiana.

Capturing a majority of states, including the largest and the main concentrations of population, Lincoln was an easy winner in the electoral college; Douglas, who had been second to Lincoln in every state carried by the Republicans, had a paltry twelve electoral votes; Breckinridge, with little more than half the Douglas popular vote, was second in the electoral vote; and Bell, with only a third of the Douglas vote, won a good third of the electoral vote. Lincoln was a minority President, but wherever he had won, he had been a clear winner; in the New England, mid-Atlantic, east-north-central, and west-north-central regions the Republicans had absolute majorities in all but 37 counties. But of all the 1,109 counties in slave states, he had carried only 2.

Another way of expressing this freak result was that in the free states there had been a straight fight between Republicans and National Democrats, with local interventions by the other two parties. In the slave states it had been a fight between the states' rights Democrats and the Constitutional Unionists, with the National Democrats occasionally mustering enough local strength to make it a three-cornered contest. Echoes of the old battles between Whigs and Democrats had clouded the issue, and many who voted for Breckinridge in the upper South were Jacksonian Democrats strongly opposed to secession and planter domination. Thus, though strongly sectional, the vote in the South was not a mandate for secession, while in the North the large majority in all parties was for leaving slavery undisturbed where it existed by a state law.

If men had been content to wait upon events, the election would have settled very little. The Republicans would control the national administration but not Congress, and their total lack of support in the South would severely limit their effectiveness. The extension of slavery into the territories would almost certainly be stopped by some means or other, but the threat of secession would make further legislation against slavery very unlikely. No national administration could govern the country without federal-office holders, and southerners could easily exact a price for cooperation. Ironically, therefore, the sectional divide and the lack of southern support for the new President could have actually increased the bargaining power of the slave states. This case was argued by some southern Unionists, but they were at a disadvantage in controversy with the secessionists, who could point to established fact rather than hypothesis. For them the election had demonstrated that the Union was divided, that there no longer existed the basis of consent upon which a national political system must rest, and that the northern vote had demonstrated hostility to the institution upon which southern civilization rested. For months they had argued that the election of Lincoln must be the signal for southern secession, and the magnitude of his victory in the free states played into their hands.

Secession was the southern version of romantic revolution. The rhetoric was intoxicating, and its attraction was increased by the refusal to recognize ugly or material facts. Enthusiasm could not fail to produce a glorious future, and the goodwill of foreign nations would be won as much by sympathy for people struggling to be free as by the power of King Cotton. On some points the fire-eaters had to reassure the cautious or conservative. Secession was and always had been a constitutional right; if one southern state took the first step, others would follow, a separate Confederacy could be formed, and the North would never be able or willing to use force. By these arguments the cooperationists and conditional Unionists were disarmed, and though it is doubtful whether there was ever a majority for immediate secession except in South Carolina and perhaps in Florida, men who wished to apply the brakes were hopelessly outmaneuvered. South Carolina led the way; Alabama, Mississippi, Louisiana, and Florida followed. So did Georgia after a slightly stiffer resistance by Unionists, and so did Texas after Sam Houston's unshakable Unionism had been bypassed. By the end of February, 1861, the Confederacy had been formed, and Jefferson Davis, of Mississippi, was President of what claimed to be a new and independent nation.

When assessing the northern response, it is important to remember that secession in the lower South was rapid but not instantaneous. President Buchanan, the President-elect, and all political leaders in the North had to make decisions in a developing situation with an uncertain outcome. When Congress met in December, 1860, South Carolina was still a state in the Union; in January there was still hope that immediate secession would fail when put to popular vote, and there were important divisions among public men in Georgia that might have defeated or at least delayed the secession of that important state. When the southern convention met, it was still not certain that plans for a confederation would be agreed or that proposals for reconciliation or voluntary reconstruction would be rejected. Northerners could not fail to be aware of the large Constitutional Union vote in the South, of the personal unpopularity of many leading secessionists, or of the propensity of southern leaders to prefer abstraction to action. Nor was it unreasonable to hope that Jacksonian nationalism would reassert itself among the plain people. The Confederacy was not formed until less than two weeks before Lincoln's inauguration and included only seven of the fifteen slave states. At every stage men who upheld the Union had therefore to face a classic political dilemma: Would firm action do more to encourage potential friends or stiffen the will and increase the following of known enemies?

Given this situation, it is difficult to maintain that the unfortunate Buchanan took any steps that were wrong, but he did nothing that inspired confidence. He succeeded in averting the use of force but at the cost of losing whatever reputation for leadership he retained. Not only the public at large but also men who observed him at close quarters saw little more than a bewildered, indecisive, and self-pitying old man. His first hope was to maintain official contacts with the seceding states, and to this end he retained secessionist sympathizers in his Cabinet until their attitudes became publicly incompatible with loyalty to the Union. His second aim was to avoid the confrontation that would have made armed conflict inevitable and turned waverers into firm advocates of southern independence. In common with many others in the North he looked with incredulity upon the triumph of the secessionists and refused to believe that a resurgence of Unionism would not occur as soon as the folly of destroying the United States became clear. His third aim, linked with the first two, was to prevent the secession of the upper South, and in this he was joined by a wide variety of politicians from all parties. He maintained that no state had a legal right to secede but that the Union had no right to coerce a seceding state, and hoped that this formula would keep open the road to voluntary reconstruction. Secession must die from its own weakness, overcome by the revival of dormant loyalties.

Buchanan has been severely condemned—not least by Allan Nevins, the foremost historian of the Civil War—for failing to summon a national convention, but it is difficult to imagine what such a meeting could have accomplished. It is possible but improbable that a prolonged exercise in rhetoric would have discovered some consensus. In 1787 there had been no national assembly capable of enacting laws that would be binding upon all and no way of propos-

ing amendments; in 1861 there was a Congress in being,
and a new one freshly elected in full knowledge of the issues at stake. A convention would have been chosen by the
same voters, probably organized in the same constituencies, and open to the same influences. It is possible that
the consummation of secession would have brought a
swing toward Douglas or Constitutional Union in the
North, but it might equally well have produced an even
stronger Republican body. It is possible that in the South
an appeal for a national convention would have stimulated Unionist efforts, but it might well have called forth a
decided commitment to southern independence. These are
hypotheses that cannot be tested, but it is necessary to
question the existence of some reserves of calm and superior wisdom that could have been revealed by a national
convention. There was no such magic waiting for a call
from the master, and there is no reason to suppose that the
men who sat in Congress were collectively less wise, less experienced, or less aware of the true gravity of the situation
than others who had failed to win election or refused to
participate in public life.

In Congress the senators and representatives of the states
where secession was expected spoke from the outset as
members of a separate nation. They might conceivably
accept terms for a new alliance, but they would not themselves make any offers. As the states seceded—and particularly after the formation of the Confederacy—the tone of
the few who remained hardened. Some made farewell
speeches when their states seceded, declaring that the
Union was not only broken but also irreparable. Never, at
any time, did any of them offer to consider terms that had
the slightest hope of acceptance in the North. The Republicans, on the other hand, kept the tone of debate in as low
a key as possible. They persisted in treating Lincoln's election as a normal political event and suggested that it was
inopportune to debate the actions of an administration
that had not yet taken office. If that administration acted
as its enemies predicted, there would be time enough for

opposition; if it acted with restraint, difficulties could be resolved by normal political process; but no leader could concede before taking office an essential part of the program he had been elected to implement.

As soon as Congress met in December men from the lower South moved to defend secession. On December 10 Jefferson Davis, his state not yet out of the Union, proclaimed his love of the Union but defended the secessionists:

It is because of their conviction that hostility and not fraternity now exists in the hearts of the people, that they are looking to their reserved rights, and to their independent powers for their own protection. . . . [The United States had] the best government which has ever been instituted by man, but an association of fraternal states could not exist when their relationship became poisoned. It is only by laying bare the disease that we are to find a remedy. It is an ulcer. Cautery, not plasters, must be applied to it.[4]

Senator Alfred Iveson, of Georgia, used no circumlocutions when he said:

We know what is coming in this Union. It is universal emancipation, and the turning loose upon society in the Southern States of the mass of corruption which will be made by emancipation. These border States can get along without slavery. Their soil and climate are appropriate to white labor; they can live and flourish without African slavery; but the cotton States cannot. . . . African slavery is essential not only to our prosperity but to our existence as a people.[5]

At the outset the argument was principally between the lower South, the Constitutional Unionists of the upper South, and a few northern Democrats. The Republicans maintained a prudent silence that exasperated those who hoped for some compromise. Their hope was to avoid commitment until their President was inaugurated. Lin-

---

[4] *Congressional Globe*, 36th Cong., 2d sess., December 10, 1860, pp. 29 and 30.

[5] *Ibid.*, p. 49.

coln made no speeches but privately urged his followers to make no concession on the extension of slavery and early in December told his closest associate in the party, Senator Lyman Trumbull, that "if there be, all our labor is lost, and ere long, must be done again. . . . The tug has to come, and better now than at any time hereafter." [6]

This position has been much criticized. It meant death to the compromise solution proposed by J. J. Crittenden, of Kentucky, who hoped, in this crisis, to take up the role of his mentor, Henry Clay. The heart of his proposal was the restoration of the Missouri Compromise line in the territories, with slavery prohibited north of it and protected to the south. A solution that promised to protect slavery in New Mexico, where it had just been recognized by the territorial legislature but where it had little prospect of flourishing, seemed innocuous enough, but the proposal was framed to recognize and protect slavery in any subsequent acquisitions south of the line. In Republican eyes this meant a commitment to conquest and annexation, with slavery following the flag, in Central America and the Caribbean. Democratic administrations had already shown an unhealthy interest in this kind of expansion, and the next election in a restored Union might well return power to a reunited Democratic party, with the R publicans bound by their own votes to support the extension of slavery by conquest. Appealing to acquisitive instincts in all parts of the nation, slavery would ride the crest of the expansionist wave as it had done before 1850. As Representative Mason W. Tappan put it:

If we compromise today, we will be required to yield more tomorrow, and when the North is sufficiently humiliated, there will

---

[6] December 10, 1860. Quoted in Roy P. Basler (ed.), *The Collected Works of Abraham Lincoln*, Vol. IV (New Brunswick, N.J.: Rutgers University Press, 1953), pp. 149–150. Three days later Lincoln wrote to another Illinois friend, Elihu B. Washburne, in the same vein (*ibid.*, p. 151).

be no difficulty . . . in "reconstructing" the Government so as to place it in the hands of the slave power forever.[7]

Even if the language was exaggerated, it contained an important truth. If the lower South could not tolerate continuance in the Union under a President who condemned slavery, the northern majority could not contemplate a national commitment to slavery. Over a generation the slave power had been presented as the enemy of progress in every aspect, and Republicans were conscious of a historic mission. Freedom was defeated in France and Germany; it appeared to flounder in Italy and made no progress in England. The Republicans came fresh from a surprising victory, and it was unlikely that they would voluntarily abandon the principle that gave strength to their party, cohesion to their diverse elements, and international significance to their cause.

Was it wise to adhere to this position? To this there can be no certain answer. History is littered with the sad wrecks of political movements that have failed to adhere to their promises or to honor their obligations. In 1861 everyone remembered how 1850 had been followed by 1854, and then by Lecompton and Dred Scott; nor was there the slightest indication that the Crittenden formula would be accepted by the lower South. In the last days of Congress Senator Louis T. Wigfall, of Texas, who remained at Washington pending instructions from his state to withdraw, scornfully rejected the compromises that had been offered:

The Wilmot proviso north of 36° 30′ . . . a lawsuit south of it . . . [and giving] the Federal Government the right to declare a free Negro a citizen. . . . Those propositions would do enough of themselves to dissolve the Union, if nothing else were offered.[8]

He believed that nothing less than an amendment declar-

7 *Congressional Globe*, 36th Cong., 2d sess., February 5, 1861, p. 759.
8 *Ibid.*, March 2, 1861, p. 1373.

ing the rights of states to secede would persuade the seceders even to consider compromise.

You must admit that the masters are free; that they have a right to live under such a Government as they see fit; that they can peaceably, quietly, constitutionally change their Government if they see fit. When you do that, then they will entertain the proposition as to whether the form of government you offer them is satisfactory or not.[9]

A formal recognition of the right to secede was, however, something never seriously discussed, though it could have been a better recipe for reconstruction than tinkering with slavery in the territories. As Calhoun had argued, the principle of the concurrent majority (however recognized or institutionalized) would give minorities precisely the safeguards that would reconcile them to majority rule, because it would ensure that majorities would never go beyond the limits set by minority consent. Yet even Buchanan denied the right to secede, Douglas passionately defended the integrity of the Union, and old Clay Whigs could not entertain the proposition. The true barrier to reconstruction was not, therefore, Republican intransigence upon a single point, but a nationalism that repudiated even a theoretical possibility of dismantling the Union. If secession was a southern version of romantic nationalism, devotion to the Union was inspired from the same deep springs of nineteenth-century faith, and the two were completely and hopelessly incompatible with each other.

Secessionists in the lower South were confident of the future; Republicans were sure that secession would collapse if they held firm and avoided provocation. In the upper South the true agony was experienced by those who realized the folly of secession but knew its strength on their own doorstep and accepted the rationality of its theoretical justification. Throughout the upper South some leaders were deeply loyal to the Union (as befitted the heirs of

[9] *Ibid.*

Washington, Madison, Jefferson, and Jackson) but were also conscious of the ties that joined the southern upper class in a common cause. Strong Unionists were therefore rare among the large slave-owners. The principal opposition to secession came from the inland and mountain counties where there were few slaves and few men of wealth. Western Virginia, western Maryland, western North Carolina, and eastern Tennessee were strongly Unionist; so were the small farmers of Missouri who had once given their support to Thomas Hart Benton, and so, of course, were many in Kentucky, the former stronghold of Henry Clay.

The wisest Republican heads in Congress turned their attention to the urgent need to keep these border states in the Union. They professed themselves ready to guarantee slavery where it existed by state law. Subject to a few safeguards for personal rights, they promised to execute the Fugitive Slave Law. They refrained from advocating coercive action against the seceding states. In a surprise move Henry Winter Davis, of Maryland, supported by Seward and Charles Francis Adams, of Massachusetts, proposed the admission of New Mexico as a slave state. This was a shrewd move, for though New Mexico had legalized slavery in conformity with the Dred Scott decision, the majority would probably abolish it as soon as they acquired statehood. The proposal therefore forced the extreme pro-slavery men to reject the principle of popular sovereignty, even when it produced a decision in favor of slavery.

The conciliatory tone of the Republicans on every point except the extension of slavery may have done something to strengthen the Unionist position in the upper South and was reinforced by a complex series of negotiations and tacit understandings between Seward and unofficial Virginia delegates. The crux of the position was an assurance that force would not be used against the seceding states provided that the seceders refrained from hostile action. Unionists in the South could also deny the need to counter in advance the effects of Lincoln's victory. The Republicans would not have an absolute majority in either House as long as enough southern Democrats remained to join with northern Democrats and Constitutional Unionists. Even an alliance of northern Republicans and Democrats would fall short of a two-thirds majority. The incoming administration would be inexperienced and ineffective. The next elections would almost certainly see a swing against the Republicans. Some even argued, with prescience, that maintenance of the Union was the best safeguard for slavery, for as long as there were slave states in the Union, a frontal attack upon the institution was unlikely. These theoretical and hypothetical arguments were reinforced by the the close economic ties of the upper South with the North and Midwest. These things combined to give the Unionists victories over the secessionists during the spring of 1861, and when Lincoln was inaugurated, eight slave states were still in the Union. Buchanan could claim that he had achieved this by resisting all demands for hasty action against secession. The Republicans could claim that this result had been obtained without yielding to compromise. The southern Unionists were convinced that they had won a notable victory with little help from anyone and least of all from the Republicans.

The Unionist success in Virginia had been secured partly by a promise to initiate a movement to call a national peace conference. It met in Washington on February 4, with former President John Tyler in the chair. The majority of the members belonged to an elderly and passing generation; only twenty-one states were represented, with the seceding states, Arkansas, Wisconsin, Minnesota, the Pacific states, and (at first) Michigan absent. After a good deal of somewhat spiritless discussion the conference presented resolutions similar to the Crittenden compromise; these proposals, coming at a stage when their principles had already been dismissed, made little impression, and both houses of Congress refused even to discuss them.

The principal effect of this gathering of well-intentioned old gentlemen was to encourage upper South secessionists after their earlier setbacks. The arguments with which men had played for so long—the Missouri Compromise line, popular sovereignty, slavery prohibited or protected, slavery in the District of Columbia—no longer had any vitality; minds were exhausted, and there was a yearning for action whatever the consequences.

One class of men in the North had been assiduous in their support of compromise. The banking and commercial interests of the northern cities had extensive investments in the South, and a good deal of their prosperity depended upon their role as middlemen in the cotton trade and as suppliers of imported goods to the South. Just before Lincoln's inauguration a western senator complained that

the influence which surrounds this metropolis, which pervades this Chamber, and which clusters around the Representatives of the people at the other end of the Capitol, is strongly in favor of any surrender, no matter how humiliating; no matter how degrading; no matter how violative of the principle of liberty and justice such surrender may be, provided that the moneyed interests of the commercial and trading districts of the country can be upheld and sustained.[10]

He urged those who were disposed to yield to this influence "to go home to the pure atmosphere of the country to meet the frowns of a betrayed and outraged constituency, who are too pure to be bought, too shrewd to be betrayed, and too brave to be frightened into a degrading and base surrender of their principles." In this way Republicans fortified themselves in the knowledge that they represented the simplest and the best in American life; their people were farmers, small-business men, plain artisans, country lawyers, pious ministers, and the educated elite. For good or ill it was a far more powerful combination than any that

10 Morton S. Wilkinson, of Minnesota, *ibid.*, p. 1369.

could have originated from the mere calculation of economic gain. Whatever the Republicans may have owed to the economic character of the society from which they sprang, their thrust came from the moral climate of churches, colleges, small towns, small entrepreneurs, and skilled labor. Of this ethos the incoming President was truly a part.

With the possible exception of Zachary Taylor, Lincoln had less experience of public affairs than any other President of the nineteenth century. No member of his Cabinet had held high national office, and the great majority of Republican leaders were new men who had come to the front since 1850 and most of them since 1856. An untried President, an inexperienced Cabinet, and a party distinguished by enthusiasm rather than maturity faced the most severe crisis that could have been imposed upon any nation. The separation of the lower South was complete, and the choice lay between recognition of secession, nonrecognition but no coercion, and the use of force to restore the authority of the Union. The upper South was in the Union but suspicious of Republican intentions, likely to be swayed by events, and convinced that secession was legal though inexpedient. In the North there was bewilderment and a good deal of false hope; few could understand the depth of southern feeling, most attributed secession to a conspiracy, and many expected Unionism to revive. In addition, the divisions within the section were deep and seemed to be abiding; Republicans and Democrats not only belonged to different parties but were different kinds of people divided by temperament, tradition, and social aims. Even within the Republican party there were important though largely unexplored areas of disagreement.

Lincoln had given much thought to his Cabinet, and the result was surprisingly successful. With the exception of Simon Cameron at the War Department, all were to prove effective. Cameron resigned before the end of 1861 and

Salmon P. Chase in the summer of 1864; apart from these two changes, Lincoln kept the same team throughout the war. This was in marked contrast to the experience of Jefferson Davis and is matched by that of few other Presidents. The key positions went to Seward as Secretary of State, Salmon P. Chase at the Treasury, Simon Cameron at the War Department, and a former Democrat, Gideon Welles, in charge of the Navy Department. Edward Bates, of Missouri, became Attorney General; Montgomery Blair (of a family that had given devoted support to Andrew Jackson and Martin Van Buren) became Postmaster General; and Caleb Smith, of Indiana, a former Whig, became Secretary of the Interior. At first it looked as though Seward might be a weak link; he had been bitterly disappointed by losing the nomination, was exhausted by three months' labor in Congress, and hoped (against all precedent) that the Secretary of State would be recognized as a kind of prime minister. The result was an extraordinary memorandum in which he offered to assume the responsibilities of government and proposed aggression against Britain, France, Spain, or all three as a means of reuniting Americans. Lincoln's reply was tactful but firm, and in course of time Seward became a loyal supporter and an effective Secretary of State. In the early days of the war he also acted as a minister for internal security and organized an efficient operation of questionable legality by which large numbers of Confederate sympathizers found themselves unexpectedly in prison.

Lincoln's inaugural address promised adherence to principle and restraint in action. There was no reasonable cause for the apprehension among the people of the South "that by the accession of a Republican Administration, their property, and their peace, and personal security, are to be endangered," for under his government there would be no breach of rights guaranteed by the Constitution. But "in the contemplation of universal law, and of the Constitution, the Union of these states is perpetual," and in a

Union that could not be lawfully disrupted, it was the duty of the President "to take care that the laws of Union be faithfully executed in all the States." Then in a carefully phrased sentence he added:

In doing this there needs to be no bloodshed or violence, and there shall be none, unless forced upon the national authority. The power confided to me will be used to hold, occupy and possess the property and places belonging to the government, and to collect the duties and imposts; but beyond what may be necessary for these objects, there will be no invasion—no using of force against, or among the people anywhere.

Southerners, with justice, viewed this sentence with suspicion. How could the property of the United States be held and the duties collected within the boundaries of what now claimed to be an independent state? Lincoln might promise forbearance, but could his declared aim avoid a collision? Their alarm would have been even greater if he had retained, from his first draft of the inaugural, a promise to *reclaim* property that had been seized. This could only have meant invasion.

Moving to a theoretical argument, Lincoln said that a majority, restrained by constitutional checks, was "the only true sovereign of a free people"; and if rejected, the alternatives were anarchy or despotism. This was language applicable to a single political system, but by April, 1861, there existed two, and a secessionist might argue that the alternative was falsely stated; it did not lie between anarchy and despotism, but between recognition of a political fact and the use of force to reverse events. To argue that the Union was perpetual when it had patently ceased to be so, and to talk of sovereignty when the basis of consent no longer existed, provided no solution in a dispute between rival governments.

Lincoln was on stronger ground when he argued that "physically speaking we cannot separate." The two sections must have relations with each other, and "intercourse, either amicable or hostile, must continue between them." In this passage Lincoln hoped to remind southerners of the complex network of economic relations between North and South, which could not be severed without great damage to both. An independent Confederacy might attempt to foster its own industry, open direct trade with Europe, or establish its own banking system, but it could do so only by sacrificing the advantages of association with the dynamic northern economy and by adopting the politics of regulation, restriction, and protection that had long been anathema to southern free traders. Nor would separation settle long-standing controversies over the territories, fugitive slaves, and antislavery agitation. The arguments and their implications were both rational and unreal; they were addressed to men who had not yet decided for independence but heard by men who already claimed a place among the independent nations of the world.

The inherent contradictions between the vocabulary of a unified political system and negotiation between separate governments were exposed by the insoluble problem of Fort Sumter, garrisoned by Federal troops but commanding the entrance to Charleston harbor. The Confederates could hardly convince foreign nations of their independent existence while the Union flag flew at the entrance to one of their two principal ports. They were ready to arrange a peaceful evacuation, but the Union Government could not negotiate without de facto recognition of southern independence. Lincoln could communicate with the governor of the state of South Carolina on the assumption that secession was void; he could not negotiate with Jefferson Davis, who alone had authority to decide the issue. The problem was complex because northern attention had been focused on Sumter since December and had come to regard its surrender as a virtual recognition of disunion; but the garrison on Sumter was too small to withstand an attack and (with supplies from the mainland cut off) would soon run out of provisions. It could be reached by sea, but an attempt at reinforcement would be a certain signal for southern attack; only overwhelming military strength could therefore succeed, and this the Union did not possess. Secrecy was impossible, for every movement in northern ports was reported in the press, and a Federal relief expedition might expect to encounter well-prepared resistance. Lincoln hoped at first to postpone decision by ordering Major Robert Anderson, in command at Sumter, to hold on but to make no provocative move, but before his first month of office was out, he knew that shortage of food would compel Anderson to surrender early in May.

On April 6 Lincoln sent a personal message to the governor of South Carolina saying that he intended to send provisions but no reinforcements to Sumter. But if provisions came in once, they could come in again, and the Confederacy would face for an indefinite period the prospect of Federal presence in their territorial waters. On April 12 Jefferson Davis took the fateful decision to forestall the Union move by demanding the surrender of Sumter, and when Anderson refused, to capture it by force. With a tiny force on Sumter, commanded by the shore batteries, and with no prospect of reinforcement, Anderson had no alternative but honorable surrender after a few hours' bombardment. No Federal troops were killed, but the flag had been under fire as the result of orders deliberately issued and enthusiastically executed. Everywhere in the North the action was seen as the fulfillment of Daniel Webster's prophecy: There could be no such thing as peaceable secession. On April 15 Lincoln issued a proclamation declaring that the law was being resisted "by combinations too powerful to be suppressed by the ordinary course of judicial proceedings" and called upon the states to furnish, from their militias, 75,000 men "to suppress said combinations and cause the laws to be duly executed." Thus, with words reminiscent of a county sheriff summoning a posse to deal with outlaws, the war for the Union began.

Lincoln's political strategy in this crisis has been scrutinized by each generation of Civil War historians, but all conclusions must rest upon surmise. Lincoln did not commit his reasons to paper, nor is there any record of consultations with others. We know that most members of his Cabinet were doubtful, if not opposed, and that Seward and others had labored for months to avoid the situation in which only the stark alternatives of force or recognition of secession remained. It has been maintained that Lincoln worked with skill to create a situation in which the Confederacy had to commit the first act of violence; alternatively, he has been pictured as a harassed and bewildered President blundering into a position that could have been avoided. The most convincing explanation is derived from a study of Lincoln's own public utterances, to which he constantly referred questioners in the months before inauguration. He believed the nation could not continue permanently half slave and half free; therefore it was necessary, at some time, to decide which it was to be. The moment of decision would be a moment of crisis and could not be evaded by postponement. The division into two hostile societies solved nothing and would leave to posterity a legacy of conflict. Within the Union one principle or the other must prevail, and ultimately the choice must be that of the majority. If these ideas were sacrificed, the great experiment had failed, and it was the duty of Americans to see that it did not fail. The preservation or restoration of the Union was therefore a political and moral necessity. It would be best if those who tried separation abandoned the attempt voluntarily, and as long as they refrained from hostile acts, they might be allowed time to decide this for themselves; but the possibility of conflict could not be ignored. Like any wise statesman whose country may be involved in war, Lincoln took steps to see that the immediate cause would unite the people who would have to fight, and nothing would do this more effectively than a deliberate act of violence against the United States. In his inaugural Lincoln said that armed conflict need not come unless the South chose it; his Sumter policy ensured that the South could not make secession permanent without demonstrating that peaceable secession was impossible.

Thus far the logic of Lincoln's policy can be followed, but political actions can seldom follow a direct and rational sequence. The moves can be made, but the information on which they are based is not likely to be complete or accurate, and misunderstanding was all the more probable when two societies had ceased to communicate with each other through most of the usual channels of information and argument. There seems little doubt that Lincoln, in common with a majority of other Republicans, believed that secession did not represent the "real will" of the southern people. The language of conspiracy had become so much a part of American political discourse that men had come to accept its suppositions as true. Moreover, the events in the lower South, from the disruption of the Democratic party to evasion of a direct popular vote on secession, gave support to the belief that the secessionists were a minority who would be repudiated once the true men of the South realized the consequence of their action. A demonstration of force would be enough to set voluntary reconstruction in motion; hence Lincoln's hope that 75,000 men mustered for three months would serve his purpose. In the event the threat of force killed Unionism in the lower South and gave secessionists the edge in the upper South, while the inadequate force enlisted encouraged the Confederacy to expect an early victory.

There are other approaches to the problem of war in 1861. It was Lincoln's misfortune to stand at the parting of the ways traveled by nineteenth-century liberalism; one road led to self-determination, local autonomy, and limited government, and the other to sovereign majorities, great states, and the concentration of power. Some of the quality of the great experiment could be preserved only by following the first, but many of its objectives demanded the second. The rights of states and of individuals had to include the right to be wrong, but the promotion of the general welfare meant that sooner or later the majority must demand the means to suppress error. If slavery could be forgotten, the South had an excellent case. The basis of agreement upon fundamentals had ceased to exist, and the Declaration of Independence had asserted that when a government ceased to enjoy the consent of the governed, "it is the right of the People to alter or abolish it, and to institute new Government . . . to effect their Safety and Happiness." The hope of a perpetual Union in 1776 or 1787 was irrelevant in 1861; so were Jackson's action in 1832, Webster's speech in 1830, and southern rejection of secession in 1850. There was a sound lawyers' argument that secession could not have the force of law, but there were equally sound political reasons for saying that the law must now be changed.

Nor was it convincing to argue that a state could secede only with the consent of all the other states. Even less convincing and more metaphysical was the argument that every individual in the Union had entered into a contract with all the other individuals and that states could not therefore take their citizens out of the Union. These arguments may have some appeal in small societies—where the interests, classes, and ethnic groups are so intermingled that separation is impossible—but cannot apply when the political societies that wished to separate were geographically distinct and internally cohesive. Nor was it realistic to argue that secession was anarchy. Indeed, government in the seceding states was vigorously effective, and the supposed dangers to life, liberty, and property could rest only upon hypotheses about what might happen in other parts of the Union. Southern statesmen had often been accused of neglecting reality and arguing about abstractions; in 1861 it was the case for preserving the Union that rested upon supposition and refused to face the facts.

The immediate and practical consequences of Lincoln's decision were dramatic. On April 17 the Virginia convention, remaining in session since the earlier Unionist victory, voted by a substantial majority for secession, and on the twenty-fourth the Old Dominion entered into formal alliance with the Confederacy. North Carolina, Tennessee, and Arkansas quickly followed. In this second wave of secession several factors were of enormous significance. The decision in these states was clearly based on the constitutional issue and not upon the need to protect slavery, so their adherence to the Confederacy raised the southern cause to a higher plane of argument. The statesmanship of Virginia was a poor echo of its golden age but still commanded respect and an enormous weight of venerable tradition. Tennessee was the home state of Jackson and epitomized the spirit of fierce democratic nationalism that had carried the flag across the continent. It is true that many old Jacksonians remained strong Union men, and at their head stood the redoubtable Senator Andrew Johnson; but Tennessee left the Union nevertheless, and two months after Sumter this was confirmed by a vote of more than two to one for secession. The state would remain bitterly divided—for in the eastern half only two counties were carried by the secessionists—but its government was firmly with the Confederacy.

In material and military terms the secession of the upper South had momentous consequences. Alone, the states of the lower South were economically weak, thinly populated, and vulnerable in every way. The four states of the upper South added not only people but also manufactures, mineral deposits, and useful railroad links. The frontiers of the Confederacy were carried to the Potomac; Tennessee held the mountain and river gateways to the lower South; and Arkansas could prevent Federal advance down the west bank of the Mississippi. Thus the decision for war came in a way that united the North but ensured that the South would be able to sustain a long struggle.

Further Union disasters were narrowly averted. In Maryland secessionist sympathies were strong, particularly on the eastern shore and in Baltimore, and accident rather than design turned the trick for the Unionists and avoided a situation in which the Federal capital would have become an enclave in Confederate territory. To this day, in Baltimore, the Civil War monuments to the Union and to the Confederate dead stand within a few yards of each other. Kentucky, occupying a vital strategic position in the Midwest, wavered, tried neutrality, and then came down on the Union side while thousands of volunteers joined the Confederate armies. Missouri remained nominally a Union state but was long disturbed by a savage local conflict that earned little credit for the humanity of either side.

In 1868 Alexander Stephens, who had opposed secession but accepted the will of the majority and spent four unhappy years as Vice-President of the Confederacy, reflected upon the true nature of the Union in sentences that could have been derived from Edmund Burke and reflected the views of constitutional secessionists:

The chief strength of the system, in its proper administration, lay . . . in that moral power which brought the several members into Confederation [in 1776]. It lay in the hearts of the people of the several States, and in no right or power of keeping them together by coercion. The right of any member to withdraw . . . was . . . one of the greatest elements of strength, looking in its practical workings to the attainment of the objects for which the Union was formed. This right is not only the basis upon which all Confederated Republics must necessarily be formed, but without it there is, and can be, in such systems, no check, no real barrier, nothing indeed, that can be successfully relied upon to prevent their running, sooner or later, into centralized despotic Empire.[11]

[11] *A Constitutional View of the Late War between the States,* Vol. I (Philadelphia: 1868), p. 532.

Recognition of the *right* to secede would have made its exercise unnecessary. Even (according to Stephens) voluntary reconstruction would have been possible on this basis, for "had this foundation principle of the system been generally acknowledged—had no military force been called out to prevent the exercise of the right of withdrawal," there would have been no war and a speedy restoration of harmony.

The theoretical strength of the argument for secession does not mean that independence would be wisely used, and the attraction of the case against centralized power should not conceal the avowed purpose of secession. In the eyes of many humane and pacific men the lower South was seceding not only from the Union but from nineteenth-century civilization. Whether secession was or was not the work of a minority, it seemed that the leaders were carrying millions of white and black people into an obscurantist world where education, enterprise, science, and humanitarian impulses were not allowed to exist. This persuaded northern intellectuals that what was at stake was the right to be civilized. They could not see the struggle for southern independence in the same light as the uprising of Italians, Hungarians, or Poles against foreign rulers; it was rather the rebellion of a reactionary minority against the best and freest government ever offered to mankind. This northern view was crystallized before Sumter and before the secession of Virginia brought constitutional issues to the fore; for until April, 1861, there was plenty of evidence (drawn from southern speeches) that the defense of slavery was the exclusive purpose of secession. Jefferson Davis would try to make northern aggression and southern independence the major issue and had some hope that he might win support among northern defenders of states' rights and even acquiescence from abolitionists welcoming divorce from slavery; but if there was ever a hope that the case for peaceable secession might be accepted, it faded between December and March and was irretrievably lost at

Sumter. From that moment every prominent northern leader of both parties, and the leading representatives of every interest and shade of opinion, became committed to the preservation of the Union as a battle for civilization. Even if the leaders had faltered, they would have been pressed forward from behind by the tremendous surge of popular enthusiasm. It was this sentiment that Lincoln gauged so accurately and expressed so eloquently in his first message to Congress, appropriately dated July 4. It was, he said "essentially a people's contest. On the side of the Union it is a struggle . . . to elevate the condition of men—to lift artificial weights from all shoulders . . . to afford all an unfettered start, and a fair chance in the race of life." For men in Congress and throughout the North who studied his words, the message was not seen in the narrow context of antislavery but in the broad perspective of an advancing civilization in which slavery must eventually be abandoned.

The conflict meant different things to different men; its causes can be studied at varying levels and with different questions in mind. Some attempted explanations have concentrated upon the differences between the sections, without which there would have been no war, but do not of themselves explain why war came. Others have concentrated upon the secession movement in the lower South, without which there would have been no war, but several options remained open by which armed conflict might have been avoided. In the next phase Buchanan's policy, Republican attitudes, and the failure of compromise are brought under microscopic examination; at this stage many contemporaries believed that a compromise could have been found (either in the bold move of a national convention or in greater flexibility of political maneuver), and many subsequent historians have agreed. The Sumter crisis comes next under scrutiny; and again minor differences in timing or calculation might have altered events, and if acute tension was by then inevitable, armed conflict might have been avoided. The secession of the upper South has received rather less attention than it deserves. In the light of all that had been said, Lincoln's call to arms made it extraordinarily difficult to resist secessionist arguments in Virginia, but comparatively small changes in emphasis and in the internal balance of power might have allowed the Unionists to hold the day, and the Confederacy would not have acquired the resources for fighting a long war. Finally, the bid to preserve the Union would have failed if the northern response had been weak, confused, and divided. As it was, not only did Republicans close ranks, but Douglas pledged immediate support, thousands of his followers rushed to volunteer, and his campaign manager, August Belmont, was to render important financial services to the Union. Merchants who had hoped for compromise announced their support of the war, and Garrisonian abolitionists—who had for so long proclaimed "No Union with Slaveholders"—announced that Union victory would mean the death of slavery.

In each separate aspect men did not draw the same conclusions from the same facts, so one has to reckon not only with things as they were but also with things as men imagined them to be. This was a matter not merely of miscalculation, but of deep-rooted habits of mind. Considerable emphasis had been placed upon Republican overestimates of Unionist strength in the South, but a more interesting speculation is why a belief that depended upon so little evidence commanded so much support. Again, it is clear that secessionists continually represented the northern people as physically and temperamentally weak, though there was no historical evidence for the proposition that town dwellers could not fight and incontrovertible census figures to show that the vast majority of northern people lived and worked on farms. The origins of this southern myth of Yankee decadence would be interesting to investigate, as would its use in secessionist propaganda. Equally misleading was the northern myth that omitted from its picture of southern society the great mass of the plain people and saw only a conspiracy of slave-owners; but the real problem is to explain how the people of what purported to be one nation knew so little of each other's character.

An investigation of the causes of the Civil War cannot therefore stop with the hard facts of policy, crisis, and decision. It must go on into the shadowy realms of communication, imagery, psychology, and character formation. The attitudes and responses of slaveholders were conditioned by a lifelong experience and traditional exercise of absolute authority. The opinions of the plain white people were molded by the black presence. The whole drama of southern history was played in front of an audience of black men and women whose bodies they could command but whose minds they could not penetrate. The unique experience of the South had led, to an extraordinary degree, to the substitution for reality of romantic fictions in the guise of rational propositions. All white men were equal, though there were enormous inequalities of wealth, education, and opportunity. The southern gentleman was high-principled, humane, and considerate, yet in dealing with slaves his behavior was governed by a different moral code. This dual standard applied to all aspects of southern life, but its deepest psychological effects came from two separate and distinct codes of sexual behavior. Another important aspect of southern life was rural isolation. A great planter lived as lord and master of a community in which his authority was unchallenged, and his meetings with equals were special occasions on which (whether the purpose was politics or pleasure) a formal ritual was observed. The northern politician could meet his constituents every day on Main Street or by traveling around small towns; the southern politicians came in from their plantation kingdoms to transact business at courthouses that were seldom commercial or social centers. With a weak press and few schools the fundamental assumptions of public or private conduct were seldom challenged. The issues were provincial and narrowly defined; even highly educated southerners were not prepared to step beyond these bounds.

Southern life had its charm, and many foreign visitors were genuinely impressed by what they saw. It was in many ways an attractive way of life and one for which a great many were prepared to fight; but it was also one that depended to an increasing extent upon assumptions at variance with experience. The rapid economic and intellectual changes of the nineteenth century had widened the gap between fact and fiction; in order to preserve self-respect, southerners had to live more and more in a world of romantic assertions in which a demand for proof was regarded as intellectual treason. This helps to explain the southern desire for separation and the rhetoric used to justify it. Yet under the obscurantism there remained something of the generous dignity that had made such notable contributions to the early Republic; the states' rights argument had become debased by the obsessions of a biracial society, but the hope that people could choose their own way of life in small communities was still a worthy ideal.

In the North and West the social conditions were more varied and their psychological implications more difficult to diagnose. There were wider economic opportunities, greater social mobility, and more positions that carried esteem. Business, law, politics, churches, and colleges all offered rewards and high status; below the highest there were large numbers of inferior but very respectable positions. There were very few large landowners but a great number of substantial farmers. There were many opportunities for skilled men, and even recent immigrants could find a foothold on the social ladder. It was therefore a society of unlimited expectations, which tended to build its myths around self-help and ignore or despise failure.

At the same time there was a tension, which could become acute, between the material criteria of success and ethical traditions. As far as the leaders were concerned, it

was still predominantly a moral society, and even where
life had become most secularized, it was natural to adopt
the language of religion; material aims were given religious significance, and religious belief offered material welfare as proof of its validity. Religion pointed to a higher
law as the rule of life, whereas conventional opinion
judged society by its success in satisfying material needs;
there was a Christian duty to cry aloud and spare not in
the war against sin, whereas civil duty required obedience
to the law and the Constitution. This was the classic
dilemma of Christendom, but in a democratic society it
had a special emphasis. Reform inspired by faith was not
in conflict with a tyrannical sovereign but with the will of
the people.

This was the dilemma faced by Emerson and the tran-
scendentalists; abandoning conventional religion, they
had sought a mystic union of souls in which all the petty
conceits and rivalries were canceled out and united on a
higher plane where the divinity in all men could unite in
the quest for pure good. With Emerson the crude concept
of "manifest destiny" had been joined with the Puritan
idea of Providence in an affirmation that every race had a
contribution to make toward the advance of civilization,
that this destiny must be understood and pursued, and
that peoples who failed in this betrayed not only themselves but mankind as a whole. It is doubtful whether Lincoln was influenced by Emerson, but there is a striking parallel between the closing passages of the President's first
message to Congress and the last chapter of Emerson's *English Traits*. In both there is a conscious attempt to carry
the argument from a mundane level—with Lincoln the
fact and law of secession, with Emerson the description of
English manners—to link American purpose with destiny
and duty to mankind as a whole. In a separate though similar development the historian George Bancroft, strongly
influenced by Hegelian philosophy, had seen a great moral
force working through history, with the institutions of

American democracy allowing the dialectic to proceed without check to the higher synthesis; but in 1861 the processes of democracy had been rudely interrupted, and conflict suddenly took the place of debate.

It would be idle to suppose that the ordinary American who responded to the call to arms, or the ordinary politicians, faced their decisions with a philosophic armory; but individual thinkers take up and rationalize the common sense of simpler men. One has only to read the way in which newspaper editors, ministers, and politicians explained the meaning of the war for the Union to realize how much they relied upon a common stock of arguments and how much these arguments owed to a religious interpretation of American history. Indeed, once they left the unrewarding task of chopping constitutional logic, almost all their arguments were derived indirectly from the Bible or directly from the Declaration of Independence and led to a fusion of both in a kind of political religion.

Transcendentalism had attempted to bring together a dedication to moral purpose and the hopes of ordinary men to live comfortably. Idealism and economic betterment had not always lived well together, but in the preceding years they had found common ground in the protest against slavery in the territories that was both a national commitment to a moral evil and a denial of the West to free settlers. The shock of secession carried this alliance forward so that it came to embrace not only Republicans who had wished to prohibit the extension of slavery but also Douglas Democrats who had been prepared to give slavery a fair trial by popular sovereignty but would not allow it to reverse the verdict. This discovery of a common cause helps to explain the deep semireligious response to Lincoln's call to arms. It also helps to explain why the outbreak of hostilities, though deplored, was welcome; by substituting action for argument, it helped to resolve the tensions of northern society.

Under these pressures it is doubtful whether the Constitution as it was could provide a permanent solution; yet people knew of no way to appeal beyond constitutional limits. The machinery of the Constitution had proved to be extremely successful in adjusting the differences that were bound to occur in a complex and diffuse society but could not contain the explosive forces of nationalism, romanticism, and transcendental idealism. The Constitution failed, but only a miracle could have made it work under these circumstances. Faced with a calamity of this magnitude, which touched so many sides of human life, judgment is inappropriate. One can say that the reasons for secession were based on misconception, self-deception, and a determination to defend the indefensible; yet one can also believe that when the peaceful separation of two societies was prevented by force, ugly precedents were set. One must understand the idealism that went into the Union cause, yet remember that it was mixed with other forces that have since done much injury. The melancholy verdict must be that the Civil War, like other political catastrophes, was brought on by decent men, acting upon the highest motives and following a logic that seemed inescapable.

[6]
The Challenge of War

In the politics of peace the minority must decide for the mass; but the transition to war introduces a new dimension that is easily overlooked however obvious its consequences. With the call to arms thousands must make individual decisions, and their cumulative effect determines the outcome, and this was particularly true of a society so loosely organized as the United States in 1861. There was no large professional army to take the field; both sides had to depend upon volunteers, and unless the tide of opinion flowed on the side of authority, the means by which individuals could be coerced were few and feeble. The law recognized and tradition sanctified many ways in which states, counties, and cities could interpose between their citizens and the higher powers. All wars depend in the last resort upon the willingness of men to fight, but the structure of American society made consent the first consideration. Even when both sides resorted to conscription, volunteers remained the hard and most effective core of the fighting force. Morale and the will to fight were from start to finish the paramount factors in the Civil War.

In the struggle for men's minds the Confederacy had, at the outset, immense advantages. The southerners fought for independence in an age when heroic forces were enlisted in that cause and in a society where self-government was the traditional foundation of law and right. The secession of Virginia added great moral weight to the cause and convinced waverers that great principles were at stake. Nor must the racial factors underlying many of the high-flown (and sincerely endorsed) theories of self-government be ignored. Not all southerners were convinced that slavery was a positive good, but nearly all feared that emancipation would set loose a black flood on society and looked in vain for any alternative system of race relations. If they did not fight to preserve slavery, they did so to avert "amalgamation." Their racial attitudes were shared by many in the North, and they hoped that a cause so broadly based upon the superiority of the white race would enlist sympathy in the whole civilized world. Few in the South had ever understood the opposition to slavery, and most believed that when the cards were down, the superiority of mild southern slavery to racial conflict required neither demonstration nor defense; and even though they knew that outside the South intelligent and humane men condemned slavery, they expected them to agree that only the people most affected could decide when to end it.

Two or more generations of southern rhetoric had created a picture of "the North" that was harsh, unattractive, and contemptible. Eminent southerners had long foretold a collision in which "the mean arts of snivelling tradesmen" (to use a famous phrase from Adam Smith's *Wealth of Nations*) would be deployed against everything that was disinterested, noble, and generous. Tradition and emotion, reason and prejudice, conviction and the expectation of sympathy from others all combined to endow the Confederacy at the outset with high morale and a strong will to fight. There were Unionists in the South, but they were either isolated or concentrated in remote areas of the Appalachian uplands. In the tidewater regions and in most of the piedmont a great wave of enthusiasm swept doubts aside. Many former Unionists were convinced that they must "go with their states" when the majority endorsed secession; many reluctant secessionists were convinced when the Union turned to coercion. The obdurate or hesitant felt the full weight of popular disapproval, and whatever the previous divisions, the coming of war generated a remarkable solidarity that embraced not only the traditional leaders but also the plain people who would have to fill the ranks in the field.

This solidarity was in part a consequence of the structure of southern society. The "plain people" had not behaved with cringing deference to the ruling planter class. They had developed and maintained their own vigorous culture, which has hardly yet been sufficiently explored or understood. They would listen to persuasion and would not accept dictation; but their view of the world had come through channels controlled by the upper class, and even without this pressure they were unlikely to disagree with the planter gentry upon the social fundamentals. The economic independence of the small white farmer and the exploitation of forced black labor were the bases upon which society rested its philosophy, conventions, and customs which were not open to serious discussion. However, the factors that gave the Confederacy impressive unity at the start also inhibited further development. The secession revolution could not become a social revolution, and bold confidence in southern independence began to fade once it was realized that no one was offered a better life or wider opportunities. The war's later phases would be marked by bitter criticism of Jefferson Davis, querulous obstruction from state governors, and an ever-lengthening roll of deserters; these were symptoms of a malaise in which old ties had been loosened and former isolation broken down, but new social institutions and ideas failed to emerge.

The census of 1860 gave the Confederate states a little under 1,000,000 men from eighteen to forty-five inclusive. The Confederacy relied upon volunteers for the first year of the war and then resorted to conscription in two acts of 1862 and one of February, 1864. A further 265,000 came of military age by 1864, and another 20,000, who had been forty-six in 1860, became liable for military service with the raising of the conscription age in 1864. The total manpower available for military service was therefore a little over 1,250,000, but from this it is necessary to deduct deaths by natural causes and exemptions because of ill-health or deformity. Some Unionists in Virginia, North Carolina, and Tennessee evaded service, joined the Federal army, or lived in areas early occupied by Union forces. This was offset by volunteers from the Union states of Maryland, Kentucky, and Missouri. Complicating factors, the lack of knowledge about irregular units and the confusion of records in the last stages of the war, make it impossible to estimate accurately the number of men who served in the Confederate army, but the total cannot be less than 1,000,000, or at least four-fifths of the available white manpower. This is a remarkable record, unmatched by any other country in any other war. Even though the labor force was, of course, largely black, which makes comparison with other service records misleading, the figures do demonstrate the will to fight that characterized the southern war for independence.

Total figures, however, reveal little about the actual numbers available for front-line service. In July, 1861, the Confederacy had (to the nearest 1,000) 112,000 men enrolled; in April, 1862, 401,000; in January, 1863, 447,000; in January, 1864, 481,000; and in January, 1865, 445,000. The Confederacy was comparatively economical in the number of troops retained for defense of communication and supply lines, but even so, a substantial number were necessarily employed upon the defense of rivers, harbors, and railroads, and some were deliberately kept back by the states for home defense. On top of this, there were the sick and the deserters. The disposition of forces was always a major problem, for although small-scale maps appear to give the South the advantage of interior lines, the distances were great and the communications poor, making it necessary to keep large numbers of troops dispersed over long frontiers. The army of northern Virginia always had the lion's share but never more than a quarter of the enrolled forces until the closing stages of the war, by which time many Confederate forces had been captured or scattered in remote areas. In spite of the high level of manpower enlisted, the Confederate commanders were constantly complaining of inadequate numbers, asking for recruits who failed to materialize, or receiving them too late to replace the losses by casualty, disease, and desertion. There were several occasions when greater willingness to sacrifice territory to facilitate a concentration of force might have yielded results, but in a fight for independence the loss of territory might damage morale and weaken bargaining power if the need for negotiation arose. A soldier's war can best be fought in the enemy's country, where maneuver will not be unduly hindered by such considerations. As it was, the Confederacy lost on both counts: The armies were widely dispersed, but the territory was not saved; for if the South won some notable big battles, it lost a majority of the small ones.

The Confederates began the war confident that they possessed economic assets of major importance. They were the major producers of a raw material upon which the textile industry of Great Britain, and to a lesser extent of France, depended. They believed that a great agricultural region would suffer little from deprivation, and many expected that the artificial barriers of war would breathe life into southern manufactures (so long frustrated by northern competition) and that European suppliers would rush to fill whatever void was revealed in the southern supply. Most of them expected that industrial distress and loss of trade would persuade European governments to intervene, failed to reckon the many aspects of national interest that would weigh with advanced nations before embarking upon the hazards of war, and were oddly oblivious to the hostages to fortune provided by a long coastline and easily blockaded ports. The Union came to the brink of committing a great folly in entangling with Great Britain over maritime disputes but drew back in time; thereafter armed intervention by Great Britain was improbable. The Confederacy had, however, some reason to hope that Great Britain and France would offer mediation and, if this were refused by the Union, recognize southern independence; but neither European power would act until convinced that the Confederacy was de facto independent and likely to remain so. Goodwill was not enough without the assurance of northern military failure, and foreign recognition would come only with decisive southern success or clear indications that the North had no longer the will to fight. The European powers might help a South that had demonstrated its capacity for survival but would risk nothing themselves to bring about this result.

The Confederate belief in economic strength appears naïve in the light of events, but this is unjust to men who, though unsophisticated by some standards, were aware of the facts of commercial life. Of course they expected privations, but their hope for survival was not wholly unfounded. Whatever the difficulties, the southern leaders did keep armies in the field supplied with arms, ordnance, and ammunition. They fell behind in the supply of clothing and boots, but hardened soldiers (most of them accustomed to low living standards) were less perturbed by these deficiencies than their modern descendants. Shortages of food were more serious and made the soldiers more susceptible to disease, but no Confederate army was ever so badly undernourished that it failed to fight. The Confederacy was indeed fortunate in having as its chief of ordnance General J. Gorgas, a man of driving energy and administrative genius. He described the achievements of the South in the following way:

We began in April 1861 without an arsenal, laboratory, or powder mill of any capacity, and with no foundry or rolling mill, except in Richmond, and, before the close of 1863, or within a little over two years, we supplied them. . . . And in that short period created, almost literally out of the ground, foundries and rolling-mills at Selma, Richmond, Atlanta and Macon; smelting-works at Petersburg, chemical works at Charlotte, North Carolina; a powder-mill far superior to any in the United States and unsurpassed by any across the ocean; and a chain of arsenals, armories, and laboratories equal in their capacity and their improved appointments to the best of those in the United States, stretching link by link from Virginia to Alabama.[1]

The record in other fields was far less impressive. On the railroads repairs were improvised but often inadequate, track was not maintained, and rolling stock deteriorated. No new lines were laid in spite of many obvious gaps in the railroad network. It was the misfortune of the Confederacy that several important railroads in northern Virginia and Tennessee were particularly vulnerable to Union attack, but even so, a Gorgas in charge of the entire railroad system might have worked wonders. Such a bold handling of interstate communications was, however, beyond the political grasp and imagination of the Confederacy.

The Confederacy suffered perennial financial troubles, and C. G. Memminger, who was Secretary of the Treasury during the crucial period of the war, had more integrity than insight.[2] There was little precedent to guide the financial operations of a government committed to fight a war without fluid assets or high taxable income, and the experience of Great Britain with the paper pound during the Napoleonic Wars had been obscured by gold-standard orthodoxy. Clearly, with tiny gold reserves, an inconvertible paper currency was essential, and some degree of inflation was inevitable to meet the cost of war. At the bottom of the

[1] Quoted in Jefferson Davis, *The Rise and Fall of the Confederate Government*, Vol. I (1881; new ed., New York, 1958) , p. 481.

[2] It may be significant that Jefferson Davis in *The Rise and Fall of the Confederate Government* mentioned Memminger only once (to record his appointment) and makes no more than incidental reference to inflation.

social scale a third of the population were slaves, and half were small farmers with very little cash in hand, while the wealthy had most of their capital locked up in land and slaves; there was, therefore, comparatively little income to tax. Goods were bound to be in short supply, and prices would rise without any other agency. Memminger, a pious Charleston banker who had made a reputation by advocating hard money and strict accounting, was hardly the man to deal with this situation. Nor was he helped by niggling criticism in the Congress that refused to accept any realistic (and necessarily burdensome) way of meeting the financial crisis. The Confederacy never made proper use of cotton, its major asset, never imposed an equitable or remunerative direct tax, and continued to hope that money could be raised by imposing still further strain upon public credit. The Confederate Constitution had omitted the clause prohibiting states from making anything but gold or silver legal tender, and confusion was increased by their note issues. Nevertheless, the Confederacy did manage to survive with a financial system that defied every canon of financial orthodoxy, and it was military failure, not irredeemable paper currency, that pushed the South into runaway inflation.

These considerations did not prevent money from being made in the South by those who were prepared to take risks. As blockade-running became the principal source of imports, the profits soared. Trading with the enemy, though officially discouraged, was privately condoned. Cotton could be sold across the lines; manufactured goods could be purchased and resold. Planters with unsold crops on their hands were often desperate for any expedient to raise cash, and there were eager buyers in federally controlled territory. Nor was it difficult to dispose of northern food or manufactures when even army commissaries asked no awkward questions about the source of supplies or even of arms. In the first year of the war, before the West was virtually cut off, there was also very substantial trading with the outside world by way of Mexico. In all these transactions it was the middlemen who made the largest profits.

A Confederate official, who saw a good deal of the inside workings of government, made the following notes on the reasons for failure.[3]

1st. A bankrupt treasury. This was the prolific source of other evils: (a) high price of all supplies, and parties unwilling to furnish even for them (b) discontent of people and army for want of payment of dues and worthlessness of it when obtained; hence desertion, impressment (c) decay of railroad transportation due in part to this cause, the roads not having wherewith to keep themselves up. . . . [Bankruptcy was caused by] (a) belief of leaders in a short war (b) inability to deal with a very large subject; first Congress responsible as well as President and Memminger.

2nd. Want of men; exhaustion of supply from which recruits of effective qualities to be drawn; severity of the conscription; desertion due to insufficient supply and worthlessness of money.

He also blamed military incompetence, shortage of horses, factionalism, slavery, and

one cause which in a certain sense may be said to include them all—the absence of a Representative Man, a leader in the council as well as in the field who should comprehend and express the movement. We had no one who approached it. The country by instinct, seeking such a reliance, gave its faith to Lee in vain.

With some additions and qualifications it is possible to accept this diagnosis. Finance and manpower have already been discussed. "Military incompetence" demands some explanation, for the great reputation of Robert E. Lee and Stonewall Jackson has often obscured the failures of other commanders. The Confederacy produced an army that

[3] Edward Younger (ed.), *Inside the Confederate Government: The Diary of Frederick Garlick Hill Kean, Head of the Bureau of War* (New York: Oxford University Press, 1957), pp. 243-244.

showed fine fighting qualities in the ranks and among the regimental officers, but at the top the military hierarchy was often weak. None of the high-ranking officers had previous experience of handling large numbers of troops, and their West Point training had looked back to the Napoleonic era. The staff work was usually weak. Maps were few and inaccurate. The central planning of military operations was confused and inadequate, and here Jefferson Davis must carry considerable blame. His own experience as Secretary of War (under Franklin Pierce, when the forces of the United States had been few and their active duties confined to the western plains) led him to believe that military direction should be concentrated in the civilian administration. Until the later stages of the war he refused to set up a unified military command but established and retained an organization by separate geographical departments, each under an independent commander responsible to the central government. The loosely organized Confederacy, with its strong traditions of local autonomy, demanded a firm hand at the center; but having centralized, the next requirement was for flexibility, an adequate general staff, and a single person able to give full-time attention to strategy, supply, and deployment. The President kept too much detail under his own control, was often too harassed by other duties, and was not a good judge of men or of military exigencies. The office of Secretary of War was filled by no fewer than six men during the four years of conflict, of whom Judah P. Benjamin, George W. Randolph, and John A. Seddon were the most important. Of these, Benjamin was able but unfamiliar with military affairs and was held (unjustly) responsible for the failure to win the short war that had been confidently expected. Randolph won most respect from his subordinates and from the army but resigned when Jefferson Davis overruled him on a question of transferring troops from one military department to another. Seddon was an aristocratic and cultured Virginian without executive experience, in poor health, and though aloof and unfriendly toward his subordinates, quite content to act as a kind of chief clerk to the President, who kept strategy and military appointments firmly in his own hands. Meanwhile arrears of work piled up in the War Department.

The charge of "factionalism" requires closer examination. It is a curious fact that southerners, whose experience and skill had so often won them a commanding position in national politics, proved to be politically imcompetent in their greatest crisis. Again, an explanation may be sought in the character of southern society. Faced with the abrasive conflicts of national politics, the leaders of the South had exerted all their skill to protect the interests of their class and their states, but at home they had been accustomed to factionalism among gentlemen who were agreed upon essentials. Government had been in the hands of local oligarchies divided by party but united in social conservatism; their rule had been tempered and occasionally rebuked by democratic processes but had successfully resisted change in the structure of politics. Within the Confederacy there was another society that comprised the greater part of the southern population and lived mainly in the back country and mountainous counties. By origin, occupation, political tradition, and religion they stood apart from the planters who had controlled state politics.

The largest strain in their racial amalgam was Scotch-Irish; in religion they were Baptists, Methodists, Presbyterians—not Anglicans, the predominant faith of the more polished elements; in occupation they were small-scale farmers, cultivating with their own hands their own plots, seldom owning slaves; in politics they had been, for the most part, Whigs. These "up-country" people disliked their contemporaries of the Piedmont and coastal plains on both political and personal grounds. Constant efforts had been under way for a century to restrict their political power. Ridiculed as "hillbillies," "crackers," "poor whites," or other opprobrious names, they maintained an independent, sturdy life as far removed from the existence of a Seddon or a Lee as from that of a New England farmer.[4]

A majority of these people had been opposed to secession, and throughout the war sustained a number of secret pro-Unionist societies, obstructed recruitment, evaded taxation, and agitated for peace. Surprisingly large numbers found their way into the Federal army. In Virginia the western part of the state seceded to form the Union state of West Virginia; in Tennessee the eastern counties accepted secession with reluctance and remained a center of Unionist activity. This Unionist wedge, following the line of the Blue Mountains and flanking them on either side, ran deep into the heart of the Confederacy.

This "alternative society" of the South also provided the backbone for political opposition within the Confederacy and produced two men of vigor and ability: Joseph E. Brown, of Georgia, and Zebulon Vance, of North Carolina. Brown came from western Georgia and rose in the ranks of the prewar Democratic party to become governor in 1857. A pious, patriarchal, and fanatical man, he was devoted to the principle of state sovereignty and unlike others of the same social antecedents was a strong secessionist. Vance was a prewar Unionist who opposed secession until after Sumter; a man of affable manners, exceptional ability, and an outstanding orator, he was for over forty years the most influential man in his state and died in 1894 as a United States senator. Brown was not backward in raising troops but insisted that their first allegiance was to the state, with home defense under his command as their first duty. Vance took the same line and was a formidable political critic of the Davis Administration. In March, 1862, a peace movement was launched in North Carolina, and though Vance strongly opposed separate action by the state, his de-

---

[4] Burton J. Hendrick, *Statesmen of the Lost Cause* (Boston: Little, Brown, 1939), p. 332. The passage refers especially to Virginia and North Carolina; in western Georgia and northern Alabama the up-country was Democratic and the cotton belt predominantly Whig until the 1850's.

fense of state sovereignty remained an embarrassment to a government that was compelled to resort to nationalist measures to fight the war. The apparent inconsistency between Vance's prewar Unionism and ardent defense of states' rights is explained by opposition to the rule of the planter gentry, whose intentions he distrusted and whose competence he denied.

Throughout the war the Confederate Congress was an ineffective body. No strong leadership emerged, and though much time was spent in debate, little was achieved. Congress did succeed (if that is the right word) in obstructing financial policy with taxes rejected, reduced, or loaded with exemptions. Congressmen tended to be elected on their prewar political affiliations, but there was no party organization in the Confederate House or Senate, and if the Federal Congress was sometimes embarrassed by the violence of party, or of groups within parties, the southern Congress floundered along in uneasy harmony and without ever grasping important issues for discussion. The great battle for political independence saw politics become increasingly unproductive.

The sterility of politics at the center was reflected in the executive branch. Jefferson Davis had not sought his elevation and could justly claim that duty rather than ambition had cast him in the role. The Confederate Constitution laid down a single six-year presidential term, and Jefferson Davis never had to fight an election; this colored his attitude to political activity and confirmed his natural reluctance to engage in all the arts of management and personal diplomacy that normally keep governmental machinery in good order. He was dignified, correct, aloof, and apparently cold; the agonizing weight of decision was seldom revealed, and he was not readily accessible to congressmen. If things went well, respect surmounted this lack of the personal touch; when they went badly, impressions of obstinacy, refusal to take counsel, and lack of consideration accumulated. What the Confederacy needed was a leader of the Andrew Jackson stamp; what it got was a man of great integrity, enduring courage, limited imagination, and little capacity for inspiring either his immediate subordinates or the people at large.

These considerations raise the question whether the Confederacy ever became, in any true sense, a nation. The original secessionists had been inspired by the vision of a great southern civilization and (as already suggested) could be compared to the romantic nationalists of Europe; but the response to war was tribal rather than national. Men followed traditional leaders and used the rhetoric that had been forged to defend local interests and explain provincialism. The readiness to appeal to concepts such as states' rights indicates the weakness of the wider appeal to southern nationalism; and so far as there were generalized professions of loyalty to the Confederate states, they were the ideals of a class rather than of a community. National sentiment would have grown with success, but its existence during the war was largely a discovery of later years when the inspiration of the Lost Cause became a necessary ingredient in the recovery of self-respect.

Another great weakness of the Confederacy also derived from the character of southern society. Lack of economic opportunity except in planting, the decline of southern commerce, migration to the West, and poor educational standards had left the South with a very small professional, business, and clerical class. When put to the test, what the South often lacked was not soldiers but administrative or technical experience and men with enough education to assume these responsibilities. The shortage of manpower and a false order of priorities meant that the educated minority was more likely to be conscripted for the armed forces than kept for administrative duties. Offices were always understaffed, and lower down the administrative ladder key positions were occupied by the elderly, unfit, and incompetent. Only the firmest action by Gorgas kept intact the managerial and technical skills necessary to man his new factories. Southerners recognized the need to keep enough white men on the plantations, as occupiers or overseers, to control the slaves, but could never recognize the paramount need of administrative and technical skills in modern war. Even if the need had been recognized, the reserves of experienced and educated men would have been too meager for the task.

The poverty of Confederate intellectual life may be traced to the same social sources. The few scientists, men of letters, and publicists were absorbed in the tasks of war. Higher education disappeared, secondary education was reduced to a bare minimum, and the opportunities for elementary education diminished. The culture of the great houses ceased, and urban culture had always been weak. Newspapers continued, but their quality was poor, and their number diminished as the cities of the upper South and Mississippi Valley were occupied by Union forces. News was late or inaccurate, and unjustifiable optimism meant that the psychological shock of defeat was greater because unexpected. For instance, southern readers learned of the fall of Vicksburg four or more days after the event, when they had been confidently assured in the press that General John Pemberton could hold out for many weeks and that relieving armies were on the way. Periodicals ceased publication, and few pamphlets appeared. After four years of war the Confederacy was intellectually bankrupt as well as financially insolvent. This had serious though imponderable effects; nothing was added to the stock of ideas that had existed in 1861, and as confident expectations were disappointed, nothing emerged to replace them.

An analysis of the weaknesses of the Confederacy inevitably owes much to hindsight, and judgment would have been different if the achievement had been successful. Independence might have been won at the outset if northerners had accepted the situation (as most secessionists argued that they must). It might well have been won in 1862 when the Federal war effort seemed to have failed and the European powers were on the verge of recognition and perhaps intervention. It could well have been won in 1863 if Lee had not been stopped at Gettysburg and had been able to strike at the industrial heart of the North, or if the peace movement had not received a decided check in the fall of that year in northern state elections. It might have been won even in 1864 if General William Sherman had been held in western Georgia and the peace Democrats had gathered momentum in the North. For if ever the North wearied of war and agreed to negotiate, it could be only on a basis of southern independence or an autonomy so complete that the Union would be no more than a fragile league. If this had happened, the weaknesses that analysis reveals in the character and organization of the Confederacy would appear as mere incidents and difficulties overcome. It would, for instance, have been offered as confident proof that solvency is unnecessary in a struggle for survival and that an underdeveloped society could fight a successful defensive war. Above all, success would have made the South a nation. War can provide the material for nationalist epics, but national existence is the product of peaceful development.

Comparisons between North and South inevitably stress the preponderance of the former in wealth, numbers, and economic resources. Yet the onset of war in April found the Union a feeble giant, weak in the limbs and confused in mind. So far as confidence existed, it was based on the expectation that the war would be short; this, in turn, depended upon a singular lack of information about conditions in the South and the force that could be deployed by the United States. While most men in the North thought the attack on Sumter inexcusable, many blamed the Republicans as much as the secessionists for the train of events that had led to this outrage; though the majority had come to believe that affairs could no longer drift, many still hoped that a final collision could be avoided. In the Federal capital itself (said Gideon Welles, the newly appointed Secretary of the Navy)

the atmosphere was thick with treason. Party spirit and old party differences prevailed, however, amidst these accumulating dangers. Secession was considered by most as a political party question, not as a rebellion. Democrats to a large extent sympathised with the Rebels more than with the Administration, which they opposed; not that they wished secession to be successful and the Union divided, but they hoped that President Lincoln and the Republicans would, overwhelmed by obstacles and embarrassments, prove failures.[5]

Stephen A. Douglas performed a great service to the Union when he pledged immediate support to Lincoln, but the situation would have been dire indeed if the popular support had not been immediate and unequivocal in parts of the Union away from the border.

Probably the most important immediate asset of the administration was its existence as a government in being. There was no need to create new institutions, and inertia ensured that the normal processes of government would continue and be accepted. In the confused state of the public mind it was easier to continue with familiar procedures than to question or protest. The enlarged administration necessary to prosecute a war would be grafted upon a stock that was accepted as a normal part of life. In the states, too, no violent innovation was necessary, and Union governors could act quickly through established agencies. This could tide over the awkward period of transition from peace to war, but sustained effort would require something more than this; it must depend upon acceptance, by the great mass of the people, of the mystique of Union as the symbol of achievement and promise

[5] Howard K. Beale (ed.) , *The Diary of Gideon Welles*, Vol. I (New York: W. W. Norton, 1960) , p. 10. It is probable that these sentences were written some years after the war; for a history of the text of the diary see the editor's introduction to this edition.

of betterment. This was the creed that Lincoln evoked when he described the war as "essentially a people's conflict." It was a theme that was capable of development, played upon deep emotions, and could call for the great sacrifices. It lifted the struggle clear away from constitutional arguments and presented the issue as one clearly drawn between the friends of man and those who obstructed his advance.

The ideological character of the war for Union was, in the long run, vital for northern morale and success, but the issues required careful handling. The leaders of both parties were prepared to commit themselves to resolutions—proposed by Andrew Johnson in the Senate and J. J. Crittenden in the House—that the cause of war was southern disunion, that its sole objective was the restoration of the lawful authority of the Union Government, and that it was not an attack upon any existing institution or property. This was the broad proposition on which it was possible to obtain the widest possible agreement among those who had to fight; but it did not preclude men from reading more into the conflict than a contest for sovereignty. During the debate in the Senate John P. Hale, sometime Free Soil candidate for the Presidency, remarked that there might "be something in the suggestion that was made by the late Mr. Adams of Massachusetts . . . that there might be, incidental to the war power belonging to any Government, some control over this subject of slavery." [6] In the House the resolutions were divided into two parts, and on the first (declaring that southern disunionists were responsible for the war) some fifteen Democrats did not vote; on the second (which declared the limited objectives of the war) about the same number of Republicans (who were known for strong antislavery views) abstained, and two voted against. Thaddeus Stevens, who would soon emerge as the most dynamic leader on the Republican side, was ab-

[6] *Congressional Globe*, 37th Cong., 1st sess., July 25, 1861, p. 260.

sent for the second vote, though he had been in the House shortly before to vote for the first part. It is worth dwelling upon this comparatively minor incident, because the Johnson-Crittenden resolutions have so often been treated as a definitive statement of war aims and would play some part in subsequent arguments over Reconstruction; but Lincoln's message, with its broad review of the events preceding conflict and its emphasis upon the universal problems involved, had already taken the meaning of the war beyond the limitations implied by the resolutions. The resolutions should be seen as a declaration, sponsored by a southern Unionist and an old Clay Whig, to explain why Democrats and Constitutional Unionists were uniting with their recent political enemies in defense of the Union. They were accepted by the Republican majority with an eye on southern moderates who, it was hoped, might still restore their states voluntarily to the Union. Eight months later Orville Browning, a conservative but representative Republican and a close friend of Lincoln's, would say:

I believe that slavery is the sole, original cause of the present unhappy condition of affairs. . . . A large majority of the people in the free States of this Union believe as I do; and so believing, many of them, good and patriotic people, are anxious that the war shall be made the occasion of wiping slavery out.[7]

Indeed, as the promise of a better future was an essential ingredient in the northern will to fight, it was impossible to pretend that slavery had nothing to do with the struggle. Men who would not lift a finger to improve the condition of Negroes in their own states or cities were, nevertheless, convinced that victory would be fruitless if slavery remained.

In a battle for men's minds the attitude of intellectuals is vital, and it was a northern asset that so many writers, ministers, teachers, and newspaper editors were wholeheartedly convinced of the justice of the cause. Nor did

[7] *Ibid.*, 2d sess., March 10, 1862, p. 1137.

intellectual development come to a halt in 1861 but continued to explore, expand, and expound the ideals of the Union. At the outset there was a possibility that intellectuals who had learned their antislavery from William Lloyd Garrison would welcome the end of a union with slaveholders, while others recoiled from the idea that force should be used to accomplish a great moral reform. In January, 1861, the abolitionist poet J. G. Whittier had written:

> Draw we not even now a freer breath,
> As from our shoulders falls a load of death
> Loathsome as that the Tuscan's victim bore
> When keen with life to a dead horror bound?
> Why take we up the accursed thing again?
> Pity, forgive, but urge them back no more
> Who, drunk with passion, flaunt disunion's rag
> With its vile reptile blazon. Let us press
> The golden cluster on our brave old flag
> In closer union, and, if numbering less,
> Brighter shall shine the stars which still remain.

The attack at Sumter and the outbreak of war brought about a drastic reversal in this attitude; if the slave power would not go in peace, war became a providential opportunity to destroy slavery forever. After some initial hesitation Garrison came out in support of the war, and thereafter abolitionist criticism was directed at the apparent reluctance of Lincoln to move against slavery.

Religion provided a link between moral persuasion and political action. People bred on the Old Testament were quick to see the hand of God in events; again and again the orators and publicists would picture war as a divine scourge, Union troops as the hosts of the Lord, and the overthrow of false prophets and idolators as the aim of war. Typical was the utterance by Ben Wade, the vigorous antislavery senator from Ohio, in May, 1862:

As the Almighty sometimes overrules the wickedness of man to perfect a glorious end, so the hand of God was never more obvious than in this rebellion. Slavery might have staggered along against the improvement of the age, against the common consent of mankind, a scoff and a byword of the tongue of all civilized nations for a great many years, but this rebellion has sealed its fate and antedated the time when it becomes impossible. You cannot escape from this war without the emancipation of your Negroes. . . . Pro-slavery men seem to suppose that the Ruler of the universe is a pro-slavery Being; but if I have not mistaken Him greatly, He is at least a gradual emancipationist.[8]

Invocation of divine approval was a powerful aid in northern morale, but emancipation was full of political dangers for the Union cause. Lincoln was aware—critics said too much aware—of the strategic importance of the slave states in the Union. Secession was crushed in Maryland early in the war, and there was a strong indigenous movement for emancipation in the state. Kentucky was a different matter; there the nationalist traditions fostered by Henry Clay had done battle with secession and won a precarious victory; but the state sent many thousands to the Confederate army, and in the first two years of the war there was always a danger that Confederate successes in Tennessee would overthrow Unionism in Kentucky. In southern Ohio, Indiana, and Illinois (mainly settled from the South) there was strong anti-Negro feeling. In the new state of West Virginia there was little support for emancipation, and in New York and Philadelphia there were strong manifestations of popular negrophobia. Gathering up these elements, together with other and more honorable doubts, the peace Democrats became formidable in 1862 and 1863. The great majority of the so-called Copperheads were attached to the Union but believed that it could best be restored by negotiation, by accepting southern slavery, and by providing effective guarantees for southern rights. Many midwestern Copperheads looked back to a simpler rural society and resented a war that they associated with New England, commerce, and consolida-

[8] *Ibid.,* May, 1862.

tion. Their opposition to the war fed also upon the suspension of habeas corpus and arbitrary arrests, but racial prejudice provided the most fertile soil. Thus there was always a rival ideology in the North that challenged the identification of the Union cause with justice, penance, retribution, and purification.

With all these considerations Lincoln's caution upon slavery was explicable; but so was the action of some Republicans in pressing hard for emancipation. From one-third to one-half of the Republicans in Congress were becoming recognized as radicals who advocated a tough war policy, direct action against slavery, and (looking to the future) national responsibility for the reconstruction of southern society without slavery or slave-owners. Few radicals came from large cities, and a substantial number came from old antislavery strongholds such as the Western Reserve and from the newer regions of the West. There was no recognized radical leadership—indeed, men so individualistic and diverse as Thaddeus Stevens, Charles Sumner, Ben Wade, Henry Winter Davis, and Zachariah Chandler would have found it difficult to recognize any common leader—but in the House Thaddeus Stevens became a powerful influence, while in the Senate Wade was the practical but unsubtle strategist of radicalism, and Charles Sumner was recognized as a national spokesman for northern antislavery. The radicals often made errors of judgment, and their moves were sometimes embarrassing for the administration and unjust to individuals, yet they played a vital part in the northern war effort. With everything to gain from victory and nothing from compromise, they were more willing than others to work in Congress or at the grass roots and might fail in judgment but seldom in vigilance. They have been called the Jacobins, and if the Civil War was a revolution, the comparison is apt; certainly they provided the hard core of dedicated and active men without whom great movements can flounder and lose direction.

The nonmilitary achievements of Congress will be considered in the next chapter, but any discussion of northern morale would be incomplete without reference to political activity. Normal politics continued throughout the war; no election was passed by, no campaigns were omitted, and the usual acrimony was not abated. Lincoln had to stand the test of reelection while the issue of war was still undecided, state and congressional elections gave almost continuous indications of popular feeling, and party organization continued. There would be no change in institutions, as there had been in France during the course of the revolutionary wars, and no moratorium on elections, as there was in Britain during the six years of World War II. It is hard to estimate the effect of all this activity, but certainly the continuance of controversy helped to promote argument over attitudes and ends. During four years there was an enormous output of political literature, the public mind traveled a vast distance, and the turmoil of war fostered new convictions, new ideas, and a new concept of national existence.

The North began the war with great advantages in education and skill. There were great reserves of educated men for administrative tasks, the large business class could turn their talents readily to the organization of war, and there was never any shortage of clerical workers. In addition to all the men required for civil and military administration, there was enough educated manpower to keep the schools of the country going; to deluge the people with newspapers, periodicals, and books; to staff the semiofficial Christian and Sanitary Commissions which cared for the spiritual and bodily needs of the troops; and, in the last two years of the war, to engage in tremendous business activity. In the army and ancillary civilian services such as railroads, telegraphs, mail, food and clothing supplies there were reservoirs of technical skill, and though, like other armies, the Union often failed to get the right men into the right job, education and technical experience were great and imponderable assets. A small story teaches a large lesson. In April, 1861, when the fate of Washington seemed to hang in the balance, General B. F. Butler, commanding Massachusetts troops, was detained at Annapolis because the only available railroad engine had been dismantled. Butler assembled his troops and asked if any man could repair it.

"Well, General," volunteered one enlisted man, "I rather think I can. I made that engine." [9]

It should not, however, be assumed that a government in being, enthusiasm, and reserves of potential administrative skill ensured to the North an efficient buildup of strength. In the early stages of the war zeal outran the competence of those charged with the task of directing the national effort. In April, 1861, the regular army numbered 16,402, but the number ready for service was somewhat smaller and mainly scattered over the great western frontiers; this army was led by professionally trained officers, but of their number almost one-third (and a considerably higher proportion of those ready for service) joined the Confederacy, though few enlisted men did so. In both North and South there were a considerable number of trained officers who had left the army for civilian employment and might be persuaded to rejoin; one such was Ulysses S. Grant, who was carrying on a somewhat unsuccessful tannery business, and another was George B. McClellan, who occupied a rather more exalted position in a railroad company. Even these additions, however, left the Union with a desperately small body of trained officers. The navy was in no better shape. For a country so dependent upon overseas trade the United States had been extraordinary neglectful of fighting ships and had relied heavily upon Great Britain to preserve the Atlantic peace. When Lincoln ordered a blockade of the South,

[9] Quoted in Robert V. Bruce, *Lincoln and the Tools of War* (Indianapolis: Bobbs-Merrill, 1956), p. 66; from *Butler's Book* (Boston: 1892), pp. 201–202.

the ships responsible for this mammoth task were few and in poor condition.

There were three ways in which the small army could be enlarged: by taking more recruits into the national forces, by calling for national volunteers to serve only during the emergency, and by calling out the state militias. The militia was recruited by each state, and its officers were appointed by the governor; when called up by the President, it came under national control, but the overlapping spheres of state and Union were an invitation to controversy. Lincoln's first call for 75,000 to serve three months was to the militia, and though national volunteers formed the bulk of the Union forces, state governors were usually responsible for recruitment and appointed regimental officers. In the early months of the war the efforts of several governors outran what the War Department considered necessary, and states offered regiments that were refused. Another method of raising troops was to authorize individuals to form their own regiments, which resulted in further clashes with the governors and in a number of colonels who were more distinguished by wealth or political influence than military experience. One expedient that seemed innocuous was to prove vicious: the offer of a bounty to each volunteer. The practice was first used by the states and then adopted by the Federal Government. This encouraged fraudulent and multiple enlistment, used up large sums of money, and added a new character, the "bounty jumper," to the national rogues' gallery. Feeble administration at the center, overlapping responsibilities, political interference, expectation of a short war, and the universal belief that military proficiency could be quickly acquired by any active man made the Union army far less effective than it should have been if the rules of common sense had been firmly applied.

The central command was at first poorly organized. The President was the constitutional Commander in Chief, the Secretary of War was responsible for army administration, and in 1861 Lincoln appointed the aged Winfield Scott as his chief military adviser. Scott, whose brilliant campaign in 1847 had led to the capture of Mexico City, still had a good mind for the broad concepts of war but was too slow for decisive action in a novel situation. Simon Cameron, the Secretary of War, had made his reputation as an adroit party manager in Pennsylvania, but the situation demanded a driving ruthlessness rather than the subtle arts of politics. Many years later Cameron would recall that

it was impossible to find a man who had any intelligent idea of the magnitude of the struggle. We were entirely unprepared to engage in war. We had no guns, and even if we had they would have been of little use, for we had no ammunition, no powder, no saltpetre. I did the best I could under the circumstances, working day and night. . . . There were very few persons who believed that the war would last for more than a few weeks. . . . At first having no means at my command; then laughed at for predicting that the war would be a long and bloody one; and all the time harassed by contractors and others.[10]

Somehow out of the confusion order and system would finally emerge, but in the meantime urgent needs gave an opportunity for fraudulent dealing. Cameron himself does not seem to have been corrupt in office but was so overwhelmed that many irregularities were allowed. Taking the line that arms and supplies must be gathered at any price, he allowed his subordinates to enter into contracts for inferior articles at grossly inflated prices, and lobbyists acting on behalf of unscrupulous businessmen brought off some notable coups. Convinced, like most others, that the war would soon collapse, contractors felt justified in making what they could while the lush times lasted. In January, 1862, Cameron's retirement was facilitated by appointing him minister to Russia. His successor, Edwin

[10] Quoted in Erwin S. Bradley, *Simon Cameron* (Philadelphia: University of Pennsylvania Press, 1968), p. 184; from Cameron's own article in *The New York Times,* June 3, 1878.

M. Stanton, was a man of grinding efficiency who was not the least deterred by the prospect of making enemies; harsh, tactless, and often prejudiced by personal animosities, he was the man to knock the ramshackle war administration into shape.[11]

In reviewing these facts, it is impossible to avoid the conclusion that the Union would have collapsed in the six months after Sumter if it had been faced by a well-organized adversary. The Union survived because the Confederacy was no better prepared for the kind of struggle that had been opened and because it had greater resources to be deployed once the crucial period had past; even so, these advantages were almost thrown away by the folly of sending raw troops, under officers with no experience of handling large numbers, on a major offensive less than three months after the opening of hostilities. The fatal battle of Bull Run on July 21, 1861, brought disaster to the untrained Union army, left the Confederates exhausted after a lucky victory, and though its military consequences were meager, its psychological effects were far-reaching. It persuaded doubtful Confederates that since coercion had failed, the North would soon recognize southern independence, and dispelled the dangerous delusion on the Federal side that the "rebellion" would soon fizzle out. Thus the great Confederate victory had perverse effects; it lured the South on to an effort that could not, in the long run, be sustained and caused the North to reassess prospects, define aims, and reinforce determination. The impossibility of muddling through with a show of force was demonstrated, and the demoralized troops who streamed back toward

[11] Gideon Welles, Secretary of the Navy, disliked Stanton, but other evidence confirms his statement that "he took pleasure in being ungracious and rough to those who were under his control, and when he thought his bearish manner would terrify or humiliate those who were subject to him. To his superiors or those who were his equals in position, and who neither heeded nor cared for his violence, he was complacent, sometimes obsequious." (Beale, Vol. I, p. 68.)

Washington convinced many northerners that they were no longer engaged in a police action but an apocalyptic struggle.

The economic strength of the North was obvious, but contemporaries were correct in discounting the argument that industrial power would bring immediate and overwhelming advantages. Industry took time and effort to organize for war purposes; American manufactures were, with few exceptions, small-scale local concerns, and though this made for flexibility, it also made ordering, standardization, and large-scale production difficult. The major short-term economic advantages for the North were ability to feed the people entirely from the resources of the free states, ports open to the trade of the world, a railroad system in good working order, and existing factories for the manufacture of arms.

The outbreak of war caught the northern economy at a time when long- and short-term influences had been pulling in opposite directions. Economic activity and industrial production were in the early stages of the great process of expansion that would make the United States a major industrial power by the end of the century. Estimates differ on the scale and timing of this long-term boom, but the general picture of upward movement since the end of the 1837–1844 depression is clear. The number of large industrial establishments were still few, and the bulk of American industry was carried on in small concerns, usually under family management. There were already a few giants among the railroad companies, but also a great number of small lines. In the same way shipping was largely in the hands of a large number of sharply competitive owners. A few prototypes of "big business" were found in the New England textile industry, but it was in banking, importing, and distribution that the large operators were found. In 1860 the United States was in the full tide of economic growth, but the transition to capitalist consolidation was still in its early stages.

In 1857 a sharp check had occurred with the familiar sequence of financial crisis followed by depression in trade and industry, so that short-run influences had worked for contraction rather than expansion. The shock of war caught the economy when recovery was still not fully developed; the loss of the southern market and the freezing of so much northern capital in the South provoked a further setback, though most of the 1860 cotton crop had already been delivered, and the crisis was slower to hit the textile industry. Military demand was slow to develop, and the immediate consequence of war was therefore to retard recovery and to dislocate many commercial and financial operations. At its worst the war went only a tiny way toward justifying Confederate hopes that the loss of cotton and of the southern market would ruin the North, but in the first year businessmen did experience a good deal of difficulty. A dramatic change would set in before the end of 1862 with the beginning of a great boom in business activity, but until that time economic superiority did little to help the war effort.

This brief analysis of the balance of assets reveals a situation in which the South went into the war with high morale and unity of purpose, whereas the North was divided and confused. A formula for northern unity was found in a legalistic declaration of war aims, which stuck to the simple objective of restoring the Union and deliberately excluded other aims. The South could play upon the magic word "independence," whereas the North had to argue the less attractive case for union and sovereign power. The northern disadvantage was offset by the appeal to national sentiment, but the political situation prevented the presentation of the Union cause as a crusade against the slave power. Independence became, however, less attractive in the South as its benefits became less clear, as politics ran into sterility, and as intellectual life slowed down. In the North conviction built up with lively intellectual activity, political debate, and more widespread acceptance of the proposition that slavery, being the cause of the war, must not survive. Economics ran a parallel course. Though never strong, the southern economy was not, at the outset, desperately weak, whereas northern business was dislocated, and it took time before the northern economy began to surge forward in the great boom of the later war years.

The extent to which ideology fed upon economics or vice versa need not be discussed here; it is enough to say that both combined to make the North stronger and more confident as the struggle progressed. What fails to convince is any attempt to explain northern victory exclusively in economic terms; a major source of northern strength was always the ability of northern politicians and propagandists to draw upon the powerful forces of nineteenth-century liberalism: religion, nationalism, humanitarian feeling, dislike of established ruling classes, and the alliance of material betterment with moral improvement. This ideological thrust was felt inside northern society, and intensity of conviction generated tension. In parts of the Midwest there were ties of kinship with the South, strong anti-Negro feelings, traditional respect for local power and suspicion of central authority, and political organizations anxious to preserve their separate identity. In Ohio Clement Vallandigham became the symbol of a Peace Democracy that declared its support for the Union but would agree to any terms that would end the war by negotiation. In Philadelphia and more markedly in New York, there was a strong undercurrent of resistance to the war; low-paid workers among the New York Irish could feel little enthusiasm for a cause that they identified with the interests of a Protestant employer class, and among upper-class leaders the traditions of conservative Democracy were still very much alive. Horatio Seymour, elected governor of New York in 1862, was ostensibly a supporter of the Union, but his politics were those of Pierce and

Buchanan rather than Douglas, and he had no wish for a victory that would give ascendancy to Republicans and war Democrats.

These internal protests proved to be embarrassments rather than serious obstacles and, by defining the issue as one between victory and compromise, reinforced the will of the northern majority to continue the war. But a small turn of fortune's wheel might have placed the Peace Democracy in a much stronger position. Even after the great northern victories of 1863, when the scales became more and more weighted against southern military success, the reluctant recognition of southern independence remained a distinct possibility.

Thus the Civil War was exclusively neither a war for southern independence nor a war for the Union. It was not a rebellion, nor was it a revolution as the term is commonly understood. It was not primarily a crusade against slavery, though slavery was entwined in its causes, and many in the North came to agree that victory without emancipation would not be worth winning. Attempts to interpret it as fundamentally an economic conflict fail to convince, though the full range of the war cannot be grasped without understanding the relationship between a developed and a less developed society. It had been fed by religious revivalism, romanticism, rationalism, and the great hope that the United States would indeed be *novus ordo seculorum*. Its results embraced more than those who launched it had ever imagined, and the course of war transcended its causes. It was the great crisis for most of the forces that move in the modern world and is thus of universal significance.

The Civil War was an international event and was followed with keen interest in the European press, but for foreign observers a clear-cut endorsement of either side was difficult. For conservatives it demonstrated the falsity of democratic dogma, but before long it became apparent that democracy (whether of the northern or southern type) could gather formidable strength for the traditional pursuit of war. Radicals found themselves torn between the rights of a majority to insist and of a minority to resist. Antislavery men endorsed any attack on the slave power but were disconcerted by the emphatic repudiation in the North of any intention of interfering with slavery in the states and by evidence in the territories that the Republican aim was to create a white man's country. It could even be argued that Union victory would perpetuate slavery, whereas an independent South would soon be forced to abolish it. In 1861 judgment was therefore confused, but those who supported the Confederacy had the better of the argument.

European conservatives, who were instinctively opposed to all forms of popular government, joined hands with liberals such as William Ewart Gladstone and J. A. Roebuck (a philosophic radical who became an energetic friend of the South in British political circles) who saw the Confederacy struggling for self-government against a government that had become alien. Free trade, which had become the gospel of enlightenment for so many, provided another cross-current; the South had always produced the most eloquent advocates of low tariffs and thus of the international peace and prosperity that free traders preached; the Republican enactment of protective tariffs came as a shock that knocked British liberalism off-balance. Richard Cobden, with a reputation (not entirely justified) for extensive knowledge of American society, had corresponded with Calhoun and other southern free traders despite a generalized hostility to slavery; he had welcomed the lowering of the tariff in 1857 and deplored the Republican support for protection; yet in other respects Cobden had far more in common with northerners, disliked slavery, and after a short period of uneasy doubt announced his support for the Union. However, Lord Palmerston, the Prime Minister, had never been a friend of

America and was believed to welcome the breakup of the Union; Lord John Russell, the Foreign Secretary, saw the war merely as a struggle for power; Gladstone, passionately attached to the cause of Italian liberty, tended to see the southern war for independence in the same light. The London *Times,* which claimed and enjoyed enormous influence in political and upper-class circles, was consistently favorable to the South and emphatically denied that slavery had anything to do with the war. Across the Channel the Emperor Napoleon III was sympathetic to the Confederacy, as was an important segment of the French press.

It is not, however, true to see European attitudes simply in terms of class. There were pronortherners and prosoutherners in every social stratum. It must also be remembered that a great many Europeans, though interested, did not feel strong emotional commitment to either side. If the war, or either belligerent, interfered with individual or national interests, the case might be altered; they might be roused by an affront or angered by distress, but short of this they had no wish to sacrifice life by intervention. Thus a commitment to neutrality probably represented the will of the majority.

Yet neutrality had its problems. War disrupted the trade and shipping of the Atlantic; threatened to cut off the raw material from the European cotton industry and jeopardized the heavy foreign investments in the United States; and involved the nations of the world in a complex series of problems concerning the rights of neutrals. The Confederacy gambled heavily on the European need for cotton and hoped that this would lead to intervention by the European powers. Few hoped for immediate action by Great Britain and France against the United States, but there were confident expectations that they would attempt to break the Federal blockade and that this, in turn, would lead to conflict. Even without this, southerners expected recognition as soon as they had proved their determination to remain independent and their capacity to provide an effective government. At the outset the issue seemed simple in the North; the South was in rebellion, and foreigners could find no support in international law for giving aid, comfort, or recognition to men in revolt against their lawful government. In any event, and after many complicated diplomatic exchanges, no foreign government did recognize the Confederacy as an independent government, but it was impossible to act as though the Union exercised authority in the South, to ignore Confederate ships on the high seas, or to pretend that there were no southern agents in Europe. There were realities to be faced that could not be obscured by the fiction that only one authority existed in the United States. Moreover, Lincoln's proclamation of a blockade implied that one was confronted with the separation of a society, not a revolt by individuals. The solution adopted by Great Britain and France was to extend to the South the rights of a belligerent. Without making any judgment upon the legality of the Confederate Government, they recognized its right to authorize acts of war, to issue commercial documents, to enter and leave European ports, and to maintain agents abroad, but not to enter into treaties or engage in formal negotiations. Throughout the war the Confederacy remained, in the eyes of European governments, in this ambiguous position; it had the right to fight but not the right to act as a nation among nations.

In 1861 it seemed not improbable that the North would bring about the conflict with Great Britain that the South most desired. Jefferson Davis had selected James M. Mason and John Slidell for the Confederate missions to London and Paris. They traveled first to Havana and then took passage in the British ship *Trent* for England. Two days out the *Trent* was ordered to stop by Captain Charles Wilkes, commanding the U.S.S. *San Jacinto*. An American search party boarded the *Trent,* and Mason and Slidell were removed and taken as prisoners to Boston. Wilkes's action roused great popular enthusiasm, and the House of Representatives responded by passing a congratulatory resolution. Unfortunately the Americans had waded deep into the difficult waters of international law. To the American layman it seemed common sense that two prominent rebels, leaving the country with the avowed object of damaging the interests of the Union abroad, should be seized before they could do any harm. The British could hardly be expected to take this accommodating view. A neutral vessel, acting in good faith, had accepted two passengers; and once embarked, they came under the protection of the British flag. It was admitted that a belligerent power had the right to stop and search neutral ships suspected of carrying contraband, yet it was stretching this right to the limit when the vessel searched was miles from the American coast and voyaging between two neutral ports, and stretching it still further to regard individuals as "contraband." Even if the Americans had a case, the proper procedure would have been to order the *Trent* to an American port and submit the whole issue to a prize court for adjudication. If an American captain could arbitrarily decide the points of law and make himself judge of who might lawfully be carried in a neutral ship, then grave damage had been done to the delicate fabric of international maritime law. The case was put explicitly by the French Foreign Minister, Edouard Thouvenel, when he wrote:

The *Trent* did not have as its destination any place belonging to either of the belligerents. It was taking its cargo and passengers to a neutral country. If it could be claimed that under such circumstances a neutral flag did not completely cover the persons and goods it carried, then its immunity would be but an empty word: at any moment the commerce and navigation of third parties might have to suffer in their harmless or even indirect contacts with belligerents.[12]

[12] Quoted in Lynn M. Case and Warren F. Spencer, *The United States and France: Civil War Diplomacy* (Philadelphia: University of Pennsylvania Press, 1970) , p. 203.

Moreover, the offense was committed against a nation sensitive to points of national honor, jealous of maritime rights, and best able to retaliate. Incidentally, the case was analogous to the practice of impressment, against which the Americans had protested so frequently in the years before 1812. For a few weeks it looked as though the American Government would support Wilkes and hold the two prisoners while Britain would insist upon humiliating terms for settlement; both governments rode the crest of public feeling, which made it difficult to recede. Aided by an exchange of friendly letters between Charles Sumner, Richard Cobden, and John Bright, and perhaps by a timely letter from France revealing that the French Government was firmly against the Americans on the points of law and usage, Lincoln and Seward ordered the release of Mason and Slidell with an official explanation that Wilkes had acted without authority; the British accepted this settlement without demanding a formal apology or other restitution.

So ended a threat of war that would have been disastrous for the Union. The incident has some curious features. Mason and Slidell had taken some pains to publicize their movements and had actually entertained officers from the *San Jacinto* in Havana. There is no proof that the affair was engineered with the intention of promoting conflict between the United States and Great Britain, but the two emissaries made no secret of their hope that this would be the outcome. Indeed, the prospect of foreign intervention would never be brighter for the South, and with it the best chance of winning southern independence. Indeed, Mason and Slidell imprisoned in Boston were far more influential than they proved to be abroad. Mason was a well-known Virginian, but his manners were those of a provincial country gentleman, and he was the author of the notorious Fugitive Slave Law of 1850; he was thus out of place in British aristocratic circles and unlikely to win popularity in the country where *Uncle Tom's Cabin* had been a best-seller. Slidell was a courtly gentleman, with some diplomatic experience and a knowledge of French, but he accomplished little.

Lincoln made two good appointments for the key posts at London and Paris. Charles Francis Adams was a man of great ability and consistent firmness, who was able to establish good personal relations with members of the British Government. Adams was never an affable person, but temperamentally he was much better suited to the patrician atmosphere of British politics than to the equalitarian vigor of political rivalries at home. His long record of opposition to slavery was also an asset. William L. Dayton at Paris was intellectually less distinguished, but he was steady, possessed good judgment, and established good relations with the French Foreign Office. This proved to be of great use, for the Emperor Napoleon's sympathy with the Confederacy and his fondness for personal diplomacy created some difficult situations.

Both in Great Britain and in France the building and arming of ships for the Confederacy became a major issue. At the beginning of the war Norfolk was the only yard in the South capable of building large ships, and after the loss of Norfolk it was necessary to rely entirely upon foreign shipbuilders. In both countries the law forbade the building of warships for belligerents, but a good deal of uncertainty attended its interpretation. In the mid-nineteenth century there was often little difference in construction between merchant and naval vessels; a ship built ostensibly for a civilian purpose might then be armed at sea with weapons obtained from another source. This was the case of the *Florida* and the famous *Alabama,* built at Liverpool under a contract arranged by Captain James Bulloch, the Confederate naval agent in Britain, and completed in March and July, 1862. Adams presented convincing evidence that the *Alabama* was intended for use as a Confederate cruiser, and after considerable delays the government ordered its detention; but this came too late, the *Alabama* sailed, and subsequently had an outstandingly successful career as a commerce raider against northern shipping. In the course of nearly two years (until finally sunk by the U.S.S. *Kearsarge* in the English Channel) the *Alabama* sank one Union warship and sixty-two merchant ships. More important than the actual losses were the fears inspired, which caused the transfer of much trade to British ships and the transfer of many American ships to British registry. The *Alabama* was the subject of an interminable wrangle with the British, which was not ended until American claims were settled by arbitration in 1872.

However, Adams believed that the British Government had acted through error rather than malice, and he was in a strong position to take up the next case of a similar kind. Bulloch arranged for the firm of Laird to build two ironclads equipped with rams; but their offensive purpose was too clear to be concealed, and the British Government was persuaded to stop their sailing. In France a number of attempts were made by the Confederates to obtain ships, but the only one completed and delivered (ostensibly to the Danish Government) proved to be unseaworthy. In other instances Dayton was able to hold the Imperial Government to the strict letter of neutrality.

These disputes about a few ships may seem trivial in retrospect; they were not so at the time. If the Confederacy had had five or six *Alabamas* at sea, the commerce of the North could have been seriously damaged. The Laird ironclads would have been powerful enough to break the Federal blockade at one or more ports and offer the European powers cotton in return for desperately needed supplies. Even a modest success would have caused a diversion of northern effort, taken the pressure off Lee or Joe E. Johnston, raised morale, and done something to stave off economic collapse. This in turn might have affected the outcome of the 1864 election and the prospect of peace by negotiation. These hypotheses prove nothing but suggest that the Union Government was right to view these matters with grave concern. They do not substantiate the subsequent American claim that the indirect consequences of the *Alabama*'s raids, in prolonging the war, could be redeemed only by the cession of Canada and a payment of many millions.

While these disputes brought international relations to the brink of rupture, there were strong undercurrents against intervention, recognition, or even overt official sympathy for the South. Though the European powers had viewed with suspicion the rise of a young republican giant across the Atlantic, no one's interest would have been served in the long run by the breakup of the Union. A defeated North might seek compensation by working for the annexation of Canada; an independent South might be forced to seek territory, markets, and bases in the Caribbean and Central America. In any event the European powers would have been compelled to commit troops and ships to keep the peace. The experienced diplomats of Europe were far too familiar with all the hazards brought about by the weakened Hapsburg and Ottoman empires to welcome the same kind of instability in America. Great Britain had an interest in southern cotton, but the financial stake was far outweighed by investments in the northern and western states. British export merchants and international bankers shared the fears of northern merchants about the economic consequences of secession.

French initiative was paralyzed by the rash intervention in Mexico. Though the Emperor seemed sometimes to ponder the possibility of getting help from an independent Confederacy, the consequences of an open quarrel with the North outweighed any possible advantages. After the capture of New Orleans, the Union was in a position to dominate the Gulf, and even though the Confederates continued to hold Texas, western Mexico was vulnerable from California.

Even more important in Great Britain was the probability that war against the Union would be unpopular with large sections of the people. Except perhaps on an emotional issue such as the *Trent,* there would have been protest, with the war represented as a conspiracy between the British ruling class and southern slave-owners. The enthusiasm of the British working class for the northern cause can be exaggerated, but it was latent when not active. Family ties, maintained by the increasing efficiency and regularity of the mail service, were a real factor that is easily overlooked. Thousands of middle- and working-class families had relatives or friends in America (by far the largest number of them in the northern and midwestern states), and most letters home contained conscious or unconscious Union propaganda. If the unthinkable came to pass, and governments dragged the two countries into war, there were strong possibilities that brothers, cousins, and even fathers and sons might find themselves shooting at each other. Throughout British society, and especially in the middle and lower classes, the idea of an Atlantic, English-speaking family was not fancy but an expression of social reality. When the Working Men of Manchester in England sent an address to Lincoln in December, 1862, they were not using empty rhetoric in asserting that "our interests . . . are identified with yours. We are truly one people, though locally separate."

On these personal and ethnic grounds it was therefore possible to accept Lincoln's thesis that the war was "a people's contest," and when Lincoln issued the Emancipation Proclamation, whatever critics might say of its limitations, the man in the street or the factory saw it as the death of slavery. In this they were, of course, correct. Old antislavery enthusiasm was reawakened by the war, and now in a form more popular and secular than the middle-class and evangelical movement of earlier days. Lincoln was not the man to ignore this groundswell of popular sympathy and made a special point of delivering a full answer to the

Working Men of Manchester, in which he deplored the sufferings occasioned by the cotton famine and welcomed their support for the Union as "an instance of sublime Christian heroism which has not been surpassed in any age or in any country." The International Working Men of the World, a tiny group based in London, represented no one except themselves, but they were adept at identifying themselves with popular feeling and trained to detect long-term forces in the process of history. Sending a congratulatory message to Lincoln after his reelection, the International wrote:

From the commencement of the titanic American strife the workingmen of Europe felt instinctively that the star-spangled banner carried the destiny of their class. . . . The workingmen of Europe feel sure that as the American War of Independence initiated a new era of ascendancy for the middle class, so the American antislavery war will do for the working classes. They consider it an earnest of the epoch to come, that it fell to the lot of Abraham Lincoln, the single-minded son of the working class, to lead his country through the matchless struggle for the rescue of an enchained race and the reconstruction of a social world.

No special prominence was given, among the signatories, to the man who had written this message, but those familiar with the internal politics of the International knew that his name was Karl Marx.[13]

---

[13] Karl Marx and Frederick Engels, *The Civil War in the United States* (3rd ed.; New York: International Publishers, 1961), pp. 278–281. See also Marx to Engels, December 2, 1864, *ibid.*, p. 279.

[7]
War and Change

MILITARY historians are constantly confronted with problems of chance, individual decision, and significant detail. The events of a single day appear to alter the course of history, and the actions of a single man seem to determine all that follows. It is too easy to concentrate upon the dramatic and ignore administration, training, supply, communication, and medical services, which make dull reading. It is equally easy to present the story of war in epic terms and to forget the muddle, boredom, and appalling discomfort. Most men who rise to high command have been taught the importance of decisive action and to acquire habits of authority, but they are also men of limited outlook who are shielded by the requirements of military decision from the kind of criticism to which they would be subjected in civilian life. Every army has a vested interest in protecting incompetence provided that the rules have been obeyed. The Civil War was no exception, and junior officers and enlisted men paid a heavy price for errors on the field of battle and inefficiency behind the lines. To some extent the official version can be corrected, because the Civil War was the most literate of wars, with a great host of letters, diaries, and memoirs to supplement the record. It is also a war for which full archives should enable one to reconstruct in great detail its administrative history. Unfortunately it was also a war that speedily bred its own mythology; both for the Union and for the Confederacy it had to be glorified, and even while it was still being fought, the orators, preachers, and publicists were at work.

In a short survey the principal danger is to see war as a great chess game. It is necessary to pick out the turning

points, and in so doing it is all too easy to forget that one is
not dealing with grand masters but with men who had had
no opportunity of studying the rules of the grim game on
which they were embarked. To those who had studied—
and this could mean little but a study of European warfare
of the Napoleonic era—knowledge was often as much a
handicap as a help. It would, however, be unjust to blame
individuals without first realizing that the war ought never
to have been fought, that once begun it should have been
terminated as soon as possible, and that if continued it
should have been fought in a different way. The object of
the South was to prove that the Union could not be preserved; the existing structure of American politics provided ample opportunities for doing this, and if these
failed, there remained numerous ways in which an active
and organized people could make themselves ungovernable. Patience might have been demanded in a prolonged
political crisis, but this would have been the nobler course
than sacrificing hundreds of thousands of lives, disrupting society, and discrediting the constitutional arguments
that had been the most commendable aspect of the southern case. A refusal to fight might therefore have been the
best way of achieving southern ends.

Equally, the North lurched into a great war that was inconsistent with the long-term objectives of preserving the
Union. The resort to arms did not convince any southerners that they ought to remain in the Union, but reinforced
the argument for secession and persuaded many waverers.
The longer and fiercer the war became, the more remote
became the possibility of restoring that harmony on which
alone true Union could rest. Until April, 1861, most Republicans probably hoped that southern Unionism would
revive, and even after the die had been cast, every plan for
reconstruction incorporated the idea of building anew
around a nucleus of southern Unionism; yet war made it
certain that many Unionists would be forced to choose the
Confederacy and that others would be paralyzed by intense

public pressure. Coercion, by definition, failed from the start for, as Robert E. Lee wrote (and many others agreed), it was impossible to be loyal to a Union that rested upon force, not consent. An early cessation of hostilities might have made possible a reversal of these feelings, but a long war meant that they would become deeply ingrained. The prospect for harmonious reconstruction was not lost in 1865 or in 1867 but in 1861.

It would be unjust to blame individuals. Political theory, even of the mild American type, placed loyalty to government above common sense. Romanticism decreed that it was better to die for conviction than to live and prosper. Religion taught that evil must be rooted out. Nationalism saw the nation as a collective entity endowed with mystic qualities and demanding a special kind of allegiance. The difficulty was that so many of these concepts, or at least the inferences drawn from them, were inapplicable to life in a federal society that had begun its national existence by talking about the pursuit of happiness, just powers, and government by consent. The Civil War meant the failure of these political ideas, but so many continued to talk and write as though it was being fought to preserve them. William Faulkner once wrote:

This was the American Dream: a sanctuary on the earth for individual man in a condition in which he could be free not only of the old established closed-corporation hierarchies of arbitrary power which had oppressed him as a mass, but free of that mass into which the hierarchies of church and state had compressed and held him individually thralled and individually impotent.[1]

The Civil War witnessed a decisive stage in the conquest of this primitive dream.

Given these fundamental errors, there were still possibilities that the war might be fought in a way that would do least damage to its aims. At the outset Lincoln was pre-

[1] James B. Meriwether (ed.), *Essays, Speeches and Publications of William Faulkner* (New York: Random House, 1965), p. 62.

sented by the aged Winfield Scott with the so-called Ana-
conda strategy, contemplating no offensive action (save
perhaps the seizure of a few vital ports and railroad junc-
tions) but a strict and tightening blockade by land and
sea. The Confederacy would be cut off from the rest of the
world except with northern consent. An army and a navy
would have to be raised but would be used to secure limited objectives. The decision to invade the South changed
all this; it gave hostages to fortune in the shape of armies
that could be defeated and destroyed the prospect of voluntary reconstruction.

Faced with northern invasion, the South would have
done better to avoid direct confrontation and resort to har-
assing, partisan, and guerrilla warfare. This would have
been less dramatic but more effective than pitched battles
and large-scale campaigns. The nature of the countryside
gave almost unlimited opportunities for piecemeal attacks,
local activity, threats to the lines of communication, and
withdrawal into remote and mountainous areas. The Federal troops would have been driven to increasing severity,
with gathering doubts among the northern people and
growing sympathy for the South abroad. It is an interesting speculation that if the Confederates had lost the first
battle of Bull Run (which they almost did), the Federal
army would have soon been in Richmond, and the South
would have been forced to adopt warfare of this type. If
this could have been accompanied by some move, however qualified, toward gradual emancipation, the prospect
of southern independence would have been bright indeed; but this was, perhaps, beyond the range of southern
possibilities.

After the disaster of Bull Run the Federal forces in the
east were put under the command of George B. McClellan;
his initial task was to restore the morale of the defeated
troops, organize and train an army capable of effective action, and resume the offensive as soon as possible. Mc-
Clellan had been trained as a professional soldier, but for
the past ten years he had been employed in railroad man-

agement and had acquired a grasp of administrative detail that most regular soldiers so conspicuously lacked. He also had the capacity, rare in a general, of communicating his personality to the troops and winning their confidence. He had the defects of these merits: He hated to act until every preparation was complete and every precaution taken, he did not like to risk the lives of his soldiers, and there was an element of truth in the criticism that he was never convinced of the political or military wisdom of an all-out offensive. This made him appear overcautious in action. Politically he had the disadvantage of having been a Democrat and opposed to federal interference with slavery; this could be expressed more sympathetically by saying that he did not aim at conquest but at winning the war in a way that would least antagonize the southern people.

The relationship between Lincoln and McClellan has long been a subject of controversy and is likely to remain so. Neither man had any clear concept of the proper relationship between civil and military command; McClellan was tactless and always ready to blame others for mishaps; Lincoln was ignorant of the essentials of large-scale warfare. In common with most other politicians Lincoln was unaware of the complicated planning necessary to move large bodies of troops even when undisturbed, let alone in the presence of the enemy, and was naïve in his understanding of how an offensive should be launched. He would learn, but for the first year his attempts to direct the war had few fortunate results. A good deal of error sprang from trying to satisfy two requirements: to attack Richmond and to defend Washington. As McClellan realized, and as Grant would discover three years later, the best way to attack Richmond was not along the direct line between the two capitals but from the east, and the way to protect Washington was to draw off Confederate troops by pressure from the south. When McClellan decided to launch his main offensive from the Jamestown peninsula, he did so against Lincoln's wishes, and throughout his campaign his pleas for reinforcements were constantly thwarted by the requirement that enough troops should be kept in northern Virginia to protect Washington.

If McClellan had been able to deliver a quick victory, he would have gone down in history as a master of military strategy. Unfortunately the time he demanded for preparation allowed the South to build up strength, and the slow rate of his advance made it possible to anticipate and prepare for his moves. Hindsight suggests that caution was justified: The North could not afford another Bull Run, and even after twelve months the army had much to learn; but McClellan had also the misfortune to confront a master of defensive-offensive warfare, Robert E. Lee, and (thanks to defective intelligence) believed that he was outnumbered. In the Seven Days Battle of 1862 (Mechanicsville, June 26, Gaine's Mill, June 27, Savage Station, June 29, Frayser's Farm, June 30, and Malvern Hill, July 1) McClellan was thrown on to the defensive, and though he avoided defeat by victory at Malvern Hill, his advance was stalled.

In spite of slow progress and a rebuff the position, early in July, was more favorable to Federal fortunes than it would be at any other time for the next two years. In the west there had been some notable successes, with Grant capturing Fort Henry on the Tennessee (February 6), Fort Donelson on the Cumberland (February 16), and snatching victory from defeat in the desperate and bloody battle of Shiloh (April 6–7). Though it took General Henry Halleck an excessively long time to make the next move and capture Corinth, it looked as though Grant was now poised for an advance down the Mississippi Central Railroad. There had also been a number of small but significant Federal successes in amphibious operations against the coast culminating in the capture of Port Royal on the Sea Islands of Carolina and, above all, of New Orleans on April 29. With an increasing number of ships, and control of a growing number of points on the coast, the Federal blockade promised to become highly effective. Southeast of Richmond McClellan had a strong army on the James River, with good supply lines by river and sea. His army was suffering from disease, but McClellan was confident that with more reinforcements (he always wanted more) he could strike south of Richmond at Petersburg. To crown the list of Federal successes the Confederate armored cruiser *Virginia* (formerly the *Merrimack*), operating from Norfolk and creating havoc with unarmored Federal vessels, had been heavily damaged by the *Monitor,* which was the most striking technical innovation of the war. Heavily armored, with little more than an enormous turret showing above the water, and equipped with two powerful guns, the *Monitor* rendered obsolete the wooden and lightly armored warships of the world.

At this stage, therefore, it seemed that the Federals had only to keep up a steady pressure to achieve their military objectives. Lee could use the advantage of interior lines, but his maneuvers would be restricted as long as McClellan was on the James and Federal strength to the north was increasing. The lure of a quick victory brought about a fatal change in Federal plans. Lincoln decided to scrap the Peninsula Campaign, order McClellan back to the Potomac, and transfer the bulk of his force to General John Pope, who was expected to deliver the knockout blow in northern Virginia. Pope had had some success in the west but now found himself suddenly placed in command of a far larger army than that with which he had served, with corps commanders whom he did not know well, and operating in terrain with which he was unfamiliar against Lee and "Stonewall" Jackson (despite the nickname, a master of rapid movement and surprise). In a haze of misunderstandings, and under the impression that he was about to trap Jackson, Pope blundered into demoralizing defeat at the second battle of Bull Run. The situation had now altered dramatically; the peninsula had been evacuated, the army of northern Virginia was disorganized, Great Britain and France were perhaps on the verge of recognizing the Confederacy, and Lee was free to move. He chose to take the offensive by invading Maryland.

In retrospect Lee's decision was a mistake; the risks were too great and the gains too doubtful. The Federal armies and government had committed drastic errors, but there were still large numbers of troops under arms, and nothing was more likely to stimulate their recovery than the invasion of Union territory; nor did western Maryland and southwestern Pennsylvania offer fair promise that sympathizers would rally to the Confederate flag. There is a further, and more interesting, speculation. If in the summer of 1862 the Confederacy had decided to seek peace, the odds would have been in favor of extremely good terms. There were powerful southern armies in the field, only small portions of the South were under Federal control, foreign powers were sympathetic, and the Union was still committed to the limited objectives of the Johnson-Crittenden resolutions. Admittedly Lincoln could hardly negotiate without southern recognition of United States sovereignty, but this could have been a token, and in all else the South was in an excellent position to demand an autonomy little short of independence. And, once this gain had been made, who on the northern side would have risked starting another war when virtual autonomy became real independence? The South could therefore have had autonomy, retained slavery, drawn upon an awakened and vigorous sectional loyalty, and held trump cards in the political game. Peace at this stage would have been very different from peace deferred, as northern society had not yet felt the full impact and impulse of war.

Faced with the desperate situation caused by Lee's threat to Maryland, Lincoln restored McClellan to the command of troops defending the capital; it was not clear whether this included the command of a counteroffensive against Lee, and, in his own words, McClellan "fought the battles of South Mountain and Antietam with a halter around [the] neck," risking court-martial for acting without authority. The battle of Antietam (September 17, 1862) has a dubious place in military annals; it was hardly a Federal victory, opportunities were missed during the action, and Lee was allowed to escape with his shaken army. McClellan was criticized with justice for allowing Lee to withdraw without pursuit, though renewal of attack after a costly engagement is one of the most difficult of military operations and is likely to be successful only when a commander has had time to plan a follow-through with fresh troops ready for action. Though the Federal victory was tactically indecisive, it was of great importance in grand strategy. If the fruits of a year's effort had been thrown away with the abandonment of the peninsula and the disaster of second Bull Run, Antietam did something to restore the balance. It showed that the Union army was still formidable (and likely to grow stronger), it inflicted losses that the Confederacy could ill endure, and it threw Lee back into Virginia on the defensive. It persuaded Great Britain to drop, at least for the time being, the recognition of southern independence. It came too late to prevent serious Republican losses in the fall elections, but it persuaded Lincoln that the time was ripe to give the war a more distinct antislavery character. On September 22 he issued the preliminary proclamation of emancipation, promising a definitive proclamation (if the rebellion had not ceased) on January 1.

On October 26 McClellan began to move his army across the Potomac. Well equipped and with high morale, it was poised (as McClellan claimed) for a decisive advance against Lee's army. At this precise moment McClellan was dismissed from his command, and Ambrose E. Burnside (whom McClellan blamed for failure to press home an attack at Antietam) was appointed in his place. Recrimination between McClellan and Stanton, and his unpopularity with a section of the Republican party, made it difficult for Lincoln to continue with a commander whom he personally disliked and in whose judgment he lacked confidence. Nevertheless, the decision to dismiss McClellan at this juncture was astounding; seven weeks before he had thrown back an invasion, he had the enthusiastic support of his troops (who greeted his dismissal as though it were a defeat), and the man appointed in his place accepted reluctantly and had done nothing that promised better things.

Burnside continued the advance on an altered plan and though he had numerical superiority over the Confederates, failed to carry out his intention of dividing the southern army and threw his forces against strongly defended positions overlooking Fredericksburg (December 13, 1862). Troops were sacrificed in gallant attacks upon impregnable positions, and though Burnside was able to disengage his army, he lost 12,600 men (1,284 killed) against Lee's loss of about 5,300 (600 killed). Burnside's attempt to renew the offensive in January bogged down in heavy rain and the mud of appalling Virginia roads. Even worse was to follow for the Union armies: Burnside's successor, Joseph E. Hooker, was outmaneuvered by Lee and Jackson and decisively beaten in the prolonged battle of Chancellorsville (May 1–5, 1863). Hooker had been successful in pulling the army together after the debacle of Burnside's command, but in the time of crisis he lost control of the large forces (about 130,000) under his command, and the later phases of the battle were fought largely by corps and divisional commanders without any clear idea of Hooker's intentions or of each other's movements. One whole corps was routed, and the army was saved from complete disaster only by the inspired action of General Alfred Pleasanton, commanding the cavalry, who succeeded in massing artillery to fire at close range into Jackson's advancing division.

With two great victories to his credit Lee once more took

the debatable decision to invade the North. Arguments in favor of doing so were the dangerous developments in the West (where, by contrast with the East, the Federals were winning the war), the worsening supply position in the South, the well-stocked farms of Maryland and Pennsylvania to the north, the possibility of striking at the Pennsylvania iron industry, and the chance of encircling Washington. All this persuaded Lee to move north on the campaign that ended on the fatal field of Gettysburg.

With greater justification than in his dealings with McClellan, Lincoln decided that Hooker's record at Chancellorsville did not recommend him as the man to stop Lee on the offensive. Once more commanders were changed, and George G. Meade (to his own surprise and that of the army) found himself in command on the eve of one of the decisive battles in history. Meade was an unassuming and competent soldier who would rise to the occasion but no further. He was fortunate in being called upon to fight a defensive battle rather than take the offensive against strong positions. Lee's action in accepting battle is difficult to understand; he had not chosen the ground, the initial clash came about by accident rather than design, and he was badly informed of the Federal dispositions and movements. Clearly he could not continue to move north with a powerful Federal army on his flank, but it was probably the time for tactical withdrawal to ground where Meade would be compelled to attack. Even if Lee had succeeded in driving the Union forces from their good but hastily assumed positions at Gettysburg, he would have achieved little. Federal commanders may not have earned his respect, but were capable of pulling an army out of danger, and anything short of total victory would leave a Federal army capable of fighting another day. Lee gambled on total victory, but in three days' furious fighting the Confederates were defeated. The final episode was a desperate attempt to break the Federal center by throwing General

George Pickett's infantry division into a frontal assault, preceded by a tremendous artillery bombardment; but when the attack began, the Federal positions were still intact and their batteries in action. Within a short space of time one of the finest divisions raised by the South had been destroyed.

Like McClellan after Antietam, Meade was not ready to counterattack and allowed Lee to withdraw and (though extremely vulnerable when crossing the Potomac) pull his army safely back into Virginia. Lincoln was bitterly disappointed by the failure of one more attempt to destroy the Confederate army, but in many respects Gettysburg had been decisive. Never again would a large Confederate army be able to take the offensive; northern strength was growing, and southern resources were weakening every day. As the South learned of the failure at Gettysburg, they also learned that Vicksburg, on the Mississippi, had surrendered to Grant's besieging army. Two months later Chattanooga, in eastern Tennessee, a vital railroad junction at the foot of passes leading through into northwestern Georgia, was evacuated by the Confederates.

Grant's encircling movement against Vicksburg was a classic. Unable to advance from the north or carry the commanding heights of Vicksburg from the river, he had taken his army on a great sweep, first to the west of the Mississippi, then crossing the river about thirty miles south of the town. The Federal river gunboats came down the river, running the gauntlet of the Vicksburg batteries, and guarded the crossing. Grant then moved northeast to capture Jackson, Mississippi (May 14), and then due west to attack Vicksburg. His first assault on the town was a costly failure (May 19–22), but after a six-week siege, the Confederate general, John Pemberton, surrendered with thirty thousand men. The whole campaign demonstrated not only Grant's quality as a "fighting general" but also a fatal weakness in Confederate strategic planning. If Joe

E. Johnston's army in eastern Mississippi had been reinforced rather than weakened by demands for the Gettysburg campaign, Vicksburg might have been relieved. A
week later General Nathaniel P. Banks captured Port
Hudson lower down the Mississippi; the whole river was
now open to Union movement, and the Confederacy was
cut in two.

The campaign in Tennessee was slower going. In the fall
of 1862 the Confederate general, Braxton Bragg, had invaded Kentucky but withdrew into Tennessee after the indecisive battle of Perryville. This western campaign closely
paralleled that in the East, with the northward move coin-
ciding with second Bull Run and the withdrawal
following shortly after Antietam. On the last day of the
year a fierce battle was fought at Murfreesboro; the Federal commander, William S. Rosecrans, forced Bragg to
withdraw, but his own army was so severely handled that it
took time to recover. In September, 1863, Rosecrans occupied Chattanooga, but his attempt to move south met
with disaster at Chickamauga, where only the stand by
General George H. Thomas saved the Union army from an
overwhelming defeat. In this instance the Confederate
command made rare use of the advantage of interior lines,
for, unknown to Rosecrans, Bragg had been reinforced by
James Longstreet's corps, moved by rail from the eastern
front by way of Charleston and Atlanta, and arriving just
in time for the battle. Grant was now placed in supreme
command in the West, with Thomas replacing Rosecrans,
and together they planned to clear the Confederates out
of Tennessee. The Union, too, was able to exploit the
advantages of mobility, and two corps were moved from
the eastern front. In the battles for Lookout Mountain and
Missionary Ridge (November 23–25), with some luck and
Confederate mismanagement but mainly due to this concentration of force, the Federal troops dislodged the Confederates from the heights overlooking Chattanooga and

the Tennessee Valley. Virtually the whole of the state was now under Federal control, and the gateway to the deep South was open.

By the end of 1863 the Confederates had lost the war, but the Federals had not won it. The South still had two effective armies—under Lee and Bragg—and numerous scattered units. Most of the lower South was still intact, and after twenty months of struggle in Virginia, the Union controlled only a narrow belt south of the Potomac. The Confederacy could therefore continue for a long period before abandoning the struggle; but again it may be asked whether the wisest course would not have been to admit defeat, cut the losses, and make peace while there was still much to bargain with. Dissension in the South was muted but growing; the economic position was worsening and could not improve; few reserves of manpower remained, and losses exceeded new enlistments. Yet in many ways, whatever the voice of realism might urge, it was harder to accept defeat in January, 1864, than it had been in the summer of 1862. So much effort had been expended, so much emotional capital invested, and so often had it been reiterated that death was better than surrender. For many southerners it was now better to bring down the house in ruins than to occupy it by grace of northern landlords. Moreover, the Confederacy still hoped that opposition in the Union would bring the war to a halt. Even while Gettysburg was being fought, New York was torn apart by riots against the draft, and Clement Vallandigham—the best-known Peace Democrat—was running well for the governorship of Ohio. These events fortified the Confederate hope of winning independence and so prepared the way for eventual and total ruin.

If southern attitudes had become more recalcitrant with defeat, the mood of the dominant party in the North had hardened with the prospect of victory. The state elections occurring in 1863 showed firmer support for the administration, and Vallandigham was decisively defeated in Ohio. Within the Republican party Radicalism had a firmer hold, and Radicals were not interested in a negotiated peace. In December, 1862, Thaddeus Stevens, the Radical leader, had said:

This talk of restoring the Union as it was under the Constitution as it is, is one of the absurdities which I have heard repeated until I have become sick of it. This Union can never be restored as it was. There are many things which render such an event impossible. This Union shall never with my consent be restored under the Constitution as it is with slavery protected by it.[2]

And a month later he added,

The Almighty has made use of the evil passions of the South to so far repeal the obligations which we were under to them, as to open the door to enable us to get rid of that great evil.[3]

He admitted that perhaps a considerable majority of the Republicans did not go so far as he did; "they are coming along behind, and will be up shortly, but they are not yet up."

In the spring of 1864 a speech by Henry Winter Davis, a leading Radical, indicated that Stevens's confidence in the drift of opinion was justified.

Our success will be the overthrow of *all* semblance of government in the rebel States. The Government of the United States is then, in fact, the *only* government existing in those States, and it is there charged to guarantee them republican government.[4]

In other words, what was now required was not merely surrender, not merely abolition, but a willingness to surrender their existing governments, submit to the authority of the United States unfettered by traditional constitutional limitations, and accept whatever form of society the north-

---

[2] *Congressional Globe,* 37th Cong., 3d sess., December 9, 1862.
[3] *Ibid.,* January 9, 1863.
[4] *Ibid.,* 38th Cong., 1st sess., March 22, 1864, Appendix, p. 83.

ern majority might regard as "republican." There was a
widening gap between what the northern majority would
demand and what the South could accept, and the war to
preserve the Union had produced a situation in which the
two sections stood further apart than ever before. Whereas
war had arrested development in southern intellectual life,
it had stimulated in the North a vigorous attempt to formulate new concepts and to examine their implications. It
is in this changing climate that Lincoln's decision for
emancipation must be understood.

It is not known precisely when Lincoln set his mind on
emancipation. On July 13, 1862, when the war had been in
progress just over a year, Seward and Gideon Welles first
heard from Lincoln himself of emancipation as a possibility; on July 22 it was briefly discussed in the Cabinet.[5] Between this date and the issue of the preliminary proclamation on September 23, Horace Greeley's "Prayer of Twenty
Millions," which urged immediate action against slavery,
had been answered by Lincoln on August 22 in the famous
letter claiming that his paramount object was to save the
Union and that emancipation would come only insofar as
it would help or hinder this objective. At the time (and by
many subsequent historians) this was seen as a decided rebuff to antislavery men, as indeed it was to those who di-
vorced slavery from all other issues; but it could also be
read as a hint that emancipation would come under the
guise of military necessity.

Constitutionally Lincoln's power to act was limited. In
common with the great majority of his fellow-countrymen,
he believed that Congress had no power to legislate upon
slavery in the states; nor was he prepared to accept the argument that citizens whose states were in rebellion had forfeited their constitutional rights. Action by sponsoring an
amendment to the Constitution would be lengthy and the

[5] Howard K. Beale (ed.) , *The Diary of Gideon Welles,* Vol. I (New
York: W. W. Norton, 1960) , p. 70. David Donald (ed.) , *Inside Lincoln's Cabinet: The Civil War Diaries of Salmon P. Chase* (New York
and London: Longmans, 1954) , p. 99.

outcome uncertain. This left only action as Commander in Chief acting under the war power and directed against individuals in arms against the United States. The carping criticism directed against the Emancipation Proclamation —that it liberated no slaves and affected only slave-owners over whom the Union had no control—is unfair. Lincoln did everything that could be done within the framework of the Constitution.[6]

The proclamation declared free all slaves in states (or parts of states) still in rebellion against the United States, and for the remainder of the war Lincoln would insist that further action could be taken only by amending the Constitution unless states would end slavery voluntarily. Yet the psychological effects of the proclamation were more important than its legal or practical limitations. In the words of a leading historian of the Civil War:

It cannot be said that Lincoln's proclamations specifically made abolition a war aim of the North. . . . Yet the truth of the matter was that the proclamation became a species of shibboleth; its dramatization in the popular mind was of more effect than its actual provisions. Despite the absence in the proclamation of any express design to produce such a result, it came to be pretty generally assumed that in September of 1862 the war somehow took a new turn, and that thenceforward it was being prosecuted as a war against slavery. It was with this interpretation that the abolitionists favoured the edict, and that those indifferent to or unfriendly to emancipation opposed it.[7]

In 1861 many had hoped that slavery would not survive the war, but few had endorsed a frontal attack upon it; by the summer of 1862 momentum was building up behind

[6] The legality of a proclamation abolishing slavery in Kentucky would certainly have been challenged and could hardly have been sustained in the courts.

[7] James G. Randall and David Donald, *The Civil War and Reconstruction* (2d ed.; Lexington, Mass.: D. C. Heath, 1969), p. 384. Comparison with the earlier edition indicates that this comment is attributable to David Donald.

the demand that some positive step against slavery must be taken; the proclamation took this step and made it official policy. Whatever objections might be made, slavery could hardly hope to survive when the armies of the Union would carry emancipation into the South.

Emancipation left those who adhered strictly to the doctrine of the Johnson-Crittenden resolutions in a minority and turned a breach between moderate and Radical Republicans into a cautious alliance. This understanding was sometimes marred by suspicion on both sides and almost broke down in the approach to the election of 1864, but was nevertheless a new and powerful factor in American political life. Among its more important consequences would be a growing Republican consensus behind the Radical proposals for reconstruction, while providing many abolitionists with grounds for relaxing their demand for an immediate and total end to slavery. Conversely, emancipaton divided the Democrats; the War Democrats accepted emancipation and became, for the time being, almost indistinguishable from Republicans with whom they formed the Union party and fought the election of 1864 with Andrew Johnson, the most prominent War Democrat, as vice-presidential candidate. Other Democrats, however, were driven closer to the peace wing of the party and while still protesting their devotion to the Union, became more firmly committed to peace by negotiation and unequivocal opposition to emancipation and other "unconstitutional" acts of the administration. Thus the proclamation became—like Jackson's veto of the bank charter bill thirty years before and William Jennings Bryan's presidential campaign thirty-three years later—a great rock around which the waters of political life flowed and parted.

Abroad the Emancipation Proclamation had a decided effect. Although prosouthern newspapers and politicians in Britain were quick to point out its limitations in practice, and its lack of social realism toward problems of a biracial society, the public at large saw it as a refutation of the argument that the war was merely a struggle for power. The men who had consistently supported the North, and claimed that slavery was the cause and emancipation the real aim of the war, were now amply justified. The attitude of the British hardly became friendly, but Charles Francis Adams in London was able to detect a distinct change in the atmosphere. In the crisis in Anglo-American relations over the building of Confederate ships in British yards, Adams was helped to take a firm line by the knowledge that public opinion was moving away from southern sympathies and toward the view that the British Government must take no steps to save slavery from extinction.

Lincoln, always sensitive to maintaining a just balance between the political case for preserving the Union and the ideals that would reinforce northern morale, struck a new note in his second annual message to Congress on December 1, 1862. It is essential to see this message and the proclamation in relation to each other, for while the latter was presented as a measure of military necessity, the former proposed practical means for achieving in peace the transition from slavery to freedom. He first drew attention to the vigor with which long-standing evasions of the law against the slave trade had been stopped (in 1862 for the first and only time the captain of a slaver had been convicted and executed). He then recommended amendments to the Constitution that would authorize Congress to compensate any state abolishing slavery before 1901, to compensate loyal owners whose slaves had been freed as a result of war, and to appropriate funds for the voluntary colonization overseas of persons of African descent. Thus the drastic surgery of emancipation by military action was to be superseded, as soon as war ended, by a gradual program that would restore no man to slavery, accomplish the freedom of those who remained, and spread the burden of financial loss over the whole nation. Lincoln's advocacy of colonization has often been criticized but should be studied in this context. The proposal was by no means unrealistic in the light of the huge numbers that had crossed the Atlantic since 1845 from the British Isles and Germany; it did not propose forcible transportation but was based on the hope that many free blacks might find the proposal attractive; it did not contemplate removal of the whole black population, but the relief of pressure in areas where race relations might deteriorate. Lincoln had rejected the naïve argument that with the end of slavery free blacks would move from the North to the South, may have anticipated the great migration from the South to the North, and hoped to direct some of this flow away from northern cities (where race relations were already bitter) to destinations overseas.

Lincoln's argument about voluntary emancipation and colonization was followed by a peroration that demanded recognition of the new character of the war.

We cannot escape history. We, of this Congress and this Administration will be remembered in spite of ourselves. No personal significance, or insignificance, can spare one or another of us. The fiery trial through which we pass, will light us down, in honor or dishonor, to the latest generation. We *say* we are for the Union. The world will not forget that we say this. We know how to save the Union. The world knows that we do know how to save it. We—even *we here*—hold the power and bear the responsibility. In *giving* freedom to the *slave,* we assure freedom to the free—honorable alike in what we give, and what we preserve. We shall nobly save, or meanly lose, the last best hope of earth. Other means may succeed; this could not fail. The way is plain, peaceful, generous, just—a way which, if followed the world will forever applaud, and God must forever bless.

Shorn of its fine rhetoric, this went beyond the earlier thesis of a limited struggle to restore the Union; what was now at stake was the reconstruction of society on principles claimed as traditional but revolutionary in their consequences.

Many years ago Charles Beard propounded the argument that the Civil War was "the second American Revolution." His thesis was marred by a forced marriage with an oversimplified economic interpretation, yet there was truth and vitality in presenting the essence of the struggle as "a social cataclysm in which the capitalists, laborers and farmers of the North and West drove from power in the national government the planting aristocracy of the South." The formulation must, however, be modified. What happened was not a "cataclysm," but a movement from a "constitutional" phase—in which both sides expected accommodation after a show of force—to a "revolutionary" phase in which the northern majority agreed that power must be used to ensure that things would never be the same again. In preceding pages of this book it has been argued that the "capitalists" were by no means unanimous and that the most influential among them had favored compromise to the latest possible moment. Nor is it enough to speak of farmers and laborers without specifying which farmers and which laborers, for there was an internal conflict in northern society that is not amenable to economic explanation, cuts across classes and interests, and can be better explained in ethnic, religious, and intellectual terms. The real thrust behind the "revolution" came from small towns dominated by New England influences and by comparatively recent immigrants from England, Scotland, and Germany. With these qualifications one can accept the thesis of "a second American Revolution" and date the beginning of the revolutionary phase from emancipation and the second annual message. Lincoln took a large side step toward the radical antislavery position, and the northern majority accepted a new definition of war aims.

The apparent caution of Lincoln's move ensured that more conservative elements in his party were not alienated. City magnates, railroad promoters, and industrial entrepreneurs were drawn into the mainstream, so that the Union party became economically more aggressive and socially more conservative; but this did not mean losing the more idealistic elements. Though old abolitionists had long been critical of the dominant attitudes in business and the churches, most of them had never pretended to be social revolutionaries except in the single field of race relations. Garrison had championed other causes but had not attacked the social structure; he was now one of the first to welcome new converts to antislavery who agreed that material betterment could be best advanced by adopting a great moral reform. Nor were the wealthy and educated minority, who had clung to old federalism and deplored universal suffrage, alienated from the new revolution which they interpreted as the triumph of sound principles over the deplorable legacy of Andrew Jackson.

Old antislavery men proclaimed that God, in His mysterious way, was using the evil of secession to destroy the greater evil of slavery; other northern spokesmen saw benefits flowing from the discipline, dedication, and organization of war. Even gentle intellectuals such as Emerson were stirred by the thought that the dull debasement of prewar politics was being dispelled by men who knew what was right and would strive for it. Other representatives of the old Puritan tradition welcomed the return of a disciplined society, in which educated and upright men would mold and monitor the ideals of the nation. Some of the new political leaders, brought to the fore by the Republican surge, were indeed rough-hewn characters of limited education, but they appeared to have a firm grasp upon moral principles; their predecessors might have appeared more gentlemanly, but this had masked their corruption. The most typical representative of this new alliance between politicians and the educated elite was Senator Henry Wilson, of Massachusetts, who was self-taught and self-made, a successful manufacturer, an astute politician, entirely sincere in his undying hostility to the slave power, and subsequently the author of a three-volume history on sectional conflict.

The idea of politics as the instrument of reform was combined with nationalism and had novel implications. At the outset of the war the problem of "loyalty" had presented itself. To *what* was an American loyal? And what tests could be applied to distinguish loyalty from disloyalty? The difficulty was not at first apparent, for a disloyal person was surely and simply one who refused to support the Union and aided its enemies; but there proved to be many gradations. A man could profess loyalty to the Union, with the mental reservation that his Union was not that proclaimed by the Republicans. He could stop far short of giving active aid to the Confederacy while doing a great deal to obstruct the operations of the Federal Government. The traditions of American society sanctified the right to attack government in public, but at what point in war did legitimate criticism become a hindrance to recruitment or an incitement to desert? When did a newspaper move from justifiable though hostile comment to the encouragement of resistance to the laws and agents of the United States? The question of loyalty would become more pressing when problems of reconstruction arose; how could one define and discover "loyalty" in a state whose elected government had been at war with the Union?

Often an immediate solution to these problems had to be found by military commanders on the spot, who were neither lawyers nor political philosophers, and their answers left a long trail of knotty and debatable problems. The government could not abandon its army commanders or fail to recognize a prima facie case when they acted in good faith, but the suspension of habeas corpus, the right of military courts to try civilians, acquiescence in imprisonment without trial, and authority to forbid publication of "disloyal" newspapers left too much to the discretion of generals. Lincoln tried to keep matters under control by using his power as Commander in Chief to issue pardons, order the release of prisoners, and occasionally countermand military instructions, but this was, at best, a clumsy way of meeting a difficult problem. Edward Bates, the Attorney General, was a man of experience and integrity but lacked the industry and imagination to be of more than routine assistance to the President. The suspension of habeas corpus and the introduction of military justice created great dissatisfaction, but a more fundamental cause for complaint was the erratic administration of measures that most men grudgingly supported as necessary for the prosecution of the war.

The most embarrassing incident was the arrest, under military authority, of Clement L. Vallandigham, who was a prominent Ohio Democrat and former congressman. Vallandigham was tried by a military court for making a violent speech against the conduct of the war and emancipation; he was denied the privilege of habeas corpus and sentenced to imprisonment for the duration of the war. Lincoln, alarmed by the prospect of placing behind bars a man with much popularity and many friends, commuted the sentence to deportation over the Confederate lines. The whole incident illustrated the danger of leaving zealous soldiers to make politically explosive decisions. Indeed the whole structure of jurisdiction under the war power rested upon shaky foundations. As early as May, 1861, Chief Justice Taney, in the case of *Ex parte Merryman,* had denied the right of the President to suspend habeas corpus; fortunately for the administration (and indeed for the security of the Union) this remained the opinion of a single judge and the issue was not brought before the Supreme Court until after the war. Then, in the case of *Ex parte Milligan,* the Court decided that trial by a military court was unconstitutional where civil courts were open and unless actual invasion occurred.

Less evident but still of fundamental importance was the question of United States citizenship. In the celebrated or notorious Dred Scott case, Taney had said that a Negro was not a citizen of the United States but had not defined citizenship in a positive way. The argument had said, in effect, that in 1787 Negroes had not been a part of the political people included in the phrase "We the people" and were not therefore "citizens" as understood by the Constitution. Immigrants became citizens by the legal process of naturalization, but there was no means by which a state could confer upon Negroes United States citizenship. But the word "citizen" is not found in the Constitution, and Taney's attempt to define it negatively bristled with contradictions. The Fourteenth Amendment would ultimately define "citizen of the United States" in the broadest possible way as everyone born in the United States or subsequently naturalized, but before that many difficulties would arise in trying to describe the rights belonging to a status that had not been defined. This illustrates many incidental difficulties that arose when men in a federal society began to talk of it as a "nation" and assume that the institutions of unitary states were readily transferable and easily understood.

In spite of the military preoccupations, the Civil War years formed a period of intense legislative activity at Washington. Many laws were direct consequences of the war, but taken as a whole the work of the wartime sessions of Congress opened a new chapter in legislative history that went far beyond measures of immediate necessity. In this the contrast between the Federal and Confederate Congresses is sharp and significant. The many legislative acts of the Thirty-seventh Congress (1861–1863) included such measures of permanent importance as the Homestead Act, the Pacific Railroad Act, the National Banking Act, and the act establishing land grant colleges. The range of legislation can be illustrated from the first session of the Thirty-eighth Congress (December, 1863, to July, 1864). A total of 253 public acts were passed, and one major measure (the Wade-Davis bill) was much discussed but finally vetoed. The acts passed ranged from such useful but minor measures as an appropriation for rebuilding the stables at the White House and authority for the appointment of a warden at a prison in the District of Columbia to the partial repeal of the Fugitive Slave Law; the admission of Colorado, Nevada, and Nebraska; the encouragement of immigration; the ending of discrimination against Negro voters in municipal elections in the District of Columbia; land grants for railroads in Minnesota, Wisconsin, Iowa, and Michigan; amendments to the Pacific Railroad and Homestead acts; a tariff act and an internal duties act (which included the novelty of an income tax); an act establishing a postal money-order system; and an important measure for the regulation of passenger vessels. While a political journalist at Richmond complained that the Confederate Congress could find nothing to occupy its time, the problem at Washington was to find enough time for all the legislative proposals that flooded into the Capitol.[8] In addition to the public acts, there were a huge number of private acts dealing with individual claims and petitions. Thus the measures of Congress in Lincoln's administration touched a wide range of activities, affected the daily lives of individuals and communities to an unprecedented degree, and marks a watershed between the eras of negative and positive government.[9]

[8] The Thirty-seventh Congress (1861–1863) passed 428 public acts, and the Thirty-eighth (1863–1865) 411. This can be compared with 201 passed by the Twenty-seventh Congress (1841–1843), which set a record for the amount of legislation prior to 1860. Legislation continued at a high level after the war; between 1865 and 1881 only one Congress (the Forty-fourth: 1875–1877) passed fewer than 300 public acts; the highest number passed was in the Forty-second Congress (1871–1873) with 531.

[9] Allan Nevins concludes that "the Civil War brought a systematic shift in American society from an unorganized society to a well-organized nation is undoubtedly much too strong a statement. But that the Civil War accentuated and acted as a catalyst to already developing

It was inevitable that war would bring about an enlargement of federal administration, but even so the scale of change is startling. It goes without saying that the Departments of the Army and the Navy grew out of all recognition, but so did departments less directly affected by war. The nerve center of government, the Treasury, increased from 4,025 employees in 1861 to 10,390 in 1865; it had added to its prewar functions the survey of over fifteen hundred national banks, the supervision and receipt of the income tax, the issue of huge sums of paper currency, and the management of an enormously enlarged national debt. The Department of the Interior, which handled a miscellaneous range of duties in 1861 with a payroll of 1,916, increased to 2,564 by 1865; major increases resulted from the Homestead Act, the College Land Grant Act, a growing number of patents, and a greatly enlarged volume of government printing. Surprisingly enough, the Interior was also responsible for the suppression of the slave trade and schemes for colonization of free Negroes. Somehow during the war J. C. G. Kennedy, superintendent of the census whose bureau was also in the Department of the Interior, managed to compile from the census of 1860 the fullest and most accurate reports ever made. The Post Office introduced some notable improvements in addition to improvising mail services for the armies in the field; free delivery of letters in cities was introduced in 1863, postal money orders in 1864, and throughout the war there were steady improvements in the methods of contracting with private railroads and steamships for the carriage of mails. The rapid development of a telegraph system was in private hands, but in November, 1861, the army set up its own organization for military telegraphs. There are difficulties

local tendencies towards organization there can be no doubt." *The War for the Union: The Organized War* (New York: Charles Scribner's Sons, 1971), p. 272.

in making exact estimates of the number of civilian employees of government, but a good authority suggests an increase from 40,651 in 1861 to about 195,000 in 1865.[10]

Too little attention has been paid to the part played by military administration during the war. Of the quartermaster general, Montgomery Meigs, Allan Nevins observes that "in any just view of the Civil War, he should stand as one of the central figures, although he was long almost totally ignored because few men had any clear understanding of the crushing load of pressures on his time and strength." [11] He had to estimate accurately what supplies and clothing would be required, set standards, decide who should share contracts, and thus indirectly influence the methods of manufacture. He was responsible for horses and wagons; sometimes he had to take personal responsibility (beyond the limits of his authority) for seeing that supply points were established to meet sudden changes in the fortunes of war; frequently and caustically he had to draw the attention of commanders in the field to the fact that they squandered supplies, carried too much impedimenta, or failed to economize in the use of wagons. Above all, he had to see that the troops in the field had enough food. By the end of the war the Union army was the best-clothed, best-shod, and best-fed army ever to take the field. If they were sometimes outfought by the ragged and poorly nourished Confederate soldiers, this does not mean that the administrative services should be denigrated. By 1865 the capacity of the Federal army to maintain this high standard month after month, for years if need be, and so

[10] P. P. Van Riper and Keith A. Sutherland, "The Northern Civil Service, 1861–1865," *Civil War History*, XI (December, 1965), 354–358. *Historical Statistics of the United States* (Washington, D.C.: U.S. Government Printing Office, 1960) gives 36,672 in 1861, rising to 51,020 in 1871; the number employed in Washington rose from 2,199 to 6,222. This indicates that the reduction at the end of the war was proportionately less in Washington than in services outside the federal capital.
[11] Nevins, pp. 289–290.

long as there were men to fight and the will to continue, was a powerful factor in northern morale. Another man who made decisive contributions to Union success was Herman Haupt, who was appointed to direct military railroads in the spring of 1862.

In the technology of land warfare there was surprisingly little advance. In 1861 breech-loading rifles and guns were already known, and during the summer of that year the government was offered the first modern machine gun, nicknamed (by Lincoln) the "coffee mill" gun. The government had all the resources of "Yankee ingenuity" to call upon, and people who had developed the cotton gin, the mechanical reaper, and the sewing machine would hardly have been defeated by technical obstacles. A Union army equipped with breech-loading rifles, improved artillery, and repeating guns would have made short work of the war, but ingrained military conservatism saved the Confederate army from early humiliation in spite of Lincoln's personal interest in the adoption of new weapons. General James Ripley, chief of the ordnance, carries a major responsibility for preventing the adoption of new weapons, but he was merely the most influential exponent of the view that experiments should not be encouraged until they had been tested in combat and one failure was usually sufficient to terminate a trial. A few regiments of sharpshooters were armed with breechloaders and performed with deadly effect, but for most troops the Ordnance Bureau preferred to stick to muzzle-loaders which were available and comparatively cheap. It is difficult to realize that the great infantry battles of the war were fought by men who took a minute to load each round. The "coffee mill" gun was given a few trials in the field but (as might be expected with an intricate weapon) developed some faults, and no further orders were placed. Richard J. Gatling could never obtain a fair trial for his more efficient weapon. Lincoln had a sound instinct for effective novelty but neither the knowledge to press his opinion against the so-called experts nor the time to give personal attention to the needs of inventors. On this, as on many other occasions, military experience was able to defeat civilian enthusiasm. General Ripley performed excellent service in equipping the Union army with weapons that were at least the equal of those available to the Confederacy, but effectively prevented the North from deriving real advantages from mechanical ingenuity.

Much controversy has gone into discussion of the war's economic consequences. It was once textbook orthodoxy that the Civil War gave a stimulus to industrialization, which started the country along the road to economic revolution. Recently economic historians have come to treat the war as an incident—perhaps even a setback—in the Industrial Revolution that had begun years before. Statistics show that the decade after 1850 was a period of rapid growth. The census of 1880 estimated an increase in the gross value of manufactures of 85.05 percent between 1850 and 1860, of 79.54 percent in the next ten years, and of 58.59 percent from 1870 to 1880. The net value (after deducting the cost of raw materials) was 84.13 percent, 63.31 percent, and 41.40 percent respectively. This is certainly enough to establish that 1850 to 1860 were years of striking growth and that (as one might predict) the maturing of the economy saw deceleration in the rate of increase. No one would now suggest that industrialization began with the Civil War. Much emphasis has been laid on the figures for the production of pig iron as an index of industrial activity. This reached a peak in 1860 at 920,000 tons, fell in 1861, and recovered slightly in 1862; but in 1863 the figure was higher than in any previous year, and in 1864 it was higher still (948,000 and 1,136,000 tons). A reasonable deduction seems to be that production was restricted in the 1857–1858 depression, began to recover in 1859, and hit a new high peak in 1860. With the coming of war there was a temporary dislocation of civilian business, and the small but significant production of Virginia and Tennessee was lost. By 1863 the northern production had recovered and moved to a new high level; there was a minor fall in 1865 (probably caused by the shift from military to civilian markets), and thereafter iron production moved upward again. If there is little in these figures to suggest a sudden upsurge in industrial activity, there is equally little evidence of retardation.

Production figures (even when of unimpeachable accuracy) do not tell the whole story. One wants to know so much more about organization, markets, and investment. The second half of the war saw prosperity, speculation, and much entrepreneurial innovation. A good deal of the activity was feverish and unsound and led to much moralizing among gentlemen of the old school; but unlike other speculative booms, it led to no panic or spectacular crash. This suggests that there was some solid ground for optimism. Wartime demand was most marked in consumer industries, and most armaments were too primitive to stimulate heavy industry; in some cases (e.g., iron) war demand may not have offset the fall in civilian activity. The experience of subsequent years suggests, however, that a great deal of profitable long-term investment went on alongside the rush for quick takings and profitable government contracts. In the army and civilian government service, a great many Americans had an unprecedented opportunity for studying large-scale administration, and there is a long list of high-ranking officers who subsequently applied their experience to the problems of private business.

It is difficult to assess the part played by wartime financial measures. In 1862 the North faced a situation that was alarming to contemporaries but less so in retrospect. The Union was rich in resources, but it was desperately short of hard cash. The export of cotton had formerly played a vital part in earning foreign currency, and though the export of wheat was increasing, the purchase of arms and supplies abroad created a heavily adverse balance of payments. At the same time the government was borrowing heavily and forced to offer high rates of interest. Somewhat reluctantly Salmon P. Chase at the Treasury was forced to meet the deficiency by issuing inconvertible paper dollars (greenbacks). Inevitably these depreciated in value, and businessmen were embarrassed by the continuing demand for gold in international transactions. As the war progressed, demand plus the large quantity of paper money in circulation raised prices but made it comparatively easy to borrow. Thus the exigencies of war had brought a victory for easy money and alarmed the orthodox by threats of inflation. Farmers, with splendid prospects at home and a growing export market, borrowed to great advantage; so did many small entrepreneurs. People on fixed incomes (a comparatively small element) did badly, and wages lagged behind prices; but the demand for skilled labor meant that the main burden of falling real wages was carried by the unskilled. As in other wars, the greatest sufferers from depreciation were the soldiers, whose pay rose but slowly and was often months in arrears.

Wisely the government adopted one great stabilizing measure that helped to control a potentially explosive currency situation. The National Banking Act of 1863 aimed at the kind of stability desired by old Whigs but without incorporating a single central bank. The intention was to give national charters to local banks with the right to issue notes secured by a deposit of government bonds with the Comptroller of the Currency. The new system made little headway at first and was amended in 1864 and 1865 but became firmly established after the war. In 1865 a heavy tax was imposed upon notes issued by state banks, and this entrenched the national banks with the exclusive right to issue universally acceptable paper currency of uniform value.

Thus the Civil War occupies an ambiguous place in economic history. For those who look first for quantifiable evidence it takes its place in the general expansion of the

American economy rather than as the cause of movement in new directions, and some would add to this the suggestion that the diversion of production from normal channels to war demand, and the fall in long-term investment due to the attraction of government bonds, temporarily interrupted the process of steady growth. On the other hand, historians who stress business behavior may claim that the Civil War introduced many to experience in large-scale operations, encouraged innovation, and provided entrepreneurs with the cheap money necessary for expansion. It was a golden age for the small entrepreneur, but also the period during which the foundations for many large fortunes were laid. Wherever the balance of argument is struck, however, one fact of outstanding importance remains: Engaged in a terrible civil war, with enemies at home and abroad predicting economic ruin, northern society displayed a vigor that was not thwarted by military disappointment. It is difficult to calculate imponderables, but the effect of prosperity cannot be ignored; at least one can venture the opinion that depression and deprivation would have dealt a fatal blow to morale, when even with prosperity the issue was sometimes in doubt.

If confidence and growing conviction of the need for fundamental change characterized the dominant party, their views were not unchallenged. Some Democrats had never accepted the necessity for war, and their doubts increased as more radical consequences were forecast. The number of active southern sympathizers was very small, but large numbers of anxious men who loved the Union grew increasingly unhappy as the war progressed. The view of the "loyal opposition" was that the Union must be preserved, that the secessionists were responsible for the war, but that the political objective should be to seek a favorable moment for negotiation. Democratic leaders did not forget that until the disastrous events of 1860, they had cooperated with southern colleagues in a national party and were more confident than Republicans that equitable terms could be arranged if representative men could be brought to the negotiating table. They deplored the suspension of habeas corpus and the use of military courts, attacked conscription, and above all opposed emancipation on both social and constitutional grounds. This was the attitude of such prominent Democrats as Horatio Seymour, who became governor of New York in 1862, and S. S. Cox, of Ohio, whose wit and urbanity made him a popular member of the House even among Republicans who detested his views. The Democrats made substantial gains in the elections of 1862 and looked forward with some confidence to 1864, when the greatest efforts had failed to produce military victory, conscription was unpopular, and emancipation stimulated racial prejudice.

The "loyal opposition" was, however, handicapped by a number of circumstances. Electoral success would depend upon winning over former Constitutional Unionists, winning back the War Democrats, and keeping their fair share of the soldiers' vote. None of this was likely to be achieved if their association with the "disloyal" was too blatant and if they denigrated too openly the efforts of the fighting men. There was also a more fundamental difficulty in the Democratic position. Their best hope lay in developing underlying popular protest against the war, but their conservatism had little to offer to the poor, and the Republicans had firmly established themselves as the champions of skilled labor and small business. Thus the Democratic leaders were forced to thread their way through a maze of difficulties, and circumstances made it harder than usual to bind together the normal American alliance of dissimilar groups. In time of war the opportunities for equivocation were greatly diminished, and ultimately the only issue was whether the war should go on to total victory or stop with its aims unfulfilled. If there had been any indication that terms short of independence would be accepted in the South, the task of the Democrats would have been easier; but no official spokesman of the Confederacy would ever give this essential aid to the northern peace movement. The Peace Democrats were left in the weak position of urging that negotiation ought to be tried without any assurance that it would succeed, while their hope of Unionist support made it impracticable to join with the extreme dissenters in advocating the recognition of southern independence.

Under these circumstances it is not surprising that Democrats found themselves embarrassed by would-be friends. The activities of avowed Confederate sympathizers, or Copperheads, in the Midwest encouraged Republicans to put all but their War Democrat allies into this category. The most ardent Peace Democrat of the Midwest, Clement Vallandigham, was indiscreet and unwisely emphatic in his attacks; if he supported the Union (as he said he did), it was a very different Union from that which Republicans were fighting to preserve. The Democrats had an excellent chance of winning the governorship of Ohio in 1863, but their nomination of Vallandigham alienated Unionists of all types and lost the soldiers' vote.

More acutely embarrassing for the "loyal opposition" were the draft riots that convulsed New York for five days in July, 1863. In a favorable light the riots could be seen as a spontaneous protest by the depressed and mainly Irish poor against the demands of the Anglo-Saxon and Protestant upper class. Governor Seymour maintained that the draft quotas were unfairly high in predominantly poor and Democratic wards and that the methods by which the rich could avoid service were many and questionable. Protest first concentrated upon the draft, the police, and armories; but then, in the words of a contemporary, "Having stopped the draft in two districts, sacked and set on fire nearly a score of houses, and half-killed as many men, it now, impelled by a strange logic, sought to destroy the Colored Orphan Asylum on Fifth Avenue." [12] From this time onward the riots became antiblack rather than antidraft, though there was also an unsuccessful attack on the office of the New York *Tribune*. Negro hunting became a sport, and

a sight of one in the streets would call forth a halloo, as when a fox breaks cover, and away would dash half a dozen men in pursuit. Sometimes a whole crowd streamed after with shouts and curses, that struck deadly terror to the heart of the fugitive. If taken, he was pounded to death at once; if he escaped into a negro house for safety it was set on fire, and the inmates made to share a common fate. Deeds were done and sights witnessed that one would not have dreamed of, except among savage tribes. [13]

By the second day rioting had taken hold in several parts of the city, and the attacks were directed against any buildings or individuals associated, however indirectly, with the army, upper-class respectability, Republicanism, or Negroes. Troops were called in, but on the third day a vast crowd moved down Eighth Avenue sacking houses and hanging Negroes from lampposts, and on First Avenue the troops opened deadly fire on the crowd. On the fourth day there were further confrontations between soldiers and the crowd, with the troops firing cannister shot into the mob on Second Avenue. A storm in the evening helped to keep people off the streets, and the fifth day saw the restoration of something approaching order as large numbers of troops arrived from the battlefields of Pennsylvania.

In Philadelphia antiwar feeling did not degenerate into similar violence, but the degree of opposition was, nevertheless, remarkable. Here the Democrats included many of the city's social elite, with strong prewar southern associations. In March, 1863, a new opposition newspaper, *The*

---

[12] Joel Tyler Headley, *The Great Riots of New York 1712 to 1873* (New York: 1873; new ed., Dover, 1971) , p. 169.

[13] *Ibid.*, p. 207.

Age, was launched with the avowed "national" aim of re-union with southern Democrats. The Emancipation Proclamation was vigorously attacked as a wretched error that left the South with "no other choice but war to the knife." [14] A large meeting publicly condemned the treatment of Vallandigham and passed peace resolutions without reference to preservation of the Union, and there was a poor response in June, 1863, to a call for local volunteers when Lee's army moved into Pennsylvania. At the end of the year prominent Philadelphians were quoting with approval the proslavery arguments drawn from the Bible, attacked the employment of Negro troops, and continued to condemn conscription. Unlike New York there was little violence against Negroes, and popular protest was directed against the dissenting Democrats. The Republicans, campaigning in Pennsylvania as the People's party, claimed to lead a revolt against the Democratic establishment and used the antiwar movement to build the popular foundations for postwar Republican ascendancy.

The antiwar protest reached its high-water mark in 1863. Thereafter there was a reaction against negrophobia, and the prospect of victory inspired the Republicans to greater efforts. It would be possible to illustrate the movement of opinion in many ways, but of all the symptoms of change those in Maryland were most striking. Nowhere had the Constitutional Unionists been stronger, resistance to war more open, and free Negroes more unpopular. In 1860 Lincoln received a tiny vote, and in 1861 Union troops were attacked in the streets of Baltimore. Thereafter Republicans multiplied but had little expectation of carrying the state until Democratic defeatism caused many Unionists to join them early in 1864; even then fierce rivalry continued between the conservative and radical elements. In October, 1864, Maryland voted on a new con-

14 Quoted in William Dusinbeere, *Civil War Issues in Pennsylvania* (Philadelphia: University of Pennsylvania Press, 1965), p. 157.

stitution that included emancipation. Residents voted to reject by a majority of about 2,000 (29,536–27,541); the soldier vote was about ten to one in favor and gave an affirmative majority of 375.[15] If Marylanders serving in the Confederate forces had voted, slavery would, of course, have been preserved. The slenderness of the victory for emancipation was striking; but so was the development of an antislavery movement in this vital border state.

These reflections throw some doubt upon the oft-repeated assertion that the Democrats would have won in 1864 but for military successes in the fall. Whatever alarms might be sounded by experienced political observers, it is likely that the pendulum was swinging, from the summer of 1863, in favor of emancipation and total victory. Radical attempts to deprive Lincoln of renomination shook the pendulum but did not alter its direction. The basic contradiction of the Democrats was displayed in the nomination of McClellan (who favored continuation of the war until the Union was safe) and the adoption of a platform that proclaimed that the war was a failure, advocated a negotiated settlement, and did not exclude the possibility of southern independence. Against this platform the Union alliance of Republicans, War Democrats, and former Constitutional Unionists swept the board in an overwhelming victory in 1864. The old Senate had stood at 36 Republicans, 9 Democrats, and 5 Unionists; the Democrats gained one seat, but (with two additional senators from Nevada) the new Senate would consist of 42 Unionists and 10 Democrats. The House, which had stood at 102 Republicans, 75 Democrats, and 9 others, became 149 Unionists and 42

[15] On the first return the Maryland soldiers voted 1,160–268 for emancipation, but a large number of votes were disallowed on technical grounds. Lincoln took a keen interest in the outcome, and his letters on the subject indicate a shift away from gradualism. On March 17, 1864, he wrote, "It need not be a secret that I wish success to emancipation in Maryland." He also allowed emancipationists to say that he preferred abolition to any form of gradual emancipation.

Democrats. It is difficult to believe that a landslide of this magnitude could have been brought about in a few weeks. Lincoln's popular majority was about 400,000 out of 4,000,000, and though this does indicate the dimensions of dissent, a 10-percent majority would be regarded as overwhelming in twentieth-century elections.

The best comment on 1864 came from Lincoln himself:

The election, along with its incidental, and undesirable strife, has done good too. It has demonstrated that a people's government can sustain a national election, in the midst of a great civil war. Until now it has not been known to the world that this was a possibility.

This election, fought in the midst of war, therefore vindicated American confidence in their democratic system; it was also the death knell to all Confederate hopes. The vote of 1864 was a decision to fight to the end and could also be read as an announcement to the world that slavery would not be allowed to survive.

The determination in the North to fight until unconditional surrender, and in the South to continue in the face of predictable ruin, distinguished the Civil War from all preceding conflicts. No ruler of the *ancien régime* would have continued a costly war when victory could be secured by negotiation, nor would the loser have risked the destruction of his army, the loss of his capital, and the humiliation of foreign occupation; but these calculations no longer applied in a people's war. Both Lincoln and Jefferson Davis were representatives rather than rulers, and neither felt free to depart from the mandate received from their people. In 1861 Lincoln had believed that he was obliged to preserve the Union because he was the constitutionally elected chief executive; in 1864 he was equally certain that he had no discretionary power to end the war without winning the whole game. Jefferson Davis did not get the same formal authority to fight on—and there were peace movements in the South as in the North—but he had no authority to bargain away southern independence. On both sides majorities were committed to objectives that could lead only to total success or total failure. The Civil War was "a people's contest" in which vast numbers had come to believe that fundamental political, social, and moral issues were at stake. It could not stop inconclusively, because war was no longer aiming to satisfy dynastic claims, control strategically important points, or secure colonial commerce. War had assumed a different character, and this alone explains its continuation—with appalling losses on both sides—long after the old rules would have suggested a peace dictated by the victor that permitted the loser to retain self-respect.

The eastern front was comparatively quiet for a long period after Gettysburg, and activity did not resume until the spring of 1864 when Grant was appointed to supreme command of the Union armies with the rank of lieutenant general. The problem of command had been a vexing one since the beginning of the war. Lincoln's constitutional responsibility as Commander in Chief was clear, but he rightly considered his function to be political rather than military. Halleck, brought to Washington to direct operations, had proved a disappointment; knowledgeable, painstaking, reluctant to commit himself except in small matters, he was essentially a good administrator rather than a strategist or leader. Stanton was a hard-driving organizer, but it was not the function of the Secretary of War to direct military operations. Lincoln told Grant in their first interview that "all he wanted or had ever wanted was someone who would take the responsibility and act, and call on him for the assistance needed, pledging himself to use all the power of the government in rendering such assistance." Grant respected Lincoln but had a poor opinion of his strategic judgment and was warned by Halleck and Stanton that the President was liable to talk too freely; Grant was prepared to "take the responsibility" and divulged his plans to no one. His overall plan was simple. He would launch two major offensives, one against Lee in Virginia and the other from the positions won in Tennessee against the Confederate forces in Georgia. At the same time there would be two secondary drives, one in the Shenandoah Valley and the other advancing from the coast up the south bank of the James; both were aimed to prevent Lee from concentrating his forces and eventually to encircle the whole Confederate army. In the far South a combined operation was launched against Mobile, and there were to be minor offensives and cavalry raids at other points. Much to Grant's annoyance, the army under General Banks in Louisiana had already been detached to advance up the Red River, in the mistaken belief that Texas could be restored to the Union by a comparatively minor operation.

Grant thought of eliminating armies rather than capturing places. In Virginia he hoped to destroy the Confederate army before Lee could withdraw to the defenses of Richmond, and to do so by drawing the enemy into a position of confrontation, outflanking to the left, and choosing the moment to attack when he could catch Lee with his back to a river. In Georgia Sherman was instructed to seek out and engage the Confederate army under Joe E. Johnston, to destroy if possible and at least to prevent troops being sent to reinforce Lee. The developments leading to the march through Georgia were planned by Sherman and accepted only reluctantly by Grant.

Grant intended to move himself with the Army of the Potomac, which was already commanded by the experienced Meade, victor of Gettysburg. Grant refused Meade's offer to stand aside in favor of someone who had already worked closely with him and tried to operate a kind of double-headed command, issuing all his orders through Meade. The arrangement was not a happy one. Meade was self-effacing and had a strong sense of duty, but he was irascible with his subordinates and often had difficulty in concealing his disapproval of some of Grant's decisions, while he himself, though the commander of an army in the field, could not make a major decision without the consent of the General in Chief. To make matters more complicated, some troops in the campaign did not belong to the Army of the Potomac and came under Grant's direct command. It was good fortune rather than good management that prevented this clumsy command structure from having serious consequences.

Grant's qualities as a general have always been controversial. Everyone concedes his determination and pertinacity. Most, too, agree that he was at his best in moments of crisis. One of his staff officers later described the way in which he received the news that one Union corps appeared to have collapsed:

It was in just such emergencies that General Grant was always at his best. Without a change of a muscle of his face, or the slightest alteration in the tone of his voice, he quietly interrogated the officers who brought the reports; then, sifting out the truth from the mass of exaggeration, he gave directions for relieving the situation with the marvellous rapidity which was always characteristic of him when directing movements in the face of the enemy.[16]

The boldness with which he tackled the offensive commended him to the Washington government, and it was a tonic for the army to have a commander who did not begin with a sense of inferiority when faced by Lee; but determination to achieve his objectives led him to underrate Lee's marvelous insight into his opponent's intentions and to rely too much on his own strategic grasp and weight of numbers. On the other hand, he was resilient and kept an extraordinarily close hold on events on the battlefield; other commanders might not always execute the tasks he

[16] Horace Porter, *Campaigning with Grant* (New York: 1897), p. 68, quoted in Paul M. Angle and Earl Schenck Miers, *Tragic Years 1860–1865*, Vol. II (New York: Simon & Schuster, 1960), p. 794.

set them, but he never lost control and was able to extricate his troops or to adopt alternative plans as the needs arose. Against these qualities one must set the terrible losses suffered by the Union forces in Virginia.

Grant's greatest asset as a general was his instinctive understanding of modern warfare. The kind of campaign that he waged was logical in a "people's war" with total victory as its objective. Weight of numbers, ample reserves, industrial strength, and a measure of ideological commitment made repeated blows possible, and as there could be no negotiated peace, attack must be maintained until unconditional surrender was the only course open to the enemy. No doubt Grant would have relished a brilliant victory, but short of this, he kept up the kind of pressure that was possible only when men believed that fundamental principles were at stake.[17]

Moving south toward Richmond, Grant swung to the east between Chancellorsville and Fredericksburg, hoping that the inhospitable area known as the Wilderness would protect his flank. This maneuver was too transparent to deceive Lee, who attacked and brought the Union forces to battle in this forest of stunted trees, often impassable undergrowth, few clearings, and fewer roads. Incidentally, it was an area in which the Union preponderance in artillery was of small advantage. The losses on both sides in the battle of the Wilderness (May 5–6) were terrible, but Lee failed in his major objective of forcing the Federals to abandon their flanking movement. Instead, Grant moved his army quickly south and east but not quite fast enough to forestall Lee, who blocked him again in the five-day bat-

[17] According to Adam Badeau, who perhaps knew Grant better than any other man, "He often explained to those in his confidence that he did not expect by a single effort to overthrow the fabric [of the Confederacy]; it was too firmly established; its leaders too able and too desperate, its soldiers too experienced and gallant for this; but persistent and repeated attacks in every quarter . . . would finally complete the ruin of the so-called Confederacy." *Military History of U. S. Grant* (New York: 1881), p. 131.

tle of Spotsylvania (May 8–12). It was at this point that Grant sent his famous message to Halleck, "I propose to fight it out along this line if it takes all summer." In fact, Grant did not mean to settle down to fight on a line but to continue his wide flanking movement if he failed to break Lee. On June 1–3 he thought that an opportunity presented itself at Cold Harbor (perhaps for the last time before Lee was safe behind the defenses of Richmond) and attacked in force with devastating losses and without success. For a moment it looked as though Cold Harbor was another Chancellorsville, but if Lee had preserved his army and countered every move by Grant, he had not prevented the movement to the south. He had hoped to keep Grant north of the James River, and in this he failed; having crossed the river, Grant could force the withdrawal of Confederate forces blocking the minor offensive (mismanaged by B. F. Butler) south of the river and move against the vital road and rail center of Petersburg. Nevertheless, the great hammer blow did not destroy Lee's army, the first assault on Petersburg failed, and the Federal army was committed to a nine months' siege; but in spite of all, the Confederacy was now in a precarious position. There were few reserves, a powerful Federal army was south of Richmond based on good river communications, and new troops were replacing their losses.

In the month's fighting that began in the Wilderness, the Federal army lost, killed or wounded, about 60,000, or approximately the number in Lee's army at the outset of the campaign. Included among these losses were over 14,000 out of some 100,000 killed or wounded in the Wilderness, 6,000 out of 66,000 at Spotsylvania, and 12,000 out of 108,000 at Cold Harbor. A further 8,000 were lost in the attack on Petersburg. The Confederate losses are less certainly known but were probably between 25,000 and 30,000 from the Wilderness to Cold Harbor. The total casualties suffered by both armies were therefore not far short of 100,000 in the six weeks from the Wilderness to Petersburg.

At this cost Grant had kept control of the situation and placed his army in a good strategic position; Lee, by his skill in defense, had prolonged the war and won for the Confederacy a further nine months of waning strength.

While Grant menaced Petersburg, the Confederates showed themselves still capable of dramatic strokes in the more traditional style of warfare. At the beginning of July General Jubal Early moved from the Shenandoah Valley with about 10,0000 troops and threatened Washington, where the defense works were good but the troops few, and succeeded in isolating the principal Federal force on Maryland Heights. The situation was partly saved by energetic action on the part of General Lew Wallace at Baltimore, who quickly gathered together a small force to defend the Monocacy River and an important junction on the Baltimore and Ohio Railroad. The Federals were heavily outnumbered and after a tough fight (July 9) were forced to withdraw, but the short time gained was enough to allow seasoned reinforcements from Virginia to take up positions in Washington. As Grant wrote in his memoirs:

If Early had been but one day earlier, he might have entered the capital. . . . General Wallace contributed on this occasion, by the defeat of the troops under him, a greater benefit to the cause than often falls to the lot of a commander . . . to render by means of a victory.[18]

Indeed, the repercussions might have been momentous, for it is difficult to know how Lincoln's presidential campaign, already handicapped by the terrible losses in the Virginia military campaign, would have fared if the Confederates had occupied Washington, even for a short period. On July 12, however, Early, with the force available for assault numbering not more than 8,000, received confirmed reports that Federal troops were now arriving in great num-

---

[18] *Personal Memoirs of U. S. Grant* (New York: 1885; new ed., 1895), p. 522. General Lew Wallace would later earn fame in another field: as the author of *Ben Hur*.

bers and reluctantly decided to abandon the attempt. He succeeded in evading all Federal attempts at pursuit and escaped with prisoners, livestock, and loot.

To the south Sherman was fighting a campaign that would eventually yield spectacular results. His advance into Georgia was timed to coincide with Grant's offensive, and with almost 100,000 men he moved against 50,000 Confederates under General Johnston. The Federal advance was slow but steady going. Johnston chose to avoid major battles, withdraw in the face of superior numbers, and keep his army intact. Unfortunately for the Confederates continued withdrawal lowered morale, the cumulative losses from rearguard actions, stragglers, and desertion were considerable, while Federal advance into the heart of the Confederacy had damaging political repercussions. By the middle of July, with Sherman threatening Atlanta, Jefferson Davis decided to replace Johnston by the more aggressive John Bell Hood. Nevertheless, Hood was forced to abandon the city, and on September 3 Sherman was able to telegraph Washington, "Atlanta is ours and fairly won." The news came at an opportune moment for the fall elections.

Hood believed that he could break up the Federal offensive by leaving Sherman in Atlanta and striking north along his lines of communication and into Tennessee. At the same time Sherman was intent upon marching through Georgia and living off the country until he could reopen communications with the sea. Sherman's reasoning was partly strategic, for he did not wish to exhaust half of his army in trying to defend the communications between Atlanta and Chattanooga, and partly political, for he was convinced that the civilian population of the South must be made to feel the weight and devastation of war. In this he showed an understanding of the nature of modern war and earned a contemporary reputation for pointless destruction.

From Atlanta, therefore, the two principal armies moved off in opposite directions: Hood toward Tennessee and Sherman toward Savannah. One of Sherman's corps commanders subsequently described the systematic destruction: "All that was of a public nature in Atlanta which could aid the enemy was destroyed. Wrecked engines, bent and twisted iron rails, blackened and lonesome chimneys saddened the hearts of the few peaceful citizens who remained there." [19] In the march through Georgia Sherman depended on foragers, under orders but acting independently, to bring in provisions. Mills, railroads, and sometimes houses were deliberately destroyed. The foragers were expected to observe military discipline and confine their depredations to what was needed by the army, but often exceeded their instructions. Around the fringes of the army the authorized "bummers" were supplemented by deserters from both armies and escaped criminals; everywhere normal respect for property disappeared, for there was no law to observe. Another feature, often grotesque in its incidents, was the flood of fugitive slaves who came asking for protection, hampering troop movements, creating much embarrassment, and forming a long straggling rear guard behind the advancing army. These by-products of Sherman's march startled contemporaries and had consequences that were sometimes tragic and often pathetic; but, like Grant's massive assault, Sherman's style of warfare was the logical consequence of a people's war aimed at the subjugation of a rival society. Sherman, himself a humane and intelligent man, merely faced squarely the question whether the "rules of war" should restrain actions likely to hasten victory and, like others since, justified the means by the end.

In the last month of 1864 Hood was defeated by George H. Thomas at Nashville in the only major battle of the war in which a Confederate army was completely broken and disorganized. In the same month Sherman occupied Savannah. A Confederate army under Johnston still barred his

[19] O. O. Howard, "Sherman's Advance from Atlanta," *Battles and Leaders of the Civil War,* ed. Robert U. Johnson and Clarence C. Buel, Vol. IV (New York: 1887; reprint, Thomas Yoseloff, 1956) , p. 663.

way north, but the writing on the wall was clear for the Confederacy. Delaying actions might prolong the war, but Federal victory had become only a matter of time; if white recruitment in the North faltered, thousands of Negro troops were available for service and beginning to acquit themselves well in action. With Republican successes in the elections the Democratic minority in the lame-duck session of the Thirty-eighth Congress could no longer offer serious criticism of the administration. The North was prosperous, and inflation, though significant, was kept within bounds. Once more the Confederacy had the choice between admitting defeat and continuing a struggle that could only bring further ruin and distress.

Under these circumstances Jefferson Davis agreed to some informal explorations, and three men who had been held in high respect in prewar Washington—Alexander H. Stephens, R. M. T. Hunter, and former Supreme Court justice J. A. Campbell—crossed the Union lines as peace commissioners. Lincoln laid down four indispensable conditions: the restoration of national authority, no "receding by the Executive of the United States on the slavery question," no cessation of hostilities short of an end to the war, and the disbandment of all forces hostile to the United States. The Confederate commissioners neither accepted nor rejected these terms, but Jefferson Davis refused them unequivocally. After four years, and facing imminent defeat, Davis expected, as a preliminary to negotiation, the recognition of southern independence that the war had been fought to deny.

At the beginning of April, Lee found it necessary to abandon Petersburg and advised the evacuation of Richmond. On April 4 President Lincoln was in Richmond, and on the tenth Lee—surrounded, short of rations, and cut off from his supplies—surrendered to Grant at Appomattox Court House. On April 18 Johnston surrendered to Sherman. The Civil War was virtually at an end, but four days earlier the man to whom most credit was due, and whose experience and charity the nation now most needed, had been assassinated at Ford's Theater in Washington.

In its four years the Civil War had produced fundamental changes in American society and even in the American character. It had affected everyone and remains the pivot in the history of the nation. It had ruined hopes, released energies, and altered fundamental attitudes. For many in the Union it had begun as a conservative response to southern rebellion; as it closed, conservatives themselves saw it as a revolution and were glad of the fact. Awareness of having ended a chapter and opened a new one pervaded every aspect of life. The passage by Congress of the Thirteenth Amendment abolishing slavery in January, 1865, was the great symbol of change, but the idea of a new departure spread across political, constitutional, and economic life. Inevitably this change left many men confused and clinging to the past; for however fast some had moved, others could not readily abandon familiar assumptions. In any period of upheaval it is not only institutional and social attitudes that are swept away; traditional moral restraints may also be eroded. The euphoria with which Republicans and War Democrats welcomed the triumph of the Union and the end of slavery could not conceal the seamy side of the war or the frequent occasions on which dubious means had been justified by the end. For the defeated all the form and meaning seemed to have gone out of life; individuals entered upon a grim struggle for survival, and communities fell back upon the bare foundations of fear and prejudice. On both sides the loss of life had been prodigious; privately if not publicly men were forced to ask whether the sacrifices had been necessary. In the North they had already begun but not completed the long quest to find a meaning for the war and raised deep questions about the character of the Union, race relations, the use of force, and the nature of democratic government. Indeed, the consequences of the war were but dimly perceived when the last southern army surrendered.

8

The Aftermath of War and the Reconstruction of a Nation

PHYSICAL devastation was not the worst injury suffered by the South; the ruin of plantations and the reduction of once affluent families to poverty were outward symptoms of damage to the spirit that could not be repaired. In the closing stages of the war few had looked with any confidence to the future; most men had lost their bearings and their faith. In other societies the defeat of a ruling elite has provided opportunities for new leadership, but in the South the defeat of the planter gentry left a void that only they themselves could fill. The plain people wished to return to their farms and to pick up the broken threads of their simple lives, and the urban middle class was too feeble to respond to any political challenge. When the quest for independence failed, there was nothing left save a desperate hope that the clock could be turned back to 1860; trial by battle had proved that secession was void, and paradoxically southern leaders now clung to this Unionist dogma in order to recover lost influence and forfeited rights.

The old leadership was hardly able to bear the responsibility now cast upon it. A generation had been decimated, those who survived were preoccupied with the personal problems of economic survival, and even the mildest plan of reconstruction assumed that men who had held high civilian or military office under the Confederacy must be excluded, temporarily at least, from public life. Prewar southern politics had not generated alternative leadership but erected two party ladders by which men could climb to the same point; now former Democrats and former Whigs fell under the same shadow of defeat, and there was no "loyal opposition" ready to transfer allegiance to the new masters. What emerged were competing groups of minor prewar politicians, a few who had done well out of the war (for profits had been made from cotton trading and blockade running) , and opportunists on the alert for economic gain or political popularity. It was not the best material to lead a defeated people, and the situation was made more precarious by the extreme difficulty in guessing which way the cards would fall. Even with Lincoln living it was not easy to predict the course that Reconstruction would take or the way in which the North would wield a power that was now absolute; with Lincoln dead all was in confusion.

Perhaps the experience of war was not entirely sterile. Rural isolation was broken down, the necessity for large-scale organization was accepted, social mobility was accelerated, and in many ways the South was shaken from a stagnant way of life into a mood in which change would be accepted if not welcomed. However, there had been signs of change before 1860, and the backwardness of the South (by many civilized standards) in the later nineteenth century supports the counterargument that by impoverishing the section war retarded it drastically. The South did revive, but in doing so earned a reputation for prejudice, violence, evasion of the law, and striking failures to achieve a fair distribution of opportunities and rewards. The southerners themselves attributed this to the experience of Reconstruction, but a broader perspective must see war as the fundamental cause and number the lost opportunities of Reconstruction among its consequences.

The manner of defeat made it impossible to learn lessons from it. The original southern theory of politics had been fresh and productive; it had degenerated by 1850 and by 1865 became a mere parade of lifeless arguments to justify the least attractive aspects of southern society. The humane liberalism of Jefferson, the constructive analysis of Madison, the vigorous equalitarianism of Jackson, or the unyielding logic of Calhoun were replaced by a nostalgic cult of the Old South. The Lost Cause became heroic, and its memories and memorials were carefully cherished; a society that faced problems of acute difficulty in economic adaptation and race relations became preoccupied with the glories of a past that had only misleading relevance for the present. This cult of the past served one purpose that was not altogether unworthy, for in a demoralized society it helped the recovery of self-respect and did something to dignify the gentler aspects of southern culture. The ladies of the upper class, whose zeal for independence had often exceeded that of the fighting men, played a special part in preserving memories of the Lost Cause, though it was often hard to distinguish their devotion from simple hatred of the Yankees. In course of time many Confederate leaders rallied to defend their record; as early as 1869 a number of them formed the Southern Historical Society to forestall the calumnies expected from the officially sponsored *War of the Rebellion,* and even before that Alexander Stephens was at work on his *Constitutional View of the Late War between the States.* As Vice-President, Stephens had been a consistent and troublesome critic of Jefferson Davis, but in his book he justified the principles of the Confederate President, expounded the compact theory of the Union, and worked out an elaborate constitutional argument against the preservation of the Union by force. Jefferson Davis did not publish his own *Rise and Fall of the Confederate Government* until 1881 and was then too much preoccupied with forgotten personal rivalries; but the core of the book was a sustained elaboration of the constitutional argument advanced in his first message to Congress in 1861. Lesser men tried to underwrite the same thesis, and most southerners were convinced that though they had been overwhelmed by northern strength, they were winning the battle of the books. Accepted articles of faith were the nobility of southern character, the humane side of slavery, and the theoretical soundness of states' rights.

This revival of southern pride reconciled white southerners to life in a new era of diminished influence but also paralyzed will and led decent men to condone behavior that they would have deplored in an earlier generation. Violence and evasion of the law were excused by the need to defend the southern way of life, and the compensation for defeat was defensive psychology and suspicion of all ideas or institutions associated with the North. In economic behavior southerners of the rising generation would prove themselves adaptable and often aggressive, but most areas of the South continued to stand low in such criteria of civilized society as literacy, higher education, science, cultural activity, distribution of wealth, and health. In an age of scientific discovery, technological innovation, and pioneer effort in social studies the South initiated nothing and remained hostile to ideas that elsewhere aroused the imagination and stimulated effort. Religious fundamentalism spread among the farming people in the lower South, and though this raised standards of personal conduct, it was profoundly conservative in its social consequences. Beneath the rural middle class that filled the churches and came to provide the voting base for the revived Democratic party, poor whites and poor blacks lived somehow at the lowest level of subsistence. Thus the disastrous war cast a lengthening shadow over the later years; it could not be forgotten, the psychological damage was ineradicable, and valiant efforts to recover self-esteem were directed toward justification rather than improvement. This was a tragedy for the whole American people.

Thus the sad paradox of the war for the Union was that the South became more self-conscious, more introspective, less ready for intellectual enterprise, and more resistant to outside influences than ever before. Tendencies that had developed between 1820 and 1860, when southerners receded from Jeffersonian cosmopolitanism, reached their climax after 1865. The price for real reunion would be northern tolerance and perhaps acceptance of southern racial attitudes, and a tacit recognition that secession had aimed to protect not slavery but an "agrarian" society. In this the southerners would receive powerful support in later years from historians who lamented "the triumph of American capitalism." In 1861 many southerners had seriously argued (for foreign edification) that the tariff had forced the South into a position of colonial dependence and was the real cause of conflict; the war, by dissipating capital and the slender stocks of entrepreneurial and technical skill, had made this dependence real. The stage was set for a more diversified economy, but the capital had to come from the North, as did also most of the entrepreneurial effort. There was, therefore, a marked contrast between cultural separatism and economic dependence; in the "New South" southern manufacturers, railroad men, and cotton producers would obtain the semblance of independence, but the reality lay in control by capitalists in New York, Philadelphia, and the midwestern cities. Only the merchants of Baltimore and New Orleans could enjoy real independence in their dealings with the rest of the world, and of these cities one had never left the Union and the other had been recaptured early in the war.

The history on which cultural separatism flourished was highly selective. The plain people were generally ignored except when they were held to have rallied to the cause of independence in 1861, and southern history became largely the history of the planter class. Party battles of the early nineteenth century were forgotten as apologists for the Old South drew pictures of a wonderfully harmonious society. The history of southern Unionism during the Civil War remains largely unwritten, and only in recent years has it been realized that desertion played so large a part in depleting the southern armies in the second half of the war or that conscription was virtually unworkable in many parts of the back country. The natural (and often rational) doubts with which so many regarded the war aims were either ignored or treated as untypical exceptions. In

1924 a southern historian concluded a book, devoted to a close study of the wrangling over conscription, with the observation that "the dereliction of many sets in a brighter light the heroic devotion of the masses. The unsurpassed sacrifices and heroism of the Southern armies and civilian population—the proudest and most sacred tradition of the South—stand unassailed." [1]

An important aspect of southern reactions to defeat was a denial that slavery had had anything to do with the war. As Jefferson Davis wrote, years after the events,

The question of the right or wrong of the institution of slavery was in no wise involved in the earlier sectional controversies. Nor was it otherwise in those of a later period, in which it was the lot of the author . . . to bear a part. They were essentially struggles for sectional equality or ascendancy—for the maintenance or the destruction of that balance of power or equipoise between North and South, which was early recognized as a cardinal principle in our Federal system. [2]

It was reasonable to question the role of slavery in sectional conflict, but to assert that "the question of the right or wrong . . . was in no wise involved" was a dangerous delusion and a leading illustration of the way in which an imaginary past prevented a realistic appraisal of the present. The great economic changes of the later nineteenth century made life difficult for all predominantly rural societies, but the Civil War made it especially difficult for the South, where the forces that obstructed social change were elevated into great principles sanctified by heroic effort. What developed was not conservatism dedicated to the principles of gradualism and organic theories of society, but reaction (in the most literal sense of the word) that was exercised to exploit the ample opportunities

---

[1] Albert B. Moore, *Conscription and Conflict in the Confederacy* (New York: 1924; reprint, Hillary House, 1963) , p. 361.

[2] Jefferson Davis, *The Rise and Fall of the Confederate Government,* Vol. I (1881; new ed., New York, 1958) , pp. 13–14.

for obstruction allowed by the political system. The descendants of the great Virginians were reduced to the unhappy position in which the northern majority made the law while they were dedicated to preventing it from taking effect.

The impact of war upon northern society came at a time when economic revolution and social adjustment were already taking place, and it is therefore difficult to identify the trends that were accelerated, retarded, halted, or initiated.[3] Preoccupation with quantitative analyses and broad generalizations may also obscure the effect upon individuals, just as small-scale maps offer little indication of the features that give character to a countryside. For most Americans the outbreak of war in 1861 changed their lives, and for many it provided a deep emotional experience that could never be forgotten; for individuals it was therefore discontinuity and an abrupt break with the past that seemed the most obvious characteristic. For most men who were active in politics and business in the later years of the nineteenth century the war was a new starting point, and to a later generation it would appear as a great divide that cut them off from their past.

To be separated from the past did not mean that it was ignored; indeed, from the start, the northern justification for fighting to preserve the Union depended heavily upon a particular reading of American history. The war had hardly begun when the historian John Lothrop Motley (whose work on the history of the Dutch Republic entitled him to speak with authority on the origin of nations) explained to the British public that "the Constitution of 1787 had made us a *nation*," and wrote:

It is strange that Englishmen should find difficulty in understanding that the United States' Government is a nation among the nations of the earth—a constituted authority, which may be overthrown by violence, as may be the fate of any State, whether Kingdom or Republic, but which is false to the people if it does

[3] For discussion of this question see pp. 243–244 and 286–289.

not its best to preserve them from the horrors of anarchy, even at the cost of blood.

This was a characteristic expression of what would become a common northern rationalization of events. There was the assertion that past events had made the United States a nation, the assumption that nations had an inherent right to retain their indivisible character, and the inference that governments had an implied obligation to prevent separation. It was admitted that there was a right of revolution —no American could deny this—but implied that secession had not been the true will of the people but the result of a slaveholders' conspiracy. Unlike the government of George III, that of the United States had not lost its moral right to act upon the whole people; it resulted from an election in which all had participated, the Constitution provided the means for its own amendment, and the Union did not depend upon a spurious claim to legitimacy but upon a network of obligations that all had accepted. This moralistic argument was also combined with assertions of the right to fight for material interests when these were threatened; Lincoln and many others from the West saw the claim for a separate sovereignty over the lower Mississippi as a prime argument for action, and Motley told his British readers that it was the loss of the Gulf Coast that would be fatal for the Republic. Northern spokesmen never came to grips with Calhoun's argument that the concurrent or local majority had rights that must be recognized by the numerical or national majority but simply denied that such a conflict could exist. In this way wartime nationalism combined defense of the Union with the theory of absolute democratic sovereignty. The traditional demands of allegiance by a sovereign, the romantic concept of a "nation" with a soul and purpose, and the revolutionary idea of government by the people were blended together and quickly fused with the moral force of a crusade. The fact of secession had released the northern majority from constitutional commitments to respect slavery where it existed under state law and replaced it by the moral obligation to attack it wherever national power could reach.

A northern "take-over" of the past began in 1861 and was complete before the end of the war. It was as unreal as the cult of the Old South, because history does not illustrate a one-way movement toward national solidarity but evolution toward consolidation *and* fragmentation. The fact that consolidation was claimed as the only legitimate development laid a trail of misunderstanding for the future. Nationality was explained, but not in a way that opened the path to real reconciliation, while the Constitution, which still commanded enormous respect, was in many ways at variance with the inferences drawn from nationalist premises. The issue was to be of immediate importance during Reconstruction and survived as an obstacle and confusion for the future. There was to be an abiding contradiction between a patriotism with universal claims to represent the rights of man and a denial that minorities had the right to be wrong.

The historians drew upon English and German sources for inspiration with strong undertones of Puritanism, but democratic nationalism claimed to be both American and universal. The foreign-born were welcomed; the Union was for all peoples under a single political banner, and the great error of the South had been the rejection of multiracial democracy. Most Democrats still qualified the word "race" with the adjective "white," but many of them came to accept the case for emancipation though not for equality. In other respects, too, northern people appropriated the ideas of Jacksonian democracy so that the cause of the Union was rendered synonymous with that of the common man and equal rights, while the aristocratic and antidemocratic character of southern society was claimed as a justification for war.

Though the Civil War plays this important part in the development of modern nationalism, it also demonstrates the difference between American and European varieties.

In Europe nationalists usually appealed to simple ethnic and traditional characteristics; in a nation with no ethnic unity and short traditions it was necessary to speculate more and speak more fervently. The war fractured the Anglo-Saxon ascendancy that had constituted the real centerpiece of earlier ideas about national existence, failed to provide a viable alternative, and left a void to be filled by assertion rather than argument. Foreign observers (and many Americans) have often been puzzled by the violent obscurantism of the self-professed watchdogs of American patriotism, but a study of Union rhetoric during the Civil War can do something to explain the phenomenon. One finds the same assumption that opponents are the root of all evil, that critics are in some way un-American, and that subversion is as dangerous as the external enemy. It is not difficult to find modern parallels to the way in which writers and speakers on behalf of the Union spoke of secessionists and Copperheads and condemned their views as not merely mistaken but wicked. It was this spirit that Lincoln condemned when he asked for malice toward none; but seed so firmly planted could hardly fail to flourish.

If the patriotism bred by war was blatant and intolerant, it was not anti-intellectual. Indeed, the men of letters found themselves recognized as spokesmen for the people in a way that was both welcome and unexpected. In the years before the war most leading writers had had strong antislavery views, and a majority had been willing recruits for the Republican party. Even Democrats such as George Bancroft had little respect for their party leadership in the days of Pierce and Buchanan, while Walt Whitman belonged by temperament to the radical Democrats of New York. Suddenly, with the inauguration of Lincoln and the coming of war, they were no longer an outgroup but articulate members of a new establishment. It was a sense of purpose as well as an instinct for profit that led to an unprecedented outflow of books, pamphlets, and newspaper articles explaining the war. If the new President did not come to the White House with the kind of learning that impressed the New England intelligentsia, he soon showed that he could turn a phrase and grapple with an idea. Indeed, Lincoln would soon become a symbol of identity between the wisdom of the ages and the institutions of a free society.

Thus the men of books, the poets, the philosophic clergy, the college professors—all who would now be called collectively the intelligentsia—felt that they had a government they could respect, a cause that they could serve, and a popular audience that they had never before enjoyed. Among those who regarded themselves as the educated elite, many who did not write books or articles found themselves engaged in voluntary activities such as the Sanitary or Christian Commissions and widely praised for their services.

It was not until comparatively recently that it has become customary to speak of "the intellectuals" as a group apart and distinct from society. The intellectual elite of the Civil War period certainly did not wish to think of themselves in this light, and the role to which they aspired was active leadership, not introspection on the sidelines. Their models were the British spokesmen of upper-middle-class culture who had acquired such standing on both sides of the Atlantic: the Edinburgh Reviewers, the philosophic radicals, Thomas Macaulay, John Stuart Mill, Alfred Tennyson, Charles Dickens, William Thackeray, and a host of other luminaries who gave to the upper levels of British life so rarefied an atmosphere. This aspiration helps to explain the great prestige of Charles Sumner, who appeared to contemporaries to unite learning, moral conviction, and leadership in a way that was at once unique and hopeful for the future. The experience of war in a cause that they believed to be just enabled American men of letters to reconcile the claims of an educated elite with those of a democratic people in a way that had never before been possible. They reacted by presenting the war as a great challenge to which the people had nobly responded and won the battle for a better world.

There is inevitably a gap between the way in which writers and preachers rationalize and dignify war and the view of the ordinary soldier. There was, indeed, among the northern troops, and particularly among early volunteers, a conviction that settled down into a grim determination to see the thing through, but it required conscription to keep up the flow of soldiers, and, as in the South, desertion became a serious problem in the later years. A good many of the nominal deserters were "bounty-jumpers" who enlisted to receive a bounty, deserted or failed to report, reenlisted under another name to earn another bounty, and so on. The facility for drafted men to offer substitutes could be grossly abused, and though there was great exaggeration in the southern jibe that the northern armies were filled by foreign mercenaries, a large number of recent immigrants and men recruited in Europe came for money rather than glory. Inevitably the middlemen appeared, and bounty-brokers became a regular feature of the Civil War scene. The broker would contract with cities and counties to fill their quotas, often taking a substantial part of the bounty as commission. The methods used to obtain men were frequently none too scrupulous and sometimes criminal, but it seems that few local authorities could dispense with the services of brokers or ask awkward questions about the enticements or fraud used to find men. Most brokers also undertook to provide substitutes for cash. This business was conducted quite openly, with advertisements appearing in the newspapers, but it meant that a great deal of money was being made out of the anxiety of many to avoid the draft and the gullibility of those who were prepared or cajoled into offering their services.

At a higher level there were frequent complaints of moral decline induced by the war. Illegal pressure to obtain government contracts, inflated prices, substandard goods, or simple frauds were often alleged. Railroad companies could make handsome profits out of the conveyance of troops and army supplies, and the Illinois Central—commanding access to highly important military areas—was popularly believed to have wrung wholly unreasonable profits out of the war. Large sums could be made from trading with the Confederates across the lines or by roundabout means; high-ranking officers in the Southwest were reputed to have made a good deal of money from this trade or by accepting bribes from those engaged upon it. Buyers were not likely to question the source of such a highly desired commodity, and even the United States Government was anxious to find cotton that could be released for British or French buyers and so reduce the pressure from those governments. Government finance seems to have been honestly handled, and Jay Cooke, the great financier who handled government loans, was a man of integrity, but there was no denying that wartime finance offered enormous profits for men who knew enough to make the right offer at the right time. Thus, alongside the heroics of popular journalism and the rhetoric of writers and preachers, there was a seamy side of the war that gave a less favorable picture of the northern cause. In fairness it should be said that some Republican newspapers and congressmen were very active in exposing fraud, and even the abused Committee on the Conduct of the War did valuable work in investigating dubious contracts.

It is more difficult to decide whether these activities were temporary phenomena, endemic in the system, or indications of a real decline in moral standards. One is tempted to trace back the more outrageous examples of predatory capitalism in the later nineteenth century to the wartime experience, and it may be argued that the war not only led men to fraud and crime but also made officials and the public insensitive to the results. Alternatively it could be said that these practices were as old as history, but public interest in the war focused light upon them. Probably there is truth in both propositions: The war did not make men wicked, but the opportunities for fraud multiplied while the profits increased. At the lower end of the social scale it can be said that war usually undermines moral conventions, and the Civil War was no exception. There is, however, no evidence that things reached the point at which the provision of brothels for soldiers was regarded as a public service. If soldiers were not saints, the voluminous literary evidence provides singularly little evidence of depravity.

Another feature of the war was the comparatively humane manner in which it was conducted. There were dozens of atrocity stories but few that could be verified. Everyone in the North came to know of the sufferings of Union prisoners in the Andersonville camp and the massacre (some would say overzealous pursuit) of black soldiers at Fort Pillow, but these were isolated incidents that would hardly have attracted attention in twentieth-century conflicts. It is testimony to the nineteenth-century scale of values that the enormity that attracted worldwide attention (including a furious letter from Lord Palmerston to the American minister in London) was General Butler's order that ladies who insulted Union soldiers on the streets of New Orleans were to be treated as common prostitutes by the authorities. Between the officers on both sides (especially among former West Pointers) formal courtesies were observed, and there are plenty of examples of fraternization between troops. Whatever civilians might say, the soldiers did not regard each other as monsters of iniquity, and stories of atrocity were mainly for consumption behind the lines.

The war for the Union had therefore been one in which the people had nobly fought and suffered, but it had also been a war of bummers, bounty-jumpers, and fraudulent contractors; it had been conducted on both sides with as much decency as one could perform a beastly business but had also hardened hearts against suffering; it had purged the national spirit of base emotions and precipitated a severe decline in moral values. Through this mass of contradictions it was unfortunately clear that on both sides the rival leaders had been execrated to a point at which even grudging respect was impossible. To a majority in the North there could be no real peace while secessionists remained in power, and to southerners the continued domination of the Republican party made real reunion impossible, and for years they would continue to believe that Yankees were responsible for all the evil in the world.

Whatever the damage done by the war to white American civilization, black Americans had good reason to rejoice. For them more than for anyone else the war had changed the world. Slavery was gone, never to return; many thousands of black soldiers had fought in the Union armies and after some humiliating refusals won equal payments and conditions with white troops. For the first time some black men had won reputations not confined to small groups of abolitionists. Frederick Douglass had become one of the best-known Americans; throughout the North men had heard of Robert Smalls, who ran the *Planter* out of Charleston Harbor to join the Union forces; the heroism of black troops in their first major engagement at Fort Wagner had become an epic. In the great cities, where negrophobia had seemed to have reached a high pitch in 1863, there had been dramatic breaches in the pattern of discrimination. The nature of the change in white attitudes can be measured by the Republican willingness, in 1861, to guarantee slavery against federal interference by an amendment to the Constitution and the passage five years later of an amendment guaranteeing citizenship and equality under the law. This was the most striking development within the shortest period in the whole history of race relations in modern times.

It is easy to say that these things ought to have happened without war, but certain that no peaceful event could have brought them about with this rapidity. In a subsequent chapter some of the difficulties, inevitable in so rapid a movement, will be discussed; and some may argue that gradualism would have provided a better and more permanent solution. This can be neither proved nor disproved; the situation was unique, and there is no comparable experience by which the hypothesis can be tested. The simple fact is that the war did kill slavery and did produce a marked improvement in the status of all blacks, freedmen and free.

In this there lies a further paradox. The war had been begun to end or preserve the Union among white Americans; on one side it was said with emphasis that slavery had nothing to do with the war, and on the other that the outcome need have no effect upon the status of blacks. Its direct consequence was to produce a Union of white and black upon the basis of common citizenship and equal rights. Yet the black race remained distinct just as the southern culture had become distinct, and the same problem of majority rule and minority rights would appear under a different guise. In this way the problems of the late twentieth century can be traced by direct descent to the experience of the Civil War.

After four years of agonizing war the South had to come to terms with defeat, and the North to discover the meaning of victory. By May, 1865, the armies of the Union exercised undisputed authority in the South; the once proud sovereign states of the Confederacy exercised no shadow of public responsibility, and order depended exclusively upon military commanders acting upon orders from Washington. Provisional governors had been appointed by the President, and in many areas it was possible to reconstitute the framework of courts and administration; but these local authorities were able to do only that which their military masters permitted. The victorious North had the power to act, and having the power, could not avoid the responsibility to decide for withdrawal or continuance of military rule, for the speedy restoration of state governments or for a long period of tutelage, for the rights of states as they once had been or for the reform of southern society. A quick abdication of responsibility would have results as far-reaching as deliberate and positive action.

Under any circumstances reconstruction would have been difficult. There were precedents for dealing with rebellion, but none could apply to rebellion undertaken by millions of the people. International law could guide the making of peace between nations but was of little assistance after a war fought to prove that there could be only one nation. Even if there had been a Confederate government capable of negotiating on behalf of the South, it would have been a negation of Union aims to admit that it had the right to do so. The Confederate states had fought to become an independent nation, but defeat meant that sooner or later they must rejoin the United States with their own governments, their own courts of law, and the same rights and responsibilities as all the other states. Men argued over their theoretical position; Lincoln and many others had maintained that since secession was void, the states had remained in being, though temporarily controlled by rebellious individuals; Charles Sumner, on the contrary, argued that the act of secession had been "state suicide" and that the states could be brought back to life only by the government of the United States; Thaddeus Stevens maintained that legalistic argument was a waste of time and that in practice the states of the Confederacy should be treated as "conquered provinces." Whatever abstractions one might contemplate, Stevens maintained that the wisest and simplest course would be to treat the "conquered provinces" as territories of the United States, recognizing loyal legislatures for local purposes but maintaining the sovereignty of Congress as long as it seemed necessary to do so.

The argument over Reconstruction had begun as early

as 1861, when optimists expected a quick Union victory. The treatment of secessionist leaders had been a matter of speculation, with a fairly general agreement that they could not be allowed to continue in control of their states; and men began to consider the problem of loyalty. What did it mean to be "loyal" to the United States? Was it a formal undertaking to obey the laws of the United States, or did it mean acceptance of a political philosophy? Was it enough to respect the flag, or did it mean an undertaking to conduct one's life in a way agreed by the majority? Americans already had some familiarity with these concepts when wrestling with the rights of immigrants and the processes of naturalization, but they had arrived at no agreed position. Moreover, Radicals were somewhat reluctant to draw upon nativist arguments, for if one were to treat a rebel as analogous to an unnaturalized alien, the same argument might apply to Negroes. The procedure for naturalization did, however, suggest that "loyalty" could be tested by requiring individuals to take oaths. Radicals insisted that the only loyal men in the fullest sense, and thus fit for full citizenship, were those able to take an "ironclad" oath that they had given no aid to the rebellion. Others, including Lincoln, were content with an oath of future allegiance to the United States. Behind this disagreement was uncertainty whether "loyalty" meant acceptance of a political philosophy or a formal undertaking to obey the law.

As long as the war continued, insistence upon the ironclad oath was a practical embarrassment to administration and detrimental to "loyal" governments established in the Confederacy. While the Confederate armies were in the field, a promise of future loyalty to the Union was a risk, and courage and conviction were required to accept office in a Union-sponsored government. Insistence upon the ironclad oath would reduce the willing collaborators to an ineffective fragment, and both Lincoln and a majority of the military commanders wished to accept "loyalty" with-

out inquiring into its antecedents. Lincoln carried this policy to its limits when he ordered that if 10 percent of
the 1860 legal voters took an oath of loyalty, a government
for their state could then be established and recognized by
the executive. But Congress alone could decide whether
to admit senators and representatives, and Republican
opinion hardened against doing so. At one point they did
admit a representative from Louisiana on the same basis
as a territorial delegate but subsequently withdrew this
concession.

Whatever the practical advantages of a simple oath of
loyalty during the war, the whole question was thrown
wide open when peace was restored. Now it required not
courage but common sense to take whatever oaths were required as a condition for the restoration of normal rights.
In the later stages of the war men had been aware of this,
and the majority in Congress sought safeguards against
formal professions of loyalty by "unrepentant rebels."
Lincoln agreed with the Radicals that some secessionist
leaders should be excluded, and exempted from pardon
men who had held high civilian and military offices under
the Confederacy; but this seemed too timid a measure for
the Radicals, who wanted a tight control over how the
South should be governed and by whom.

The Wade-Davis bill of July, 1864, is usually represented as a Radical measure; actually (and in common
with all subsequent Reconstruction measures) it was a
compromise between Radicals, who wanted to treat the
southern states as territories, leaving Congress full freedom
to decide how and when they should become states, and
moderates, who wanted a clearly defined mechanism for reconstructing the Union. With some ingenuity the authors
of the bill utilized both concepts of loyalty. Reconstruction
would begin when 50 percent of the legal voters were prepared to take an oath of future loyalty, but only men who
could take the oath of past loyalty would be allowed to
vote in elections for a constitutional convention. The new

constitution must include the abolition of slavery and disqualify from office persons who had held high office or military rank under the Confederacy. When this process was complete, Congress would decide whether to admit the state to the Union. The 50-percent requirement meant that Reconstruction could not begin until after the end of the war, or at least until a greater part of the state was under Union control, and then demand a willingness to confer exclusive responsibility upon hard-core Unionists.

The Wade-Davis bill was an embarrassment to Lincoln's plans for Unionist governments in Louisiana, Arkansas, and Virginia, and it was possibly unconstitutional to order abolition by act of Congress. Just as many Republicans feared that emancipation that rested upon a presidential proclamation, relying upon the war power, might not stand legal scrutiny once the war was over, so Lincoln thought that the courts, relying upon a strict interpretation of the Constitution and earlier Republican recognition that no such power existed, might void congressional abolition. Abolition in this form would also derange Lincoln's hope for gradual emancipation with compensation for slave-owners. Arguing on these lines Lincoln vetoed the Wade-Davis bill; as it came to him at the end of the session, he was able to kill it with a pocket veto, but he chose to explain his reasons in a public message, perhaps to conciliate Republicans or reassure the weak southern Unionist governments that he did not intend to destroy them. His wisdom in vetoing the bill is debatable; it was not perfect, but it represented a consensus among the Republicans, provided a workable procedure, and could have been modified later. In any event no further constructive steps were taken while Lincoln lived, and the war ended without agreement upon the processes or objectives of Reconstruction.

The early Republican arguments on Reconstruction had been influenced by the need to ensure that the Union had power to damage slavery irretrievably even if there were constitutional objections to abolition. By April, 1865, however, the great majority of southern slaves were either free or on the brink of freedom. The Thirteenth Amendment had passed Congress, and its ratification seemed certain. The emphasis had therefore shifted, as policy had, to take account of between three and four million freedmen. What was the status of these freedmen, and who was to decide? Were they citizens of the United States? The Dred Scott decision had said that no Negro could be a United States citizen, and though disputed by most Republicans, the courts might be bound by it. If the freedmen were citizens, to which rights, privileges, and immunities were they entitled? If they were, at present, qualified to exercise *some* rights, who was to decide when they would enjoy *equal* rights? If they needed education, experience, and economic opportunities, who was to decide how these things should be supplied? Traditionally the states had defined the rights of their citizens and defended them against a remote federal government, but could the rights of Negroes be defended by those who had enslaved them? And if the federal government were to interpose between the states and their black citizens, would not this mean a fundamental change in the balance of responsibility in the federal republic?

These questions crowded in upon politicians in the months after Lincoln's assassination, and for them there could be no ready or easy answer. It was clear that some responsibility for the freedmen must be assumed by the federal government, for the masters were now released from the responsibilities they had normally assumed. The great mass of Negroes entered the era of freedom with no money, no property, and only their labor to sell; their natural ambition was land of their own or a living wage in a freely chosen occupation. As early as March, 1863, Lincoln had recognized the responsibility by setting up a Freedmen's Inquiry Commission to investigate and report. There was also much interest in the Port Royal experiment on the Sea

Islands of South Carolina, occupied by Union forces early in the war, and since then a testing ground for the education of Negroes and their establishment as independent farmers; the results (among slaves regarded as the most backward in the South) encouraged cautious optimism but also emphasized the need for firm direction, a judicious use of military discipline, and philanthropic enthusiasm. Lincoln's commission recommended the establishment of a freedmen's agency within the War Department, and a bill on these lines passed the House. In the Senate the bill was amended by Sumner's Committee on Slavery and Freedom to place the proposed agency under the Treasury on the ground that this department had custody of abandoned lands that could be transferred to freedmen. As a consequence of the disagreement no bill was passed in 1864. Early in 1865 Sumner proposed a separate Freedmen's Department with a head of Cabinet rank, and the future might have been very different if a man of high authority had had exclusive responsibility for all the complex issues involved. Sumner's proposal was, however, defeated in the Senate after being passed in the House, and finally, in the last days of the Thirty-eighth Congress, a Bureau for Refugees, Freedmen, and Abandoned Lands was established in the War Department for a single year. Characteristically Congress had muddled through, under pressure of events, to a compromise solution that was weak in many respects and denied to the great task the importance it deserved. Nevertheless the Freedmen's Bureau was the first, and in some respects the most important, of all the great agencies for social welfare created by modern governments. If imperfect, it was also a fitting addition to the massive enlargement of government functions that resulted from the Civil War.

The limited time for which it had been established hampered the bureau's work, for it was restricted to short-term remedies for long-term problems. General O. O. Howard, whom Stanton appointed as its head, was a distinguished soldier with a genuine concern for the Negro, but he was a good chief of staff rather than an army commander. When President Johnson showed himself unsympathetic—particularly in disputes between the bureau, local authorities, and the owners of abandoned land—Howard had neither the determination nor the will to fight for his bureau's policy. As the bureau had to recruit staff quickly from among the officers of the army, some mistakes were made. In the early days there was little of the corruption later alleged against bureau officials, nor were they involved in politics; but in a job that demanded imagination, efficiency, tact, and dedication there were many who fell short. Nevertheless, it is fair to judge the bureau by imagining what chaos, suffering, and frustration would have ensued if the federal government had entirely evaded responsibility.

The men of the South had to live with defeat. For many of them it was both public humiliation and personal ruin. Many planters had lost savings and capital invested in slaves, returned to neglected or wasted estates, and faced the future with neither the assets nor the labor to recover their fortunes. The smaller planters and farmers suffered proportionately less, for though their property might be in desperate condition, they had never expected high returns and found it easier to adjust to subsistence agriculture while waiting for better times; but nevertheless many humble men had to accept a total change in their way of life. In all classes there were surprisingly few regrets over the end of slavery. The experience of war had convinced many that slavery was doomed whatever the outcome, but there were many psychological shocks to be met and overcome. It was often the most valued and apparently faithful household slaves who took the first opportunity to leave their former masters. Southern ladies endured much irritation as the black servants from whom they had learned to expect immediate and unqualified obedience, and rewarded with numerous favors, asserted their independence in many small ways. Planters were genuinely confused by the problems of wage labor and failed to realize that adequate wages had to be paid if laborers were to be held to their accustomed tasks. In some cases the Freedmen's Bureau officers cooperated with the planters to organize labor for production and enforce contracts, with the approval of northern textile manufacturers and merchants anxious for a quick revival of cotton production. Humbler white southerners were irritated by Negroes wandering about the country at will, alarmed when they congregated in towns, and horrified by black soldiers. It was admitted that former slaves must now enjoy life, liberty, and property under the law, but in practice these rights could be strictly limited. Negro testimony (except against other Negroes), Negro jury service, and Negro suffrage seemed abhorrent. It was no argument to say that some Negroes were educated and owned property, for the Negro who aspired to middle-class status was of all the most feared and despised.

Yet, in spite of defeat, members of the southern upper class retained their prestige and influence. The decline in morale and the high rate of desertion may have been in part a symptom of class conflict or of a tacit decision by many plain men that it was not their war; but when peace came, there were few areas where upper-class ascendancy could be challenged. There were exceptions in parts of the upper South, particularly in West Virginia, North Carolina, and Tennessee where dissent during the war echoed long-standing distrust of planters and their commercial allies; some, including President Andrew Johnson, hoped to build a Unionist revival on this base. Johnson had succeeded in his own Tennessee as military governor, though by cruel irony the Unionism that he had fostered came under the control of W. G. Brownlow, a bitter personal enemy. At the end of May Johnson made a further move by issuing a reconstruction proclamation for North Carolina, where Unionism and peace movements had been strong. He exempted from his amnesty proclamation the same groups as Lincoln, with the significant addition of persons owning property valued at more than twenty thousand dollars who had aided the rebellion. This was, however, accompanied by an indication that he might give pardons to individuals who applied to him in person. The inference is that Johnson hoped to build loyal states upon a broad basis of the southern farmer vote, while keeping the old ruling class in a cooperative mood by a judicious use of the pardoning power. Following the Wade-Davis model, he required 50 percent of the legal voters to take an oath of loyalty, but when this was done, a convention could be elected on the 1860 electoral registration. The convention was required to ratify the Thirteenth Amendment and declare void the secession ordinances, but beyond this it had a free hand in framing a constitution.

There might have been good cause, at this point, for a pause in Reconstruction while the ground was tested in North Carolina and Virginia and the earlier experiments in Louisiana and Arkansas were reviewed. There would have been rough justice in making the first states to secede wait longest for readmission, and the experience of states where genuine Unionism formed a nucleus for Reconstruction might have been valuable. Against this Johnson was anxious to push ahead as fast as possible before the strongly Republican Thirty-ninth Congress met in December, and the North Carolina proclamation was quickly followed by others on the same model for the remaining Confederate states. This was, perhaps, a fatal error, for the extension of the process meant that President Johnson soon lost control of Reconstruction in the South.

The conventions that met in the southern states during the summer and fall of 1865 have left little mark upon history. Most of them were brief. They ratified abolition and repealed secession, though in some conventions a form of words was adopted to indicate that these acts recognized military might, not constitutional right. The 1860 state constitutions were restored, eliminating amendments made in consequence of secession and all references to slavery. The provisional governors appointed by the President then ordered elections; before the end of 1865 every southern state had restored legislatures, and upon them the tasks of social adjustment and economic revival devolved.

Behind the smooth operation of presidential Reconstruction significant forces were at work. In most of the 1865 conventions the bulk of the delegates were men who had played little previous part in public life—smaller planters, farmers, some lawyers—but it also seems that members of the old upper class who had escaped disqualification quickly established their authority. In the elections for the legislatures many unpardoned persons were chosen, and the social composition of the new assemblies was very similar to that of the prewar days. Johnson had already shown himself generous in his pardoning policy. Though suspicious of the large landowners, he had orthodox views about the sanctity of property and wished to avert any wholesale occupation of the land by freedmen. A pardon automatically restored the rights of property, and it was this rather than political considerations that moved him in the first instance. Quick to exploit the situation, some men established themselves as pardon brokers; the President himself was above suspicion, but there were many ways in which an astute man could ensure that cases were brought quickly to his notice and presented in a favorable light. Perhaps the cruelest blow to the freedmen was the restoration of property rights to several of the Sea Islands planters, where blacks had enjoyed four years of comparative prosperity on small farms, carved out of the great estates, from which they were now evicted. The political developments in the South put further pressure on Johnson. The men who had been elected in the South had succeeded through democratic processes; to insist that some were disqualified as unpardoned rebels would deny the validity of the popular movements upon which the President had relied, and there seemed to be little option but to ratify the choice of the people by a lavish issue of pardons.

As 1865 moved to its close, Republican suspicions were aroused. The old ruling class of the South was back in the saddle, nothing had been done to safeguard the rights of freedmen, and the efforts of the bureau were being thwarted by the President's lack of sympathy with its aims and his refusal to sanction a homestead policy for the freedmen. News also began to come in of measures adopted or under consideration in southern legislatures affecting the status of freedmen, from which it appeared that the southerners intended to keep them as a laboring class, subject to a rigid contract law, and severely limited in their freedom of movement. A different issue also caused concern. Under the apportionment clause in the federal Constitution, which had counted a slave as three-fifths of a man, abolition would automatically increase southern representation at the next census by fifteen or twenty members; it seemed unfair that they should receive this bonus on account of a measure that they had resisted and on behalf of people to whom they had no intention of giving the vote.

All Republicans shared these doubts and questioned the assumption that Reconstruction was an executive responsibility. It was not unreasonable that the representatives of the people who had fought the war should have the right to decide the conditions of peace. Many experienced legislators felt that they had already conceded too much to Lincoln under the guise of the war power, and the Wade-Davis veto still rankled. It was therefore with some relief that Republicans contemplated the provision of the Constitution that "each House shall be the Judge of the Election, Returns and Qualifications of its own Members." The President might authorize provisional governments in the states, but only Congress could decide whether their senators- and representatives-elect were qualified for admission to Congress. With the Vice-President of the Confederacy and several high-ranking Confederate soldiers among those knocking at the door of Congress, there seemed to be ample justification for delay; but the real point at issue was whether inquiry should be confined to the personal loyalty of individuals or extended to the whole character of the provisional governments. Moderate Republicans hoped that the President would accept the addition of "guarantees" to safeguard freedmen's rights and to check the revival of the secessionist power; Radicals hoped for an opportunity to draw more support for their hard line of territorial status and a reconstruction of southern society.

The man of the hour was Thaddeus Stevens. Seventy-four years of age, he was an old man in a hurry; experienced, tough, and formidable in debate, he had longed for the power that was now within his grasp; domineering, cynical about the motives of others, he had, nevertheless, been a lifelong advocate of racial equality. During the Civil War he had been chairman of the House Ways and Means Committee and alarmed the orthodox by his championship of paper currency. He was unmarried, kept a mulatto housekeeper, had a club foot, wore a brown wig, enjoyed flattery, and was a compulsive gambler. His political speeches were short, pointed, and devoid of oratorical flourishes; he was a master of practical politics, who marked out his objectives early in the campaign but was always aware that the best must not be allowed to destroy the good. Charles Sumner, of Massachusetts, is often coupled with Stevens as an architect of Radical Reconstruction, but no two men could have been more unalike. Sumner was almost twenty years younger but had thirteen years' service in the Senate and was now one of its senior members. He was a good chairman of the Foreign Affairs Committee but otherwise played little part in the day-to-day business of Congress (though most regular in attendance) and preferred occasional prepared orations, heavily laden with historical learning and literary allusion. He embarrassed more cautious Republicans by his premature advocacy of Negro suffrage, was a captious critic of most of the great Reconstruction measures, but usually ended by voting for measures that he had attacked. His strength lay in his acknowledged spokesmanship for the antislavery conscience of the North. He could also claim that events had proved his wisdom in opposing compromises, and in retrospect his reputation grows as a man who consistently maintained that a presumption of equality was the only possible basis for a biracial society.

There was no clear-cut division within the Republican party between moderates and Radicals, and it is only on a few procedural votes that they separated. Indeed, on all the substantive votes during the Reconstruction period, the Republicans achieved a remarkable unity. Once they had broken with President Johnson, all the major Reconstruction bills had to be carried over the veto by two-thirds in both houses. The early days of the New Deal offer the only comparable example of sustained solidarity, and this commanded full presidential support. This unity can be explained only by exceptional circumstances, powerful emotional drive, and strongly shared views. The Radicals had no common economic policy, they came from all parts of the Union states, and they represented very varied constituencies. Only one of them (William G. Kelley, of Philadelphia) represented a large city, and only in the new western states of Wisconsin, Minnesota, Iowa, and Kansas did they form a large majority of the Republican members. In New England, the Middle Atlantic States, and the Midwest they shared the Republican delegations in approximately equal numbers with moderate and conservative colleagues. A few came from Missouri and Maryland. If they shared any common factors, it was representation of old antislavery districts in the East, small-town America, and the new rural West. Some had business interests, but neither they nor their policies were popular with the commercial magnates of the northeastern cities.

The first fruit of Stevens's initiative was the appointment of a Joint Committee of Fifteen on Reconstruction (under the chairmanship of the influential William Pitt Fessenden, of Maine) and concurrent resolutions that no senator or representative from a seceding state should be admitted until it had reported. Congress refused to make an exception of Tennessee, even though it was the President's own state, reconstructed by him as military governor, and had his nephew (of unimpeachable Unionist credentials) as one of its senators-elect. The Joint Committee became the most influential body in the country, and though modeled on the Committee on the Conduct of the War, played a more constructive role. It was one of the rare occasions on which Congress made an effective bid to initiate policy. The committee was not a judicial tribunal but appointed to report measures that the majority could approve; its investigations were thorough, but the object was to document a case.

At this juncture President Johnson committed a series of acts that were evidence of courage rather than wisdom. It was clear that a price would have to be paid if the structure of presidential Reconstruction were to be preserved, but it could be kept low if moderate Republicans were not driven into close alliance with the Radicals. Instead the President broke down the bridges between himself and the congressional party. Incensed by the refusal to admit Tennessee, he treated Republican leaders as hostile emissaries. He vetoed a bill extending the life and power of the Freedmen's Bureau, and though Congress might well have been asked to reconsider some of its provisions, he took the general ground that protection of the freedmen must be left to the states and challenged the legality of any measure passed while the Confederate states were excluded. Congress failed by one vote in the Senate to override this veto, but when Johnson vetoed a civil-rights bill guaranteeing individual rights, it was repassed by two-thirds in both houses. Between the two vetoes Johnson had made a public utterance in which he referred to Stevens, Sumner, and

Wendell Phillips as "disunionists" and traitors. This attack upon two leading Republicans and the best-known campaigner for equal rights was hardly calculated to win friends for the President in the North. Concurrently the President began to use federal patronage and his power of dismissal to reward his personal supporters and punish faithful Republicans.

The principal outcome of the Committee of Fifteen's labor was the Fourteenth Amendment. A cumbersome measure, designed to include in one package all the "guarantees" required by the Republican majority, the amendment is, nevertheless, the most important added to the Constitution since the original ten. Its unique significance lay in its first clause, which declared that all persons born or naturalized in the United States were citizens of the United States—thus reversing the Dred Scott decision and firmly establishing the right to determine citizenship—and then made a fundamental alteration in the constitutional balance of power. Hitherto the states had been seen as the natural protectors of the rights of their citizens against infringements by the federal government; now the federal government assumed responsibility for the protection of civil rights against the states. Indirect wording slightly obscured its effect; it did not give to Congress a positive duty to protect rights but prohibited the states from abridging the privileges or immunities of citizens of the United States, depriving any person of life, liberty, or property without due process of law, or denying to any person the equal protection of the law. In later years the amendment was to pass through some curious perversions in judicial interpretation, but in the twentieth century it became the constitutional basis for all decisions advancing equal rights, while the final clause of the amendment—giving Congress the power to enforce its provisions by legislation—was the grant of power that produced in 1875 an abortive, and in 1957 the first effective, Civil Rights Act.

The other clauses were of temporary significance but of great importance in the Reconstruction drama. In a single provision it tackled apportionment and suffrage by reducing proportionately the congressional representation of any state that denied the vote to a portion of its adult male citizens, so that southern white representation might well be decreased if they refused to give black citizens the vote. Its operation might, however, be inequitable, for the effect would be severe in South Carolina, Mississippi, and Louisiana, but hardly noticeable in northern states with few blacks, though the Union states of Maryland, Kentucky, and Missouri would lose representation. On the other hand, any aggrieved state had the remedy in its own hands, and this clause of the amendment, by making it in the interest of a state to introduce Negro suffrage, offered a hopeful road to the future. The process might be slow but promised to be sure. It would soon, however, be superseded by the Fifteenth Amendment and has never been enforced even to prevent illegal disenfranchisement.

Many Republicans attached most significance to an ingenious formula for forcing the old ruling class of the South out of public life; this disqualified from state or federal office all men who had once taken an oath of allegiance to the United States and subsequently aided the rebellion. This disability could be removed only by two-thirds of both houses of Congress. This affected all prewar holders of federal or state office (including justices of the peace), members of Congress and state legislatures, and officers in the armed forces. This sweeping proscription disqualified a large majority of the old upper class and many in humbler stations, but it did not disenfranchise anyone and did not prevent pardoned rebels from recovering their property.

The remaining clauses of the amendment guaranteed the national debt, forbade payment or assumption of the Confederate debt, and gave Congress legislative power to carry the amendment into effect. The Fourteenth Amendment passed Congress with the almost unanimous support of the Republicans. Radicals welcomed disqualification, would have preferred a stronger version of the civil-rights clause (perhaps, as Stevens had suggested, an unequivocal declaration that all laws applied equally to all persons), and had mixed views on the suffrage and apportionment clause. Sumner regarded the evasion of direct action on Negro voting as a betrayal, but Thaddeus Stevens was not an enthusiast for immediate Negro suffrage. In the Committee of Fifteen Stevens had supported a plan that would give all adult males the vote not later than 1876; this had been proposed by Robert Dale Owen (distinguished son of a famous father) and would have allowed a realistic interval to elapse while both races prepared for color-blind suffrage. However, the clause as it passed met the difficulty raised by apportionment based on unenfranchised blacks, and a state that refused to extend the suffrage would lose representation; but many Radicals believed (rightly) that the section would be unworkable and would have preferred a straightforward apportionment based on legal voters. It is possible that President Johnson would have accepted this proposal, but it was unpopular in New England, where the proportion of adult males was falling.

The parting of the ways between Radicals and moderates was over the resumption of normal relations. The moderates regarded the Fourteenth Amendment as the Union terms of peace and assumed that the southern states would be admitted if and when they accepted it. Radicals wished for a much longer period of tutelage, during which the reconstruction of southern society could be effected. If the southern states had moved quickly to accept the amendment, the Republican party might have split on this issue. Fortunately for the Radicals, Johnson and the southerners saved the situation for them and opened the way to a more drastic experiment in Reconstruction.

President Johnson had placed himself at the head of the opposition to Republican policy. His ill-judged impromptu attacks on Stevens, Sumner, and Phillips were vividly recalled by later utterances. His veto messages gave no hope to moderate Republicans of achieving even the minimum guarantees for the Union and freedmen's rights. He hoped to place himself at the head of a new National Union party (formed from Union Democrats, former southern Whigs, and conservative Republicans) and used executive patronage to dismiss regular Republicans. The Republican majority in the Senate replied by refusing confirmation to many of his nominations. When the Fourteenth Amendment finally passed Congress, the President advised southern states against ratification, while in his administration of the Freedmen's Bureau Act he had displayed hostility to the officials most active in protecting the freedmen. His issue of pardons seemed precipitate and responsive to the wrong kind of pressure. Finally he decided to campaign personally against the Republicans in the congressional elections of 1866.

This speaking tour in the North demonstrated the President's real weakness; his basic error lay in insensitivity to the issues as seen by men who had been deeply affected by the war and craved to find in it some transcendental purpose. To be told that the object had been to restore the Union as it had been in 1860 was not enough, particularly when coupled with the assertion that southerners must be left free to decide the status of the Negro without federal intervention. In addition, Johnson's style was ill suited to northern audiences, and men who might have been prepared to consider his views on paper were repelled by their presentation in a manner that had won votes in rural Tennessee. Wherever Johnson spoke he seems to have increased the Republican vote, and in the Union states as a whole the Republican victory was impressive. It was also noticeable that Radicals had done better than moderates, and all conservatives had lost ground. Meanwhile the Fourteenth Amendment was being ignominiously rejected in the South.

The pattern of events was similar in most former Confederate states (except Tennessee), but the example of Virginia was particularly important. As the keystone state of the Confederacy, the seat of its government, and the home of its most heroic leader, Virginia's traditional role as the guardian of southern traditions had been reinforced. On the other hand, it was the state from which conciliatory gestures might be expected. It had always had a strong minority of Whigs, the state had been carried by Bell in 1860, and a considerable number in both the northern and the western counties had remained Unionist in sympathy. Planters, merchants, and railroad men had a lively appreciation of the need to restore association with northern business, and many hoped that well-chosen policies would lead to voluntary reunion with West Virginia. Finally the state ended the war with a shadow government recognized by the Union, so it was unnecessary to go through the process of holding a convention before beginning reconstruction.

In May Francis Pierpont, the Union governor, moved to Richmond, was officially recognized as governor of the whole commonwealth, and welcomed warmly by local leaders. Observers were surprised to notice what was apparently a complete change of sentiment in the state; no one seemed to lament the end of slavery, most seemed to accept the need for a new start, and only a minority showed any inclination to refuse cooperation with the government of the Union. Pierpont recommended the sale of land to Negroes in small lots, in June the legislature legalized Negro marriage, and two Unionists were chosen as United States senators. In October elections for Congress, six of the eight congressional representatives chosen could take the "ironclad" oath, while the state legislature consisted mainly of former Whigs and included no prominent secessionists.

In appearance, therefore, Unionism triumphed in Virginia on the morrow of defeat; but what had really hap-

pened was that the ruling class, composed partly of prewar
Whigs and partly of its younger members who had played
little part in public life before the war, had come to the
fore and established control over the state (so far as this
was compatible with the continued presence of federal
troops). While Pierpont recommended the establishment
of a public school system and a broad but expensive program of economic recovery, the legislature refused Negroes
the right to testify in cases where a white was a party, enacted a severe vagrancy law, and guaranteed payment of
the prewar debt and accrued interest. In December, 1866,
Pierpont advised ratification of the Fourteenth Amendment, but the majority were not prepared to admit federal
jurisdiction over civil rights or to contemplate the possibility of Negro suffrage. The disqualification section does not
seem to have been a great issue in Virginia, though it was
in other states. Johnson's influence against the amendment
was said by some to be decisive, but opponents also argued
that there was no assurance of readmission to the Union if
the amendment were passed. In all, and in spite of the convincing Republican victory in the northern states, they
seemed to have expected that the amendment would die
still-born and that Congress would soon recognize Virginia without further conditions. The amendment was rejected in both houses of the state legislature, with only one
vote cast in its favor, and the state that had shown the
earliest and most hopeful signs of reconstructing its own
political system was now in unqualified opposition to the
policy accepted by Radical and moderate Republicans
alike and endorsed by a convincing majority of the northern electorate.

None of the official actions of the provisional governments in the South contained better promise than this.
Unofficially, or in the twilight zone between public and
private response, the prospect seemed even bleaker.
Congressmen were receiving a mounting volume of com-

plaints from known Unionists of their treatment at the hands of former Confederates. In some cases these were no more than grievances of men who had expected reward and received contempt, but even the least admirable had cause for dissatisfaction, and some had risked much to serve the Union; they expected reproach from former Confederates, but not from the executive of the government they had served. In Virginia serious efforts were made to exclude notorious secessionists from public life, but this did not mean extending the hand of fellowship to active Unionists. Similarly, freedmen complained that the provisional governments denied them the full rights of citizenship, but their worst treatment came from private persons. At the outset in Virginia Governor Pierpont had argued that the landowners would themselves adjust to a free labor system and that no legislation protecting the rights of Negroes was necessary; after a year's experience he revised his views. Throughout the South what might be true of an occasional enlightened landowner was not true of the majority; they had been bred upon the assumption that Negro inferiority was axiomatic, that law and religion enjoined his submission, and that independence implied defiance. The irony was that most southerners believed that they had done everything that could be reasonably expected of them, whereas to those outside it seemed that they had hardly made a start. The gap was too wide to be bridged by any normal political process.

This was the situation that confronted Congress, meeting for its second session in December, 1866. Radical Republicans wanted a suspension of the provisional governments and territorial status for an indefinite period. Moderates wanted an early restoration of normal political relationships, but with the Fourteenth Amendment safely in the Constitution. President Johnson wanted the immediate admission of senators and representatives from the southern states and modified his previous views only by emphasizing that while states should be admitted, individuals could be excluded.

In the admission of Senators and Representatives for any and all of the States there can be no just ground of apprehension that persons who are disloyal will be clothed with the powers of legislation, for this could not happen when the Constitution and the laws are enforced by a vigilant and faithful Congress. Each House is made the "judge of the elections, returns, and qualifications of its own members," and may, "with the concurrence of two-thirds, expel a member."

But the exclusion of individuals could have only an indirect effect upon the situation in the South, and it was this that gave concern to members of Congress. In the first session the key word had been "guarantees"; in the second it was to be "protection," and this provided further cement to bind Radicals and moderates together while separating both from the President. Without protection loyal men would be persecuted and freedmen oppressed, but the right to vote would provide protection without constant surveillance by the federal government. Thus, by a curious turn of the wheel, Negro suffrage became the argument by which moderates hoped to resist the Radical policy of territorialization for an indefinite period; and though Radicals were content to leave decisions to the Fortieth Congress (with its stronger Radical element), moderates hoped to get a measure decided in the Thirty-ninth.

Radicals objected that even Negro suffrage would be of no avail if the southern upper class were entrusted with responsibility for making constitutions and conducting elections. A revolution was necessary in the South, and this could not be effected merely by giving ignorant and inexperienced black men the vote. When Congress rejected the Radical proposal for the replacement of the provisional governments by military rule under congressional authority, controversy shifted to a formula that would best keep the old ruling class from controlling the situation in restored states. In the last days of the Thirty-ninth Congress a solution was found in temporarily disenfranchising those whom the Fourteenth Amendment proposed to disqualify, requiring ratification of the Fourteenth Amendment and postponing admission until it had become a part of the Constitution. In its final form congressional Reconstruction required several stages before readmission. The act declared that as "no legal State governments or adequate protection for life or property" existed in the rebel states (except Tennessee), they should be placed under military rule. A constitutional convention should then be elected by all male citizens except those excluded from office by the proposed Fourteenth Amendment; if the proposed constitution were ratified by a majority of qualified voters and approved by Congress, and if the legislature subsequently ratified the Fourteenth Amendment, and when the amendment had become a part of the constitution, then senators and representatives from the state could be admitted to Congress. Disenfranchisement would then cease, but disqualification would continue under the Fourteenth Amendment until ended by two-thirds of both houses of Congress. In the hurried hours when the final form of the act was agreed, nothing was said about who should initiate the process, and a second act passed by the Fortieth Congress made the commanding generals responsible for registering qualified voters and calling conventions. Nor had authority been given to the military commanders to remove or appoint civil officers, and this, with other minor omissions, was remedied in a third act. Finally, when southern whites abstained from voting to prevent ratification being passed by the required majority of legal voters, a fourth act required only a majority of votes cast for this purpose.

Four further acts were designed to give Congress firm control over the processes of government. To avoid the normal interval between the end of one Congress and the beginning of the next, it was agreed that the next Congress should meet on March 4, immediately after its predecessor had terminated. An Army Appropriations Act contained a provision that all military orders from the executive should be issued through the general of the armies, who could not be removed or assigned to other duties without the consent of the Senate. A Tenure of Office Act deprived the President of the right to dismiss federal officials, for whose appointment the consent of the Senate was required, without the approval of that body. Finally, Congress limited the appellate jurisdiction of the Supreme Court to exclude appeals from military courts in the South.

The constitutionality of these acts has often been questioned, and some commentators have praised the President for the constitutional purity of his civil-rights veto while condemning Congress for steps that were justified by the Constitution itself. The Constitution said that "Congress shall assemble at least once in every Year, and such Meeting shall be on the first Monday in December, unless they shall by Law appoint a different Day" and that "the supreme Court shall have appellate Jurisdiction, both as to Law and Fact, with such Exceptions, and under such Regulations as the Congress shall make." The President's power of dismissal depended upon an interpretation adopted by the First Congress, not upon a strict construction of the Constitution itself. The President was Commander in Chief, but Congress had power "to make Rules for the Government and Regulation of the land and naval Forces."

The Republicans argued that these measures remedied long-standing anomalies or applied common sense to an unprecedented situation. The long interval of over twelve months between the election of a Congress and its first meeting had often caused inconvenience. The Constitution had been intended to ensure that Congress should meet at least once a year, not to give the President exclu-

sive authority to decide when a special session was necessary. It was irrational that laws passed by Congress, and
dependent upon the military for their execution, should be
thwarted because the President issued orders that nullified
their operation. The Tenure of Office Act was originally
designed to prevent the President from dismissing officials
who were acting in the spirit of laws approved by Congress; it was aimed both to limit his use of patronage in
building up a personal party and to end dismissals of
officers of the Freedmen's Bureau who had become conspic-
uous for the defense of Negro interests. During debate the
act was enlarged to include Cabinet posts, on the ground
that against the spirit of the Constitution the authority of
the President (and of several of his predecessors) had been
used to make the Cabinet subservient to his personal will.
The military courts were, in many parts of the South, the
only tribunals from which Negroes and former Unionists
could expect justice; their effectiveness lay in the rapidity
with which they could act and would be negated by the
normal but expensive delays of the law. Congress intended
and almost consummated a revolution in constitutional
practice, but this could be defended as an attempt to
get back to first principles; for it was certainly arguable
that the makers of the Constitution intended legislative
supremacy rather than presidential government.

The revolution in constitutional practice ended by over-
reaching itself. If Congress was to be supreme, the President must be subordinate, but as head of the executive he
retained extensive powers and his veto was an effective instrument except when an overwhelming majority was ar-
rayed against him. A majority of the Republicans now
moved to the view that the President's use of his authority
conflicted with his duty to "take care that the Laws be
faithfully executed," and that he should be replaced.
In Andrew Johnson's case this argument was strengthened
by the accidental nature of his succession and the condemnation of his policy by a large majority in the congressional

elections. Yet the Constitution provided no means of removing a President save by impeachment. The Republicans were caught in a dilemma; their real intention was to remove the President on political grounds, but the Constitution limited the grounds for impeachment to "Treason, Bribery, or other high Crimes and Misdemeanors." An opportunity seemed to be presented when Johnson dismissed Stanton, the Secretary of War, without the consent of the Senate and thus in defiance of the Tenure of Office Act. Unfortunately for the managers of the impeachment, which was initiated by the House in March, 1868, the President could avail himself of the technical defense that Stanton had been appointed by Lincoln and was therefore not protected by the Tenure of Office Act (which could hardly have been intended to prevent a new President from dismissing his predecessor's appointees). The arguments on this point were involved, but the effect was to shift the burden of decision from the formal to the real ground for impeachment (summarized in the eleventh article of impeachment), that the President had defied Congress. In a crucial phrase he had denied "that the legislation of said Congress was valid or obligatory upon him . . . except in so far as he saw fit to approve the same." In effect, the eleventh article said that even though Johnson might slip through the net of the Tenure of Office Act, he should be removed from office for having failed to "execute faithfully" the policy agreed by Congress.

The Republicans in the Senate had the two-thirds majority necessary for conviction, but the issue was, nevertheless, in doubt. A vital constitutional principle was at stake; if it were established that a President could be removed on political grounds, the country would have taken a significant step toward congressional government, and the ultimate power to direct policy would lie with a majority in the House and two-thirds of those present in the Senate. The trial was conducted by Chief Justice Salmon P. Chase with an impartiality that seemed (to ardent Republicans) too favorable toward the defense, and on the vital eleventh article seven Republican senators voted "not guilty" to save Andrew Johnson from conviction by one vote. If one of the dissenting Republicans had voted in the affirmative—or if two had absented themselves—the President would have been impeached, the constitutional history of the United States might have taken a different course, and presidential domination might not have developed in the twentieth century. One must, however, resist the temptation to deduce far-reaching consequences from single events, and it is, perhaps, more relevant that the misfortunes of Andrew Johnson ushered in a period of weak presidential leadership than to suggest that his narrow escape affected events that still lay far in the future.

The final measure of congressional Reconstruction was the Fifteenth Amendment that "the right of citizens of the United States to vote shall not be denied or abridged by the United States or by any State on account of race, color, or previous condition of servitude." There has been considerable controversy over the motives behind this amendment. A common-sense view suggests that while the Reconstruction acts had imposed Negro suffrage on the South, these measures could easily be repealed by a subsequent Congress, and states would then be free to restrict suffrage. It was also inequitable that Negroes should vote in the South but not in some of the northern states. There was a subsidiary argument that without the Negro vote the Republican party would collapse in the South and might be endangered in the Midwest. In arguing the case for the amendment it was natural to calm the fears of some Republicans by assuring them that the bonus of new Negro votes would offset any losses of white votes, but it seems somewhat perverse to suggest that the minor benefits that might be expected to the Republicans in some cities and midwestern districts provided the major reason for pressing the amendment through Congress. What is far more striking is the distance traveled by northern Americans on racial questions. In 1860 Negroes had voted only in Massachusetts and (on a high property qualification) in New York. In 1865 only a handful of extreme radicals favored Negro suffrage; in 1866 an early version of the Fourteenth Amendment had been killed by the objections of some Republicans who could not contemplate the promise of Negro suffrage by 1876.

The Fifteenth Amendment adopted a weaker form of words than some might have hoped. A simple declaration giving all adult male citizens, not disqualified by crime or insanity, the right to vote would have been more effective and easier to enforce; but the states were left free to impose tax-paying or literacy qualifications, and in this way a whole chapter of evasions was opened. The later years of the nineteenth century saw systematic disenfranchisement in many southern states, and not until the second half of the twentieth century would there be serious efforts to honor the spirit of the amendment. In the northern and western states, however, the amendment was accepted, and the later migration of southern Negroes into the northern and midwestern cities brought them political influence, and in the long run this would be more important than southern disenfranchisement.

Reconstruction can be seen as a logical extension of the great changes inaugurated by the Civil War and displays some of the characteristics that one expects in the "anatomy" of a revolution. It began as a constitutional attempt to write into law provisions to safeguard the gains of the war. A vigorous minority wished to go further but were forced to take what they could get in the Fourteenth Amendment. The failure of this policy to achieve its objectives served to intensify the demand for more drastic change and enabled the Radicals to increase their power in Congress. There followed a series of measures in which Radicals and moderates acted with remarkable solidarity; though they argued about details, they united in support of agreements that were reached. In this phase the objectives broadened to include important adjustments in the central machinery of government. The Fourteenth and Fifteenth amendments effected such alteration in the distribution of power that it was not inappropriate to contrast the "new" with the "old" Constitution. The revolution had, however, to take place within the framework of a political system that most men continued to respect; for this reason impeachment failed, and congressional government failed to gather momentum. In the years immediately following Reconstruction the prestige and power of the Supreme Court greatly increased, and the cutting edge of legislative supremacy was blunted on the rock of judicial vetoes. Hindsight should not, however, blind one to the possibilities that were opened by the political revolution of Reconstruction.

The Reconstruction controversies had brought the United States to the verge of a constitutional revolution. The federal courts now had jurisdiction wherever privileges and immunities were abridged, due process ignored, or equal protection denied. Policies had been initiated in Congress, and the Committee of Fifteen had demonstrated that a kind of congressional cabinet existed in the limbo of constitutional possibilities. Republican orators had emphasized the subordination of states to federal authority, spoken repeatedly of "the nation," and even invoked a sovereign will that unconsciously echoed the theories of Jean Jacques Rousseau and the German philosophers. Yet the constitutional revolution was abortive. Failure of the impeachment was a setback but not a mortal blow, and causes that weakened the dynamic of change were of deeper origin. There was simple inertia and force of habit, for whatever the rhetoricians might say, officials and lawyers instinctively turned to familiar precepts. There was a basic weakness in political mechanics, for neither then, nor on any subsequent occasion, did Congress evolve an efficient, coordinated, and coherent policy-making body. The following years would not see the concentration of responsibility but its diffusion over dozens of autonomous congressional committees. Then the Democrats, who had been overwhelmed in 1866 but not annihilated, and showed signs of revival in 1868, were committed to reversing the trend of innovation. Finally, the moneyed men of the country, alarmed by radicalism and anxious for the restoration of sectional harmony, were using their private but pervasive influence to curb radical tendencies, restore the authority of the Supreme Court, redress the balance between executive and legislature, and make the national government both sound and safe.

Whatever conclusion economic historians may eventually reach about the material consequences of the war, certain facts are clear. Cotton had been profitable and essential to the national economy; vast northern interests had been committed to the South; Boston, New York, and Philadelphia had been heavily engaged in all the commerce and banking operations of southern trade; the South had been a leading market for domestic and imported manufactures; the river cities of the Ohio and upper Mississippi valleys had been advancing their mercantile interests in the Southwest, while the rising metropolis of Chicago thrust southward the Illinois Central Railroad. Many of those concerned were anxious to send their agents into the South as soon as hostilities ceased, and along with them went dozens of hopeful men in search of a fortune; but everyone knew that large-scale revival depended upon establishing working agreements with men on the spot and securing the goodwill of whoever controlled local politics.

Active men in the South realized the need for northern capital, northern aid, and northern goods. War, economic ruin, and the shadow of political disabilities had forced the planter class to their knees and driven many to impotent poverty, but the survivors were resilient men who had learned the lesson of economic diversification the hard way. In 1865 they recovered political authority; in 1866 they were looking for a political solution to usher in a period of economic cooperation, and even at this early stage they could make common cause with northeastern merchants and textile manufacturers in pressing the Freedmen's Bureau to organize labor for the plantations. Looking further ahead, they hoped that the contract, apprenticeship, and vagrancy laws in the new black codes would stabilize the labor situation.

To this upper class, drawn from old Whig families or from men newly risen from the ranks of the yeoman farmers, disqualification proposed by the Fourteenth Amendment came as a shattering threat. Their hard-won ascendancy would be overthrown (for a majority would be affected) , and with the loss of political power would go the chance of winning the confidence of northern merchants and bankers from whom alone could come the capital for sustained recovery. Rightly they judged that it would be expedient to resist voluntary abdication, whatever the consequences, and refuse ratification; as leaders of the opposition their position would be far stronger than as tame supplicants for congressional pardon. When the Radical countermeasure proved to be Negro suffrage, these tactics were vindicated by the consequent alliance between whites of all classes. Conservative planter businessmen could appear as champions of the Old South and the white race; privately they could condone anti-Negro terrorism while demonstrating their respect for law by condemning it publicly; beyond this lay the probability of alliance with conservative forces in the North.

Nevertheless, Radical Reconstruction presented some difficult problems of judgment for white southern leaders, and not all judged correctly. Some went too far in counseling defiance of the law; others calculated that cooperation would yield the best dividends, and the "scalawags" included several bearing distinguished southern names. The legislatures under the new regime had the power to tax, and largess to bestow in the form of state bonds and guarantees for private loans to finance railroads, banks, and factories. Reconstruction legislatures that favored new entrepreneurs from the North had seemed to have it in their power to supplant the revived upper class and promote their rivals as the preferred allies of northern capitalism. Should the old upper class beat them or join them? The question was not easy to answer, but for most of them there could, in the long run, be only one answer: to lead the "redemption" and beat the Radicals at the political game. Typically, the directors of the Louisville and Nashville Railroad, who coveted and eventually obtained unique influence in the lower South, decided to back redemption and to refuse cooperation with Radical legislatures whatever immediate difficulties might ensue.

In a sense the freedmen were peripheral to this power struggle. The upper class was not particularly disturbed (once the initial shock had been absorbed) by Negro rights or even by Negro suffrage. A class that had learned political skill in handling a potentially restive white electorate was not likely to be unduly concerned by the task of handling simple black wage earners. The supposed threat of black political power was, nevertheless, an excellent cement for white solidarity, and planter businessmen soon realized that the politics of race could sublimate the conflicts of class. And whatever the overt commitments of the Republicans to safeguard Negro rights, the reunion of the old white Protestant stock—restored to command in the South and dominant in northern business—provided an excellent emotional base for a nationwide business alliance.

In the North the economics of Reconstruction were confused. Everyone was committed to expansion and prosperity, but no one could make a rational calculation of how these ends could be achieved. The war ended with what would now be regarded as a comparatively mild dose of inflation, which could be regarded as a reasonable part of the price of victory. The irredeemable paper dollars ("greenbacks") had recovered slightly from their lowest value in 1864, but their depreciation was still sufficient to alarm orthodox financiers.[4] In particular it disturbed those trying to attract foreign capital or to import from abroad; investors wanted a stable currency, and importers found it difficult to obtain credit except at rates raised to cover a possible fall in the value of the paper dollar. If importers wished to buy gold to settle debts incurred abroad, they had to pay a premium in greenbacks that acted as concealed protection for American goods. On the other side of the argument were the many small-business men who had ventured out in the war years with money borrowed when loans were not tied to gold reserves. To some extent farmers had benefited from easy money, but the principal beneficiaries had been the manufacturers, who gained from an inflationary market, the restraints upon importation, and the gold premium.

The battle over the greenbacks was fought largely among the Republicans, with the Democrats playing a wavering and opportunist role. A number of Republicans, including Thaddeus Stevens and his faithful lieutenant, William G. Kelley, were deeply committed to the nationalist economics of Henry Carey, who argued, in his later days, for a national policy of industrial protection and a controlled paper currency, expanded or contracted according to economic needs, without reference to the supplies of gold. The difficulty, of course, lay in estimating the needs and gauging precisely the quantity of money necessary to finance production without undermining confidence, but

---

[4] The gold price of greenbacks fluctuated a great deal, but the average price of $100 in gold was $113 in greenbacks in 1862, $145 in 1863, $203 in 1864, and $157 in 1865. Cf. Robert P. Sharkey, *Money, Class, and Party* (Baltimore: Johns Hopkins Press, 1959), p. 51. This book provides the best treatment of the complex question in 1865–1870; Irwin Unger, *The Greenback Era* (Princeton, N.J.: Princeton University Press, 1964), carries the story on to 1879 and sets the currency question in its social and political context.

in the deflationary postwar years the problem was presented in a simpler form. A resumption of specie payments would mean a contraction of the greenback circulation to bring the price of the paper dollar back to the gold standard. Thousands of loans would have to be called in, and a drastic curb on further advances would be necessary. At the same time the manufacturers would benefit little from lowered prices, as few manufactured goods were exported. Cotton exporters, however, stood to benefit considerably, as the fall in prices would increase demand abroad and put hard money into their pockets. Western wheat farmers were also more likely to favor contraction as a boost to their growing export trade, though this might be offset by the need to repay loans obtained to finance wartime expansion.

Hugh McCulloch, Johnson's Secretary of the Treasury, was a stolid Indiana banker trained in orthodox financial doctrines. Faced with depreciation of the paper currency, he ordered contraction in 1866 as a first step toward the resumption of specie payments, which he anticipated by 1868. Almost immediately the effect was felt, and then multiplied, as the United States felt the shock waves spreading outward from a British financial crisis. In 1866 the contraction bill had met with doubtful and halfhearted opposition; in 1867 a majority of the Republicans moved quickly to repeal it. At the same period the Democrats, traditionally committed to hard money, fastened on the national debt as a grievance and mounted an attack on the public creditors whose contracts stipulated payment of interest and principal in gold. While other citizens were managing with a depreciated paper currency, it was easy to argue that the debt should be scaled down or that interest be paid in greenbacks. From this it was a short step to demand further inflationary issues of paper money to relieve midwestern farmers from their debt burdens.

The situation was now highly confused; so much so that few contemporaries understood its complexities, and almost a century would elapse before historical investigation unraveled the various threads. Some Republicans were consistent greenbackers and favored Democratic plans for paying national debt charges in paper money at current values; others favored greenbacks but maintained that the obligation to the public creditors must be honored; others supported the contraction policy and a speedy return to gold. Some Democrats were clamoring for an end to devalued paper money and strict curbs on bank issues; others, linked with New York bankers, favored both the gold standard and freedom for state banks from the curbs of the National Banking System; others, and among them the most vocal, wanted more paper currency issued as a relief measure. Somehow out of all this later generations, echoing perhaps the issues of 1896, distilled the theory that the Republicans favored hard money and specie payments, the Democrats soft money and easy credit. It required but a further misconception to picture Radical Reconstruction as the facade behind which hard-money policies were to be imposed upon the country. It would be truer to say that northern bankers and merchants watched with growing anxiety the political success of Radicals who promised a prolonged period of inconvertible paper.

In any event the Republicans worked their way toward a compromise by which the resumption of specie payment was deferred but no further paper issues were to be made except under strict control. The expectation was that the rising tide of prosperity would gradually bring the paper currency into balance with gold and make painless resumption possible. The hope was to be delayed by the depression that began in 1873. In 1874 the Republican majority, frightened by the prospect of Democratic gains, passed a bill authorizing an issue of greenbacks as a relief measure but this was vetoed by President Grant. In 1879 John Sherman, as Secretary of the Treasury, was at last able to guide the country back to the apparently safe haven of specie resumption; but by then the country had moved into a very different era, and the struggles of Reconstruction were the bitter memories of aging men.

The greenback controversy was essentially an argument over the supply of capital for expansion. The Republicans advocated either borrowing on prospects of future growth, or postponing expansion until savings had accumulated, or creating conditions favorable for the importation of foreign capital. The Democrats called for relief measures for men who had fallen into debt—either through overexpansion or through economic fluctuations over which they had no control—together with discriminatory legislation against men who had done too well out of the war. Whatever their theoretical differences, Republicans united in looking to the future, whereas the Democrats looked back to relieve distress or punish profiteers; and if the different objectives are remembered, it will be understood why men who appeared to subscribe to similar soft-money theories found few points of agreement. The South shared characteristics of both attitudes. There was need for new investment, but the primary purpose was to recover from the losses of war, and on both counts southern leaders were likely to support any proposals that would make it easier to borrow in the North, and this was as true of scions of the Old South as it was of carpetbaggers. There was, therefore, a conflict of interest between the southern entrepreneurs and the hard-money interest of the North, and southerners found their best economic allies among some of the strongest Radicals, and their stoutest opponents among the conservative Republicans and such Democratic financiers as August Belmont. This underlines the thesis that economics was often at cross-purposes with politics, as might be expected in a period of economic change and ideological upheaval. There was pressure by the developed society of the Northeast and Midwest upon the retarded and shattered society of the South, but this pressure was diffused in many ways and applied at different points in different ways. It did not focus upon specific policies, because the men of the developed society were themselves divided on economic matters that few understood.

This serves to underline some further points. There was a ready-made basis for Reconstruction in the common interest of northern and southern businessmen in the recovery of the South and the revival of its former contribution to the national economy, but the potential southern members of this alliance were those whom the Radicals wished to drive out of public life. The compulsory divorce between economic interest and political aims was difficult to maintain, and in 1872 a majority of the Republicans (becoming increasingly responsive to business pressure) joined with the Democrats to rescind the political disabilities imposed by the Fourteenth Amendment. This was a more significant step than the supposed formation of a conservative alliance between eastern Republicans and southern Democrats in the "compromise" of 1877. By that time the planter-business class of the South had recovered power in all but three of the states, and the economic ties were closely welded. With far-reaching consequences this planter-business leadership was committed not only to white supremacy (which everyone took for granted) but also to systematic evasion of the Fourteenth and Fifteenth amendments. This had not always been so, for there had been some substance in the planters' claim that they were the freedmen's best friends. In freedom as in slavery the large employers had the most direct interest in the well-being of their labor force; equality they would not grant, but some kind of fair deal might well have been offered as the price of political ascendancy and economic recovery.

This leads to the paradoxical conclusion that Radical efforts were directed principally against the class that could have best promoted the reconstruction of southern society. If the Radicals had been materialistic, purely partisan, or cynically opportunist, they might well have brought off a deal with the southern leaders that would have been to their mutual economic advantage. If success is the sole criterion for political action, the major error of the Radicals was their failure to understand the character of the ruling class in the South and to see all as secessionist conspirators who must be deprived forever of the capacity for doing harm. They did not realize that the true secessionists had been long since squeezed out of power and that leadership now consisted of old Whigs, former Unionists, reluctant rebels, and ambitious men on the make. Instead of seeking an understanding with this ruling class, Radical Reconstruction, with its insistence upon disqualification, drove its members to racialism as the means of recovering power. Only in this way could they secure themselves against the threat of replacement by rival groups, mainly northern and midwestern in origin, who hoped to benefit from the favor of southern Republican governments. On this analysis the real reason for the initial success and ultimate failure of Reconstruction was that leading Radicals meant what they said, and like dedicated men everywhere generated equal determination among their enemies. The Fourteenth and Fifteenth amendments had been added to the Constitution, but the symbolic figure for the immediate future was the white-hooded man of the Ku Klux Klan.

9

The Transition from Slavery to Freedom

SLAVERY was never exclusively a southern problem, nor did its burden lie only upon the enslaved. It affected masters and all the dependents of slave-owning families; it molded the lives and thoughts of the nonslaveholders who lived alongside slavery. Less directly its pervasive influence was felt by every citizen of the United States, and its end created problems for the freedmen and for the whole nation. Whatever hopes may have been raised, and whatever analogies may have been drawn from experience, no American knew what society would be like without slavery, what behavior to expect from the freedmen, or how emancipation would affect white society. Everyone could predict that racial tension would remain, that somehow the problem of labor would have to be solved, and that the former slaveowners would have to discover the law and customs of a wage-earning society; but the people of the United States went headlong toward a new great experiment without any idea of how it should be tackled.

Before 1860 everyone who advocated emancipation thought of progress by stages toward freedom. In the most cautious proposals emancipation would have stretched over two or three generations, and colonizationists had added proposals to draw off free Negroes by emigration schemes. Immediate abolitionists had demanded that slavery should cease at a stroke to be recognized by law; though most of them had considered a subsequent period of training and adjustment to be necessary, the logic of the abolitionist strategy had demanded a frontal attack on slavery and a refusal to be drawn into hypothetical arguments about what should follow. Indeed, Garrison had tended to assume that as slaveholders themselves must find the way to abolish slavery, they must also learn to make freedom work.

Naturally no thought on these lines could be expected in the South itself. Since 1831 it had been impossible to discuss publicly any alternative to slavery, and the weightiest argument against emancipation was the danger of having a large free black population. Indeed, proslavery men used abolitionist proposals for immediate emancipation to threaten nonslaveholders with the prospect of a black flood once slavery ceased to exist. Voluntary emancipation became an antisocial action, and in several states masters were required to remove freed slaves from the slave states. Voluntary emancipation did go on (three thousand were freed in 1860), but mainly in the upper South or in cities where the favored slaves were often elderly domestic servants. Nowhere was there any precedent for large-scale emancipation.

It is a matter of difficult speculation to decide the capacity of the slaves themselves to meet the challenge of freedom. Socially they were more varied than is often imagined. They were field hands on large plantations, laborers on small farms, craftsmen, and household slaves; they worked in all kinds of employment and might be hired out in gangs or as skilled men. They had their own social hierarchy headed by superior house servants, drivers, preachers, and "conjurors" (or spell workers). Like other working populations, they lived in two worlds: that of the masters and that made by themselves. The first contained the harsh realities of life and demanded conformity as the price of privilege and obedience as the basic condition for survival; the other was made up of myths and fancies that nourished hope and preserved self-respect.

If status in the slave society was conferred by the master, esteem among their fellows was often secured by evasion of the master's rules. Their folktales told of weak creatures in a world of strong creatures; quick wit, cunning, and deception were the keys to success. Brer Rabbit was engaged in a lifelong battle against slow-witted, stupid, and vindictive foxes, wolves, and bears who had the power to assault, torture, maim, and destroy. The rabbit relied only upon his wits, disregarded the rules imposed by the brutal and strong, or turned them to his own purpose. The legendary slave "John" had the best of "ol' Massa" even while preserving an outward show of subservience. The tortoise won the race against the swift; the weak little terrapin escaped the predatory buzzard. In their religion these myths took on a more strongly emotional form; there was the promise of future happiness and of judgment upon the Egyptians. Preachers appeared to counsel submission while teaching their flock to preserve independence and hope in captivity. Of all the biblical symbols Jordan became the most evocative; over the sacred river God's children would cross to enjoy their own.

This alternative culture contained a rudimentary social philosophy with different values and different aims from those of the white man; yet it existed in a white man's world. The authority of the master was universal in both the real world and the world of emotion. A slave tended to identify himself by his relationship to that authority. It was a mark of superior status to be under the direct orders of "massa" or "missis" and not under an overseer. The slaves who enjoyed most privileges had also an interest in the reputation of the master. Their own servility was enriched by contact with a master who was wealthy, wise, respected, and just. When freedom came, authority had no longer the power to confer these benefits, and an entire change came over the relationship. Former owners frequently complained that the most trusted and privileged house servants were the first to leave or to assert their independence by petty acts of defiance. This sudden change of demeanor puzzled and saddened the owners and their wives, who had often exercised special responsibilities for the welfare of the domestic slaves and their children. Later white southern folklore made much play with the faithful slaves who refused to abandon the family they served, but the evidence suggests that they were not typical. Often, it is true, the house servants returned after establishing their right to go and resumed their old duties but with the undeclared assumption that they were willing but not compelled to serve. Thousands of southern households had to come to terms with the right to secede.

Folklore, religion, and the behavior of freedmen demonstrate that slaves had not been stripped bare of their personality, whatever the law might have done to them, but there were tragic implications in myths of escape and evasion. The world of the slaves can be contrasted with that of the white frontiersman; both were escapist and owed as much to imagination as to reality, but whereas the white pioneer had escaped into a hard, competitive, and individualistic mythology, the slaves had escaped into an inner life conditioned by the recognition of overwhelming authority. The culture of the slaves was often vivid and emotionally stirring, but collective dreams were a poor preparation for life in a highly competitive society. The people crossed over Jordan, but into a wilderness with long bitter years ahead.

Some four million slaves came into freedom without any understanding of what their status should be, and few had the knowledge to instruct. Most of them had no money; many had only primitive agricultural skills; few could read, and fewer still could understand the complexities of the law. Sympathetic observers often discovered a strong vein of common sense, but it fastened upon simple things that they hoped would be theirs by right.

Above all, the emblem of freedom was the ownership of land. For the freedman this meant crossing the great divide between servitude and freedom. Wage-earning was unfamiliar, and many found it difficult to realize that they would have to work in order to secure the food that had hitherto come whether they worked or not. To own one's own land and raise one's own food was a different matter, but little land was distributed, and some of that was reclaimed when Johnson's pardons restored rights to former owners. As a consequence the freedmen found themselves in a twilight world that they did not understand; they were no longer slaves but had not become free as they understood the term. For many the Freedmen's Bureau was expected to provide, but often they found the officers as anxious as the planters to get them back to gang work under contract.

It was idle to expect leadership to emerge from this mass; that would take a generation or more. The superior household servants were too attached to their accustomed routine, and once the awkwardness of freedom was over, did not seek exposure to a competitive world. One class of former slave could develop more ambition; these were the drivers, who had often been more than men with whips. They were the warrant officers of the plantation system, allocating work, investigating petty grievances as well as punishing minor crime, interpreting the master's commands to the slaves and often the worries of slaves to masters. Some drivers came to exercise large responsibilities; many were literate, and most were of considerable natural intelligence. In a somewhat different category were the Negro preachers, both slave and free, who were accustomed to speaking with authority. There were also a few highly favored slaves (some the sons of white masters) who had been brought up in white households; such was Robert Smalls, hero of the dashing escape from Charleston and subsequently a congressman and unchallenged leader in the Sea Islands of South Carolina. There were a small number of skilled slaves in other positions who could assume responsibilities. Most of the politically active blacks were drawn from the free Negroes in the towns, but there was often a gulf fixed between them and the former field hands; their background was different, and geographically they had lived apart. Leadership was not only a question of promoting a few men of superior intelligence to hold state office but of finding men in every community who could organize and accept responsibility; it was at this level that the culture of slavery and the habit of dependence persisted long after emancipation had removed its causes.

Freedom almost always came suddenly, but in different areas at different times and by different methods. In districts that were occupied by Union troops by 1862, the Negroes existed for some time half slave and half free: free to move, free to starve, but still legally enslaved, though their masters might have absconded. One particular region, the Sea Islands of South Carolina, was the scene of the most ambitious experiment in the training and education of former slaves; it attracted wide attention (and has been the subject of an excellent modern study [1]), but the results were inconclusive. Elsewhere slaves in thousands crossed into Union lines, to the great embarrassment of the military commanders, who did not know how to treat them and received no clear directives from the national government. General B. F. Butler, always fertile in expedients, decided to treat them as "contraband"—that is, as property that could be used by the enemy for warlike purposes and thus liable to confiscation under the rules of international law. As "contrabands" many slaves worked as laborers or performed other menial tasks in Union camps. A few were also freed under the confiscation acts passed by Congress in 1861 and 1862.

The Emancipation Proclamation affected some slaves before the breakthrough in 1864. Thousands joined Sherman's army as hangers-on, and many others became free as the soldiers occupied the plantations. As the southern ar-

---

[1] Willie Lee Rose, *Rehearsal for Reconstruction: The Port Royal Experiment* (Indianapolis: Bobbs-Merrill, 1964).

mies withdrew or surrendered, the news of freedom reached the slaves (often before their masters had heard of events). In other remote areas they continued as slaves for weeks after the fighting ended, and some masters insisted that the proclamation became inoperative, as war had ceased and the Thirteenth Amendment was not yet ratified. In many other cases the owners called the slaves together and told them that Union victory had made them free but that they could continue to live in their quarters until the position became clear. Soon the exigencies of agriculture demanded that some kind of contract labor should be introduced, but masters (as unfamiliar with wage labor as the freedmen) often assumed that contracts allowed them to use again the harsh discipline of forced and servile labor. The "black codes" enacted by the southern legislatures might be justified by necessity as police measures, poor laws, and labor systems, but they incorporated the views of those who believed that discipline rather than training was the need of the day.

If proslavery men had refused to contemplate alternative systems, the abolitionists had given little thought to the problem of race in a free society. They had assumed, with some justice, that efforts to improve the status of Negroes in the North could have little permanent effect as long as slavery debased the whole race. When war promised an early end to slavery, the situation changed, and it became imperative to demonstrate that Negroes everywhere were entitled to equality and qualified for citizenship. Abolitionists had always maintained a theoretical opposition to the idea of innate Negro inferiority, and in and after 1861 they began to attack the biblical and scientific arguments for racial inequality. Some investigated the African past and collected examples of African distinction in both continents and in antiquity. They sometimes got into deep water over racial differences (which might imply that Negroes were fit for some responsibilities but not for others) but were most likely to conclude that differences should be ignored and that equal rights should rest upon the broad basis of universal humanity.

During the war there were many efforts to eliminate or diminish discrimination. Churches were pressed to abandon segregation, and there were efforts to end it in schools. Charles Sumner led a national campaign to end discrimination in the courts; in 1862 he was successful in opening the courts of the District of Columbia to Negro witnesses, and in 1864 the same rule was extended to all federal courts. The District of Columbia was also the testing ground for ending discrimination in public transport. The other eastern cities were much harder nuts to crack, and the dreadful New York draft riots seemed to reverse every trend not merely to equal but even to humane treatment of the blacks; but the very violence of the mob, and the pointless murder of Negroes, produced a reaction among decent citizens, and the powerful *Tribune* and *Evening Post* backed a campaign to end segregation on the streetcars. Just a year after the riots, all streetcars were open equally to both races. Progress was slower in Philadelphia, though the antislavery men were influential and well organized; but in March, 1867 (the same month as the first Reconstruction act), the state legislature abolished segregation on all streetcars and railroads. In the Midwest the racial barriers were even harder to break down than in the East; racial prejudice was exploited by the Democratic opposition, and legal discrimination continued in many areas of life. Only in some antislavery strongholds (such as Cleveland, Ohio) were substantial changes made.

Taken individually, the moves toward racial equality were slow and the gains small, but cumulatively the results were impressive evidence of a great change taking place. If few accepted the positive proposition that the races were equal, a growing number accepted the negative conclusion that racial differences did not justify legal inequality. Opinion was more sluggish west of the Appalachians, but discriminatory practices were greatly diminished in the northern cities of the Midwest. Thus the war began a trend that would reach its high tide with the ratification of the Fifteenth Amendment.

In all these efforts the utmost significance attached to the recruitment and arming of Negro troops. In 1861 the national government not only ignored but positively rejected Negro offers of service, but by the end of that year advanced Republicans were beginning to urge the use of Negro soldiers as a matter of justice and military necessity. In July, 1862, Congress approved in principle the recruitment of Negroes; Lincoln prevaricated and told an Indiana delegation that the arming of blacks would lose the border states, but three weeks later he authorized the raising of five regiments in the Sea Islands (an area comfortably remote from the troublesome border). The First South Carolina Volunteer regiment was commanded by Thomas Wentworth Higgison, an ardent abolitionist, intellectual, and leader of men. Massachusetts raised two regiments recruited from free Negroes in the North. In Ohio John M. Langston, a wealthy Negro abolitionist, raised a regiment, and a considerable number of black troops were recruited by local commanders in Union-occupied areas of the South.

Even more important than the arming of Negroes was their excellent record. They took with enthusiasm to the parade aspects of military training, and their performance in battle was good. The engagement at Fort Wagner, guarding Charleston Harbor, in July, 1863, when the 54th Massachusetts made a vain but heroic attack, became an epic in black history and throughout the North. Nevertheless, Congress at first refused to sanction equal pay for black soldiers, and then agreed to future but not to retroactive equality. The 54th and 55th Massachusetts refused to accept any pay if they were not given equal pay from the date of enlistment, and even maintained this self-denial when Massachusetts offered to make up the difference. The leading Democratic newspaper, the New York *World,* declared that it was a libel on American citizens to declare "that the indolent, servile negro is the equal in courage, enterprise and fire of the foremost race in all the world. . . . It is unjust in every way to the white soldier to put him on a level with the black." [2] Congress was finally persuaded to concede equal pay retroactive to January 1, 1864, or to the date of enlistment for men who had been free when they volunteered. This was still unfair to the South Carolina volunteers, and Colonel Higgison continued to use his considerable influence on their behalf. Finally, on March 3, 1865, Congress (with a generosity stimulated by the imminence of victory) granted equal and retroactive pay to all Negro regiments. Abolitionists had also pressed for equal treatment in promotion, and in the later stages of the war a few black soldiers were promoted to lieutenant and some physicians commissioned as army surgeons; but suggestions that the army should be integrated were too far in advance of public opinion to command any support.

In spite of the meanness over pay, it is surely right to describe the use of Negro troops as "one of the most revolutionary features of the war." [3] A significant note was struck by Lincoln when he wrote, in July, 1863, to opponents of emancipation:

You say you will not fight to free negroes. Some of them seem willing to fight for you. . . . There will be some black men who can remember that, with silent tongue, and clenched teeth, and steady eye, and well-poised bayonet, they have helped mankind

---

[2] Quoted in James M. McPherson, *The Struggle for Equality* (Princeton, N.J.: Princeton University Press, 1964), p. 214. Most of the information in this and the preceding paragraph is derived from this work.

[3] *Ibid.*

on to this great consummation [of victory]; while, I fear, there will be some white ones, unable to forget that, with malignant heart, and deceitful speech, they have strove to hinder it.[4]

Again and again similar arguments would be used in all the battles against discrimination. It was a powerful contribution to the Republican conviction, during the struggle for the Fourteenth Amendment, that Negroes must be guaranteed equal civil rights; then followed the plea that a man who was fit to fight for the Union was fit to save it with his vote. Civil and political equality might have been achieved without the military record, but it would have taken far longer.

Black men fighting for the Union might carry their race toward equal estimation in the North but did not help and might damage race relations in the South. Indeed, the use of black troops in the South after surrender, and the later arming of black militias by Radical governments, were neither forgotten nor forgiven. Though indiscipline was probably less frequent than among ordinary white troops, every incident became an atrocity, an example of congenital depravity, and proof of deliberate attempts to "Africanize" the South. The reaction illustrated the insoluble character of the southern problem, for the transition from slavery to freedom created a white problem as well as a black problem. The attitudes, assumptions, and daily lives of the slave-owning class had been conditioned by slavery. No man can live from early years with unquestioned authority over others without a permanent effect on his character; among slave-owners this was reinforced by tradition and buttressed by many accepted reasons why this particular authority was ordained by God, socially necessary, and morally superior to that exercised by normal employers.

[4] To James C. Conkling, August 26, 1863. Quoted in Roy P. Basler (ed.), *The Collected Works of Abraham Lincoln*, Vol. VI (New Brunswick, N.J.: Rutgers University Press, 1963), pp. 409–410.

Small slave-owners were, perhaps, little troubled by the need for philosophic justification, but every publication and pulpit had taught them that though kindliness to slaves was a virtue, severity was a social necessity. Of deep psychological significance was the expectation that owners and their sons would have casual sexual relations with any slave girl whom they selected while less transient relations were strongly condemned. Not every slave-owner took advantage of the situation, but everyone was conscious of living in a society that acknowledged two different and contrasting codes of sexual morality, for in relations with white women casual intercourse was condemned and unions were expected to be permanent. Just as slaves assumed that stealing from the master was no crime, masters assumed that the ethical rules observed in white society did not apply when dealing with slaves. Slave families could be divided by sale, terrible punishments could be inflicted, slave girls could be ravished, and no man would rush to judgment. Thousands of planters were upright and decent men, who had an instinctive revulsion against abuse of the authority they possessed; but all the decency in the South had not succeeded in legalizing slave marriages, regulating the domestic slave trade, or giving public encouragement to masters who wished to improve the condition of the Negroes. The religious instruction of slaves had, indeed, won grudging approval, but only because it was supposed to teach submission and foster obedience.

These were poor foundations upon which to build a new order. Some members of the upper class made conscientious efforts "to accept the situation" by resigning themselves to defeat, accepting the end of slavery, and recognizing that if men were not slaves, they must have "inalienable rights" recognized by law. Often the master intended to administer honestly whatever responsibilities he might have toward the freedmen but found difficulty in understanding such novel conditions. Others made little attempt at adjustment and thought only of how the Negro could be made to work; many quickly realized that under a system of free labor, a wage earner was free to go and an employer was under no obligation to keep him a moment longer than he had need of his services. The untried ground of free labor had to be traversed at a time when many planters were in desperate economic plight and could ill afford generosity, nor did events allow them time to learn the conventions of an altered system.

The small farmers of the middle class were equally unprepared to face the future. For a generation or more the feeble criticism of slavery in the South had been crushed by pointing to the unimaginable dangers of a free Negro population. Sometimes the Negro was a fierce beast kept under salutary discipline by slavery; sometimes he was a weak, depraved creature who would corrupt white society by his presence. Sometimes slavery had been defended because it protected the whites from barbarism, sometimes because it protected the blacks from a war of extermination; but always it had been agreed that no society could be happy with a large free Negro population. This was accepted as axiomatic in the prewar South, and the belief was underlined by the alacrity with which new territories prohibited the settlement of Negroes. With all the Negroes suddenly free, it was still impossible to eradicate beliefs that had become so deeply ingrained. The South had fought against a known enemy; now it was necessary to combat a more insidious foe.

In the towns, where many free Negroes had long been settled, the rural freedmen were not welcome. In the best of times the opportunities for employment in small southern towns were limited, and in the wake of war economic life was often at a standstill. Freedmen who crowded in were unemployed, perhaps unemployable, and the consequent social problem was beyond the resources of small urban communities. The Freedmen's Bureau might help, but for most southerners a prime task of the bureau was to get the Negroes out of the cities and back to the fields under discipline. One suspects that many free Negroes, living comparatively stable lives, were little more prepared than the whites to welcome black migrants from the countryside.

These circumstances determined the "black codes." Most of their provisions seemed, to average southerners, necessary, expedient, and just; equally the reactions in the North were inexplicable and prompted the conclusion that Republicans intended not adjustment but humiliation. The rush into Negro suffrage with the Reconstruction acts confirmed this impression, and though most southerners decided to cooperate and to reconstruct under the acts, they maintained that Congress was not, in any sense, deriving just powers from the consent of the governed. Southern independence had been crushed on the field of battle, but had this given the North a mandate to revolutionize southern society? With doubts and reservations (but often with some relief) southerners had accepted the end of slavery, but did this imply the abandonment of racial attitudes nourished by history? By what mandate could an external authority demand new patterns of behavior?

These questions were of vital importance for the South, for the United States, and perhaps for the civilization of the North Atlantic. If the experiment of equal participation in a biracial society had succeeded under these exceptionally difficult circumstances, an example would have been set for similar experiments elsewhere. And southern questions could not be ignored, for whatever advances toward equality were made in the North, the decisive struggle would take place in the South.

Unfortunately the cards were stacked against success. Disqualification, temporary disenfranchisement, and the declared objective of ousting the old ruling class from power alienated those who had the best chance of making it work. The planter gentry had assumed immeasurable superiority to the Negroes, and this social gulf made racial hostility unnecessary. The slave-owner had been able to exploit and drive but did not need to hate or fear; but when the rights of blacks threatened the white upper class, racial animosity was an obvious instrument. Even before the war the proslavery argument had increasingly developed racial overtones, and slavery came to be explained as the means of preserving white society from corruption. Under Reconstruction this argument could not be forgotten and merged with a spontaneous reaction against the idea of racial equality. It was remarked at the time that no part of southern society was more vehemently negrophobic than the "white counties" where Unionism had flourished during the war, so that racialist policies become the instruments of both upper-class ascendancy and southern reunion. White supremacy was a cause to which men of all classes, different political traditions, and recent animosities could subscribe.

The situation would have been difficult enough if the racial question had stood alone, but the southern upper class also had to meet the challenge of rivals for power. The new political leaders came sometimes from the North, sometimes from the southern white Unionists, sometimes from educated free Negroes, and occasionally from members of the planter class itself; as their power depended upon the willingness of the federal authorities to give real meaning to the Fourteenth and Fifteenth amendments, the old leadership was naturally ready to condone all means by which the thrust for equality could be discredited. Logically it became necessary to convince the majority in the North that a terrible error had been made and that the new governments were thoroughly vicious and corrupt. The story that would survive—in the southern press, in public oratory, and in personal reminiscences—appeared to provide overwhelming evidence for this view, until one realized the extent to which the means of communication were controlled by men who had the strongest possible motive for presenting the prosecution case. There were, of course, some Republican newspapers in the South during the Reconstruction era, but their circulations were small, and government support was necessary for survival. By contrast, those southern journals that appeared to be reputable and independent could rely upon an educated readership and an adequate circulation. This southern press was supplemented by some northern Democratic journals, such as the New York *World,* which enjoyed a wide circulation. Finally, there were influential spokesmen from Maryland, West Virginia, and Kentucky, from parts of the Midwest, and from southern states that were "redeemed" at an early stage, who added their voices to the chorus of condemnation. Indeed, the attack upon Radical Reconstruction became staple fare for the revived Democratic party.

The case against Negro participation in government was therefore presented with force, eloquence, and apparently abundant evidence; and in the nature of things one good scandal outweighed anything that could be said on the other side about well-meant endeavor or the comparative rapidity with which some black men acquired political skills. The legacy of misconception has survived and in spite of much scholarly evidence to the contrary, continues to color the popular concepts of Reconstruction in the South. A modern writer has characterized the stereotypes that are still used a century after the dust of conflict subsided.

The scalawags were poor whites without character, education or position. The carpetbaggers—except those with money—were bootless ex-officers of the Union Army and unprincipled adventurers in search of political plunder. And Negro politicians were either Northern-sprung zealots in various stages of mental derangement or ignorant and deluded freedmen who moved directly from the cotton fields into office without so much as a change of clothes.[5]

There is little in this propagandist view that stands up to examination. In South Carolina, where the subject has been most closely studied, most scalawags had been Unionists (in sympathy if not actively), but they also included a few former secessionists. Some were poor, and the low standards of education in the state ensured that any cross section of the community would include some whites who were barely literate, but there were some men of wealth and high intellectual attainments. The carpetbaggers also included men of substantial wealth, and if most of them were admittedly men trying to build a new career or seeking a fortune, they included men of superior ability; several wished to identify themselves with the interests of their new state and serve it by a typical nineteenth-century blend of material drive and moral uplift. Behind the newcomers who became politically active were the large numbers of small entrepreneurs, schoolteachers, and men with technical skills. Some officers of the Freedmen's Bureau came to identify themselves closely with the interests of the district in which they worked. The writer John de Forest was a good example of the intelligent and humane bureau officer, while the novelist Albion W. Tourgée in North Carolina was a "carpetbagger" who combined personal ambition with idealistic hope for the future of his adopted state.

The Negro leaders who came to the fore formed a particularly interesting group. Some of the northern Negroes hoped to advance themselves in business or law, but a large number were genuinely inspired by a missionary call to help in the great tasks of elevating their race. A large, emancipated black population provided a better field for

[5] Joel Williamson, *After Slavery: The Negro in South Carolina during Reconstruction* (Chapel Hill, N.C.: University of North Carolina Press, 1965) , p. 373.

both kinds of ambition than the small black minorities of the northern cities, but there was nothing disgraceful in the thought of a Negro moving to that part of the country where opportunity and challenge were equally strong. Incidentally, these northern Negroes were following the course predicted by earlier antislavery men and moved South when their race was no longer enslaved.

Few of the native Negro leaders had been field hands. Some were tradesmen or craftsmen of one type or another; others were ministers, teachers, or farmers. A substantial number had been free Negroes, and the majority who had been slaves had occupied superior positions in the servile-class structure. Some were ignorant; a number were self-educated; a few had good educational achievements. In South Carolina one Negro legislator had been educated in England at Eton College, and another was a graduate of the University of Glasgow. Indeed, the Negro legislators as a whole seemed to represent exactly the type that one would expect to emerge in a revolutionary situation: predominantly lower middle class in aspiration if not already recognized as such, mixing enthusiasm with naïveté and personal ambition, while hoping to make their mark in a novel and exciting situation. Even those who had been slaves could hardly be described as "working class"; they belonged rather to skilled occupations that have everywhere produced leaders for working-class movements.

A large majority of the Negro leaders were not pure African by descent, and many were light-skinned. The problem of the mulatto in southern society has not been adequately studied by historians or social scientists. For the white South the barest physical evidence of African descent made a man indistinguishable in status from his darkest compatriot. Modern radicals tend, in the same way, to treat all as "black." In spite of this, the mulatto was conscious of being different, and in a world in which "white" was invariably equated with superiority, he could hardly avoid the implication for his own character. It was not that the mulatto thought of abandoning the blacks but that he inevitably thought that the whole race would be improved to the extent that its members moved toward white society. Thus Negro participation in Reconstruction politics did not bring out a distinctively black contribution but rather the hope that the black-, brown-, and light-skinned people would win acceptance in a society where whites continued to determine the style of life. Negro leaders did not wish to draw upon black culture but to learn the ways of white civilization; they did not wish to emphasize race but to forget it. This was seen over and over again in dress, manners, and oratory, and many a black legislator wasted time on points of order, florid speeches, and personal explanations because they believed (with some justice) that this was the way in which white men conducted the serious business of politics.

The most serious charges against the black legislators were extravagance and corruption. To many white commentators there was something ludicrous about the idea that black men should drink French wine and smoke expensive cigars; equally, it seemed absurd that they should wear new suits or starched linen and carry silver-mounted canes. To the white mind, in the North as in the South, it required only to say or picture these things to provide evidence of wasteful expenditure. Even in modern works examples of "extravagance" are cited without providing comparable information about conditions after "redemption." Negro leaders, anxious to impress, were often guilty of misplaced ostentation, and like new men in any situation, often offended against the social conventions of the upper class; but their solecisms became propaganda weapons only because the perpetrators were black.

Corruption is more difficult to assess, because there is often a fine distinction between legitimate and undue influence, or between payment in advance for official acts or votes and subsequent recognition of help received. There is a good deal of evidence that some white entrepreneurs were prepared to pay lavishly for favors received, for there was much to be done and much to be gained. Every black or white carpetbagger who received a bribe was presumptive evidence that someone was operating on a grand scale.

Among those who did steal, the most successful thieves invariably combined high intelligence and large administrative talents with generous endowments of education, wealth, and experience. Petty frauds were numerous and widespread, but the truly magnificent peculations were conceived and executed by a relatively few men, usually residing in Columbia or Charleston. However, these larger schemes frequently required the purchase of the co-operation of scores of state officers and legislators, and thus corruption was spread.[6]

In South Carolina the "truly magnificent peculations" were most frequently the issue of state bonds in excess of those authorized by the legislature. The unauthorized bonds could be sold in the open market and the proceeds taken by the conspirators; the state treasury received no cash, but the indebtedness of the state unaccountably grew beyond expectations. An advantage of this trick was that it required the connivance of only the small number of officials responsible for issuing the bonds and accounting for the sales.

In the South, as elsewhere, the promotion and building of railroads furnished a happy hunting ground for predatory capitalists. Large sums of money had to be raised, and it was often difficult to keep account of the sums actually used in construction or operation. The fortunate few found themselves in the possession of borrowed capital guaranteed by the state and extremely hard to account for accurately. The most skillful and least scrupulous could pay themselves, as directors of both railroads and construction companies, inflated prices for work that was done on the cheap.

This underlines the real problem of the Reconstruction

[6] *Ibid.*, pp. 382–383.

governments. There was so much to do; and in so many instances the money required and the extent of state participation went far beyond what had been customary in the
South. It was necessary to tax, borrow, and spend on a scale
comparable to that of modern government and deeply
offensive to men nourished on Jeffersonian precepts. A
good many of the notorious debts of the southern states
during this period arose from the need to raise capital
by guaranteed bonds for railroad construction or repair,
and much of the additional taxation was required to
meet debt charges, carry out essential public works, establish public schools, and provide relief for the indigent; but
the complaints of those who paid the taxes won sympathy
from the rising tide of laizzez-faire opinion in the North.
Radicalism, corruption, extravagance, and excessive taxation became indissolubly linked in the minds of northern
politicians, editors, and public moralists. The impression
created goes far to explain the willingness of northern men
to abandon the Reconstruction experiment.

These arguments and examples proved nothing about
the characteristics of color-blind democracy. Nor would
they have been accepted as evidence of its failure if the
story had not been told against the background of rising
disturbance in the South, and the impact of sustained violence did more than theory, evidence, or ideals to change
the course of events. Defeated in battle, politically crushed,
burdened by constitutional amendments, the leaders of the
white South turned to evasion of the law and intimidation
of those whom it was intended to protect, and despite the
cries of shocked denunciation, the majority in the North
came to accept the case for leaving the South alone. The
Radical political structure proved to be vulnerable; its
popular base was weak, and men of good social standing
were prepared to defy the law and persuade law-
abiding citizens that they had a good reason for
doing so.

Anti-Negro activity preceded political Reconstruction.

In the early days after the collapse of the Confederacy there were real fears of a revolt by the former slaves. This had been foretold by proslavery advocates, but there were very few acts of reprisal or disorder. Indeed, men who had gained freedom and expected the protection of the Union forces had no need to revolt. Calculated insubordination was more common than attacks on persons or property, and the only large-scale example was the "sack of Beaufort" in November, 1861, when field hands from the Sea Islands plantations invaded the elegant homes of their former masters, but this event took place when the owners had just abandoned their plantations and the slaves were uncertain of their future status. In 1865 Negroes could allow things to take their course, though the disturbed condition of the country produced a few ugly incidents. White reactions immediately following Appomattox were spontaneous, sporadic, and nonpolitical attempts to prove that in freedom as in slavery whites had the upper hand. The legislatures set up under Johnson's plan passed stringent patrol and pass laws and in some states moved to enact complete black codes; the white militia was also armed and mustered at full strength. Between the passage of the Reconstruction acts and the elections of 1868 there was a good deal of poorly organized violence aimed to prevent the Negroes from exercising their new rights and at intimidating whites who cooperated too readily with the federal authority. This was unsuccessful, and the white leaders themselves were divided in their counsels. The establishment of the new governments was followed by the raising of Negro militia units to preserve law and order, but this led to widespread protest and was, in many cases, the immediate cause of more disturbing violence than any yet witnessed in the South.

The Ku Klux Klan and other secret societies originated in the troubled months after the end of the war; conspiracy, bizarre costume, and intimidating behavior aimed to play upon Negro superstitions and at humiliation rather than physical assault; but when Radicalism seemed to be in the saddle, the secret societies moved to defeat the law by violence. The principal targets were no longer the simpler freedmen but politically active black and white Republicans. For the most part the outrages were organized locally, and there was no single body to direct the strategy of violence; but the separate outbreaks followed similar patterns, and one example quickly inspired another. Responsible leaders of the white South faced a dilemma. As men of property, education, and social standing they hastened to deplore murder, assault, and destruction, but privately they might welcome any indication that Republican policy was making the South ungovernable; yet they also feared congressional countermeasures and loss of conservative northern sympathy. The summer of 1871 saw a crisis of violence in the South. President Grant suspended habeas corpus in nine South Carolina counties, many arrests were made, and in the federal courts the sorry tale of violence was told in all its details. In the North this created a climate of opinion in which the Republicans were ready to underwrite the Fourteenth and Fifteenth amendments with the "force" acts and finally, after much hesitation, to pass in 1875 the Civil Rights Act to which Charles Sumner had devoted his great prestige and dying energies. In the South federal activity seemed to have achieved its objective, but the result was merely to place southern leadership in more skillful hands.

From 1874 the cause of white supremacy, now championed by "Redeemers," moved to more widespread and more subtle methods. "Rifle clubs" were formed to make a systematic display of white strength, especially at election times. Employers threatened economic coercion, and in the days before a secret ballot a Negro who voted the Republican ticket knew that he might be a marked man. The aim was to avoid breaking the letter of the law while creating an atmosphere in which black radicalism became impossible. This was the kind of legal pressure that the upper-class leaders could endorse, and many explained (with evident sincerity) that once the blacks were brought to recognize the errors of their Radical leaders, they would cast their vote for the Democrats. Many, indeed, did so. The public show of white strength would not, however, have been so effective if crude violence had not continued off-stage. Lynching, beating, and the burning of property became a part of the southern way of life. This kind of violence was usually directed against individuals rather than groups and dealt out summary punishment where the processes of law were judged to be too slow, too uncertain, and too dependent upon verifiable evidence.

In spite of the large place that it fills in southern annals, Radical Reconstruction was a comparatively short-lived experiment. In Virginia and North Carolina it can hardly be said to have taken place at all, and the political conflicts of the period were between white factions with the enfranchised Negro minority on the sidelines. In Georgia the white majority overplayed their hand in 1868 by expelling Negro members from the legislature but soon established themselves under a vigorous planter-business leadership. In Alabama a conservative governor was elected in 1870, and the Democrats carried the state in 1874; "Redeemers," "Conservatives," or Democrats won Texas in 1873, Arkansas in 1874, and Mississippi in 1875. In 1877 only Louisiana, Florida, and South Carolina remained under Radical control, and the withdrawal of federal troops in that year enabled the Democrats to establish control; indeed, it is possible that they would have done so without this gesture by President Rutherford B. Hayes.

Only in the lower house of South Carolina from 1868 to 1874 were Negro representatives in the majority; everywhere else (including the state senate of South Carolina) they were in a minority. In Mississippi, with a black majority of the population, there were only 40 Negroes out of

115 in the first legislature chosen under the Reconstruction acts, and thereafter the number diminished. In Alabama there were 26 out of 84, and in Florida only 19 out of 76. "Negro domination" was a myth that gained currency in later years when it became convenient to assume that the white South had always been solid. Except in South Carolina, no Radical regime could, in fact, have existed without substantial white support.

During their short period in power the southern Radicals wrote state constitutions on the best northern models, established public schools, and presided over the initial stages of southern economic recovery. The Redeemers made little change in the constitutions they took over, continued the educational system (though with expenditure cut and no provision for compulsory attendance), and reaped the benefit of economic advances that led the way to the "New South." By 1873 northern capital was flowing into the South; then the whole nation felt the shock of depression, but southerners, with cheap labor as an asset and a valuable export crop, were better able to survive than vulnerable manufacturers dependent upon a domestic market. Other southern staples such as tobacco, sugar, and rice flourished, and new crops such as peanuts in Virginia and peaches in Georgia became important. More spectacular was the emergence of southern manufacturing; in Georgia and North and South Carolina cotton manufacturing went ahead and would eventually beat the textile factories of New England at their own game. In North Carolina the manufacture of tobacco became big business. In the upper South the ironworks around Richmond prospered, as did those at Chattanooga, and enormous iron and coal deposits were being exploited in northern Alabama.

All classes and both races benefited from these developments, but the largest profits accrued to those members of the southern upper class who, with northern allies and financial backers, turned to merchandising, transportation, banking, and manufacturing. Many of them came from old planter families, retained land, and drew substantial profits from it. A good deal of white labor was drawn into the new factories, more money began to find its way into the back country and hitherto isolated rural districts, and a considerable number of young men from small farming families found new opportunities.

Yet the South remained apart from the nation. Except to transact business, few northern or midwestern men traveled in the South and a smaller proportion of the southern upper class than in prewar days came north for education or recreation. Though the Union had been preserved, the two sections continued to talk of each other as alien cultures. The economic advances in the South were not accompanied by cultural change of equal dimensions; the number of southern colleges increased, but their standards were low and their teaching hampered by suspicion of most developments in natural and social science. A southern version of history was being written that made a virtue of intellectual isolation and turned failure into a glorious defense of civilized life. Fifteen years after the end of the war the South showed unmistakable signs of capitalist vigor but few of the benefits that had come elsewhere as the results of economic development.

It is of some interest to speculate upon the causes of these changes. Was the southern economic development the result of the unnatural and premature stimulus of war, or did the war interrupt slow but steady developments that were already under way? What was the real consequence of the "carpetbagger" invasion that came South after the war and flourished under Radical aegis? At least their skill and competitive drive stimulated native-born southerners to comparable efforts. Many of them developed links with northern bankers, railroad promoters, and entrepreneurs which were to be vital in southern development. Some of the notorious carpetbag governors and officials were extremely successful in attracting enterprise to their states as well as lining their own pockets. There is therefore a good deal of evidence to support the view that Radical Reconstruction played a vital though unacknowledged part in the revival of the South; at least it came as a kind of shock therapy that shook southerners out of depressive apathy. Diversification, experiment, the movement of capital, and mobility of labor were by-products of the abortive political revolution in the South.

The Negroes, whose status had been the central issue, gained least. For them economic reconstruction came slowly and under pressure. The postwar attempt to tie the freedmen down to contract labor on the large plantations proved too cumbersome, too rigid, and too difficult to enforce. Freedmen might feel that they had made a bad bargain and wished to go, employers might regret taking on redundant labor, and lawyers were more likely to profit than either. Contract labor had many of the disadvantages of slavery without security for the wage earner or certainty for the employer that he could get labor when he wanted it most. With increasing frequency, therefore, the prewar system of sharecropping gained in popularity; the freedmen got land that they could occupy as long as they gave half the crop in lieu of rent. The landowner could specify what crop he would accept and the minimum quantity that he would require. As years went by, many landowners found it increasingly profitable to go into the crop lien business, under which they furnished supplies, food, and seed to the sharecroppers on security of a further portion of the crop. The sharecroppers were both white and black; both found some kind of security but paid for it by sacrificing all hope of advancement. When the share and the lien had been dealt with, there was little left to sell; money was always pitifully short; every able-bodied member of the family had to work, and education was a luxury; many remained illiterate, and few could get beyond the early grades in primary education. For thousands of freedmen, therefore, the transition from slavery came to mean a hard life, with few rewards and fewer opportunities.

Negro political leaders had made a record that was neither brilliant nor discreditable, but they had not succeeded in crossing the color line and establishing themselves as American citizens who could win votes from both races, and once thrown back exclusively upon black support, the base of their power was fragile. Not only intimidation kept the black people from the polls but also ignorance, apathy, and disillusionment. Even the small middle class and the former free Negroes began to lose hope of political salvation, though they hoped to retain their rights as citizens of the United States. The experiment of suffrage had been justified in the North by the key word "protection." The freedmen needed the vote to protect their rights and the long-term interests of the Union; in a Jeffersonian spirit they had been seen as cultivators of the soil providing a new check to balance the revived southern leadership. The concept was naïve at best and hopelessly inadequate when the newly enfranchised had to provide the popular mandate for new tasks in government against the powerful forces of economic interest, social prestige, and racial prejudice. Color-blind democracy was the boldest of nineteenth-century experiments, but it had not the slightest prospect of success.

One should not rush to judgment, and it is necessary to discount the weight of emotion built into such phrases as "white supremacy" or "racial equality." The men of the South, both black and white, faced an unprecedented situation, and no man can yet say with confidence what the solution should have been. Everywhere racial animosity has proved to be extraordinarily durable, even when differences have not been accentuated by color. It is also salutary to remember that most twentieth-century "new nations" have found western-style democracy unworkable. Lack of familiarity with constitutional procedures, the combination of ignorance with emotion, and the need for hard-headed technical and administrative skills have forced most "new nations" to one-party government.

The Radical Republicans anticipated the case for one-party government in the South. As with others who have since followed the same road, they contemplated an eventual restoration of normal political life, but their immediate aim was to proscribe the old leaders and create a new power structure based on Republicanism and black suffrage. If their aims, expressed in this way, sound less admirable than the quest for equal rights, it may be asked how else could equality be achieved against the wishes of the majority? Disqualification and temporary disenfranchisement of the opposition leaders proved to be half measures, but when Radicalism collapsed, the alternative was to accept the rival view of what southern society should be. On the other side one can understand, if one may regret, the reaction. It is no light matter to abdicate power, and the southern leaders met the threat by substituting single-party Democratic and conservative government for single-party Republican government. Neither reconstruction nor redemption could accept the normal conventions of a two-party system. The Redeemers played their hand with enormous advantage, for their leadership was customary and indigenous, while that of their rivals was novel and dependent upon external authority.

If "protection" was an inadequate rationale for a party that was required to govern, "equality" was an objective that has been notoriously difficult to implement. Since it is impossible to offer a philosophic proof that men are *created* equal, it has been necessary to make the unexplained substitution that they ought to be treated *as though they were equal*. Equality must be tested by asking how inequality is avoided rather than by requiring positive proof that men behave equally. Equality cannot be a simple concept easily applied; it demands a complex system of law, opportunity, and social convention, and even then the end eludes realization. Equal protection of equal rights seemed a definitive proposition, but equal opportunity meant unequal achievement, and equality under the law could not remedy inequality in social conditions. Equality does not necessarily mean identical treatment, but should the weak be given advantages denied to the strong? Equality has eluded the systematic efforts of men working in sympathetic societies; it could hardly succeed when external authority laid down the rules for men who rejected their premises.

At least the Republican majority in Congress believed that the Fourteenth and Fifteenth amendments laid down specific conditions and gave Congress the power to see that they were observed. Moreover, many moderates as well as Radicals were deeply impressed by the argument that the war and the amendments had altered the nature of American government. In line with contemporary European thought about the philosophic basis of the state, they believed that government ought to serve the moral will of the people. With Charles Sumner this attitude derived from the argument that the Declaration of Independence had defined the national purpose and that it was the function of the Constitution and of statute law to fulfill this intention. It followed that if the Constitution had been interpreted in the past to protect slavery, it had been wrongly interpreted, because servitude denied inalienable rights. Sumner believed that the amendments had simply made explicit what had always been implicit and that Congress had now not only the right but the duty to translate the promise of the Declaration into law. Others adopted a less sophisticated approach and simply assumed that the war had been fought to elevate the condition of men and that if this was denied, the war had been fought in vain. As Carl Schurz put it, "The war grew out of the systematic violation of individual rights by State authority. The war ended with the vindication of individual rights by the national power." John A. Bingham, who had been mainly responsible for drafting the first clause of the Fourteenth Amendment, emphasized that there was now vested in Congress "a power to protect the rights of citizens against States, and individuals in States, never before granted." [7]

In this spirit Congress passed the first Enforcement Act on May 31, 1870, to appoint federal supervisors for elections and give the federal courts cognizance of intimidation or fraud at the polls. United States marshals were to act against violators of the law, and military force could be invoked if necessary. A second act on February 28, 1871, set up more safeguards for voting rights, though military enforcement was dropped. In March President Grant requested legislation to protect life, liberty, and property, and Congress promptly responded with a third "force" act on April 20, 1871 (which is also known as the Ku Klux Klan Act), which authorized the President to suspend habeas corpus and proclaim martial law in districts where unlawful combinations threatened rebellion against the United States. In October Grant applied the act in nine South Carolina counties, and before the act expired a year after its passage, there were hundreds of arrests and several convictions in this and other states. As noted above, this show of determination led to a decline in general violence but the adoption of more calculated and less crude methods by southern leaders.

The enforcement acts marked, for almost a century, the high point of national effort to secure legal and political equality in the South. The Civil Rights Act of 1875 was wider in scope and was aimed at discrimination in transportation and all places licensed or regulated by law, but it did not provide appropriate machinery for enforcement, and even some of its supporters regarded it as a gesture

[7] *Congressional Globe*, 41st Cong., 2d sess., May 19, 1870, p. 3607; *ibid.*, 42nd Cong., 1st sess., March 31, 1871, Appendix, p. 83. I owe both references to Stephen G. F. Spackman, *National Authority in the United States . . . 1870–1875* (Unpublished Ph.D. dissertation, Cambridge University, 1970), pp. 45–46.

rather than as a serious effort to enforce the implications of equality. Few prosecutions were brought under this act, and in 1883 it was invalidated by the Supreme Court on the grounds that the Fourteenth Amendment had not intended to limit the rights of individuals or private concerns to refuse service or to provide separate facilities for both races. The third Enforcement Act had been no empty gesture and had provided the authority to secure the promised rights, but it was of temporary duration, led to no longer-term changes, and Congress would not again attempt anything on this scale.

The reasons for this slackening of the impulse for equal rights are not far to seek. The idea of a "new" constitution existed within the framework of the old. However much the bolder Republicans might plead for the legitimate use of national authority in the cause of equal rights, the forms and traditions of the Constitution provided ample arguments for its restraint. The case against "consolidation" or "centralization" could call upon some of the realities of life—that no permanent solution in the South was possible without the consent of the white majority—and suspicion that protection for the Negro was merely a cloak for Republican supremacy. In 1868 and 1870 the Democrats, despite Grant's personal popularity, made gains in Congress, and though they remained a minority, they were strong enough to argue vigorously against the enforcement acts and against the whole Reconstruction experiment. The Republicans, though generally committed to making the amendments effective, were unanimous neither in their constitutional nor in their racial views. Few accepted Sumner's argument that interpretation of the Constitution must be by the principles of the Declaration of Independence, and lawyers were deeply suspicious of appeals that bypassed precedent. For eighty years men of both political traditions had been taught to appeal to the Constitution and to avoid invoking a higher law that could not be defined. Thus in Congress many Republicans might discount the blatant appeals of the Democrats to racial hostility, or their evident anxiety to recruit their depleted ranks from the South, but were half convinced by their constitutional arguments.

This was certainly true of the Liberal Republicans who staged an unsuccessful revolt in 1872. Their dissatisfaction with Grant's administration sprang from other causes, but as they sought for Democratic support they inevitably questioned the wisdom of enforcement, and several accepted the assurances of southern leaders that if left alone, they would end violence and give fair play for both races. Their ranks included several men of abolitionist antecedents, but men who had learned their antislavery from Garrison were suspicious of all attempts to impose the moral law by force rather than conversion. Charles Sumner went halfway with the Liberal Republicans and advised Negroes to support them, because he had quarreled deeply and irrevocably with the administration over Grant's proposed annexation of Santo Domingo. The Liberal Republican movement was confused, appeared to compromise on essential points, and ran into deserved disaster in 1872 when Grant was reelected with an increased majority; but one by-product was to identify Radicalism with men such as Roscoe Conkling, Zachariah Chandler, Levi Morton, and Benjamin Butler, whom high-minded Republicans disliked and distrusted.

The fatal blow to Radical Reconstruction came, however, from extraneous sources when depression hit the American economy in 1873. Middle-class voters who would support Radicalism on the rising tide of prosperity turned to conservatism when an economic disaster threatened their livelihood, and in the 1874 congressional elections the Democrats scored spectacular victories in all parts of the country; the Republicans clung precariously to their Senate majority, but in the House they faced a large and triumphant Democratic majority. In the lame-duck session the Republicans pushed through a weakened version of the Civil Rights Act, but it was in the knowledge that, for the next two years at least, no Radical measure would pass Congress. Conversely, in the South conservatives took heart from the knowledge that the national administration would be paralyzed if there were any further question of enforcement.

Thus national intervention in the transition from slavery to freedom slowed and came almost to a halt. The commitment to equal citizenship remained, but a growing number of people were coming to the conclusion that all that could reasonably be expected had been done. They were not prepared to go forward from the formal guarantee of equal protection to provide aid for the weak that was denied to the strong. For this men can hardly be blamed in an age when advanced opinion believed that natural laws governed the development of society. There can, however, be little doubt that permanent damage was inflicted. Americans as a whole turned away from the pursuit of equality; white southerners took refuge in evasion of the law under the banner of conservatism; a few Negroes advanced up the ladder of opportunity, the majority remained as low-grade peasants or menial laborers; idealism withered away. The first experiment in the organization of a biracial society had failed, and the brotherhood of man became a lost cause.

[10]
A New Era

IN 1875, as Americans looked forward to celebrating a century of national existence, a rhetorical question was posed by the Centennial Commission: "Shall the bitterness and animosity engendered by the war remain forever? Is final reconciliation utterly hopeless?" A decade had passed since Appomattox, and the physical mementos of war were becoming obscured. "Over all, as well as over the innumerable graves of the unknown dead, kindly and loving nature is rapidly drawing her beautiful mantle of refreshing verdure to hide them away from the sight and recollection of all." Was it not time to wish that "all the errors of the past be hidden in high and holy aspirations for the future of our restored nationality"? [1]

The florid language displayed the crucial hopes and assumptions of the decade. There was, indeed, hope that "all the errors of the past might be hidden," that bitterness and animosity might be forgotten, and that the future would redeem the failure of the past; unfortunately memory was tough, and the past could not be obliterated. Northerners would see "our restored nationality" as their vindication, whereas southerners (as far as they were prepared to participate) would be thinking of the earlier and purer Republic that (they believed) had been damaged beyond repair by northern politics and northern power. Nor was it easier for individuals, however disinterested, to forget. The war had been a part of the experience of every adult male and had molded their opinions and personalities; war had generated a new set of beliefs about men and so-

[1] *Congressional Record*, 44th Cong., 1st sess., p. 1034.

ciety, and its emotional impact stood as a barrier between the present and the past. The long-term psychological consequences of catastrophic happenings are speculative and obscure, but it is certain that men who had experienced the war became a changed people, and for good or ill they would dominate every aspect of national life until the turn of the century.

For Republicans this meant devotion to the party that had preserved the Union, ended slavery, and declared a commitment to legal and political equality between races; their movement had been identified with the humane and progressive forces of the age, which their opponents had opposed, thwarted, and abused. For some politicians the Republican party was merely an instrument for personal power, but they could have advanced nowhere without the conviction among the Republican masses that the party battle was a struggle between progress and retrogression. The continuing strength of this ideological commitment explains the survival of the Republican party. Challenged by revived Democratic strength, shaken by western protest, distressed by scandals, sacrificing the goodwill of many reformers, divided by deep disagreement over financial policy and the civil service, embarrassed by the failure of Republicanism in the South, taking the full shock of economic depression, troubled by the savage conflicts between capital and labor, and disturbed by personal and factional rivalries, the party nevertheless held together. In retrospect this survival seems to have been so natural that it escapes comment; yet it was significant and not altogether predictable that the Republicans did not go the way of the Federalists, National Republicans, and Whigs. The critical period in this feat of survival was the Presidency of General Grant, when so many hopes seem to have been disappointed and so many ideals tarnished.

The Democrats did not regard themselves as the enemies of progress, but a majority were eager to appropriate the name "conservative." Indeed, in the middle ground where the moderates of both parties fought for the floating vote, the major objective was often to establish the best claim to be truly conservative. Democratic "conservatism" always meant a resistance to "centralism," a defense of states' rights, and criticism of government expenditure; these well-worn themes concealed a sincere concern over the apparent gains of federal against state government and of all government against individuals, but too often Democratic policy meant no more than undiscriminating opposition to any extension of federal responsibility, the defense of white supremacy however achieved, and blind criticism of any federal or state intervention in social or economic affairs. In northern constituencies the economic principles wavered somewhat (as did those of most men overtaken by unprecedented problems), but the national Democratic party never hesitated to support all measures taken to secure white ascendancy, establish "home rule" in the South, and defeat the purpose of Reconstruction legislation. They opposed the so-called force acts (designed to repress terrorism and safeguard the right to vote), joined with conservative Republicans to defeat proposals for a national education system which offered modest federal aid to areas with few or poor schools, and used their majorities secured in Congress in 1874 to mount investigations to document the conclusion that black participation in politics was an unmitigated disaster. At the same time the Democrats did nothing to meet the challenge of economic depression that had brought them the unexpected bonus of electoral victory.

Thus, though the Democrats achieved a surprising recovery, dominated the South, and fought neck and neck with the Republicans in the new West and the "old free states," they failed to seize an opportunity. They did not forge a permanent alliance with liberal Republicans who were disenchanted with Republican leadership, nor establish themselves as the spokesmen of discontents in the emerging industrial society. In the North they remained predominantly rural, though retaining their traditional constituency among the immigrant groups of the larger cities. In spite of their congressional majority in 1875 and the near success of their bid for the Presidency in 1876, they remained a party of "outs" linked indissolubly with groups and supporters who had least sympathy with the new civilization of the late nineteenth century.

As the party of the "outs" the Democrats were able to profit from economic difficulties, errors of government policy, and public scandals. In practice both parties were divided on economic issues, and their declarations of policy tended to embody somewhat flat compromises between factions. It was this, more than anything else, that led Lord Bryce to make his famous but misleading generalizations about the lack of principle in party battles during one of the comparatively few periods in American history when there was a real ideological gulf in politics.

For many years before the war the Democratic party had been controlled in most states by the hard-money, anti-bank faction; they emerged from the war ready to denounce the Republicans who had issued inconvertible paper money and set up a national banking system. The central core of the Republican party contained some ardent greenbackers who believed in a national paper currency, issued in accordance with economic needs and not tied to the supply of gold. However, the Republican party also contained the most influential and moralistic advocates of the gold standard, though unlike the simpler advocates of hard money, they did not think that an exclusively metallic currency could or should supply the needs of the country but believed most firmly that paper must be freely convertible and thus automatically regulated by the quantity of gold in the country. As silver was, at this time, overvalued by its official gold equivalent, there was little need to enter upon a theoretical repudiation of bimetalism.

The history of the greenback and specie controversy during the Reconstruction years has already been reviewed. By the time that Ulysses S. Grant came to the White House, the Republicans were committed to a return to specie but also to postponing resumption until an increasing volume of business brought the greenbacks up to parity. Meanwhile Republican Secretaries of the Treasury concentrated upon paying off the debt. The Democrats continued to argue among themselves, and a minority of Republicans, led by Ben Butler, were greenback inflationists. In hard times the pressure for further issues of greenbacks built up, and in 1874 Congress passed a law authorizing this; President Grant vetoed the bill. The amount affected by the veto seems to have been very small (for the bulk of the issue authorized had already gone into circulation under existing Treasury arrangements), but the veto was widely hailed as a symbolic turning point that committed the administration to resist pressure for a less stringent monetary policy. This, more than anything else, gave substance to the later myth that hard money had been a cardinal policy of the Republican party.

In 1879 John Sherman, then Secretary of the Treasury, was finally able to restore specie payments. Thus the return to the gold standard can be regarded as a Republican achievement, but it had taken thirteen years and divided both parties. The most decisive influence probably came from northern writers, economists, bankers engaged in international trade, ministers of religion, and academic writers, for whom the problem was essentially one of simple morality; a fixed standard would take currency out of politics, give money a stable value, and so safeguard the economic base of civilized life. Most of these gold-standard moralists were Republican, but they did not speak for industry or small-town business and on many other questions were bitterly critical of their party leadership.

The political history of these years was therefore marked by a recovery of the Democrats after their dismal record in 1864 and 1866 and their restoration as a national party in 1868. Indeed, it is possible that the Republicans would have lost the Presidency if they had not had Grant as their nominee. The Democrats failed to sustain this momentum and made a wretched showing, in alliance with dissident Liberal Republicans, in 1872. The depression beginning in 1873 gave a fresh stimulus to the Democrats, and the failure of Reconstruction gave them an unassailable position in all but three of the southern states by 1876. The Republicans had failed to secure a southern base, and the manner of their failure caused many northern supporters to doubt their wisdom. The Democrats seemed about to recover their prewar position as the normal majority, but their success fell far short of expectation. When, in 1876, the Republicans won only because they were awarded three contested southern states, many believed that the Democrats had been cheated and expected convincing endorsement of their position in 1880. In fact, though the Democrats would win congressional majorities in several years, they would win the Presidency only in 1884 and 1892, when Grover Cleveland, an honest but essentially commonplace New Yorker, won because he appealed to reformers whose normal affiliation was Republican. In 1896 this middle-class intelligentsia returned en masse to the Republican fold.

This brings out the surprising fact that in a period during which the parties approached equilibrium in a fully democratic society, their fate was decided by the comparatively small number of highly educated and frequently dissatisfied individuals. Their influence in the currency controversy has already been indicated, but in other fields a characteristic of the age was the emergence of an elite. Their condemnation of public ethics (as interpreted in the national capital) was expressed by young Henry Adams in his anonymous novel *Democracy* and by Mark Twain in *The Gilded Age,* which incorporated not very well informed impressions of Washington in 1872 and would provide a convenient label for a quarter century of American history. In his retrospective *Education* Henry Adams would see the Washington politicians of the 1870's not so much corrupt as gray, limited, working hard because they knew no other way of life, and spending their leisure time on whiskey and cards because they knew no other form of recreation. Adams came to Washington with a great name, unusual experience for a man of his age, and a great enthusiasm for public life; his withdrawal to a professorship at Harvard was a tacit realization that in Washington he and his kind would now be on the outside. Never again would an Adams occupy the White House, and it seemed improbable that anyone whom he could respect would do so. The politicians were becoming a breed apart; this, however, was not a sudden development but one that had been long maturing.

From this some commentators have assumed a relative decline of the influence of intellect in national life. This was far from the truth. American writers, economists, and moralists did not, it is true, wield the influence of their British counterparts, and they seldom held public office, but their number was increasing, their social status improving, and through the increase of newspapers and periodicals they wielded more influence than ever before. Hitherto college presidents (except those of Harvard, Yale, and Princeton) had not been much regarded; now, with an increasing number of universities they multiplied, and their reputation became a matter of local pride. There had been great editors before 1860, but in the late nineteenth century distinguished journalists achieved unprecedented fame and influence. In religion it was an age of platitude rather than inspiration, but the position of ministers had never been more secure nor their ethical pronouncements more generally received. For more than a generation the churches, carrying the great incubus of slavery, had failed in their approach to other problems of civilized life; by 1870 they could speak with restored confidence to a middle class that craved for assurance that moral order could prevail in society. Economists and social theorists assumed a similar authority, and even agnostics assumed the existence of great mechanical principles that would produce the greatest benefit for all, though (like God) they often moved in a mysterious way their wonders to perform. There was coming to birth a tremendous faith in man's capacity for self-improvement, which also justified the refusal to be deflected by examples of individual suffering.

Thus the 1870's did not witness a twilight of the intellect or its overshadowing by practical men in politics and business. Rather the decade saw the forging of the intellectual authority that would dominate national life for many years to come. This truth has been obscured by two things: first by the accident (thanks above all to Henry Adams) that the picture of the alienated intellectual became so firmly fixed in the public mind, and secondly by the catastrophic failure of reform in 1872. In that year the men who accounted themselves as the guardians of the Republican conscience revolted against the Grant Administration. "Liberal Republicanism" was inevitably tangled with the disappointed ambitions of politicians who did not think that their merits had been recognized and with the discontents of regions who were conscious of dropping behind. Carl Schurz, who was, more than anyone else, the inspirer of the movement, combined all three. A man of high intelligence, he deplored the national influence of stupid or self-seeking men; though his ambition had been rewarded by a United States senatorship, he resented his inability to exercise any decisive influence on policy; and as an adopted son of Missouri he came from a struggling region that had little to gain from protection or the return to specie.

Whatever the hidden motives a great deal of sincerity went into the liberal Republican campaign of 1872. It involved three things: a protest against what had become the Republican way of life, a take-over of their convention by the followers of Horace Greeley, and a successful effort to persuade the Democrats to endorse Greeley. As on other occasions (1964 and 1972 come to mind) success in the preliminary stages left so many with doubt or discontent that the presidential campaign was a disaster for the Liberals and gave President Grant an overwhelming electoral victory.

Though the new professional elite failed in direct political action, its members continued to exercise a wide influence. The men who controlled higher education, spoke from thousands of pulpits, dominated the daily and periodical press, were a power in the land. They won the battle of the books and transmitted to posterity the unflattering picture of the Grant era. This was highly significant, for it meant that a period of great stress and difficulty was viewed through the eyes of intelligent men whose ideological equipment limited their understanding of the great changes that were taking place. The problems of an emergent urban and industrial society were presented as a simple moral struggle between the best and worst in American life, between a disinterested elite and a deluded mass, between the true faith in a self-regulating society and mistaken attempts to interfere with the "natural" law of human progress.

The man who presided over this confusing decade was President Ulysses S. Grant, and no man has fared worse in the account transmitted to posterity. Reelected by an imposing majority in 1872, a popular hero to the day of his death, and admitted (even by his detractors) to have given of his best in a situation he had not sought, he earned in textbooks the reputation as one of the worst of Presidents. Only the undeniable evidence of his own memoirs, written in plain but lucid and vivid prose, preserved him from the stigma of near illiteracy. "Grantism" became the label of an era supposed to flourish on corruption and insensitivity to the decencies of life. Indeed, Grant has become the epitome of those whom the people have favored but have been found wanting at the bar of intellectual judgment.

It is comparatively easy to diagnose the reasons for this reputation. At least in the early days of his Presidency Grant deferred to Congress and made an honest attempt faithfully to administer the law. His record in trying to carry out the intentions of Congress in the South could hardly be faulted. His instructions were issued with precision, he ordered the right amount of force at the right time, and he supported subordinates under the most trying circumstances (a welcome reversal of Andrew Johnson's abandonment of military commanders who did what they conceived to be their duty); but when it seemed that Republicans in the South were relying too much upon the military, he let it be known that the federal government would not support indefinitely those who could not win consent of the governed. On only one occasion did he deliberately reject the considered opinion of Congress, and that was in his veto of the 1874 currency bill; this, characteristically, is the one measure for which he won praise from the intellectual elite. The fact is that Grant interpreted too literally the sovereignty of the people and showed too much respect for their representatives to satisfy those historians who measure the worth of a President by success in defying Congress.

It is worthwhile asking how Grant conceived the duties of the Presidency, and his style as a general is instructive. He would study a problem, keep his own counsel, issue clear but brief orders, and stand by his subordinates as long as they did all that was required of them. He was also a brilliant improviser and trusted those who could do the same within the spirit rather than the letter of his plan. Combined with this there was his refusal to be flustered by setbacks. He had never questioned civilian control whatever his private opinion, and unlike George McClellan he kept that opinion to himself. As head of government Grant tried to apply the same principles, but whereas he had an instinctive grasp of military problems, he had little understanding of the balance of political forces. Congress was master, declaring the intention and providing the legal framework; it was for the executive to decide the means. He succeeded a President who had denied the right of Congress and had used the means that lay in his power to obstruct its purpose. Grant's concept of the presidential function was in every way superior and restored confidence in the system of separate powers. Soon, however, he realized that the situation could not be stable unless supporters of the administration exercised some control over Congress, and he looked for men who appeared to understand the job to carry out this function.

The leaders of the Republican party faced a difficult task. Throughout the war their driving power and cohesion depended upon commitment and dedication, but no one can remain for too long at a high emotional pitch, and the battle over Reconstruction had exhausted the reserves. The party remained but in imminent danger of fragmentation, and to avoid this it was constantly necessary to remind the northern electorate of what had been at stake and to employ the resources of patronage to maintain a hard core of professionals who would keep the party going through the lean years. Along with this it was desirable to sustain the Republicans in the South in the hope that they would become the nucleus around which would gather former Whigs, new radicals, and the dispossessed, both black and white. All this Grant came to understand, but the better his understanding, the more he had to become a party leader and the more reliance had to be placed upon the party managers. This was the era of the "spoilsmen," but men like Roscoe Conkling, Ben Butler, Don Cameron, and Zachariah Chandler took few "spoils" for themselves; they were interested in power and became the channels through which the federal patronage reached those who would promise support in return for jobs.

To such men civil-service reform (the favorite objective of liberal Republicans) was anathema. The reformers held up the British model of a professional civil service selected by competitive examination, promoted on merit, and secure in tenure. To the party leaders this would mean sacrificing the one instrument that they could use to control the local situation and preserve their national alliance. Civil-service reform never became a popular issue, and to many Americans government by politicos was greatly preferable to rule by an administrative elite, and there were inbuilt checks upon incompetence or scandalous appointments. Of necessity every appointment meant several disappointed applicants, and their voices would soon be heard if the successful candidate was notoriously unfit. Local party organizations had strong incentives for seeing that the men they put forward commanded respect, and poor appointments inevitably weakened the party. There were therefore checks upon the abuse of power, and a balance between organization and good repute that ensured greater respectability than reformers would admit. The scandals arose not from design but from ignorance of a man's true character. The opponents of civil-service reform had therefore a stronger case than is sometimes imagined. The existing system did not fill the public service with scoundrels; it honored the old principle of rotation in office while keeping many experienced men on the job, and up to a point it performed efficiently.

It was not so much the intrinsic defects of the old system as the growing need for expertise in administration that provided the strongest argument for change. The growing trade of the country meant more customs, more officials, and more complex fiscal problems; the acceptance of new responsibilities in the regulation of shipping, the extension of the postal system, and the supervision of mail routes extended federal authority to the furthest limits; there were demands for more statistical services, more information from the census, and more attention to the manifold administrative problems created by the Homestead Act, land grants to railroads, and Indian problems. All meant more federal officers exercising tasks requiring greater discretionary powers and often operating far from Washington.[2] The suspect land grants, corrupt mail contracts, sharp practice in the construction costs for subsidized railroads, and excise frauds in the West brought about the most notorious scandals touching even members of the Cabinet; but these were by-products of the sudden extension of federal responsibilities rather than symptoms of moral disaster. Americans did not suddenly become less honest, but the inherited means of control and accountability were totally inadequate for the new scale of operations in a rapidly expanding society. Exactly the same problems could be observed at close quarters in the administration of cities that had suddenly grown too large and too varied in their problems for old easy-going methods of municipal government.

Hesitantly Grant tried to meet the more modest demands of the reformers, but he was always torn between desire for honest government, loyalty to his lieutenants, awareness of the requirement for stable political organization, and suspicion that the evils proclaimed by reformers were often exaggerated and untypical. As a result his support for reform was hesitant and wavering. In 1870 he called positively for reform in "the manner of making all appointments" while deliberately leaving aside the question of tenure. Following this message Congress debated reform inconclusively, until in its final hours the Forty-first Congress passed an appropriation bill with an amendment (approved by Grant) empowering the President to appoint a commission to draw up rules for the examination of candidates for the civil service. The commission was set up in June, 1871, with George William Curtis, a noted reformer, as chairman, and in January, 1872, Grant promul-

[2] The increase in the number of federal employees was striking. In 1871 there were 51,020; ten years later 100,020. Of these 6,222 were in Washington in 1871 and 13,124 in 1881. The increased activity of Congress is illustrated by the rise of legislative employees from 618 to 2,579 and of the federal courts from 247 to 2,762 (these figures are included in the totals given above).

gated rules requiring competitive examinations for entry
and promotion on merit; but at the same time his closest
supporters in Congress vigorously opposed its principles,
opposed attempts to make the new system semipermanent,
and obstructed appropriations. After the election of 1872
Grant, though still professing his general support for civil-
service reform, made some appointments that were anathema to the reformers, and in March, 1873, Curtis resigned
as chairman of the commission. By December of that year
Grant seems to have decided that the commission's rules
were unworkable, though he was still ready to consider
ways of making them effective. A year later he was
prepared to continue only if Congress gave positive authorization, and as Congress let appropriations for the
commission go by default, the whole examinations system
was terminated in 1875. Disappointed reformers concluded
that though the President might have accepted the logic
of the examinations system, he was not prepared to fight
for it against hostility in his party, obstruction in Congress,
and apathy among the people.

In external affairs the Grant Administration stands at
the parting of the ways between preoccupation with the
problems of the American continent and responsibilities
on a wider stage. The formal and prolonged diplomacy
that led to a settlement of the *Alabama* claims with Great
Britain was symptomatic of the American determination
to play a decisive part in international relations. Caribbean problems foreshadowed all the agonizing questions of
the American attitude to revolutionary movements in
other countries, responsibility toward weak states, and the
relationship between political commitments and economic
expansion.

Grant selected as Secretary of State a New York lawyer
named Hamilton Fish, whose conservative temperament
and unchallenged integrity won him the respect of contemporaries and high praise from diplomatic historians. His

reputation derives in part from the way in which he represented deeper currents of change. Though these changes
had originated long before and their implications would
not be apparent before the end of the century, it is not fan-
ciful to see Hamilton Fish as the symbol of America's transition from "the beacon of radicalism" to the bastion of
conservatism in world affairs. The guiding principle of his
policy was to ensure that American interests were fully
safeguarded in a stable world; this stability was to be maintained against American eagerness for conflict with Great
Britain, Cuban revolutionaries, and the involvement of
the United States in Caribbean adventures. He inherited
the work of Seward, an expansionist whose considerable
skill and conciliatory temper were often harnessed to
emotional commitments, and he served a President who
believed that the way to success was to fix ambitious objectives and hammer away until they had been gained. In the
negotiations with Great Britain Grant's practical realism
brought both men together in the quest for settlement that
would avoid the folly of war and the absurdity of trying to
couple the annexation of Canada with the *Alabama*
claims, while ensuring that reasonable demands were met
in full. Behind this was the underlying necessity of reconstructing the Anglo-American relationship on terms of
equal partnership in the Atlantic. In Cuba Fish successfully blocked Grant's intention to extend belligerent rights
to the rebels against Spanish authority; in Santo Domingo
he loyally implemented the President's desire for annexation but without enthusiasm. If Grant had had his way,
Americans would have accepted more definite responsibilities in the Caribbean but would have done so as the pa-
trons of revolution, committed to rescue weak nations
from the consequences of misrule and poverty, and on the
assumption that the outward thrust of American enterprise was the instrument of progress.

The *Alabama* had been allowed to sail from a British shipyard after the British Government had received

prima facie evidence that she was intended for use as a
Confederate warship. The subsequent success of the ship as
a commerce raider left the Americans with a justifiable
claim against the British Government for a clear breach of
international law. From the start, indeed, the British accepted some blame, and the argument was over its extent
and consequences. On the American side expansionists
joined by the former anglophile Charles Sumner (who had
been bitterly offended by the apparent favor with which
the slave power had been regarded in England) insisted
that Great Britain must pay not only for all the losses inflicted by the *Alabama* but also for the indirect damage to
American commerce and undefined consequences of prolonging the war. It was suggested that Great Britain might
settle by ceding Canada to the United States, regardless
of the fact that the Canadians were themselves embarking at this time on the bold and hopeful experiment of
confederation.

Compared with this extravagance, the decision of Grant
and Fish to seek a settlement by calm though complex
negotiation was a triumph of good sense. Fortunately
Gladstone's government in Great Britain was peacefully
inclined, and the Prime Minister may have been anxious to
repel the inference that his support for recognition of the
Confederacy in 1862 had revealed him as a defender of
slavery. It was not easy to find a way in which both nations
could recede from extreme positions, but patient efforts
led to the Treaty of Washington in 1871 which agreed to
put the claims to an international commission in Geneva
and to accept the result of arbitration. Not unexpectedly
the adjudication required Great Britain to pay rather
more, and the United States to accept considerably less,
than either had wished. Regarded as a landmark in establishing procedures for the peaceful settlement of disputes,
the Geneva arbitration brought Grant and Fish little popularity at home.

The Caribbean policy of the Grant Administration is a

preview of later arguments and events. The debates over
Cuba and the abortive attempt to annex Santo Domingo
can be seen as a rehearsal of the great debates over imperialism at the turn of the century and American involvement
in Asia a hundred years later. In October, 1868, the discontent of Spanish Cuba came to a head in a revolution that
inaugurated ten years of war. The revolutionaries demanded separate independence with echoes of 1776, but
also with a strong element of social revolution. In addition
to declaring independence, the revolutionary constitution
of Guáimaro abolished slavery, established equality under
the law, and ended the privileges given to favored groups.
The revolution was largely a rural uprising, including
large landowners as well as small, and many freed slaves
were enrolled in the army; their most determined opponents were the men of Spanish descent in the towns and
more thickly populated areas who saw Spanish authority
as the guarantee of white supremacy in the island, and the
local militia was reputed to be even more savage in dealing
with rebels than the regular troops.

American opinion as a whole was strongly opposed to
Spanish rule and anticipated the speedy triumph of independence; Grant was personally inclined to accelerate
events by recognizing the revolutionaries as belligerents. If
he had done so, there is little doubt that the action would
have been more popular than any other act of policy in his
two terms. His Secretary of War, John A. Rawlins, was
emotionally and financially committed to the revolutionary cause and though almost forgotten in his own country,
is still remembered with gratitude in Cuba. In New York a
revolutionary Cuban junta was set up to influence American opinion and organize supplies for the insurrectionary
forces. There were, however, difficulties that impressed
Hamilton Fish; even though the provisional President was
a great landowner, Fish was suspicious of the wilder
clements and believed that the revolutionary movement could not provide a stable government and was mil-

itarily weak and opposed by influential Cubans. The recognition of belligerent rights might speedily involve Americans in a clash with Spain and lead to direct intervention before long. The United States would then be committed to the support of a weak revolutionary regime of unknown intentions without appreciable strategic or economic gains. For these reasons Fish refused to grant belligerent rights and successfully maintained this position against Grant, Rawlins, pressure in Congress, and public criticism. According to the rules of the diplomatic game, Fish was undoubtedly correct, but there is a lingering shade of regret that he was strong enough to maintain his point of view. The future of American policy might have been happier if the United States had taken a bold line, whatever the consequences, in support of revolution, abolition, and social equality. Whatever the immediate consequences—and they might well have been unfortunate—a significant precedent would have been set.

Instead of direct involvement in the Cuban conflict Fish hoped to bring off a diplomatic coup in 1869 and secretly proposed that the Spaniards should accept American mediation on the basis of Cuban independence, a payment from Cuba to Spain of $100,000,000 guaranteed by the United States Government, the abolition of slavery, and an armistice pending negotiations. The American minister at Madrid, a somewhat flamboyant Civil War general named Daniel E. Sickles (who was strongly in favor of Cuban independence), persistently overestimated the flexibility of the Spaniards and misunderstood their emotional attachment to empire and their obligation to Cuban supporters. There was, indeed, very little chance that the Spaniards would throw in their hand, but failure did not incline Fish to recognition of the revolution, and he insisted that the President's message to Congress in June, 1870, originally drafted in bellicose terms, should be toned down to an anticlimactic expression of neutrality.

The interchanges with Spain now began to treat aboli-

tion as the first essential, and to stress the general consequences of obstinacy in Cuba rather than the immediate
possibility of American intervention. The Spanish Cortes
did pass a measure of gradual emancipation in June, 1870,
but this would have preserved the essentials of slavery for
more than a generation, and a second act in 1872 was still
unacceptable to antislavery opinion. In contast to his une-
motional response to revolution, Fish reacted very sharply
in 1873 when the Spaniards captured the *Virginius* (an
American ship and former blockade-runner, now engaged
in taking arms and passengers to the revolutionaries) and
summarily executed the captain, thirty-six members of the
crew, and sixteen passengers. Spanish attempts to delay
were immediately rejected, and American demands were
accepted under the threat of war. The ten years' war in
Cuba ended in 1878 with the restoration of Spanish authority; the United States had acted throughout with ex-
emplary correctness and won no friends in any quarter.

If the Cuban question saw America reject a commitment
to revolution, Santo Domingo brought the country to the
brink of new-style imperialism. Perhaps Grant did not see
it as a novelty; he had been brought up in an age of expansionist enthusiasm, and his first active service had been in
the Mexican War. Seward had recently carried through the
purchase of Alaska, without arousing either enthusiasm or
alarm. There had been a proposal to purchase the Danish
West Indies, which had got so far as a vote in the islands favoring transfer and an agreed price; this was shelved because of the impossibility of carrying anything as long as
Johnson was in the White House and had then been allowed to die for lack of interest; but no one had opposed
the principle of acquisition. Santo Domingo was weak
(probably not more than 120,000 inhabitants), poor, and
black. The internal conditions were unstable. To preserve
his own position and obtain funds to develop the resources
of his country President Buenaventura Báez was in the
market and found allies in two American speculators, Wil-

liam Cazneau and J. W. Fabens. A loan had been negotiated in London at such disadvantageous terms that not
only was the normal revenue pledged to meet interest payments but the island's best harbor might be leased to a foreign power. Altogether Santo Domingo did not seem to be
an attractive proposition, but it caught President Grant's
imagination. He sent his friend and secretary, Orville Bab-
cock, to confer with Báez, and from this came an agreement for annexation by the United States.

The message in which Grant presented the proposal to
Congress in May, 1870, contained in embryo most of the arguments that would reverberate whenever American commitments overseas were discussed during the following
hundred years. He dealt first with national security,
warned of the danger that a European power might acquire a permanent interest in the island, and enlarged the
Monroe Doctrine to embrace the principle that "hereafter
no territory on this continent shall be regarded as subject
of transfer to a European power." The strategic position of
the island was emphasized; it would guard the southern
approaches to the United States and stand athwart the new
lanes of commerce to be opened up when the isthmian
canal was built. Most of the message was taken up with the
economic case for annexation; Santo Domingo could support ten million "in luxury," produce abundant produce
that would otherwise have to come from foreign countries,
become "a large consumer of the products of Northern
farms and manufactories," while the cheapness of American food, tools, and machinery would stimulate competition in the other Caribbean islands and open "a still wider
market for our products." Santo Domingo would therefore
provide the magic key to a favorable balance of payments,
and American shipping would recover the prosperity that
had been lost to foreign competition. Using a somewhat
obscure line of reasoning, the President linked annexation
with a great moral cause by saying that American trade
and institutions would make slavery unprofitable "in

Cuba and Porto [sic] Rico at once and ultimately so in Brazil." He concluded that annexation "is, in fine, a rapid stride toward that greatness which the intelligence, industry and enterprise of the citizens of the United States entitle this country to assume among nations."[3]

Thus Grant used the classic formula for justifying intervention and expansion overseas: the danger that others would act if America failed to do so, strategy, economic expansion, moral superiority, and the small step necessary to obtain such striking benefits. Unfortunately for him rumors of shady financial transactions began to circulate, and the supposed foreign threats were discounted; suspicion was generated that America was being asked, on the strength of a fraudulent prospectus, to take over a bankrupt concern, while Báez, a handful of American operators, and London bankers would get away with the proceeds. These doubts might have been laid at rest, but the treaty also attracted the determined opposition of Senator Charles Sumner, chairman of the Foreign Relations Committee, and the more Grant pushed annexation, the stronger became the obsessive determination of Sumner to kill it. He went over all the doubtful points in the case for annexation and with typical exaggeration presented it as a measure that was not merely inexpedient but wicked. The core of his case was, however, an argument of permanent significance. Santo Domingo was a black country; it was naturally suited to the black people and presented the ideal stage for them to develop their own institutions.

[It was] the earliest of that independent group destined to occupy the Caribbean Sea, toward which our duty is as plain as the Ten Commandments. Kindness, beneficence, assistance, aid, help, protection, all that is implied in good neighbourhood,—these we must give, freely, bountifully; but their independence is as precious to them as is ours to us, and it is placed under the

[3] Quoted in James D. Richardson (ed.), *A Compilation of the Messages and Papers of the Presidents*, Vol. VII (Washington, D.C.: 1897), pp. 62–63.

safeguard of natural laws which we cannot violate with impunity.[4]

Thanks largely to Sumner, enough Republican senators were detached from the main body of the party to kill the annexation treaty. The immediate consequence was that Grant (who honestly believed that Sumner had promised in advance to support annexation) determined to destroy the senator's influence. In the next Congress the Republican majority took the almost unprecedented step of depriving Sumner of his committee chairmanship, and this in turn drove a sizable portion of the old guard of antislavery men into the Liberal Republican revolt of 1872, while committing Grant to firm alliance with the party bosses.

Considerable space has been devoted to Cuba and Santo Domingo (which normally receive but passing mention at this stage of American history), because it becomes clear, in retrospect, that they symbolize a decisive shift in Americans' view of their country's future. Intervention and annexation both failed, but the arguments were very different. Intervention in Cuba failed because the idea of national interest prevailed over a commitment to stand as foster father to small nations struggling to free themselves from European domination. Annexation failed because, in a case in which national interest was by no means clear, the commitment to independence prevailed. The relevance of both issues to twentieth-century problems is therefore clear.

The memory of the Civil War and the still vexed problems of the South blinded many to the changes taking place in society as a whole. American civilization was entering upon a period of decisive transformation in which it is difficult to isolate particular changes or give priority to any single influence. In the modern world all developing

---

[4] *Congressional Globe*, 41st Cong., 3d sess., December 21, 1870, Pt. I, pp. 227–231.

societies have experienced the cumulative effects of concurrent changes taking place over a wide range of economic activities, social structure, intellectual assumptions, and personal conduct; a brief summary cannot hope to give an adequate description, let alone an explanation. Population growth, migration, social mobility, occupational mobility, and the drift to the cities could provide one area of inquiry, but these features cannot be separated from scientific and technological change, improvements in communications, and the development of more sophisticated commercial and financial institutions to handle long-distance trade and find capital for new developments. Nor can these changes be separated from the greater emphasis upon public responsibility as a supplement to or substitute for individual responsibility. These movements have fused with intellectual changes derived from rationalism and the repudiation of traditional authority, and the quest for new secular faiths has led to the rise of the intelligentsia as a distinct social group. Of even more profound consequence have been changes in ethical conventions, alterations in family life, and new codes of social behavior. All these great changes are reflected (though not always in a manner that is immediately clear) in art, architecture, literature, taste, and fashion. Even such apparently trivial matters as dress, the design of household goods, and popular amusements are symbols of the great transformation and cannot be studied in isolation.

Any analysis of society during a period of change must therefore begin with a somewhat arbitrary choice from a very large number of related topics. However, a start must be made somewhere, and it is reasonable to take as a focal point a phenomenon that impressed most visitors: the rapid growth of American cities.

It was natural to attach most importance to large cities. In 1880 the number of people living in cities of over 100,000 was approximately equal to the total urban population in 1860 (6,200,000), and the average annual increase had been just under 200,000. The birth rate in the large cities was certainly lower than in rural areas, and a large part of this increase was therefore explained by new arrivals from Europe and by internal migration. The net migration from the countryside to the towns was considerably larger than from the towns to the country, but there is some evidence to suggest that most people who moved into the larger cities had spent some time in smaller towns, which received the bulk of direct migration from rural areas. With arrivals from abroad the pattern was reversed; migrants tended to congregate first in the large cities and move at a later stage to smaller towns. A few went direct to rural areas, but the proportion doing so was lower than in earlier periods. The middle range of towns—from 25,000 to 100,000—increased their population between 1860 and 1880 by 1,200,000 to reach 2,500,000. It is a reasonable hypothesis to think of these towns of middling size losing people by migration to the larger cities while gaining still more from rural America and smaller towns and getting some spill-over of foreign-born who had spent a period in a larger city. At the lower end of the urban scale, in 1880 there were 716 places with more than 2,500 and less than 10,000 people. In 1860 there had been 299 and in 1850, 174. A few of these small towns must have been places that failed to grow, a few may once have been larger, but the great majority of small towns in 1880 must have been new urban centers.

The features of urban change in the middle years of the century were therefore great increase in the number of people living in large towns and the large contribution to that increase made by migrants from abroad or from other parts of the United States; an increase in the number of towns of middle size with a changing population as some left for larger towns while others arrived; and a tremendous increase in the number of very small towns. Thus, while the attention of contemporaries (and of most historians) was focused upon the larger cities, less noticed but highly significant changes were taking place in the smaller towns. Of the total urban population in 1880 of 14,100,000, 6,200,000 lived in cities of over 100,000 and 6,900,000 in towns of under 50,000. Thus, almost half of the town-dwellers lived in places in which it was still possible for the leaders in business, politics, and the professions to know each other and to form a cohesive group. The small towns also had a geographical unity; even in a town of 50,000 an easy walk would take one from one limit to the other; no one need live far from his place of work, and it was still possible for the wealthy to find pleasant homes within sight and sound of their humbler fellows. The large cities were beginning to present problems in social and residential segregation that foreshadowed the future but were not yet typical of nineteenth-century society. One consequence of the contrast between large and small cities was a dichotomy between economic and political authority. The drive behind the Republican party had come from the small towns; by 1876 control of the economy had shifted decisively toward the larger towns, but the small towns still occupied the center of political gravity. Indeed, a great deal of the misgovernment endured by the greater cities springs from this cause; they had become too large for rule by a patrician oligarchy but not yet so politically important as to make their problems a matter of concern for national politicians. In the crude terms of electoral arithmetic a presidential candidate could still win easily if he lost every one of the cities over 100,000. Partly because of this neglect and partly as a result of pressures from below, the government of cities fell into the hands of new men who wanted the job as a profitable investment or an instrument of self-advancement.

Large districts in the big cities were being given over to low-paid workers and recent immigrants. Such districts were not always the haunts of crime and vice pictured in the middle-class literature of the day, and many immigrant groups made gallant efforts to create a culture of their own in an alien environment. Churches, foreign-language news-papers, and traditional customs played a major part in this struggle for cultural survival; but if there was resistance to Americanization, there had also to be adjustment, and in this the political bosses and their henchmen played essential roles. They provided a link with the official world and could do a great deal in the way of petty patronage to find employment, see that no one starved, and that some kind of community was established. The boss was interested in votes, not in good housing, clean streets, and efficient police. Even if he had been determined to improve in these respects, he would have had to draw upon funds that urban taxpayers and rural legislators were not prepared to supply and would have risked alienating business interests whose goodwill was necessary. Nor was he normally prepared to subsidize voluntary charitable organizations presided over by members of the old elite. The boss was in business to monopolize the supply of political favors and to ensure that people who wished to take advantage of lawful opportunities in urban expansion or to operate beyond the law paid for the privilege. Building contracts, streetcar franchises, and water and gas supply were subject to political approval; and municipal politicians could control matters upon which a great deal of money might depend, and it was hardly regarded as immoral for them to accept payment for their services. More dubious was the practice of inflating estimates, paying the boss a kickback amounting to the difference between the real and estimated cost, and thus silently transferring public money to private pockets. Equally dubious was the practice of taking payment from brothel-keepers and gambling establishments, though it is fair to remember that the cost was really paid by the clients who chose to spend money on these activities. This tale of fraud and crime merely emphasizes the truth that behind the new power of the bosses lay the indubitable fact that no one was prepared to pay for more desirable alternatives.

American cities had grown rapidly, and many of them had little more than village government to cope with the problems of an urban society. The old civic elite had managed well enough as long as the towns were small and relatively homogeneous, but they could not contemplate the huge sums of money necessary for providing the streets with sound paving, good lighting, and efficient cleaning; they could not come to terms with voters who lived in a separate part of the city, appeared to live in squalor, spoke an alien language, belonged to an alien church, and yet had votes to make or break the aspiring politician; nor could they readily accept the need to regulate utilities, housing, and other kinds of private property. The professional city politician, normally himself the product of urban environment, understood power and persuasion in a congested city blessed with universal suffrage; he would spend the necessary time and effort to build a stable political base, and he would do what was required for municipal improvement provided that he was paid for the job. There was, indeed, something to be said for this specialization of function by which municipal government became a business enterprise; the real drawback arose from the character of the men who thrived on the system. The performance of some welfare services in a haphazard and self-interested way does not redeem the bosses from blame for the system over which they presided. Some had criminal instincts; more were hardheaded men with poor taste and no imagination; posterity might forgive them a little graft if they had had the artistic culture and architectural vision of Renaissance despots, but in fact they were coarse and very ordinary men who contributed much to the ugliness, squalor, and low standards of urban life.

William Marcy Tweed, of New York, has passed into history as the epitome of city bosses, and the movement that led to his downfall is regarded as a classic example of civic reform. At the height of his power in 1869 Tweed seemed to be in complete command of the city, advancing rapidly in the state, and closely linked with major enterprises such as the Erie Railroad. The instrument of his power was Tammany Hall, its base the poorer and predominantly Irish wards of the city, and its sinews the flow of cash that came to him and his associates ("the Ring") from inflated estimates and payments from business for favors received. Tweed was a very large, jovial man who had grown up in the rough world of the poorer districts; he was regarded by the New York Irish as their champion, and the large sums that he and his friends gathered from the taxpayers were matters for congratulation rather than concealment. The cartoonist Thomas Nast made his reputation by his bitter attacks upon Tweed, pictured as a greasy, bloated tough with small piglike eyes. *The New York Times* became spokesman of the better-class citizens (and so established a reputation as the most honest newspaper in the nation), and, somewhat late in the day, Samuel Tilden joined in the attack as an anti-Tammany Democrat (thereby earning a fame that almost made him President of the United States). Scandals roused the "good citizens" to make a supreme effort, and exposures discredited Tweed even among loyal Democrats. In 1870 reform triumphed, and Tweed was broken, but within a short while reform had revealed the limitations of an attitude that gave first priority to the taxpayers' purse and little consideration to the welfare of the urban masses. Soon New York was back under the rule of another but more discreet and less greedy Tammany boss.

This sequence was to become familiar and appeared in various forms in several cities. Bosses gathered power, became overconfident, fell after a struggle, and were succeeded by short-lived reform administrations. The merchants, bankers, and successful lawyers who had formed the municipal oligarchy in former days no longer had the inclination to engage in the tiresome business of municipal politics in which few reputations could be made and the pleasure of office was marred by association with unpleasant people. Thus the cities experienced the basic problem of finding leadership in a democratic society and arrived at no happy solution.

Concentration upon political scandal obscures changes of more lasting importance in the life of the cities. In spite of all the frauds and errors streets were being paved and cleaned, disease (though still all too common) was being tackled, and violent crime held in check. Gas had come to most cities before the Civil War, but pure or filtered water was mainly a postwar development. Lines were laid for the horse-drawn streetcars, and these began to affect the pattern of urban development; it was no longer the privilege of the carriage-owning classes to live at a distance from the center, and clerical and a few skilled workers could now live near the end of the line in new suburban areas. In the larger towns these new residential areas would soon be invaded by the immigrants and poor. In New York middle-class settlements were established north of Forty-second Street, but within a few years the well-to-do were finding new homes farther north in the Seventies and Eighties. In many of these developments private enterprise led wherever the smell of profit lured, but there was also a good deal of municipal enterprise and regulation. No street could be dug up for a gas or water main without authority; streetcar companies had to obtain franchises; railroads required permission to build stations and carry tracks over, under, or along streets; wharves and harbors had to be supervised; some cities took a hand in the task of water supply. Of a rather different kind were the semiofficial groups of leading citizens who combined to raise funds for much-needed railroads, confer on commercial problems, organize charities, and appeal for public-spirited action on many issues. On several of these problems the businessmen sought and obtained aid from the city government. On occasions the cities were forced to meet the challenge of epidemics and in normal times maintained a rudimentary health service. Hospitals, prisons, insane asylums, and homes for the aged were other areas for municipal enterprise. Above all, the cities accepted the challenge of producing a literate people (even where the foreign-born predominated), and if the urban schools lacked the charm of the little red schoolhouse, far more children passed through their doors.

Much of what was done was sporadic, inefficient, and riddled with graft; but even so, the urban environment was being transformed, and municipal government was touching the lives of more people than ever before. The limitations were most apparent in the poor districts where action was most needed. The housing was cramped, streets narrow and dirty, crime and sickness most apparent. There was virtually no control over landlords, employers, or sale of goods, save the shadowy safeguards of the common law that were beyond the comprehension of the poor. Private baths were unknown, water taps normally shared between several families, lavatories rudimentary, and cooking stoves dirty. Things were perhaps not quite so bad as they became in later years. The areas were less crowded, and tenements that so shocked Jacob Riis and others around 1890 were still new or less dilapidated in 1870. Even so, and though class lines were a little less sharp than they subsequently became, conditions of life in these areas emphasized the social segregation of the new era. Class differences and some degree of residential separation there had always been, but in the growing cities the classes lived apart as never before. Even in the cities of middling size, the railroad track often became an easily identifiable frontier between respectability and the land of the poor.

What kind of people moved into the growing cities? The question cannot be answered with any precision until a great deal more investigation has been done. One of the persistent myths of migration is that natural selection chooses the energetic, ambitious, and enterprising. In the United States, as elsewhere, there seems to have been a considerable movement of the shiftless, rootless, and unstable people, who drifted throughout life from place to place and job to job; many of them moved into the cities, and probably few returned to the country. At the other extreme were ambitious men attracted by opportunities and anxious to succeed. At every level most men and women who moved into the cities tended to stay there; some from inertia or because city life had unfitted them for agriculture, but many because city life despite its drawbacks was varied, gregarious, and exciting. The driving force behind many poor-boys-made-good was compulsion to escape from the deadening boredom of rural isolation.

Apart from the shiftless and unemployable, most native-born migrants into the large cities hoped to occupy positions well up the urban hierarchy—at least as skilled craftsmen, and possibly as businessmen, lawyers, or doctors. Migration thus tended to emphasize the ethnic stratification of the expanding urban culture. The foreign-born moved in at the bottom of the ladder and found themselves in a social enclave hedged around with cultural, linguistic, and economic barriers. For many the best hope would be to establish a precarious livelihood in an occupation that had ceased to be attractive to native-born Americans. They provided ready-made material for exploitation in the sweated industries, and their prospects of escape were dim. A few established themselves as storekeepers or small employers within their ethnic subculture. A trickle moved on to the country, but the city, with all its drawbacks, still exercised a magnetic attraction upon people from European peasant backgrounds who carried with them traditions of rural hardship and petty oppression. But whether the new immigrants stayed because they had to, or because they preferred to do so, the result was segregation on ethnic as well as class grounds. American society was no longer a homogeneous culture.

There is a common confusion between urbanization and industrialization. Before the Civil War most cities had grown as centers for commerce, communications, and banking, and when it ended, most factories in towns were small. There was, however, a bewildering variety of industrial occupations (many carried on in tiny workshops) ; in the postwar decades these occupations were making important contributions to economic growth and to the prosperity of the cities in which they were situated. Newcomers with specialized skills were welcome, and these smaller industries provided the means by which some immigrants climbed the social ladder. The range of such occupations was impressive, and at this level America was still the land of opportunity. If the failure rate was high, and if some eager newcomers soon found themselves permanently consigned to sweated labor, enough survived to reinforce the old, hopeful belief that anyone with enterprise could succeed in the United States. Success and frustration were both illustrated in the history of the ready-made clothing industry. Many of the entrepreneurs were German Jews who first gathered savings as tailors, peddlers, or small merchants; they tended to employ others of the same faith and language, and with the introduction of cutting and sewing machines it became possible to organize large workshops that eventually became factories. By 1880 a pattern was beginning to emerge, with some extremely successful men at the top, a few skilled mechanics and foremen, a large body of semiskilled factory operatives (many of them women) , and a considerable amount of auxiliary work still carried on in very small workshops or in the home. Such industries also provided employment for a growing number of managers, technical experts, and clerical workers.

It is easy to overlook white-collar employment. Clerks had always been a part of the urban scene, but their number was increasing in both gross and relative terms. A study shows that between 1860 and 1930 the population of Philadelphia rose from 566,000 to 1,951,000. The proportion of unskilled laborers in industrial occupations remained relatively stable at 8.1 percent and 8.7 percent, but office and sales clerks increased from 3.4 percent to 13.9 percent. The proportion of the population engaged in manufacturing and mechanical industries fell from 54.9 percent to 45.3 percent, whereas nonmanufacturing rose from 45.1 percent to 54.7 percent. Among the nonmanufacturing occupations there was a considerable fall (21.8 percent to 12.8 percent) in hotels, laundries, and domestic service, but significant increases in wholesale trades (11.2 percent to 15.3 percent) and the professions (4.3 percent to 6.3 percent). One cannot make much of figures covering seventy years when only the first fifteen are under consideration, but at least one can hazard a hypothesis that the era after the war saw the beginning of a period in which "Philadelphians' economic effort shifted steadily from an early concentration on manufactures and commerce toward a modern emphasis on services, education and government." [5] It is a reasonable assumption that other large cities showed the same pattern of change.

There is little information about the character of the growing number of clerks and professional men, but it is probable that most of them were of old American or recent British origin, that a high proportion had had some secondary education, and that a majority were Protestants. It is also a reasonable guess that they were moving or wished to move to the new suburbs springing up as the streetcar lines extended from the center, but as most of these residential areas either remained within or were added to the cities for political and administrative purposes, the clerical workers remained a political counterweight to the foreign-born low-paid vote in the center. As small taxpayers they provided the popular backing for civic-reform movements and help to explain the continuing strength of the Republican party in the large cities. This white-collar working class of the cities had similar attitudes and aspirations to the middle class of the small towns. They believed in and practiced the virtues of thrift

[5] Sam B. Warner, "If All the World Were Philadelphia," *American Historical Review*, Vol. LXXIV, No. 1 (October, 1968). The figures quoted in this paragraph are drawn from this article.

and hard work, were good family men, and attached great importance to education (but not, as yet, to higher education) ; they believed that business was better run and operated on ethically superior principles than government; they had little aesthetic sense but liked simple, sentimental, and representational art; they admired material success provided that it had not been gained too blatantly at the expense of others. Toward the older commercial elite and the new railroad and industrial magnates they were usually unsympathetic. It was therefore a class of enormous significance for the future, which social analysts ignore at their peril.

The railroads dramatized the consolidation of economic power and persuaded many that there should be a distinction between business and big business, between fair and unfair competition. There had been other rich and powerful men in American history, and occasionally—as in the bank question—their power had become a political issue. The incidence of railroad power was of a different order; for while financial questions affected individuals sporadically and occasionally during the course of their lives, the railroads were always present and frequently used. Many were still local concerns, but the trend was toward consolidation and the accumulation of power in a few hands. Control was exercised through disciplined bureaucracies and became remote, invisible, and impersonal. Railroads were also vulnerable to all kinds of financial manipulation and malpractice, and it was usually impossible to distinguish increases in rates justified by a genuine need to cover costs from those resulting from operations by which a predatory capitalist had milked the corporate funds.

Several of the railroad magnates were also involved with other kinds of financial sharp practice (such as speculations in gold and commodities) and linked with unsavory politics; thus this first generation of big-business men emerged as a publicized and unpopular group, imposing unnecessary hardship upon others and defying conventional morality. Even if they had risen from humble backgrounds, their success was attributed to ruthlessness and deceit rather than to industry, honesty, and thrift. There was, indeed, traditional admiration for the "smart man," but success achieved by cunning and quick wit ceased to earn respect when painted larger than small-town life. Nothing is further from the truth than the belief that the great magnates were folk-heroes regarded as untouchable by the public; it would require a whole generation of propaganda before this stereotype was accepted, and even then it would be fragile. In the 1870's big business was viewed with equal alarm by simple farmers, white-collar workers, small-business men, and representatives of the older culture. President Grant's friendship with some of the new men of great wealth was a principal reason for the decline in his popularity during the second term.

It was not, however, until the second term that this tension within American capitalism became acute. The seven years following the Civil War presented a reassuring picture of growth and profits. Though there were setbacks in 1866 and 1868, recovery followed quickly, and in retrospect the symptoms that had alarmed contemporaries and caused a turnabout in the government's deflationary policy in 1868 appeared as mild and temporary checks. Psychologically this prosperous period was of great importance. It is hard to imagine the consequences if the political disturbances of Reconstruction had been accompanied by economic depression, but evidence of economic success confirmed many northerners in their belief that God had blessed the Union cause, and though the southern economy was in chaos after the war, prosperity spilled over to assist southern recovery.

In 1873 confidence was rudely shaken by the failure of Jay Cooke's great banking firm, by a subsequent crop of business failures, and by almost four years of depression accompanied by savage industrial disputes. This had political consequences in the Democratic victories in the congressional elections of 1874, the contested election of 1876, and the abandonment of Reconstruction policies. As the depression began with a spectacular financial crisis, it was natural for contemporaries to concentrate upon speculation and excessive borrowing as the primary cause; they were as yet unfamiliar with heavy borrowing to finance development and condemned as immoral practices that would now be regarded as normal. Once confidence was shaken, pressure mounted on the institutions that were suspected of having insufficient available cash, even though their capital was invested in enterprises with bright futures.

If railroads had become symbols of economic aggression, their image became still more tarnished as they grappled with depression. An enthusiasm that did not reckon upon the long delay between promotion and working profits, and the lure of government land grants, had drawn enormous sums into railroad investment; much of this passed straight through the accounts into the hands of construction companies (often owned by the promoters themselves) and bequeathed to the railroad a heavy burden of interest charges and meager prospects of high earnings in thinly populated regions. Events worked in an unhappy circle for the railroads. High rates to meet debt charges reduced earnings; increased charges stimulated political opposition and fostered demands for the regulation of railroad rates. Between distant points the railroads were often in competition and forced to cut rates to attract traffic; in country districts, and on branches to small towns, they often had a monopoly and could raise rates to recoup losses elsewhere. This brought farmers, aggrieved by high freight rates, and businessmen anxious to promote the interests of their towns into alliance against the railroads. To counteract this the railroads entered politics and bought off discriminatory legislation with cash, favors for individuals, or agreements to build new branches to smaller places; but this increased their financial liabilities and damaged still further their public reputation. Thus the finest technological achievement of the mid-nineteenth century raised a cloud of bitterness, generated suspicion of fraud and unfair discrimination, led to demands for public regulation, and raised profound doubts about the ethics of large-scale capitalist organization.

State regulation of private economic activities was no novelty; it was supported by many precedents from earlier periods and received impressive endorsement in the famous case of *Munn v. Illinois*. In this instance the challenge to regulation came from a grain elevator company, not a railroad, but the principle was the same. The company claimed that a state law fixing maximum rates was a violation of the clause of the Fourteenth Amendment declaring that no state should "deprive any person of life, liberty, or property, without due process of law." The core of Chief Justice Morrison R. Waite's Supreme Court judgment was the statement that

property does become clothed with a public interest when used in a manner to make it of public consequence, and affect the community at large. When, therefore, one devotes his property to a use in which the public has an interest, he, in effect, grants to the public an interest in that use, and must submit to be controlled by the public for the common good, to the extent of the interest he thus created.

This was a notable vindication of the right to regulate by the state, but some contemporaries noted with alarm the strength of the challenge to principles of public responsibility that had long been accepted. Future years were to see their forebodings fulfilled, but nevertheless the 1870's should be remembered as the era when some of the problems of overmighty economic power were first confronted. In retrospect it is the grip of laissez-faire theory on the courts in the following decades that should appear temporary and untypical, and it was the later "folklore of capitalism" that seized upon this passing phase as the norm by which the economic activities of government should be judged.

In 1869 Massachusetts set up a railroad commission upon a pattern that looked weak on paper but could be very effective. It had the right to investigate, conduct hearings, recommend action to the railroads, and make public report of its findings; but it had no coercive power. Its chairman, Charles Francis Adams, Jr., a redoubtable member of a formidable family, believed that publicity could be far more efficient than attempts to regulate by legislative action. "The commissioners," he said, "had to listen, and they might investigate and report; they could do little more," but nevertheless, "the law could not have been improved." The Massachusetts model was imitated elsewhere in New England and in New York. Illinois adopted another mode. Here the state legislature passed laws with detailed regulations and set up a commission to enforce them. This was copied in some western and most southern states. These regulatory laws were often associated with political pressure from the Grange, a farmers' organization that sprang into vigorous life during the 1870's. Railroad companies preferred the Massachusetts type even though they usually felt bound to accept its recommendations. Whatever the method chosen, these experiments brought into focus all the problems of regulated capitalism and rehearsed, in many ways, developments of the twentieth century.

The great sectional quarrel had focused on the future of the West, but when the struggle was over, few eastern Americans knew much about the vast region west of the Mississippi. Not until the last decade of the century would western settlement be claimed as the key to American development, and then the generalizations of the frontier thesis would be based on the experience of the old Northwest rather than the Great Plains, the mountains, and the

Pacific regions. Nor would the Wild West assume a firm place in American mythology until a later generation, although railroad companies were beginning to advertise the blessings and future prospects of the region. Indeed, there was little to romanticize in the experience of the 1870's. The three north-west-central states of Iowa, Wisconsin, and Minnesota saw the development of a new agricultural civilization to which immigrants from Germany and Scandinavia made substantial contributions. Iowa was also the starting point for many who moved farther west during the decade. In 1860 these three states had totaled about 1,700,000 people; by 1880 there were almost that number in Iowa alone, the total was 3,700,000, and a number of growing cities provided markets and commercial services for a prosperous farming region. Farther south Kansas and Nebraska were the fastest-growing states in the Union between 1870 and 1880, with increases from 364,000 to 996,000 and 123,000 to 452,000.

The north-central states were, with Illinois, the scene of what was virtually an agricultural revolution. The war drained young men away to join the Union army, while others moved off to Canada or the western mining regions to avoid the draft. This meant an acute shortage of labor at a time when prices were running high, and consequently an incentive for labor-saving mechanization. After the war demand for wheat ran high in Europe; and though the worldwide depression caused some slackening of demand, exports of wheat continued to rise. Yet labor remained scarce and expensive to hire. Fortunately most of the ideas for improving machinery had already been thought out and patented before 1860 and were ready for development and adaptation. Almost every agricultural operation was touched by the hand of innovation, but perhaps the best-known improvement was in harvesting and binding. By 1880 it was estimated that two men and a team of horses could reap and bind twenty acres of grain in a day. Steam power on the farm was still a novelty, but would soon become more general.

The bald figures of agricultural expansion conceal tough, undramatic, and often frustrating experiences. The climate was hot, often excessively dry in summer, subject to fierce storms in the fall and spring, and very cold in winter. The rhythm of life was dictated by the need to sow fast, grow quickly, and harvest before the rains and frost arrived. Too little rain in the spring could create killing drought before the summer was through. A historian of western agriculture observes:

The person who has never traveled through the subhumid regions when the temperature is 118° in the shade, and the shade is "all in the next county," can neither understand nor believe the truth of the situation. . . . In the West, when the temperature is above 110°, the arrival of a breeze is a calamity. Wheat in the milky stage shrivels in the husk and becomes worthless except for chicken feed. Corn wilts and the blades turn crisp on the stalks. The man in the open feels no perspiration, but wishes he could. To all appearances he sweats dry salt till his face becomes white and his eyebrows are encrusted.[6]

Even worse than the hazards of climate were the grasshopper plagues of 1874, 1875, and 1876. In incredible numbers the insects traveled in dense clouds, settled wherever things grew, and left the land bare. Nor did the settlers enjoy many advantages to offset these ills. Timber was rare, firewood often unobtainable, and sod houses were normal dwellings. Water had often to be obtained from deep-dug wells, and wind pumps were yet to make their appearance.

These difficulties were compounded by man-made problems. Though so remote, the region depended heavily upon the resources of developed capitalist civilization. Serving a distant market, their livelihood depended upon

[6] Fred A. Shannon, *The Farmers' Last Frontier* (New York: Reinhart, 1945), p. 150.

a whole range of railroad magnates, merchants, shippers, brokers, and distributors. Long-distance trade required a complicated financial system. Development dependec upon an adequate supply of money for investment and created an inevitable tension between borrower and banker that was never satisfactorily resolved.

The United States Government was the greatest landowner in human history, and much would depend upon the way in which the public domain was distributed. The intention of the 1862 Homestead Act could not have been purer, but its execution bristled with error. There was a basic flaw in the expectation that a region such as this could be settled by sturdy cultivators of the soil who would take up the free 160-acre homesteads. The act probably did something to attract the German and Scandinavian settlers and provided splendid advertising matter for the railroads, but a family required cash to move, capital to invest in seed and stock, and sufficient reserves to last out until the land began to yield. In order to get the railroads built Congress had used land grants as an inducement, and the alternate sections of public land along the proposed tracks were reserved from allocation to homesteaders. This meant that settlers had often to buy from the railroads or site their farms in more remote spots. The pattern of settlement that therefore tended to develop was that of tolerably prosperous farms along the tracks, started by men with available capital, and scattered homesteads struggling for existence in the hinterland. The economics of farming favored very large units and expensive irrigation schemes, and there were strong incentives for land companies to acquire homesteads by deception and then consolidate the holdings. By 1880 much land was already owned in huge blocks and often by absentee owners.

Another human foe of the farmer was the rancher who was building up great herds of cattle. Many of the cattle barons had acquired legal rights to riverbanks and illegal but uncontested grazing rights over wide areas before the homesteaders arrived. However, most of these great ranches were on the more arid grasslands, and the major clash with farmer settlers did not come until after 1880.

In many respects the West stood in relation to the East as an underdeveloped stands to a developed country today. There was a strong case for association between the two, judicious federal aid, and effective executive supervision to ensure that it got into the right hands; but the basic plan for development was ill conceived, and the homestead policy conflicted with the use of land grants to subsidize essential means of communication. Instead of planned partnership the course of events was determined by conflict between homesteaders (with a voting majority in elections for territorial or state legislatures), railroads, land companies, and ranchers. Occasionally Indian resistance or raids provided another theme. Indian agents of the federal government, officials of the land offices, mail-coach contractors, and officers of the United States army all sought to advance their legitimate or less admirable interests. Congress acted an uncertain part, sometimes responding to one pressure, sometimes to another, and more often to agreements made on terms that no one wished to discuss.

It is perhaps too easy to exaggerate the mistakes and forget the achievement. Somehow, after many setbacks, settlement survived and even thrived in what had been regarded thirty years before as the outlying portion of the great American desert. When Daniel Webster said in the Compromise Debates of 1850 that nature had fixed the limit to westward expansion of slavery, he meant that civilized settlement was unlikely or impossible. By 1880 there were still very large areas unsettled, and some that would never be settled, but there had sprung up an agricultural society that was a unique addition to American civilization.

Even more extraordinary in their way were developments on the Pacific Coast. Thanks to gold, California had grown from 93,000 to 380,000 between 1850 and 1860; by

1870 it was 560,000 and in 1880, 865,000. Oregon had moved more slowly but grew threefold between 1860 and 1880 to reach 175,000 in the latter year. Four major cities —San Francisco, Los Angeles, Portland, and Seattle—now looked across the Pacific; in California many gold towns had become deserted, but several newer towns served the more prosaic needs of agriculture and commerce. The people were drawn from all parts of the United States, Europe, and Mexico, and, for the first time, Americans encountered Chinese immigrants in considerable numbers.

The early years of the "golden state" epitomized (often in the crudest form) the conflicts and anxieties of the modern world. The gold rush had left a legacy of violence, uninhibited scramble for wealth, and callous disregard for failure. Things were calmer by 1860, but new problems crowded in upon a society that had grown rapidly in a fiercely competitive environment. Organized capitalism at its most aggressive confronted organized labor in its most militant mood. Small tenant farmers suffered at the hands of landowners who had established titles by setting legal ingenuity to work on the uncertainties of Mexican land grants. In a state with abundant land it was impossible for a newcomer to acquire an acre without paying a speculator's price, and the frustration of optimistic migrants fed into a politically explosive situation. The rise of San Francisco as a great seaport produced a racially mixed city with ostentatious wealth, much poverty, and a good deal of crime. Chinese coolies (imported mainly to work on railroad construction) added a new element to the population, and produced an explosion of racial hatred and mob violence. "The Chinese," said the governor of California in 1869, "are a stream of filth and prostitution pouring in from Asia, whose servile competition tends to cheapen and degrade labor."

Circumstances favored both predatory capitalism and organized labor. In a new country the men who were first on the spot and held on to their gains could deploy power in a way that would have been impossible in a society with stronger traditions and older institutions. By 1860 it had become clear that the men who controlled transportation would hold the keys of power. The authorization of the transcontinental railroad in 1862 meant that the Central Pacific with its terminus at Oakland was the great prize. Collis P. Huntington and Leland Stanford, the owners of Central Pacific, also controlled the Southern Pacific and thus a majority of the railroad tracks in the state; these internal modes of transport were of even greater significance for Californians than the transcontinental line, for prosperity in the central valley depended entirely upon transportation to the sea.

Until the completion of the transcontinental railroad in 1869 skilled labor was scarce and protected from competition. It might take months to get alternative unskilled labor if a strike occurred, and men who had learned trades might be impossible to find. The compact area of San Francisco offered an ideal environment for the organization of labor; though some of the many craft unions went through uncertain periods, by 1870 more occupations worked an eight-hour day than in any other American city. The degree of organization was made evident in 1864; employers in the iron industry sent east for strikebreakers to use against molders and boilermakers, but representatives of the workingmen met the newcomers at Panama and enrolled them in the union.

Conditions changed in 1869 when easier access to the East coincided with the release of thousands of Chinese from railroad construction work. By 1872 half the workers in San Francisco factories were Chinese working at rates well below the American standard. Conditions grew still worse in 1875 when depression struck two years later than in the East, brought down the Bank of California (the dominant financial institution on the Pacific Coast), and spread ruin and unemployment. Newcomers to the land of opportunity found the state in the throes of poverty, raging discontent, and incipient violence. In 1871 nineteen Chinese had been lynched in Los Angeles purely on grounds of race, and in 1877 the mob invaded the Chinatown of San Francisco and spent two days destroying and looting property. "The Chinese must go" was the most popular slogan of the newly formed Workingmen's party.

This short-lived political movement was of interest for more than its racialist fervor. Primarily a combination of city labor and farm workers, the party aimed "to wrest the government from the hands of the rich and place it in those of the people where it belongs." It secured a majority in the legislature, and in 1877 tried to implement its aims by writing a new constitution to establish popular control over government. The new document was less radical than might have been expected but was the first of those attempts to reorganize the state on democratic lines that have given Californians the longest ballot sheet in the world and the least easy to comprehend. The Workingmen's party lost power in 1880 and broke up soon after, but its practical protest against the rule of wealth and its exploitation of anti-Chinese sentiment had shown the rough side of American radicalism.

There was a significant footnote to these events. The Workingmen's party attracted the support of a San Francisco editor called Henry George, who had been born in Philadelphia, worked as a printer, gone as a seaman to Asia, and like many others came to California in search of freedom and fortune. He failed at first, but eventually established himself in precarious solvency as a journalist. In 1869, on a visit to New York, he was profoundly moved by the contrast between the opulence of the rich and the degradation of the poor. Back in California, and observing a young society where improvement seemed only to widen the gap between the few and the many, he concluded that the root of the evil lay in the private ownership of land. The transfer of land to public ownership might be the best theoretical remedy, but the most practical was a tax on increments in the value of land. As a moralist George argued that a private individual had no right to enjoy wealth from land that he had done nothing to improve but owed its increased value to the progress of the people as a whole. The "single tax" would restore the unearned increment to society and create a fund that government could spend for the benefit of all. He did not attack other forms of property, but

> in allowing one man to own the land on which and from which other men live, we have made them his bondsmen in a degree which increases as material progress goes on. There is a subtle alchemy that in many ways they do not realize is extracting from the masses of every civilized country the fruits of their weary toil . . . that is bringing political despotism out of political freedom, and must soon transmute democratic institutions into anarchy.

Progress and Poverty, published in 1879, is the only work of social and economic philosophy to become a best-seller. The reason is not far to seek, for *Progress and Poverty* was really a book about the morality of society rather than its economic organization. Apart from his own experiences there were two powerful influences upon Henry George: Thomas Jefferson and the British classical economists. He rejected many of the inferences drawn from the economists but believed with them that economic laws and the pursuit of happiness could lead men along the road to social justice. Where he parted company with laissez-faire economists, and with those who preached "iron laws" in economic behavior, was in his belief that man had the power to create an environment of freedom and justice. The subjection of man to wealth would end, and the fruits of progress would be distributed to all.

To many throughout the world, but especially in English-speaking countries, Henry George's doctrine came as a revelation. It promised that poverty *could* be eradicated, that the power of overmighty business *could* be restrained, and that industry and science *were* the servants of mankind. Jefferson had feared the corrupting influence of manufactures and crowded cities; George maintained that industrialization and the organization of economic life could yield unlimited benefits if their operation were properly understood. It was natural that this doctrine should be repudiated by the orthodox, and though the single tax won many followers, they had to exist outside the limits of academic life, where it became conventional wisdom that *Progress and Poverty* should be unanswered and unread. The single tax could not have provided all the funds necessary for modern government, but the principle of taxing capital gains and development values has since been accepted in many countries. The real importance of *Progress and Poverty*, however, lay in its combination of a full-scale attack upon the economic and ethical assumptions of nineteenth-century society with ideas and institutions that were a part of the American heritage.

This book began with the annexation of Texas and ends with a critique of capitalism. The men of 1844 contemplated with anxiety the consequences of slavery and in pessimistic moods could predict the imminence of sectional conflict; but the strikes of 1877, the settlement of the Great Plains, the rise of California, and *Progress and Poverty* lay beyond their range of comprehension. The period gave enlarged dimensions to old problems but also inaugurated a new order. The Civil War had played its part but also obscured the nature of the transformation. Later generations would compound this difficulty by relating to the war long-term changes that might have happened in any event. The war affected the timing and speed of developments, but it did not initiate nationalism, industrialization, the enlargement of government, the settlement of the West, the rise of towns, or the perplexity of race relations. What the war did ensure was that these long-term movements took place under a single flag. The Union remained, and one federal government continued to exercise authority over the whole. This meant more than political mechanism; it meant that the growing United States continued as one market, struck a single balance of payments with the rest of the world, and enjoyed free movement of money, men, and ideas.

If the one government remained, the men who governed had changed. It is always difficult (if not impossible) to say who governs America, but it is sometimes possible to decide who influences government and to place them in some kind of rough priority. A contrast between 1844 and 1876 reveals some obvious facts and others more obscure. The southern upper class had commanded a major influence in 1844, and experience in government and a concentration on political objectives had secured for them an importance even greater than their numbers and social status deserved. By 1876 this southern influence was greatly diminished, and the most that southerners could hope was to play off one northern interest against another. Moreover, the character of the southern upper class itself had changed; the leaders were becoming capitalist farmers, business entrepreneurs, and to a limited extent pioneers of an industrial revolution. In the past their natural affinity had been with the professional elite of the North and merchants who handled the cotton trade; they were now more likely to seek understandings with bankers, industrialists, land speculators, and railroad promoters. Whether it is correct (or has any meaning) to label the prewar slaveholding upper class as precapitalist, it is true that its most influential members had thought more of status, prestige, and a genteel way of life than of balance sheets; now the economic calculus had become essential, and southern leaders sought to influence the men with economic power.

The North and West contained many diverse interests, but businessmen provided a common factor across the nation. They shared common assumptions, tended to use the same arguments, and could readily move from one location

to another. Though nationwide business clubs were yet to
be formed, their clientele already existed. This business
culture should be distinguished from "big business." The
business magnates were men who had succeeded at the expense of other businessmen. The "public" that Commo-
dore Cornelius Vanderbilt damned was mainly a business
public of men who could understand company accounts,
might detect sharp practices, and were directly interested
in the railroads as shippers and consignees. Nor was the
new businessman a small speculator out for quick gains; he
was a stable citizen, conscious of a place in his community,
and probably proud to remind his fellow citizens of his
services to their town. If the "big businessman" wanted to
get something done, he had to use all the legitimate or ille-
gitimate arts of persuasion, but the influence of ordinary
businessmen was so pervasive that special efforts were
seldom required.

Merchants, bankers, and lawyers in the smaller market
centers were not cut off from the countryside. Their businesses were usually affected directly by agriculture, many
of their clients were farmers, and every farmer knew that
his own prosperity depended upon the commercial success
of his region. There was nothing forced or hypocritical
about the way in which businessmen were coming to see
themselves as the late nineteenth-century legatees of the
rural freeholders in whom Jefferson had placed so much
trust; and this appropriation of Jeffersonian rhetoric symbolized a real community of interest.

Lawyers continued to play an important part in political life. Most congressmen were trained lawyers, and so
were most men active in local affairs. Closely associated
with business and farming interests, lawyers provided a
link between the world of economic and political activity.
Indeed, congressmen and state legislators almost unconsciously assumed the posture of lawyers representing
clients; it was not so much the public as a particular interest that engaged their attention. There was nothing mor-

ally wrong in this, but the fact that so many congressmen thought it their duty or interest to give priority to serving vocal groups in their communities goes far to explain why Congress failed to develop firm leadership. The committee structure in Congress was admirably designed to allow individuals the greatest opportunity of bringing pressure to bear upon the legislative process, while the authority of the Speaker ensured that an informal system of checks and balances was preserved between factions and interests.

The growing influence of the professional intelligentsia has already been noted. Despite the relative economic decline of New England, intellectual life continued to have a strong Yankee flavor. The two most prestigious universities (Havard and Yale) were in New England; Columbia and Princeton were within the New England orbit. Most of the eminent writers, college presidents, teachers of history, and pioneers in the social sciences had been educated at one of these four institutions. The newer colleges claimed distinct identities but also served as outposts of traditional northeastern culture. Few in numbers but strong in influence, the professors, editors, and men of letters sustained a nationwide culture of growing weight.

Below the elitist groups the substructure of political life was changing. If small towns in rural districts were still the most typical bases of political power, most of them were becoming more and more caught up in the web of national power. Railroads provided not only the communications to facilitate the operation of a national economy but also a common set of problems and aims. Less obviously but as effectively, the National Banking System provided loose control and uniform standards for financial institutions throughout the nation. The rise of organized labor and the vicissitudes of strikes and violence furnished a common stock of experiences and attitudes for employers and employed. The cities aspiring to become metropolitan centers for great agricultural regions looked in two directions: toward regional consolidation and toward integration within the national economic system. Thus the localism of American life, though still strong, existed more and more within a framework of national ideas and institutions.

This trend could not, however, take in all the powerful new currents of urban and immigrant life. The goal of assimilation was set, but older Americans found it difficult to make the necessary effort (particularly when this meant the expenditure of large sums on education, housing, and city services), and those of alien birth clung to their ethnic churches and customs. The "melting pot" has always been a poor analogy. It might be more appropriate to think of a machine for polishing semiprecious gems, in which the rough stones are immersed in a mildly abrasive liquid, turned for weeks, and emerge with similar external appearances but remain with distinct and indestructible cores. Equally, the attempt to bring blacks within the political community was palpably failing. The nation in the centennial year was therefore predominantly white, Protestant, and of Anglo-Saxon descent; it was led by lawyer-politicians responsive to business and farming pressures, with the southern element reduced to a junior partnership; the constituency that counted most was still the small or middle-sized town in a rural district, though forces were at work to provide a stronger sense of national interest.

The period immediately following the Civil War saw moves in several directions to give the federal government a more positive function. There were civil rights and a national guarantee against racial discrimination in fixing suffrage qualifications; national acts to enforce the rights given by law; proposals for federal initiative in education and railroad regulation; demands (occasionally met) for federal intervention to protect property during labor disputes; and the beginning of a demand for federal control over immigration. Yet at the very moment when government seemed about to implement the new nationalism, a setback occurred. An ingrained suspicion of politicians cast doubt upon any action that might given them more power and patronage and linked up with the fashionable theory that government intervention interfered with the benevolent balance of nature. Impressed by the truth that the fittest survived in nature, and that the evolutionary process achieved the correct balance between living things and their environment, the majority of intellectuals applied these dogmas to social life. Thus while government responded in many ways to pressures from local and special interests, the authoritative voice of science vetoed the evolution of a general philosophy of intervention.

Holding government to the noninterventionist line meant resisting popular pressure from many quarters, and there was thus a fundamental contradiction between the social philosophy of an elite and the demands of a democratic electorate. In a new form, therefore, an old dilemma was repeated. Before the Civil War the central issue had been the determination of a minority to retain slavery whatever the national majority might wish. By 1880 the principal issue had become the determination to use or prohibit the use of national authority according to rules laid down by a minority whatever social needs the majority might formulate. So far the democratic pressure for enlarged responsibility had been diffused, focused on a few specific issues, and advanced by groups or individuals acting in isolation. The reception of *Progress and Poverty* was the first indication that an alternative philosophy of government might find a national constituency; but the attempt was premature, and businessmen, lawyers, and intellectuals closed ranks against the symptoms of widespread but poorly coordinated disquiet. If the thirty-year period that can be labeled "the era of the Civil War" closed one chapter in American history, it opened another in which democratic society would encounter the opportunities and conflicts of an advanced civilization.

A Select Reading List

The historical literature for this period is voluminous but unevenly distributed. There are probably not less than sixty thousand books dealing with the Civil War, but the years before 1854 and after 1868 yield a meager harvest. In the central period it is necessary to be ruthless in eliminating many worthwhile studies, but at the beginning and end of the central period it is difficult to compile an authoritative list.

In the following list preference is given to recent books and to those that have successfully held the field as definitive studies. For those who wish to seek further sources there is guidance in the first section, and in addition many of the works cited have extensive bibliographies. With regret, works concerned exclusively with military history have been omitted; this does not imply that campaigns and battles are unimportant but that the literature is so vast and specialized that even a highly selective list would have filled many pages. The arrangement is not alphabetical. The list is divided into a number of sections, and in each section the most important general works are placed first, followed by books on more specialized topics, arranged, so far as possible, in the chronological order of the events to which they refer.

I. Aids to Study
1. Guides

Handlin, Oscar, et al. *Harvard Guide to American History*. Cambridge, Mass.: Harvard University Press, 1954.

Johnson, Thomas H. *The Oxford Companion to American History*. New York: Oxford University Press, 1966.

Morris, Richard B. *Encyclopedia of American History*. New York: Harper & Row, 1970.

U.S. Bureau of the Census. *Historical Statistics of the United States to 1957*. Washington, D.C.: Government Printing Office, 1960.

2. Bibliography

Many of the books listed below contain extensive bibliographies. Special mention must be made of that in James G. Randall and David Donald, *The Civil*

War and Reconstruction (Lexington, Mass.: D. C. Heath, 1961) ; this is the best starting point for specialized work on the period. More selective but useful is the Goldentree Bibliographies in American History Series; the two volumes covering this period are Don E. Fehrenbacker, *Manifest Destiny and the Coming of the Civil War* (New York: Appleton-Century-Crofts, 1970) , and David Donald, *The Nation in Crisis* (New York: Appleton-Century-Crofts, 1969) . A comprehensive bibliography of the war is Allan Nevins, James I. Robertson, Jr., and Bell I. Wiley, *Civil War Books: A Critical Bibliography* (2 vols.; Baton Rouge, La.: Louisiana State University Press, 1967) . This lists books and pamphlets but not articles or unpublished dissertations. The usefulness is limited by the lack of a comprehensive subject index and by the inclusion of sources and secondary works in the same list. Also useful is James M. McPherson et al., *Blacks in America: Bibliographical Essays* (Garden City, N.Y.: Doubleday, 1971) . The best way of keeping up to date on the historiography of the period is by consulting the *Journal of American History, Civil War History,* the *American Historical Review,* and the *Journal of Southern History.* Abstracts of articles are printed in *American History and Life,* published by the American Bibliographical Center.

II. Sources and Historiography

  1. Letters, Papers, and Diaries

      Lincoln, Abraham. *The Collected Works of Abraham Lincoln.* Edited by Roy P. Basler. 8 vols. and Index. New Brunswick, N.J.: Rutgers University Press, 1958.

      Douglas, Stephen A. *The Letters of Stephen A. Douglas.* Edited by Robert W. Johannsen. Urbana, Ill.: University of Illinois Press, 1961.

      Welles, Gideon. *The Diary of Gideon Welles.* Edited by Howard K. Beale. 3 vols. New York: W. W. Norton, 1960.

      Polk, James K. *Polk: The Diary of a President.* Edited by Allan Nevins. New York and London: Longmans, 1929.

Strong, George Templeton. *The Diary of George Templeton Strong, 1835–1875*. Edited by Allan Nevins and Milton H. Thomas. 4 vols. New York: Macmillan, 1952.

2. Collections of Source Material

Johannsen, Robert W. *The Union in Crisis, 1850–1877*. New York: Free Press, 1965.

Knoles, George H. (ed.) . *The Crisis of the Union*. Baton Rouge, La.: Louisiana State University Press, 1965.

Post, C. Gordon (ed.) . *John C. Calhoun: A Disquisition on Government and a Selection from the Discourse*. New York: Liberal Arts Press, 1953.

Stampp, Kenneth M. *The Causes of the Civil War*. Englewood Cliffs, N.J.: Prentice-Hall, 1959.

Potter, David M., and Manning, Thomas G. *Nationalism and Sectionalism in America, 1775–1875*. New York: Holt, 1949.

Source collections that deal exclusively with one topic are listed in the appropriate section below.

3. Historiography

Pressly, Thomas J. *Americans Interpret Their Civil War*. Princeton, N.J.: Princeton University Press, 1962. New York: Collier Books, 1962. An important analysis of Civil War historiography.

Beale, Howard K. "What Historians Have Said about the Causes of the Civil War," in *Theory and Practice of History* ("Social Science Research Council Bulletins," No. 54 [New York, 1946]) .

Rozwenc, Edwin C. (ed.) . *The Causes of the Civil War*. Lexington, Mass.: D. C. Heath, 1961.

———. *Slavery as a Cause of the Civil War*. Lexington, Mass.: D. C. Heath, 1963. Both Rozwenc volumes contain well-chosen selections from writers offering contrasting views.

Geyl, Peter. *Debates with Historians*. The Hague: Nijhoff, 1955. London: Fontana Library, 1962. Chapter XII, "The American Civil War and the Problem of Inevitability."

Woodward, C. Vann (ed.) . *A Comparative Approach to American History*. New York: Basic Books, 1968.

Essays by David Brion Davis ("Slavery"), David
M. Potter ("The Civil War"), Eric McKitrick
("Reconstruction").

III. Works Covering the Whole or Large Parts of the Period
   1. General Histories
      Nevins, Allan. *The Ordeal of the Union.* New York:
      Charles Scribner's Sons. Vol. I: *The Ordeal of the
      Union: Fruits of Manifest Destiny, 1847–1852* (1947).
      Vol. II: *The Ordeal of the Union: A House Divid-
      ing, 1852–1857* (1947). Vol. III: *The Emergence of
      Lincoln: Douglas, Buchanan, and Party Chaos, 1857–
      1859* (1950). Vol. IV: *The Emergence of Lincoln:
      Prologue to Civil War, 1859–1861* (1950). Vol. V: *The
      War for the Union: The Improvised War, 1861–1862*
      (1959). Vol. VI: *The War for the Union: War Be-
      comes Revolution, 1862–1863* (1960). Vol. VII: *The
      War for the Union: The Organized War, 1863–1864*
      (1971). Vol. VIII: *The War for the Union: From
      Organized War to Victory, 1864–1865* (1971). This
      eight-volume history of the period 1847–1865 is one
      of the foremost historical achievements of this
      century.

      Randall, James G., and Donald, David. *The Civil War
      and Reconstruction.* Lexington, Mass.: D. C. Heath,
      1961. A new edition, much revised, of an older text
      by Randall alone. The best single-volume history.
      Excellent bibliographies.

      Smith, Elbert G. *The Death of Slavery: The United
      States, 1837–65.* Chicago: University of Chicago Press,
      1967. Interesting on some aspects of politics before
      the war but deals very briefly with other major issues.

      Franklin, John Hope. *From Slavery to Freedom: A
      History of Negro Americans.* 3rd ed. New York:
      Alfred A. Knopf, 1967. New York: Vintage Books,
      1969.

   2. Economic and Social History
      The period is covered by four volumes in the Economic
      History of the United States Series (New York: Holt,
      Rinehart and Winston): George Rogers Taylor,
      The Transportation Revolution (1951); Paul Gates,
      The Farmer's Age (1960); Fred A. Shannon, *The

Farmer's Last Frontier (1945) ; and Edward C. Kirkland, *Industry Comes of Age* (1961). A brilliant history of industrial society is Thomas C. Cochran and William Miller, *The Age of Enterprise* (New York: Macmillan, 1951). Two volumes in Arthur M. Schlesinger and Dixon Ryan Fox (eds.), *History of American Life* (New York: Macmillan), are still essential for social history: Arthur C. Cole, *The Irrepressible Conflict* (1934), and Allan Nevins, *The Emergence of Modern America* (1927). A conventional economic history that devotes considerable space to developments in this period is Harold Underwood Faulkner, *American Economic History* (8th ed.; New York: Harper & Row, 1960). A new approach incorporating econometric analyses is Douglas C. North, *Growth and Welfare in the American Past* (Englewood Cliffs, N.J.: Prentice-Hall, 1966) and *The Economic Growth of the United States, 1790–1860* (Englewood Cliffs, N.J.: Prentice-Hall, 1961). Two special studies with wide implications are Bray Hammond, *Banks and Politics in America from the Revolution to the Civil War* (Princeton, N.J.: Princeton University Press, 1957), and Irwin Unger, *The Greenback Era: An Economic Study of Civil War and Reconstruction* (Princeton, N.J.: Princeton University Press, 1964).

3. The South, Slavery, and Antislavery
   a. The Old South
      Eaton, Clement. *The Growth of Southern Civilization, 1790–1860.* New York: Harper & Row, 1961.
      Sydnor, Charles S. *The Development of Southern Sectionalism, 1819–1848.* Baton Rouge, La.: Louisiana State University Press, 1948.
      Craven, Avery O. *The Growth of Southern Nationalism.* Baton Rouge, La.: Louisiana State University Press, 1953.
      Olmstead, Frederick Law. *The Cotton Kingdom.* Edited by Arthur M. Schlesinger. New York: Alfred A. Knopf, 1953. Original edition: New York: 1861.
      Cash, Wilbur J. *The Mind of the South.* New edi-

tion with Introduction by Sir Denis Brogan. London: Thames and Hudson, 1971. Original edition: New York: Alfred A. Knopf, 1941.

Owsley, Frank L. *Plain Folk of the Old South.* Baton Rouge, La.: Louisiana State University Press, 1949.

Heath, Milton S. *Construction Liberalism: The Role of the State in Economic Development in Georgia to 1860.* Cambridge, Mass.: Harvard University Press, 1954.

Green, George D. *Finance and Economic Development in the Old South: Louisiana Banking, 1804–1861.* Stanford, Calif.: Stanford University Press, 1972.

Eaton, Clement. *The Freedom of Thought Struggle in the Old South.* New York: Harper & Row, 1964. A revised and enlarged edition of *Freedom of Thought in the Old South* (1940).

b. Slavery

Two works, using similar materials, which present contrasting views of slavery, are Ulrich B. Phillips, *Life and Labor in the Old South* (Boston: Little, Brown, 1929), and Kenneth M. Stampp, *The Peculiar Institution* (New York: Alfred A. Knopf, 1956). Provocative analyses that have stimulated much discussion are Stanley M. Elkins, *Slavery: A Problem in American Institutional and Intellectual Life* (2nd ed.; Chicago: University of Chicago Press, 1968), and Eugene D. Genovese, *The Political Economy of Slavery* (New York: Pantheon Books, 1965) and *In Red and Black: Marxian Explorations in Southern and Afro-American History* (New York: Pantheon Books, 1968). Two books that add important new discussions to the study of slavery are Richard C. Wade, *Slavery in the Cities: The South, 1820–1860* (New York and London: Oxford University Press, 1964), and Robert S. Starobin, *Industrial Slavery in the Old South* (New York and London: Oxford University Press, 1970). Firsthand accounts and sources are Frederick

Douglass, *Narrative of the Life of Frederick Douglass, an American Slave,* edited by Benjamin Quarles (Cambridge, Mass.: Harvard University Press, 1960) ; Frances Anne Kemble, *Journal of the Residence on a Georgian Plantation in 1838–1839,* edited by John A. Scott (New York: Alfred A. Knopf, 1961) ; Eric L. McKitrick, *Slavery Defended: The Views of the Old South* (Englewood Cliffs, N.J.: Prentice-Hall, 1963), a collection of proslavery writings; and Allen Weinstein and Frank Otto Gatell, *American Negro Slavery* (New York: Oxford University Press, 1968), a collection of modern writings. Further material can be found in Laura Foner and Eugene D. Genovese (eds.), *Slavery in the New World* (Englewood Cliffs, N.J.: Prentice-Hall, 1969); George M. Frederickson, *The Black Image in the White Mind: The Debate on Afro-American Character and Destiny, 1817–1914* (New York: Harper & Row, 1971) ; and Otto H. Olsen, "Historians and the Extent of Slave Ownership in the United States," *Civil War History,* XVIII (June, 1972), 101–116. There has been much controversy about the profitability of slavery. Important articles and further discussions are to be found in John R. Meyer and Alfred H. Conrad, *The Economics of Slavery and Other Studies in Econometric History* (Chicago: Aldine-Atherton, 1964), and Robert W. Fogel and Stanley L. Engerman, *The Reinterpretation of American Economic History* (New York: Harper & Row, 1971), Part VII (the notes provide a useful bibliography of the subject).

c. Blacks in the Free States

Litwack, Leon F. *North of Slavery: The Negro in Free States, 1790–1860.* Chicago: University of Chicago Press, 1961.

Berwanger, Eugene H. *The Frontier against Slavery: Western Anti-Negro Prejudice and the Slavery Extension Controversy.* Urbana, Ill.: University of Illinois Press, 1967.

Voegli, V. Jacque. *Free But Not Equal: The Midwest and the Negro during the Civil War.* Chicago: University of Chicago Press, 1967.

d. Antislavery

Filler, Louis. *The Crusade against Slavery, 1830–1860.* New York: Harper & Row, 1960.

Dumond, Dwight L. *Anti-Slavery: The Crusade for Freedom in America.* Ann Arbor, Mich.: University of Michigan Press, 1967.

Duberman, Martin B. (ed.). *The Anti-Slavery Vanguard.* Princeton, N.J.: Princeton University Press, 1965. A collection of original essays.

Wolf, Hazell Catherine. *On Freedom's Altar: The Martyr Complex in the Abolition Movement.* Madison, Wis.: University of Wisconsin Press, 1952.

Kraditor, Aileen S. *Means and Ends in American Abolitionism: Garrison and His Critics on Strategy and Tactics, 1834–1850.* New York: Pantheon Books, 1967.

Quarles, Benjamin. *Black Abolitionists.* New York: Oxford University Press, 1969.

Thomas, John L. *The Liberator: William Lloyd Garrison.* Boston: Little, Brown, 1963.

——— (ed.). *Slavery Attacked.* Englewood Cliffs, N.J.: Prentice-Hall, 1965. A collection of abolitionist writings.

Wyatt-Brown, Bertram, *Lewis Tappan.* Cleveland, Ohio: Case Western Reserve University Press, 1969.

Sherwin, Oscar. *Prophet of Liberty: The Life and Times of Wendell Phillips.* New York: Bookman Associates, 1958.

4. Political Parties

Binkley, Wilfred E. *American Political Parties: Their Natural History.* 2nd ed. New York: Alfred A. Knopf, 1947.

Silbey, Joel H. *The Shrine of Party: Congressional Voting Behavior, 1841–1852.* Pittsburgh, Pa.: University of Pittsburgh Press, 1967.

Mayer, George H. *The Republican Party, 1854–1966.*
2nd ed. New York: Oxford University Press, 1967.

Holt, Michael F. *Forging a Majority: The Formation
of the Republican Party in Pittsburgh, 1848–1860.*
New Haven, Conn.: Yale University Press, 1969.

5. Religion and Intellectual Life

Ahlstrom, Sydney E. *A Religious History of the American People.* New Haven, Conn.: Yale University
Press, 1972.

Reimers, David M. *White Protestantism and the Negro.*
New York: Oxford University Press, 1965.

Smith, Timothy L. *Revivalism and Social Reform:
American Protestantism on the Eve of the Civil War.*
New York: Abingdon Press, 1957. New York: Harper
Torchbooks, 1965.

Frothingham, Octavius Brooks. *Transcendentalism in
New England.* New York: Harper Torchbooks, 1959.
First published 1876.

6. The West

Billington, Ray A. *Westward Expansion.* New York:
Macmillan, 1949.

————. *The Far Western Frontier, 1830–1860.* New
York: Harper & Row, 1956.

Lamar, Howard Roberts. *The Far Southwest, 1846–
1912.* New Haven, Conn.: Yale University Press,
1966. New York: Norton Library, 1970.

Webb, Walter Prescott. *The Great Plains.* New York:
Ginn, 1931.

7. Foreign Affairs

Merk, Frederick. *Manifest Destiny and Mission in
American History.* New York: Vintage Books, 1963.

Adams, Ephraim D. *Great Britain and the American
Civil War.* New York: Russell & Russell, 1925.

Case, Lynn M., and Spencer, Warren F. *The United
States and France: Civil War Diplomacy.* Philadelphia, Pa.: University of Pennsylvania Press, 1970.

IV. Works Dealing with Personalities, Problems, and Specific Events

Included in this section are the biographies of men whose
careers spanned a major part of the period. Other biographies are listed in the appropriate sections.

1. Biographies

Sellers, Charles G. *James K. Polk.* Vol. II: *Continentalist, 1843–1846.* Princeton, N.J.: Princeton University Press, 1957.

Milton, George F. *The Eve of Conflict: Stephen A. Douglas and the Needless War.* Boston: Houghton Mifflin, 1934.

Randall, James G. *Lincoln the President.* 4 vols. New York: Dodd, Mead, 1945–1955.

Thomas, Benjamin. *Abraham Lincoln.* New York: Alfred A. Knopf, 1952.

Donald, David. *Charles Sumner and the Coming of the Civil War.* New York: Alfred A. Knopf, 1960.

———. *Charles Sumner and the Rights of Man.* New York: Alfred A. Knopf, 1970.

Brodie, Fawn M. *Thaddeus Stevens: Scourge of the South.* New York: W. W. Norton, 1959.

Van Deusen, Glyndon G. *William Henry Seward.* New York: Oxford University Press, 1967.

Duberman, Martin B. *Charles Francis Adams.* Boston: Houghton Mifflin, 1961.

2. 1845–1854

Merk, Frederick. *Slavery and the Annexation of Texas.* New York: Alfred A. Knopf, 1972.

Brauer, Kinley J. *Cotton versus Conscience: Massachusetts Whig Politics and Southwestern Expansion.* Lexington, Ky.: The University Press of Kentucky, 1967.

Morrison, Chaplain W. *Democratic Politics and Sectionalism: The Wilmot Proviso Controversy.* Chapel Hill, N.C.: University of North Carolina Press, 1967.

Sewell, Richard H. *John P. Hale and the Politics of Abolition.* Cambridge, Mass.: Harvard University Press, 1965.

Hamilton, Holman. *Prologue to Conflict: The Crisis and Compromise of 1850.* Lexington, Ky.: The University Press of Kentucky, 1964.

Russell, Robert R. *Critical Studies in Antebellum Sectionalism.* Westport, Conn.: Greenwood Press, 1972.

Campbell, Stanley W. *The Slave Catchers: Enforcement of the Fugitive Slave Law, *1850–1860*. Chapel Hill, N.C.: University of North Carolina Press, 1968.

Nevins, Allan. *The Ordeal of the Union*. Vol. I: *The Ordeal of the Union: Fruits of Manifest Destiny, 1847–1852*. Vol. II: *The Ordeal of the Union: A House Dividing, 1852–1857*. New York: Charles Scribner's Sons, 1947. The most comprehensive treatment of 1847–1854.

3. 1854–1861

Foner, Eric. *Free Soil, Free Labor, and Free Men: The Ideology of the Republican Party before the Civil War*. New York: Oxford University Press, 1970.

Nichols, Roy F. *The Disruption of American Democracy*. New York: Macmillan, 1948.

Jaffa, Henry V. *Crisis of the House Divided: An Interpretation of the Lincoln-Douglas Debates*. Garden City, N.Y.: Doubleday, 1959.

Fehrenbacher, Don E. *Prelude to Greatness: Lincoln in the 1850's*. Stanford, Calif.: Stanford University Press, 1962.

Angle, Paul M. *Created Equal?: The Complete Lincoln-Douglas Debates*. Chicago: University of Chicago Press, 1958.

Johannsen, Robert W. *The Lincoln-Douglas Debates*. New York: Oxford University Press, 1965.

O'Connor, Thomas H. *Lords of the Loom: The Cotton Whigs and the Coming of the Civil War*. New York: Charles Scribner's Sons, 1968.

Wooster, Ralph A. *The Secession Conventions in the South*. Princeton, N.J.: Princeton University Press, 1962.

Potter, David M. *Lincoln and His Party in the Secession Crisis*. New Haven, Conn.: Yale University Press, 1942.

Stampp, Kenneth M. *And the War Came: The North and the Secession Crisis*. Baton Rouge, La.: Louisiana State University Press, 1950.

Current, Richard N. *Lincoln and the First Shot*. Philadelphia, Pa.: J. B. Lippincott, 1963.

Helper, Hinton Rowan. *The Impending Crisis in the*

South. New edition with Introduction by George M. Frederickson. Cambridge, Mass.: Harvard University Press, 1968. First published 1857.

Bailey, Hugh C. *Hinton Rowan Helper.* Montgomery, Ala.: University of Alabama Press, 1965.

4. The Civil War
   a. The Union at War

Though military history is excluded from this bibliography, mention should be made of *Battles and Leaders of the Civil War,* new edition by Roy F. Nichols (4 vols.; New York: Thomas Yoselof, 1956 [original edition: New York: 1887]). These accounts by participants throw abundant light upon all aspects of life during the war. David Donald (ed.), *Why the North Won the Civil War* (Baton Rouge, La.: Louisiana State University Press, 1960; New York: Collier Books, 1962), contains essays by five leading historians. Two books by Bell I. Wiley are as important for social as for military history: *The Life of Johnny Reb* (Indianapolis, Ind.: Bobbs-Merrill, 1943) and *The Life of Billy Yank* (Indianapolis, Ind.: Bobbs-Merrill, 1952). Robert Cruden, *The War That Never Ended* (Englewood Cliffs, N.J.: Prentice-Hall, 1973), concentrates upon the way in which the war affected people and social groups. So do the readings collected in William R. Brock (ed.), *The Civil War* (New York: Harper & Row, 1969).

   b. Politics in the North

Considering the importance of the war years in political and administrative history, there has been amazingly little serious study of the subject. There is no comprehensive history of the two wartime Congresses, and the older writings focused almost exclusively upon the relationship between Lincoln and the radicals. The following selection gives preference to recent works that indicate a new trend in the political historiography of the war.

Curry, Leonard P. *Blueprint for Modern America:*

Non-Military Legislation of the First Civil War Congress. Knoxville, Tenn.: University of Tennessee Press, 1968.

Linden, Glenn M. "Radicals and Economic Policies: The House of Representatives, 1861–1873," *Civil War History,* XIII (1967), 51–65.

Bogue, Allen G. "Bloc and Party in the United States Senate, 1861–63," *Civil War History,* XIII (1967), 221–241.

Stampp, Kenneth M. *Indiana Politics during the Civil War.* Indianapolis, Ind.: Bobbs-Merrill, 1949.

Trefousse, Hans L. "The Joint Committee on the Conduct of the War: A Reassessment," *Civil War History,* X (1964), 5–19.

———. *The Radical Republicans.* New York: Alfred A. Knopf, 1969.

Belz, Herman. *Reconstructing the Union: Theory and Practice during the Civil War.* Ithaca, N.Y.: Cornell University Press, 1969.

Thomas, Benjamin, and Hyman, Harold M. *Stanton.* New York: Alfred A. Knopf, 1962.

Jellison, Charles A. *Fessenden of Maine.* Syracuse, N.Y.: Syracuse University Press, 1962.

Donald, David (ed.). *Inside Lincoln's Cabinet: The Civil War Diaries of Salmon P. Chase.* New York and London: Longmans, 1954.

Beale, Howard K. (ed.). *The Diary of Gideon Welles.* 3 vols. New York: W. W. Norton, 1960.

Brodie, Fawn M. *Thaddeus Stevens: Scourge of the South.* New York: W. W. Norton, 1959.

Trefousse, Hans L. *Benjamin Franklin Wade.* New York: Twayne, 1963.

Donald, David. *Charles Sumner and the Coming of the Civil War.* New York: Alfred A. Knopf, 1960.

———. *Charles Sumner and the Rights of Man.* New York: Alfred A. Knopf, 1970.

McPherson, James M. *The Struggle for Equality: Abolitionists and the Negro in the Civil War and Reconstruction.* Princeton, N.J.: Princeton University Press, 1964. A study in great detail of a special aspect of radical political activity.

c. Society, Economics, and Technology

Andrew J. Cutler. *The North Reports the Civil War*. Pittsburgh, Pa.: University of Pittsburgh Press, 1955.

Smith, George W., and Judah, Charles (eds.). *Life in the North during the Civil War*. Albuquerque, N.M.: University of New Mexico Press, 1966.

Quarles, Benjamin. *The Negro in the Civil War*. Boston: Little, Brown, 1953.

Andreano, Ralph (ed.). *The Economic Impact of the American Civil War*. Cambridge, Mass.: Harvard University Press, 1962.

Cochran, Thomas C. "Did the Civil War Retard Industrialization?," *Mississippi Valley Historical Review*, XLVIII (1961). Also reprinted in many collections of readings.

Vartanian, Pershing. "The Cochran Thesis: A Critique in Statistical Analysis," *Journal of American History*, LI (1964), 77–84.

Scheiber, Harry N. "Economic Change in the Civil War Era: An Analysis of Recent Studies," *Civil War History*, XI (1965), 396–411.

Fogel, Robert W., and Engerman, Stanley L. *The Reinterpretation of American Economic History*. New York: Harper & Row, 1971.

Bruce, Robert V. *Lincoln and the Tools of War*. Indianapolis, Ind.: Bobbs-Merrill, 1956. Casts important light upon the technology of war as well as upon Lincoln's interest in the subject.

Weber, Thomas. *The Northern Railroads in the Civil War*. New York: Columbia University Press, 1952.

d. Intellectual History

The war had profound effects upon intellectual attitudes and assumptions, but at present one study stands almost alone in this field: George M. Frederickson, *The Inner Civil War: Northern Intellectuals and the Crisis of the Union* (New York: Harper & Row, 1965). Much can be learned, however, from Thomas J. Pressly, *Americans Interpret Their Civil War* (Princeton, N.J.: Princeton University Press, 1962; New York: Collier Books, 1962), and from the relevant passages in Merrill D. Peterson, *The Jefferson Image in the American Mind* (New York: Oxford University Press, 1960).

e. Protest and Dissent in the North

Klement, Frank L. *The Copperheads in the Middle West.* Chicago: University of Chicago Press, 1960.

———. *The Limits of Dissent: Clement L. Vallandigham and the Civil War.* Lexington, Ky.: The University Press of Kentucky, 1970.

Curry, Richard O. "The Union as It Was: A Critique of Recent Interpretations of the Copperheads," *Civil War History*, XIII (1967), 25–39.

Dusinberre, William. *Civil War Issues in Philadelphia, 1856–1865.* Philadelphia, Pa.: University of Pennsylvania Press, 1965.

Murdock, Eugene C. *Patriotism Limited: The Civil War Draft and the Bounty System.* Kent, Ohio: Kent State University Press, 1967.

f. The Confederacy

Roland, Charles P. *The Confederacy.* Chicago: University of Chicago Press, 1960.

Coulter, E. Merton. *The Confederate States of America.* Baton Rouge, La.: Louisiana State University Press, 1950.

Eaton, Clement. *A History of the Southern Confederacy.* New York: Free Press, 1956.

Vandiver, Frank E. *Their Tattered Flags: The Epic of the Confederacy.* New York: Harper & Row, 1970.

Patrick, Rembert W. *Jefferson Davis and His Cabinet.* Baton Rouge, La.: Louisiana State University Press, 1944.

Ransdell, Charles W. *Behind the Lines in the Southern Confederacy.* Baton Rouge, La.: Louisiana State University Press, 1944.

Wiley, Bell I. *The Plain People of the Confederacy.*

Baton Rouge, La.: Louisiana State University Press, 1943.

Brewer, James H. *The Confederate Negro: Virginia's Craftsmen and Military Laborers.* Durham, N.C.: Duke University Press, 1969.

Moore, Albert B. *Conscription and Conflict in the Confederacy.* New York: Hillary House, 1963. Original edition: New York: 1924.

Black, Robert C. *The Railroads of the Confederacy.* Chapel Hill, N.C.: University of North Carolina Press, 1952.

5. Reconstruction
   a. General

   Stampp, Kenneth M. *The Era of Reconstruction, 1865–77.* New York: Alfred A. Knopf, 1965.

   Franklin, John Hope. *Reconstruction after the Civil War.* Chicago: University of Chicago Press, 1961.

   Patrick, Rembert W. *The Reconstruction of the Nation.* New York: Oxford University Press, 1967.

   Du Bois, W. E. B. *Black Reconstruction in America, 1860–1880.* New York: S. A. Russell, 1956. Original edition: New York: 1935. Though often undervalued by modern writers, remains a work of seminal importance.

   b. Collections of Writings and Source Material

   Stampp, Kenneth M., and Litwack, Leon F. (eds.). *Reconstruction: An Anthology of Revisionist Writings.* Baton Rouge, La.: Louisiana State University Press, 1969.

   Lynd, Staughton (ed.). *Reconstruction.* New York: Harper & Row, 1967.

   Hyman, Harold M. (ed.). *The Radical Republicans and Reconstruction, 1861–1870.* Indianapolis, Ind.: Bobbs-Merrill, 1967. An invaluable collection of source material.

   Shenton, James P. *The Reconstruction: A Documentary History.* New York: G. P. Putnam's Sons, 1963.

Current, Richard N. *Reconstruction*. Englewood Cliffs, N.J.: Prentice-Hall, 1965.

Wish, Harvey. *Reconstruction in the South*. New York: Farrar, Straus & Giroux, 1965.

Reid, Whitelaw. *After the War: A Tour of the Southern States, 1865–1866*. Edited by C. Vann Woodward. New York: Harper & Row, 1965. First published 1866.

Dennett, John Richard. *The South as It Is, 1865–1866*. Edited by Henry M. Christman. New York: Viking, 1965.

Tourgée, Albion W. *A Fool's Errand*. Edited by George M. Frederickson. New York: Harper & Row, 1966. First published 1879. Fiction but based upon extensive firsthand experience in North Carolina.

c. Northern Policy

Beale, Howard K. *The Critical Year: A Study of Andrew Johnson and Reconstruction*. New York: Frederick Ungar, 1958. Original edition: New York: 1930. A major study, but many of its conclusions are disputed by modern writers.

Brock, William R. *An American Crisis: Congress and Reconstruction, 1865–67*. New York: St. Martin's, 1963. London: Macmillan, 1963.

Cox, Lawanda and John H. *Politics, Principle, and Prejudice, 1865–66*. New York: Free Press, 1963.

McKitrick, Eric L. *Andrew Johnson and Reconstruction*. Chicago: University of Chicago Press, 1960.

Donald, David. *The Politics of Reconstruction, 1863–1867*. Baton Rouge, La.: Louisiana State University Press, 1965. An interesting but not wholly convincing analysis of congressional voting figures.

Coben, Stanley. "Northeastern Business and Radical Reconstruction," *Mississippi Valley Historical Review*, XLVI (1959).

Rose, Willie Lee. *Rehearsal for Reconstruction: The Port Royal Experiment*. Indianapolis, Ind.: Bobbs-Merrill, 1964.

McFeely, William S. *Yankee Stepfather: General O. O. Howard and the Freedmen*. New Haven, Conn.: Yale University Press, 1968.

Bentley, George R. *A History of the Freedmen's Bureau*. Philadelphia, Pa.: University of Pennsylvania Press, 1955. New York: Octagon Books, 1970.

Sefton, James E. *The United States Army and Reconstruction, 1865–1877*. Baton Rouge, La.: Louisiana State University Press, 1967.

Sharkey, Robert P. *Money, Class, and Party: An Economic Study of Civil War and Reconstruction*. Baltimore, Md.: The Johns Hopkins University Press, 1959.

Nugent, Walter T. K. *The Money Question during Reconstruction*. New York: W. W. Norton, 1967.

Unger, Irwin. *The Greenback Era: A Social and Political History of American Finance, 1865–1879*. Princeton, N.J.: Princeton University Press, 1964.

d. In the South

Williamson, Joel. *After Slavery: The Negro in South Carolina during Reconstruction, 1861–1877*. Chapel Hill, N.C.: University of North Carolina Press, 1965.

Wharton, Vernon L. *The Negro in Mississippi, 1865–1890*. Chapel Hill, N.C.: University of North Carolina Press, 1947.

Shugg, Roger W. *Origins of Class Struggle in Louisiana, 1840–1875*. Baton Rouge, La.: Louisiana State University Press, 1939.

Current, Richard N. *Three Carpetbag Governors*. Baton Rouge, La.: Louisiana State University Press, 1967.

Conway, Alan. *The Reconstruction of Georgia*. Minneapolis, Minn.: University of Minnesota Press, 1966.

Maddex, Jack P. *The Virginia Conservatives, 1867–1879*. Chapel Hill, N.C.: University of North Carolina Press, 1970.

Olsen, Otto H. *Carpetbagger's Crusade: The Life of Albion W. Tourgée.* Baltimore, Md.: The Johns Hopkins University Press, 1965.

Singletary, Otis A. *Negro Militia and Reconstruction.* Austin, Tex.: University of Texas Press, 1957. New York: McGraw-Hill, 1963.

Donald, David. "The Scalawag in Mississippi Reconstruction," *Journal of Southern History,* X (1944).

Trelease, Allen W. "Who Were the Scalawags?," *Journal of Southern History,* XXIX (1963).

Alexander, Thomas B. "Persistent Whiggery in the Confederate South, 1860–1877," *Journal of Southern History,* XXVII (1961).

6. The Grant Era

When one turns to national history after 1869, one experiences a strange quiet after the heightened controversy and intensive study of Reconstruction and the South.

Hesseltine, William B. *Ulysses S. Grant: Politician.* New York: Frederick Ungar, 1957. Original edition: New York: Dodd, Mead, 1935. Remains the most authoritative study, though some judgments may deserve revision.

Josephson, Matthew. *The Politicos, 1865–1896.* New York: Harcourt, Brace, 1938. Very lively but so biased that one is left with fiction rather than fact.

Bryce, James. *The American Commonwealth.* 2 vols. London: 1888. Still, in many ways, the best introduction to late nineteenth-century politics.

Woodward, C. Vann. *Reunion and Reaction: The Compromise of 1877 and the End of Reconstruction.* Boston: Little, Brown, 1951.

Kirkland, Edward C. *Dream and Thought in the Business Community, 1860–1900.* Ithaca, N.Y.: Cornell University Press, 1956.

McKelvey, Blake. *The Urbanization of America, 1860–1915.* New Brunswick, N.J.: Rutgers University Press, 1963.

Unger, Irwin. *The Greenback Era: A Social and Politi-*

cal History of American Finance, 1865–1879. Princeton, N.J.: Princeton University Press, 1964.

Weinstein, Allen. *Prelude to Populism: Origins of the Silver Issue, 1867–1878.* New Haven, Conn.: Yale University Press, 1970. A discussion of the political implications of the currency issue.

Index

THE FREE AND THE UNFREE
A New History of the United States

Peter N. Carroll and David W. Noble

The Free and the Unfree is a "counterculture" survey of American history from pre-Columbian times to the post-Watergate era. Based largely on firsthand sources, the book focuses, in each period, on the dynamic relationship between the nation's ruling elite and its various "out-groups"—native Americans, blacks, women, ethnic minorities, and, most recently, young people. The book's bold conclusion is that these groups will be the saviors of the country's future—for they regard America as a "home" to care for, not as a "frontier" to be exploited.

GOLDEN DOOR TO AMERICA
The Jewish Immigrant Experience

Abraham J. Karp

Letters, poems, documents, and memoirs tell the story of Jewish immigrants in America—from the seventeenth century, when a trickle of Spanish and Portuguese Jews arrived, through the mid-nineteenth century, with its steady flow from Germany, to the late nineteeenth and early twentieth centuries, when wave after wave of Eastern Europeans unfurled upon New York City. "A lovely companion to Irving Howe's massive *World of Our Fathers,* and an absorbing collection in its own right"—*Kirkus Reviews.*

The Pelican History of the United States 6

COMING OF AGE
The United States during the 1920's and 1930's

Donald R. McCoy

In this panoramic review of American politics, economics, and diplomacy between the two world wars,
Donald R. McCoy discusses the development of big
government, the rise of mass production and consumption, and the nation's new role in the international sphere. The turbulence of the interwar
period is shown to have accelerated, rather than
reversed, long-term trends in American history.
Although the differences between the prosperity of
the twenties and the depression of the thirties are
covered in detail, the book's major theme is continuity, not contrast. Donald R. McCoy is Professor
of History at the University of Kansas.

The Pelican History of the United States 8

RISE TO GLOBALISM
American Foreign Policy, 1938–1976
Revised Edition

Stephen E. Ambrose

This is a searching review of American foreign policy between 1938 and 1976. American involvement
in World War II, the Cold War, the Korean conflict,
the Berlin crisis, the invasion of Cuba, and the war
in Vietnam are among the events that Professor
Stephen E. Ambrose surveys as he relates them to the
larger themes of America's rise to, and maintenance
of, her enormous global power. Yet going far beneath these vast currents, he looks at traits of the
American character—economic aggressiveness, ra-
cism, fear of communism—and shows how they have
helped shape the nation's foreign policy. It is this
probing beneath the surface of history that makes
Rise to Globalism a uniquely valuable work. Stephen
E. Ambrose is Professor of History at the University
of New Orleans.

COMMON SENSE

Thomas Paine
Edited and introduced by Isaac Kramnick

Published anonymously in 1776, *Common Sense*, more than any other factor, kindled the movement for American independence. Thomas Paine wrote it out of a belief in those fundamental principles that must stand, he felt, no matter what excesses are committed on their behalf. It contains some of the most famous words of the time: "Government, even in its best state, is but a necessary evil; in its worst state, an intolerable one." George Washington said of it, "I find *Common Sense* working a powerful change in the minds of men."

Also

THE RIGHTS OF MAN
Thomas Paine

REFLECTIONS ON THE REVOLUTION IN FRANCE
Edmund Burke

ON LIBERTY
John Stuart Mill

THE WEALTH OF NATIONS
Adam Smith

A HISTORY OF LATIN AMERICA

George Pendle

About Latin America and its problems there prevails what the *Economist* called an "awe-inspiring ignorance." An authoritative and concise introduction to an area of such great economic potential is certainly needed. This history has been written by a specialist who has been closely associated with Latin America for the last forty years. His text emphasizes how many races and classes have contributed to the civilization of this great land-mass, with its vast mountain ranges, rivers, prairies, forests, and deserts: Indians, European conquistadores, priests, planters, African slaves, caudillos, liberal intellectuals, commercial pioneers. George Pendle successfully integrates the histories of the principal countries into one continental story, and in this latest edition he analyzes the pattern of recent developments in Argentina, Brazil, Peru, and Chile.

THE MAN ON HORSEBACK
The Role of the Military in Politics

S. E. Finer

This definitive book on the part played by the military in politics has now been updated. Studying "political colonels" as a type, Professor S. E. Finer discusses the strengths and weaknesses of the military as a political force, the factors that promote or inhibit armed intervention in politics, and the limits, types, and methods of the military's role and style. He concludes that with the rise of new states in Africa and Asia, military interventions will increase. Acclaimed by both political and military specialists, *The Man on Horseback* has already proved invaluable to students. The new material in this edition includes an additional chapter, a revised bibliography, and tables setting out the number, distribution, and provenance of military coups in the past fifteen years.

KARL MARX: MAN AND FIGHTER

Boris Nicolaievsky and Otto Maenchen-Helfen
Translated by Gwenda David and Eric Mosbacher

This is a portrait of Karl Marx as a politician and socialist militant rather than as a philosopher and economist. It ranges from his early life in Germany through the period of the *Manifesto* to the controversy with Mikhail Bakunin and the years in London. Here readers will find the Marx of the Communist League and the International Working Men's Association as well as the brilliant journalist and the family man beset by poverty. First published in 1936 in an English translation from the German, *Karl Marx: Man and Fighter* is still generally regarded as the best one-volume life of Marx. Its principal author, Boris Nicolaievsky, was a prominent revolutionary activist and historian in Russia and, later, within the Socialist International in Germany.